T0211062

Lecture Notes in Computer Science   14702

Founding Editors

Gerhard Goos
Juris Hartmanis

The series Lecture Notes in Computer Science (LNCS), including its subseries Lecture Notes in Artificial Intelligence (LNAI) and Lecture Notes in Bioinformatics (LNBI), has established itself as a medium for the publication of new developments in computer science and information technology research, teaching, and education.

LNCS enjoys close cooperation with the computer science R & D community, the series counts many renowned academics among its volume editors and paper authors, and collaborates with prestigious societies. Its mission is to serve this international community by providing an invaluable service, mainly focused on the publication of conference and workshop proceedings and postproceedings. LNCS commenced publication in 1973.

Pei-Luen Patrick Rau
Editor

Cross-Cultural Design

16th International Conference, CCD 2024
Held as Part of the 26th HCI International Conference, HCII 2024
Washington, DC, USA, June 29 – July 4, 2024
Proceedings, Part IV

 Springer

Editor
Pei-Luen Patrick Rau
Tsinghua University
Beijing, China

ISSN 0302-9743 ISSN 1611-3349 (electronic)
Lecture Notes in Computer Science
ISBN 978-3-031-60912-1 ISBN 978-3-031-60913-8 (eBook)
https://doi.org/10.1007/978-3-031-60913-8

This Springer imprint is published by the registered company Springer Nature Switzerland AG
The registered company address is: Gewerbestrasse 11, 6330 Cham, Switzerland

If disposing of this product, please recycle the paper.

Foreword

This year we celebrate 40 years since the establishment of the HCI International (HCII) Conference, which has been a hub for presenting groundbreaking research and novel ideas and collaboration for people from all over the world.

The HCII conference was founded in 1984 by Prof. Gavriel Salvendy (Purdue University, USA, Tsinghua University, P.R. China, and University of Central Florida, USA) and the first event of the series, "1st USA-Japan Conference on Human-Computer Interaction", was held in Honolulu, Hawaii, USA, 18–20 August. Since then, HCI International is held jointly with several Thematic Areas and Affiliated Conferences, with each one under the auspices of a distinguished international Program Board and under one management and one registration. Twenty-six HCI International Conferences have been organized so far (every two years until 2013, and annually thereafter).

Over the years, this conference has served as a platform for scholars, researchers, industry experts and students to exchange ideas, connect, and address challenges in the ever-evolving HCI field. Throughout these 40 years, the conference has evolved itself, adapting to new technologies and emerging trends, while staying committed to its core mission of advancing knowledge and driving change.

As we celebrate this milestone anniversary, we reflect on the contributions of its founding members and appreciate the commitment of its current and past Affiliated Conference Program Board Chairs and members. We are also thankful to all past conference attendees who have shaped this community into what it is today.

The 26th International Conference on Human-Computer Interaction, HCI International 2024 (HCII 2024), was held as a 'hybrid' event at the Washington Hilton Hotel, Washington, DC, USA, during 29 June – 4 July 2024. It incorporated the 21 thematic areas and affiliated conferences listed below.

A total of 5108 individuals from academia, research institutes, industry, and government agencies from 85 countries submitted contributions, and 1271 papers and 309 posters were included in the volumes of the proceedings that were published just before the start of the conference, these are listed below. The contributions thoroughly cover the entire field of human-computer interaction, addressing major advances in knowledge and effective use of computers in a variety of application areas. These papers provide academics, researchers, engineers, scientists, practitioners and students with state-of-the-art information on the most recent advances in HCI.

The HCI International (HCII) conference also offers the option of presenting 'Late Breaking Work', and this applies both for papers and posters, with corresponding volumes of proceedings that will be published after the conference. Full papers will be included in the 'HCII 2024 - Late Breaking Papers' volumes of the proceedings to be published in the Springer LNCS series, while 'Poster Extended Abstracts' will be included as short research papers in the 'HCII 2024 - Late Breaking Posters' volumes to be published in the Springer CCIS series.

I would like to thank the Program Board Chairs and the members of the Program Boards of all thematic areas and affiliated conferences for their contribution towards the high scientific quality and overall success of the HCI International 2024 conference. Their manifold support in terms of paper reviewing (single-blind review process, with a minimum of two reviews per submission), session organization and their willingness to act as goodwill ambassadors for the conference is most highly appreciated.

This conference would not have been possible without the continuous and unwavering support and advice of Gavriel Salvendy, founder, General Chair Emeritus, and Scientific Advisor. For his outstanding efforts, I would like to express my sincere appreciation to Abbas Moallem, Communications Chair and Editor of HCI International News.

July 2024   Constantine Stephanidis

HCI International 2024 Thematic Areas and Affiliated Conferences

- HCI: Human-Computer Interaction Thematic Area
- HIMI: Human Interface and the Management of Information Thematic Area
- EPCE: 21st International Conference on Engineering Psychology and Cognitive Ergonomics
- AC: 18th International Conference on Augmented Cognition
- UAHCI: 18th International Conference on Universal Access in Human-Computer Interaction
- CCD: 16th International Conference on Cross-Cultural Design
- SCSM: 16th International Conference on Social Computing and Social Media
- VAMR: 16th International Conference on Virtual, Augmented and Mixed Reality
- DHM: 15th International Conference on Digital Human Modeling & Applications in Health, Safety, Ergonomics & Risk Management
- DUXU: 13th International Conference on Design, User Experience and Usability
- C&C: 12th International Conference on Culture and Computing
- DAPI: 12th International Conference on Distributed, Ambient and Pervasive Interactions
- HCIBGO: 11th International Conference on HCI in Business, Government and Organizations
- LCT: 11th International Conference on Learning and Collaboration Technologies
- ITAP: 10th International Conference on Human Aspects of IT for the Aged Population
- AIS: 6th International Conference on Adaptive Instructional Systems
- HCI-CPT: 6th International Conference on HCI for Cybersecurity, Privacy and Trust
- HCI-Games: 6th International Conference on HCI in Games
- MobiTAS: 6th International Conference on HCI in Mobility, Transport and Automotive Systems
- AI-HCI: 5th International Conference on Artificial Intelligence in HCI
- MOBILE: 5th International Conference on Human-Centered Design, Operation and Evaluation of Mobile Communications

List of Conference Proceedings Volumes Appearing Before the Conference

https://2024.hci.international/proceedings

Preface

The increasing internationalization and globalization of communication, business and industry is leading to a wide cultural diversification of individuals and groups of users who access information, services and products. If interactive systems are to be usable, useful and appealing to such a wide range of users, culture becomes an important HCI issue. Therefore, HCI practitioners and designers face the challenges of designing across different cultures, and need to elaborate and adopt design approaches which take into account cultural models, factors, expectations and preferences, and allow development of cross-cultural user experiences that accommodate global users.

The 16th Cross-Cultural Design (CCD) Conference, an affiliated conference of the HCI International Conference, encouraged the submission of papers from academics, researchers, industry and professionals, on a broad range of theoretical and applied issues related to Cross-Cultural Design and its applications.

A considerable number of papers were accepted to this year's CCD conference addressing diverse topics, which spanned a wide variety of domains. A notable theme addressed by several contributions was that of user experience and product design from a cross-cultural point of view, offering insights into design, user interaction, and evaluation across different domains and how cultural contexts shape user preferences, expectations, and behaviors. Furthermore, a considerable number of papers explore how individuals perceive, attend to, and process information within cultural contexts. Furthermore, the impact of culture across different application domains is addressed, examining technologies for communication, cultural heritage, and digital transformation and bringing together cutting-edge research, innovative practices, and insightful studies. Finally, the influence of culture on emerging technologies is a prominent theme, with contributions discussing extended reality, aviation and transportation, as well as artificial intelligence, addressing a multitude of aspects such as narrative design, interaction design, evaluation of user experience and performance, artificial empathy, and ethical aspects.

Four volumes of the HCII 2024 proceedings are dedicated to this year's edition of the CCD conference:

- Part I addresses topics related to Cross-Cultural Design and User Experience, and Cross-Cultural Product Design;
- Part II addresses topics related to Cross-Cultural Communication and Interaction, and Cultural Perception, Attention and Information Processing;
- Part III addresses topics related to Cross-Cultural Tangible and Intangible Heritage and Cross-Cultural Digital Transformation;
- Part IV addresses topics related to Cross-Cultural Extended Reality, Cross-Cultural Design in Aviation and Transportation, and Artificial Intelligence from a Cross-Cultural Perspective.

The papers in these volumes were accepted for publication after a minimum of two single-blind reviews from the members of the CCD Program Board or, in some cases, from members of the Program Boards of other affiliated conferences. I would like to thank all of them for their invaluable contribution, support and efforts.

July 2024   Pei-Luen Patrick Rau

16th International Conference on Cross-Cultural Design (CCD2024)

The full list with the Program Board Chairs and the members of the Program Boards of all thematic areas and affiliated conferences of HCII 2024 is available online at:

http://www.hci.international/board-members-2024.php

HCI International 2025 Conference

The 27th International Conference on Human-Computer Interaction, HCI International 2025, will be held jointly with the affiliated conferences at the Swedish Exhibition & Congress Centre and Gothia Towers Hotel, Gothenburg, Sweden, June 22–27, 2025. It will cover a broad spectrum of themes related to Human-Computer Interaction, including theoretical issues, methods, tools, processes, and case studies in HCI design, as well as novel interaction techniques, interfaces, and applications. The proceedings will be published by Springer. More information will become available on the conference website: https://2025.hci.international/.

General Chair
Prof. Constantine Stephanidis
University of Crete and ICS-FORTH
Heraklion, Crete, Greece
Email: general_chair@2025.hci.international

https://2025.hci.international/

Contents – Part IV

Artificial Intelligence from a Cross-Cultural Perspective

Cross-Cultural Extended Reality

Characteristics and Development of Digital Curators for Virtual-Physical Integration

Yueh Hsiu Giffen Cheng[1](✉) iD and Ying-Chi Chiu[2]

[1] National Taiwan University of Arts, 59, Sec. 1, Daguan Rd., Banqiao Dist., New Taipei City 22058, Taiwan, R.O.C.
giffen.cheng@gmail.com
[2] National Yunlin University of Science and Technology, 123 University Road, Section 3, Douliou, Yunlin 64002, Taiwan, R.O.C.

Abstract. This study employs an action research methodology to implement digital-physical integration curation practically, utilizing the "Creative Life Corridor" as a physical exhibition space. Through leveraging social media platforms such as Facebook, Instagram, and Pinterest for digital content curation and promotion, it investigates the characteristics and development of curators, essential elements of digital-physical integration curation operations, and the conditions necessary for proficient digital-physical integration curators. The findings indicate that in terms of the characteristics and development of digital-physical integration curators, individuals need to possess insight akin to a talent scout, a spirit of eclectic learning, unique perspectives, and compelling copywriting skills. Additionally, they should adeptly utilize digital and physical platforms, discern the meaning behind data, keep abreast of trends, engage in empathetic thinking, and demonstrate effective communication and leadership skills to facilitate fluency.

Keywords: Curators · Social Media Platforms · Digital Content Curation

1 Introduction

With the development of the internet in the private sector for nearly 30 years and the continuous rise in the usage of mobile devices, global internet usage has surged to over 80% in less than three decades, as indicated by the recent "2017 Global Internet Usage Survey Report" jointly released by We Are Social and Hootsuite. The increasing use of mobile internet has also contributed to the development of social media platforms. For instance, Facebook has amassed over 1 billion users, with the report highlighting an average daily usage time of 2 h and 19 min per person on social media platforms. This underscores the integral role of internet and social media usage in people's lives, with over half of global internet traffic originating from smartphones. Consequently, these trends have influenced information acquisition, learning, and entertainment habits.

Moreover, due to the influence and exposure of Internet communities, many fields have begun to prioritize managing online communities as part of their operations. Consequently, community management and maintenance have evolved to incorporate the

P.-L. P. Rau (Ed.): HCII 2024, LNCS 14702, pp. 3–19, 2024.
https://doi.org/10.1007/978-3-031-60913-8_1

concept of curation for information dissemination. As curation extends beyond the traditional realms of art galleries and museums into the digital world, curators have also ventured into digital virtual spaces for curation. The rapid development of the internet has led to endless possibilities and business opportunities, giving rise to new industries such as Facebook page managers, bloggers, and internet influencers. Among these, online publishing content is also considered a form of digital content curation. This type of curation, distinct from traditional physical curation, challenges traditional curators' adaptation to digital content curation. Thus, exploring the evolution and characteristics of "curation" in the online sphere is the starting point for this research.

This study is divided into three parts: The first part involves conceptual derivation, utilizing literature to explore the definition and evolution of curation concepts, platform transitions and utilization, and the functional transformation of different curators. Through literature review, the concept of "digital-physical integration curator" is derived, embodying traits of traditional and general digital content curators. The second part entails the execution of curation, employing the "Creative Life Corridor" for a physical curation experiment combined with digital content curation. Observations, recordings, random interviews, and deductions regarding the operational characteristics and benefits of digital-physical integration are made from the experiment. Lastly, the data collection and analysis phase utilizes expert interviews and focus group discussions with online and physical visitors. The research will ultimately propose the characteristics and conditions of digital-physical integration curators and the essential elements of digital-physical integration curation operations.

2 Literature Review

2.1 Application of Physical Curation Concepts in the Online World

Physical curation primarily involves selecting exhibits based on themes and meticulously planning and executing the selection, arrangement, and interpretation of exhibits to create context and imbue them with new meanings and perspectives (Gaskill, 2011). On the other hand, digital content curation borrows concepts from physical curation, with curated content derived from existing online information. It undergoes theme selection, data collection, filtering, organization, contextualization, and the infusion of new viewpoints (Cui, Wang, Zhou & Yokoi, 2013; Floyd, 2015; Mullan, 2020). However, the final distinction lies in the sharing and resonance generated through the dissemination via the internet and social media platforms, making the spread faster and broader than traditional physical curation.

2.2 Emergence of New Types of Curators

The nature of physical curators involves exhibition planning, exhibit selection based on themes, establishing connections between objects, and conveying perspectives to viewers. Each exhibition requires considerable knowledge background and extensive coordination, making physical curators conveyors of knowledge and perspectives and caretakers of objects. Their traits include profound professional knowledge, leadership and communication skills, empathy, curiosity, responsibility, and resilience (Lin, 2013; Chen, 2016). With the advancement of the internet and social media platforms, digital content curators have emerged. They curate content and platforms on the internet, known as editors, bloggers, internet opinion leaders, YouTubers, etc. They utilize social media platforms to disseminate messages according to different themes and purposes, engaging audiences. Their content generation and dissemination process constitute digital content curation tailored to different audience needs. Their traits include curiosity about new things, creative and humorous copywriting skills, insightful observation and perspective abilities, quick response, service enthusiasm, and responsibility. This study suggests complementary traits between these two types of curators, proposing the concept of digital-physical integration curators who operate both physical and digital content curation. Hence, the operation of this curation concept requires the traits of both types of curators.

2.3 Emergence of New Curation Platforms - Social Media Platforms

In the digital age, the emergence of online communities has significantly impacted various fields, breaking geographical barriers and bringing together individuals with shared interests, beliefs, and ideologies on common online platforms for information exchange and sharing. With the trend towards platformization of the internet, the development of social network sites such as Facebook, Instagram, YouTube, and Pinterest has surged. These platforms, referred to as social platforms in this study, enable cross-platform integration and connectivity and facilitate digital content curation in the vast expanse of online information.

Aghaei et al. (2012) and Patel (2013) noted that platforms can transcend, integrate, and connect due to advancements in networking technology. In response to the need to stand out amidst abundant information, the digital world has increasingly engaged in digital content curation, with social platforms emerging as the primary curatorial arenas. Based on trends and economic viability, this study selects social platforms as the online platforms for digital-physical integration curation. Considering that the presentation of creative lifestyles in the gallery channel is relatively static, Facebook, Instagram—primarily image and hashtag-based—and Pinterest—utilizing its pinning feature for digital art galleries are chosen as this study's digital content curation platforms.

2.4 Communication Functions of Social Media Platforms

Regarding social marketing and audience behavior, the study analyzes the relationship between social media platform operation and audience. Leveraging the function of community aggregation and the intense traffic guidance of social media platforms, many enterprises choose social media platforms as channels for marketing and communication with customers, improving the quality of services for both parties. Compared to traditional media communication, which is generally harder for the public to access, the application of social media platform functions has developed into accessible self-media, allowing the public to participate in media communication and production through platforms. This has become a bridge tool for individuals, artists, museums, and enterprises for marketing and communication with the public, and depending on platform attributes and functions, it also affects the presentation of content, allowing audiences to choose information reception based on their preferences (Cheng, 2016).

2.5 Driving Social Marketing with Curation Concepts

The considerations in social marketing can be divided into platforms, content, managers, and users, with content presentation and interaction being the critical factors for successful social marketing. Social managers who manipulate content are crucial. Social marketing success depends on the audience's response and interaction with the content. Social managers need to consider the nature of audience engagement on social media, such as information exchange and acquisition, learning, leisure, socializing, self-realization, and expression, as the basis for content creation. This influences audience behavior to achieve the purpose of social marketing (Ashley & Tuten, 2015). This study integrates the concept of digital-physical curation into social marketing, serving as the basis for community management.

From the literature review, it is evident that the development of digital content curation is a significant trend for the future. While its concept originates from physical curation, existing practical cases mostly explore content presentation in digital content curation. There are fewer studies on the operational methods of combining physical and digital curation. Therefore, this study will utilize the digital-physical integration curation proposed in the literature to conduct experiments using the Creative Life Corridor as the physical venue, combined with social media platforms. It aims to explore the future trends and market of digital-physical integration curators, operational benefits, and the relationship between curators, platforms, and curation subjects, providing a reference for future operations integrating physical curation with digital content curation.

3 Research Methodology

This study utilizes the "Creative Life Corridor" at the Department of Creative Living Design, National Yunlin University of Science and Technology, Taiwan, as the venue for action research, abbreviated as the "Corridor." The display cabinets along the corridor were originally intended to showcase students' design works, serving as inspiration, aesthetic cultivation, and teaching aids for students. The corridor is a mandatory route for students of the Creative Living Design Department, similar to this study's proposed physical curation function. Since the exhibits in the cabinets are periodically replaced and lose their original display function, and because this venue is easily accessible to people, it was chosen as the platform for the physical curation experiment in this study. Integrating digital content curation is aligned with the trend of using internet communities and platforms. Thus, the experiment involves the practical operation of digital-physical integration curation and is renamed as the "Creative Life Corridor." The researcher assumes the role of curator, collects data, and performs analysis through the experiment.

The research adopts an action research cycle consisting of three iterations. Each iteration includes planning, execution, observation, reflection, and adjustment. The first iteration, "Everyday-Illustration Exhibition x Carpe Diem," is a pilot phase. After completing the first cycle, adjustments and corrections are made based on reflections from the first iteration, preparing for the second iteration, "Tao Hao-Good Daily Exhibition." The second iteration focuses on correction, utilizing experiences from the first iteration for adjustment and observation. After the first and second iterations, a comprehensive review and strategy adjustment are conducted. The final iteration, "Artisan-Commonplace" serves as the period for overall strategy reorganization. Data collection and analysis are performed using three cycles.

Each iteration involves three main stages: theme exploration, pre-phase, and execution and reflection. During the theme exploration phase, the curator selects the theme and conducts physical and digital content curation as preparatory steps for producing viewpoints and writing content. The first step is theme collection and screening, followed by collecting and filtering online data related to the chosen theme, facilitating data organization and contextualization in the next stage. This phase lays the groundwork for content collection for physical exhibition posts.

In the pre-phase of physical curation, the exhibition concept is designed and developed based on the theme, influencing exhibits' collection, filtering, organization, and contextualization. The digital data organization and contextualization steps may be influenced by the exhibition concept and exhibits, prompting a return to the previous step for additional data collection and filtering to generate viewpoints, content writing, and value assignment. The third part involves the execution phase of digital and physical content curation, using virtual and physical platforms to connect and share with the audience. Feedback from the audience, continuous observation, and reflection are utilized for subsequent curation adjustments (Table 1).

Table 1. Data Collection and Coding.

Identity Code	Research Period Code
Digital-Physical Integration Curator (C)	Pre-experiment Period (E1) 2017/9/28–2017/12/27
Physical and Digital Audience Code A (A1, A2, and so forth)	Post-experiment Period (E2) 2017/12/28–2018/5/25
Social Media Audience Code D (D1, D2, and so forth)	
Expert Coding: (P1, P2, P3)	
Data Coding: Post Observation Reflection Form J, Random Interview I, Group Focus Interview GI, Expert Interview PI	

4 Research Analysis

4.1 Traits and Development of Curators

Ability to Select Curatorial Themes. The selection of themes was a crucial aspect during the initial phase of the action research. For the first exhibition theme selection, due to the repositioning of the corridor space and its significance as a passage for students majoring in Creative Lifestyle Design, which integrates graphic, product, and spatial design, there was a wide range of interests among the students. As the curator of this research, through regular observations of the audience, it was noticed that while the corridor was a part of the daily lives of Creative Lifestyle Design students, it was neglected in terms of maintenance, and most passersby did not have a significant impact from it. To make the corridor audience rediscover this space and generate resonance and discussion more efficiently, it was decided to select "Everyday Life" as the core concept for this space and "Illustration" as the primary curatorial theme for the first exhibition. Everyday, quickly observable items, issues, designs, crafts, and arts from everyday life were utilized to connect with the audience and resonate with them.

Starting from Everyday Items Among the Audience Facilitates Resonance. The first to the third exhibitions were respectively titled "Everyday-Illustration Exhibition x Carpe Diem," "Tao Hao-Good Daily Exhibition." and " Artisan-Commonplace ". In the first exhibition, commonly accepted illustrations were linked with the core concept of the corridor, "Everyday Life," marking the beginning of the first digital-physical integration curation. As it was the first attempt at digital-physical integration curation, many aspects were still in the experimental stage. During communication with illustrators to collect exhibition works, "Everyday Life" served as the basis for collecting exhibits and determining the theme of the first exhibition. "Everyday Life" also became the central axis for subsequent social media posts and exhibition themes, including "Tao Hao-Good Daily Exhibition." and " Artisan-Commonplace," as well as the primary focus for subsequent image exposures and positioning of the corridor (Figs. 1, 2 and 3).

Fig. 1. "Everyday-Illustration Exhibition x Carpe Diem," poster and actual exhibition

Fig. 2. "Tao Hao-Good Daily Exhibition." poster and actual exhibition

Fig. 3. " Artisan-Commonplace" poster and actual exhibition

Insight into Audience's Daily Life to Find Themes. The "Everyday-Illustration Exhibition x Carpe Diem" exhibition ran from 2017/10/18 to 2017/12/20, emphasizing the repositioning and activation of the hallway. Before showcasing physical artwork, the promotional groundwork was laid on three digital community platforms: Facebook, IG, and Pinterest. Additionally, invitations, likes, exposure, and promotions were initiated, leveraging the curator's social network. The hallway's illustration image was utilized as native content posts to attract audience attention and increase anticipation. This image also became the symbol for subsequent digital content curation and theme alignment. To maintain its image, the curator also crafted copy based on the hallway's curation core and theme. The audience's response to the "everyday" theme was positive (E1-A3-I3). Moreover, the second event, "Tao Hao-Good Daily Exhibition," was relevant to the audience's daily life and provided benefits, effectively attracting attention (E1-A1-I10; E1-A5-I1; E1-A4-I2).

Outward to Inward Focus in Copywriting. After selecting themes and collecting online data, three interconnected aspects influence each other: digital content curation's data organization and contextualization, physical curation's design development, planning, exhibit collection, filtering, organization, and contextualization. Only then can viewpoints be generated and copywriting initiated. These parts interact and adjust during practical operation. However, once these three parts are preliminarily determined, the advantage of the speed of digital content curation is utilized to initiate viewpoint generation and copywriting. This refers to the primary curation copywriting for each exhibition. At this point, posts are first published and promoted on online social platforms, initiating the first interaction with the community to observe audience reactions and adjust the direction of subsequent posts.

Early Exposure to Gather Attention. After collecting and filtering online data relevant to the theme, the design, and planning of physical exhibition concepts, as well as the organization and contextualization of exhibits, interact and adjust with the filtered online data organization and contextualization. If data inadequacies or mismatches are discovered during organization and contextualization, returning to the previous step for online collection and filtering is necessary. Before executing the physical exhibition, a primary copy is officially released through online social platforms, serving as the pre-exhibition promotion period and setting the direction for promotion.

Diverse Presentation, Conciseness, and Focus on Daily Life. The ability to describe outwardly focused, point-based copy is essential for curators. Post-description skills are the first step in influencing whether the audience wants to click and effectively attract them, helping them understand the content (E2-A11-GI6; E2-A11-GI7; E2-A14-GI6). Given the rapid flow of information, concise narrative skills are crucial (E2-A11-GI9; E2-A11-GI10). A narrative or presentation also helps increase reading length and attention (E2-A12-GI9). In addition to text, appropriate graphics are necessary, and the curator's ability to respond quickly is essential, allowing the audience to understand the content more quickly amidst a large volume of information (E2-A13-GI26).

Perspectives and Providing Diverse Information—Facilitating Topic Creation and Increasing Audience Engagement. After the exposure of primary curation copy posts, other posts mainly use daily concepts for presentation. These posts also require factors such as copy, topics, discussions, events, etc., to attract audience attention. Key operations include: understanding audience interests, finding suitable post types, leveraging theme associations to evoke resonance and create topics, timely changing tastes to stimulate curiosity and providing unique insights on daily events.

Knowledge Accumulation and Exhibit Selection Contribute to Maintaining Fan Page Image, Direction, and Quality. As mentioned earlier, under the mutual influence of the curator's understanding of the exhibited works, exhibition concepts, and existing online information, viewpoint generation is a prerequisite task. After the physical exhibition, the overall process primarily focuses on the cycle of digital content curation, while the physical aspect influences the interaction between data, exhibition concepts, and exhibited works. Since the audience of the hallway mostly has a design-related background, the curator must have the ability to select and design data and works, as well as organize and contextualize existing online information, leading to viewpoints, copywriting, and value attribution. The choice and category of exhibits will also determine the audience's retention (E1-A1-I9). Therefore, key operations include providing professional knowledge, creating resource sharing, using exhibits to extend knowledge, maintaining curation quality and image, and using curiosity and empathy to acquire broad knowledge and select exhibits to maintain quality.

Broad Knowledge Accumulation and Exhibit Selection Contribute to Maintaining Fan Page Image, Direction, and Quality. The final step in curating digital-physical integration involves audience interaction and feedback. This encompasses sharing, connecting, and delivering messages to the audience, as well as receiving feedback, observing, and reflecting. It also marks the period between posting digital content and the subsequent post. This phase serves as an opportunity for observation, information gathering, and adjustment. In random interviews conducted after the initial phase, some audience members noted that curators often attempt to narrate articles of similar types in new ways but with unsatisfactory results (E1-A1-I3). This can be attributed to the fact that the initial phase is still exploring the audience. The overall content of the posts primarily focuses on introducing exhibits, and excessive similarity among the posts leads to audience fatigue. This phase tests the curator's insight, which includes understanding the relationship between the audience, current events, post content, and exhibits, and how to discern and capitalize on trending topics.

Following trends is a powerful tool for creating topics and is considered a fundamental skill for corridor curators (E2-A13-GI5; E2-A13-GI10). As mentioned in the above analysis, utilizing the famous game character as a starting point to write posts, as seen in E2-C-J110, is an example of leveraging trends. Bringing the "Travel Frog" puppet into physical display cases creates topicality in the physical realm, thereby influencing the community (E2-A13-GI19). Simultaneously, it adds interest, readability, and stickiness to task-oriented posts introducing exhibits (E2-D1-I6). However, mindlessly following trends is only sometimes necessary. It is essential to grasp the trends based on corridor management strategies, harnessing trends to create topics (E2-A11-GI27). Therefore, understanding the relationship between the audience's environment, events, and exhibits and effectively utilizing trend-following is a crucial fundamental characteristic for curators.

4.2   Elements of Digital-Physical Integration Curatorial Operations

In the operation of digital-physical integration curation, it is necessary to integrate the elements of both physical and social media platform curation. Additionally, it is essential to effectively transform the content of both curation types to enhance efficiency. This involves identifying the interests and values that attract the audience from the physical aspect of presentation form and content and utilizing technology to extend into social media platforms for presentation.

Lighting and Ambiance Creation. In physical curation, corridors affiliated with academic units are subject to spatial and temporal constraints. The primary spatial limitations include lighting, long corridor spaces, and display cabinets. Expert P1, who is both a physical storefront operator and utilizes social media for marketing, shares similarities with the digital-physical integration curation discussed in this study. Expert P1 emphasizes decoration, display, and lighting in physical curation, focusing on creating ambiance and utilizing lighting as critical elements to attract audiences. While the use of lighting in corridors primarily emphasizes display lights within cabinets, expert recommendations suggest that besides cabinets, corridors could also focus on enhancing overall space lighting (E2-P1-PI21). Audience feedback from focus interviews indicates that lighting in corridor physical spaces is indeed one of the attractive elements (E2-A11-GI1; E2-A12-GI3). Hence, lighting emerges as one of the essential elements in physical curation.

Digital-Physical Transformation for Enhanced Effectiveness. Besides lighting and ambiance, the next step is transforming the atmosphere created by physical exhibitions and creativity into valuable social media content. At this point, curators need to utilize internet communities and technology to overcome physical curation's spatial and temporal constraints. First and foremost, before transforming into online community content, curators must utilize their insight into what interests the audience, understanding the personalities and preferences of the audience. As the style of the corridor is oriented towards design and art knowledge-based communities, curators must consider how to transform the physical into valuable and relevant information for the audience (E2-P2-PI1; E2-P2-PI2), thereby achieving the benefits of digital-physical integration. Therefore, the primary operational element for physical entry into online communities is insight into the relationship between the physical and the audience and transforming it into beneficial and valuable information.

After gaining insights into the relationship between the audience and the subject, the next step is to use online community platforms as a medium to overcome the limitations of physical curation. At this stage, curators need to harness the power of technology, such as using fast-editing apps as marketing tools (E2-P1-PI30), the built-in categorization features of online communities (E2-P3-PI11), or innovative content strategies like the ones used in this study (E2-C-J122) to create interaction. This extends the physical curation into online communities, facilitating communication with the audience, asking questions, and maintaining audience relationships through social media platforms (E2-P3-PI10).

Platformization Trends, Echo Chamber Benefits, and Sustainment. Integrated curation of physical and digital realms can complement and leverage the strengths and weaknesses of physical and online community aspects. For instance, the speed of information dissemination in online communities can compensate for the spatial and temporal limitations of physical curation. The sense of presence in physical curation is more complex to achieve in online communities. In contrast, online communities can serve as a free marketing platform and promote physical curation content. This section will analyze and discuss the benefits and sustainability of integrated curation. In the overall integration of physical and digital curation, it is evident that due to the internet platformization trend, online communities have become the preferred choice for the masses to receive information (Walker, 2016). Expert P3 has also found in their own business experience that many collaborators and clients primarily use social media to communicate and inquire about issues (E2-P3-PI9).

Understanding Community Platform Origins to Capture Attention Effectively. Therefore, many museums, galleries, and even physical businesses and storefronts opt for social media as their choice of self-media for promotion (Gillmor, 2006). Utilizing physical spaces, issues, and current events as original content combined with relevant apps as aids, along with the connectivity and interactive features of social communities, creates the benefits of integrated curation.

Although online community platforms are rapid and convenient in message delivery, audiences, bombarded with a plethora of information, have relatively brief windows in which they choose to consume information. Expert P2 believes the critical seconds to attract audience attention range from 0.3 to 3 s (Fan, 2018), while expert P1 suggests it is between 3 to 7 s (E2-P1-PI10). Within this short period of less than 10 s, as mentioned earlier, curators must craft content to be concise, impactful, and brief to swiftly capture audience attention amid the information flood (E2-P2-PI8). To leverage the characteristic of online communities to attract audience attention for efficiency, it's crucial to understand that these platforms are not sales platforms but information exchange platforms for promotion and advertising. Merely bombarding audiences with direct messages about products or subjects can easily lead to neglect and aversion from the audience (E2-P3-PI19). Therefore, the role of content copywriting lies in using precise words, images, and videos to engage the audience. It requires long-term maintenance and accumulation, akin to managing reputation and brand (E2-P1-PI36).

Maintaining Warmth within Echo Chambers. Building upon the previous discussion, the primary motivation for most online community users lies in exchanging messages, experiences, and viewpoints, obtaining entertainment, and maintaining social connections (Koh & Kim, 2004). Therefore, it is essential first to meet the audience's needs mentioned above and motivations. As mentioned earlier, curators need to accumulate a wealth of humorous, concise, and diverse information to provide varied content, which can then persuade the audience to engage in interaction or even make purchases.

The audience gathered on online community platforms through integrated curation forms what is known as an echo chamber. Experts emphasize the importance of creating content from the audience's perspective within these echo chambers, using different topics and common language to convey messages (E2-P1-PI28). This helps maintain cohesion among the audience in the curated online community and even attracts them to physical venues or storefronts through content shared within the echo chamber (E2-P1-PI38). The benefit of echo chambers lies in their ability to use the audience to find potential new audiences, such as using advertising targeting features to select friends of the audience (E2-P3-PI15).

Regarding echo chambers, Expert P1 manages different platforms, while Expert P3 utilizes different platform features. For example, Expert P3 utilizes Instagram's "#" feature to break through echo chambers and algorithmic restrictions to reach new audiences (E2-P3-PI17). Expert P3 also points out that Instagram's "#" keyword function and image-based layout, compared to Facebook, can help reach audiences beyond Taiwan (E2-P3-PI18). Therefore, it is evident that the benefits of integrated curation can be achieved through the functionality of different platforms and the diversity of echo chambers on these platforms.

Incentives and Audience Benefits Facilitate Interaction. Taking Expert P1 as an example, their primary goal in managing communities is to promote the products sold in their physical storefront. Therefore, besides empathizing with the audience's needs and finding relevant topics for their benefit (E2-P1-PI33), incentives play a crucial role in attracting attention. Expert P1 offers gifts and tangible benefits to create audience interest and encourage interaction through comments and questions (E2-P1-PI29; E2-P1-PI32). As interaction occurs within online communities, the algorithms of these platforms can generate free promotional benefits (E2-P1-PI31). Thus, generating interaction leads to promotional benefits in community marketing operations.

For curators involved in community marketing, incentives and audience benefits are two primary tools in their operations. These incentives and benefits stem from understanding what consumers care about and transforming it into genuinely helpful and valuable information for the audience (E2-P2-PI1; E2-P2-PI2).

Understanding incentives and audience (consumer) benefits as the two primary tools for community content, when utilizing online community content for community marketing, Fan (2018) proposed the following posting principles and focus points for Facebook to attract audience attention and achieve community marketing benefits:

Posting principles: Keep it concise and regular.

Posting focus points: Timing, algorithms, and post content.

Post content categories: Direct promotion, indirect promotion, providing information, and lifestyle sharing.

Tips for engagement: Design content that sparks high-interaction comments and native content, optimize videos (self-made videos), seize trends at the right time, and use the proper methods to increase fans and friends (without buying fans with money).

Facebook is just a platform medium; content and copywriting are key.

Regarding the third point about post content, its effectiveness ratio is 1:4:3:2. This means that, compared to directly promoting products or conveying messages, indirect promotion and providing valuable information are the incentives and consumer benefits for the audience. Indirect promotion refers to the power of outward-inward copywriting, where the audience is more interested in content composed of peripheral relevant information (Feng & Cheng, 2015), such as integrating current events, gift events, and lifestyle topics into content, or designing original posts that are interesting and can prompt interaction. Therefore, integrating the above analysis, the operational model of community marketing and attracting audience attention mainly revolves around understanding the audience and using incentives and consumer benefits to generate interaction. The generation of interaction requires curators to combine the posting as mentioned earlier principles and focus points to spark interaction, thereby achieving the marketing and promotional benefits of integrated curation.

4.3 Qualifications of Integrated Curators in the Virtual and Real World

Insight into Platforms to Reach Audiences and Create Benefits. In expert interviews, it was found that insight is used in three dimensions: platforms, audiences, and subjects. Insight into platforms is crucial to understanding various platforms' attributes and their audiences' usage habits (E2-P1-PI2; E2-P1-PI3). For example, all three experts believe the best time to use social media is from 9 pm to 10 pm (Fan, 2018; E2-P1-PI5; E2-P3-PI20). However, the timing speculation also needs to consider the usage habits of one's community audience. Understanding the characteristics and needs of the audience and thinking from their perspective helps create "consumer benefits" (E2-P1-PI14). For example, based on the analysis of the "Daily" illustration exhibition x Carpe Diem and the "Good Pottery, Pleasing Daily Life" exhibition, it was found that the audience of the community is more interested in knowledge, fun, and tasks. Therefore, the content was adjusted in the third exhibition to include tasks combined with knowledge and fun, creating beneficial content for the audience (E2-P1-PI19).

Insight into the Subject to Identify the Stage. Insight into platforms and audiences is essential to understand audience needs clearly. Therefore, curators can express appeals more clearly, provide beneficial and valuable information, and achieve goals based on the audience's needs, habits, and concerns (E2-P1-PI17; E2-P2-PI1). Curators also need insight into the attributes, suitable platforms, market, and audience of the subjects they want to appeal to (E2-P1-PI9; E2-P3-PI14). This insight helps curators resonate with the audience using the same language and precise copywriting (E2-P1-PI6; E2-P1-PI8). Therefore, insight is a necessary condition for curators, and the target of insight must include the audience, the platforms used by the audience, and the subjects. These three must be connected by the curator's insight to generate benefits through the platform.

Brief and Humorous Content Expression. Digital integrated curation involves transforming physical entities with spatial limitations into online content distributed on social media platforms. However, the information on the Internet is like a flood to the audience. Therefore, curators must capture the audience's attention quickly and convey messages to them in a short time. Concise text expression is essential to immediately convey the intended content to the audience (E2-P1-PI7). In addition to understanding the audience, experts also emphasized that the key to content delivery lies in a single appeal and purpose, conveying only one point to the target audience clearly at a time (E2-P2-PI4).

Utilizing the Internet to Absorb Information and Knowledge for Inspiration. Besides insight into platforms, audiences, and subjects, extensive knowledge and diverse information accumulation are necessary for curators to provide quality, diverse, and creative content to the audience (E2-P1-PI16; E2-P1-PI20). Curators must also pay attention to current events, famous phrases, and timely trends to create content that resonates with the audience (E2-P1-PI19). This knowledge accumulation requires continuous training and accumulation of knowledge similar to traditional physical curators. However, digitally integrated curators need to utilize the power of the Internet to accumulate information quickly and keep up with trends to cope with the rapidly flowing information on social media. This enables them to use knowledge to transform the wording and communication frequency suitable for the target audience, ensuring a constant flow of inspiration and content (E2-P1-PI19).

Not Blindly Following Trends or Over posting. While following trends can break the echo chamber of social media and find new potential audiences, relying too much on trends can lead to losing focus. Quality content and maintaining relationships with the audience are crucial, especially during downtime. Providing diverse daily topics is essential for maintaining audience engagement (E2-P1-PI35). Moreover, depending on the attributes of one's subject and audience habits, curators must find the appropriate frequency for community content to avoid excessive posting that lacks quality (E2-P3-PI12).

Multitasking Skills to Shape Style. Providing quality virtual and actual content requires multitasking skills. In addition to being content creators, curators act as gate-keepers (E2-P3-PI12). They need to have skills in copywriting, photography, video editing apps, and visual comprehension to create engaging posts (E2-P1-PI18; E2-P2-PI9). By integrating the subject of physical curation, writing skills, and photography and editing abilities into online community management, curators can create high-quality content, maintain their image and quality, and shape their style. Therefore, integrated curators are multitasking gatekeepers, and maintaining the image and style of the community acts as a barrier to filtering the audience (E2-P2-PI6).

Style as a Filter. Regarding style and image, the community focuses on providing knowledge, fun, and topics related to design and art. Therefore, the audience belongs to a community-oriented toward design, art, and knowledge. Among the experts interviewed in this study, expert P3's community has a strong style and image. As a professional glaze craftsman and community manager, P3 adopts a question-and-answer format in community content and uses authentic Taiwanese dialect to connect with the audience. The style shaped by expert P3 comes from an extension of a series of works and has been set as a style and feature due to its excellent effectiveness (E2-P3-PI1). Expert P3's use of a question-and-answer format in posts creates a unique style and generates topics, increasing audience browsing and dwell time (E2-P3-PI3). Moreover, the unique style and operating methods act as barriers to filter the audience and attract the right audience (E2-P3-PI8; E2-P3-PI13).

Expert P3's community page has accumulated positive impressions due to its particular style and high-quality content, even resulting in audiences actively searching for and viewing posts on the fan page despite changes in the algorithm prioritizing friend posts in 2018 (E2-P3-PI6). Expert P3 relies on their aesthetic sense and editing skills to generate graphics and text, treating community content as creative works with their image and style (E2-P3-PI22). Style and image are essential for curators to control and filter the audience, ensuring the delivery of quality, good, and correct information. Through the above analysis and examples, it can be seen that curators act as gatekeepers for information reception by the audience and maintainers of community image and style, acting as filters for the audience (E2-P2-PI6).

5 Conclusion and Recommendations

Insightful Topic Selection. Curators must demonstrate sensitivity and insight in selecting themes and topics, considering their relevance, novelty, and audience appeal. This is especially crucial when combining physical exhibitions with online community curation, as each periodical exhibition has its theme. After the physical exhibition, online community curation involves selecting exhibited items, related topics, and knowledge for social media posts, continuing until the exhibition period ends. Therefore, curators must carefully evaluate the value, significance, topicality, and feasibility of selected themes and related topics before execution. Utilizing existing online data and preliminary conceptual design is also essential at this stage, requiring insightful collection and filtration of relevant information to lay the groundwork for the communication process with the audience.

Polymathic Spirit Facilitating Insight and Unique Perspectives. Curators must organize and contextualize selected data, integrating them with physical exhibition concepts and items. This process, akin to a polymath's approach, involves comprehensive insight, organization, and contextualization of data, exhibition concepts, and items, fostering the development of unique perspectives. While traditional physical curators require aesthetic sensibilities and background knowledge, digital-physical integration curators can leverage online data with lower entry barriers. However, they must rigorously filter the information for accuracy. Therefore, maintaining curiosity and seeking verification from experts or relevant literature are crucial steps in this process, ultimately leading to diverse perspectives.

Copywriting as the Initial Attraction. Crafting engaging copy is the first step in attracting audience attention, whether for physical exhibitions or online communities. The copy is the first impression for each curation cycle, conveying design trends, artistic viewpoints, craftsmanship, and other relevant knowledge. Given the abundance of information and the audience's shortened attention span, adequate packaging through copywriting is essential. Curators must possess concise, humorous, and engaging writing skills to organize and focus the content, guiding the audience to understand the intended message comprehensively. Additionally, visual elements like images, graphics, and video editing complement the textual content, making copywriting a powerful tool to stand out amidst the information overload.

Leveraging Platforms and Interpreting Data. With well-crafted copy, curators must utilize various platforms to disseminate content to the audience. This requires a deep understanding of platform characteristics and functionalities, enabling the strategic placement of content on suitable physical or online platforms. Leveraging backend data for audience insight is essential, as it informs content customization, optimal posting times, and adjustments for future curation cycles.

Trend Awareness and Responsive Content Creation. Curators should stay updated on online trends, internet jargon, and current events to maintain relevance and audience engagement. Responsive content creation, aligned with trending topics, demands quick decision-making and content generation while ensuring suitability for the target audience.

Empathy, Communication, and Leadership Skills. Throughout the curation process, curators must demonstrate empathy, communication, and leadership skills to understand the audience's perspective, meet exhibitors' needs, foster positive collaborations, and address challenges effectively, ensuring smooth execution and timely completion of the curation process.

In summary, developing digital-physical integration curators requires a combination of insight, polymathic spirit, copywriting skills, data interpretation abilities, trend awareness, and communication and leadership skills. Unlike traditional physical curators, digital-physical integration curators face lower entry barriers but rely heavily on audience engagement and feedback. Therefore, continuous learning, curiosity, platform trend awareness, and content creation are essential for survival and success in the competitive online environment. The curator's journey involves continual adaptation and self-improvement to maintain creativity, perspective, and productivity.

Acknowledgments. This study was funded by National Science and Technology Council Taiwan (112–2420-H-224–001-).

References

Aghaei, S., Nematbakhsh, M.A., Farsani, H.K.: Evolution of the world wide web: From WEB 1.0 TO WEB 4.0. Int. J. Web Semant. Technol. **3**(1), 1–10 (2012)

Ashley, C., Tuten, T.: Creative strategies in social media marketing: an exploratory study of branded social content and consumer engagement. Psychol. Mark. **32**(1), 15–27 (2015)

Chen, M.T.: An investigation of the requirements of curators in science museum. Technol. Mus. Rev. **20**(2), 5–24 (2016)

Cheng, H.W.: Ai Weiwei's Social Media Utilization and Identity Development. Contemp. Art Media Cult. **31**, 9–31 (2016)

Chi, B.U., Wang, W.H., Zhou, W., Shigeki, Y.: An exploration of protecting local culture via content curation in local online museum. In: Paper presented at the IEEE (2013)

Floyd, L.: A little more curation. IEEE Ind. Appl. Mag. **21**(6), 2 (2015)

Fan, G.R.: E-commerce copywriting skills (lecture) (2018)

Feng, T.Y., Cheng, Y.H.: Marketing in a social media environment: the impact of interactivity and argument quality on consumer purchase intentions. J. Inf. Commun. **5**(2), 47–71 (2015)

Gaskill, K.: Curatorial cultures: considering dynamic curatorial practice. In: ISEA - The 17th International Symposium on Electronic Art (2011)

Gillmor, D.: We the Media: Grassroots Journalism by the People, for the People O'Reilly Media, Inc. (2006)

Koh, J., Kim, Y.: Knowledge sharing in virtual communities: an E-business perspective. Expert Syst. Appl. **26**(2), 155–166 (2004)

Lin, T.Y.S.: The cultivation of curators: examining the US principles and standards. J. Des. **18**(4), 23–40 (2013)

Mullan, E.: What is Content Curation? http://www.econtentmag.com/Articles/Resources/Def
ining-EContent/What-is-Content-Curation-79167.htm. Accessed 12 Feb 2024

Patel, K.D.: Incremental journey for world wide web: introduced with web 1.0 to recent web 5.0–a
survey paper. Int. J. Adv. Res. Comput. Sci. Softw. Eng. **3**, 112–125 (2013)

Walker, D.: Mobile exceeds desktop as the most used internet platform (2016). http://www.itpro.co.
uk/mobile/27503/mobile-exceeds-desktop-as-most-used-internet-platform. Accessed 07 May
2024

Research on Interactive Design of Guangxi Bronze Drum Tourism and Cultural Creative Products Based on AR Technology

Feng He[✉] and Zhengcheng Duan

Guangxi Normal University, Guilin 541006, China
dzc1999@qq.com

Abstract. Guangxi is one of the birthplaces of bronze drum culture, and bronze drum culture is rich in resources, which provides precious cultural genes for the research and development of cultural creative products. However, at present, the relevant products are not personalized enough, the expression form is single, and the culture and connotation contained in them are difficult to be understood and cognized by most people, and the empathy degree between the products and consumers is low. Based on this phenomenon, this thesis will explore the methods and strategies of AR technology intervention in the design of Guangxi bronze drum tourism cultural and creative products, so as to empathize with consumers in an interactive way and let users feel the experience of rich culture in the interaction, thus providing new ideas for ethnic minority cultural and creative products to increasingly go digital, mobile, scenario-based and experience-based.

Keywords: Augmented Reality · interaction design · Guangxi Bronze Drum · cultural and creative products

1 Introduction

With the advancement of technology and the development of China's cultural and creative industries, the design of cultural and creative products has evolved from content design to experience design. The focus of design has shifted from a product-centric approach to a human-centric experience design. Traditional cultural and creative products primarily showcased static displays of objects, whereas modern cultural and creative products emphasize the integration of technological means. They accentuate interactive experiences that allow consumers to better perceive and understand the cultural context of products, guiding them to establish an emotional connection with the product during the experience, thereby achieving a higher level of cultural awareness. Augmented Reality (AR) technology, which combines virtual information with the real world, can add more interactivity, fun, and experiential elements to cultural and creative products. This paper will discuss the methods and strategies of integrating AR technology into the design of cultural and creative tourism products related to the Guangxi Bronze Drum, incorporating the historical and cultural aspects of the Guangxi Bronze Drum into digital

P.-L. P. Rau (Ed.): HCII 2024, LNCS 14702, pp. 20–32, 2024.
https://doi.org/10.1007/978-3-031-60913-8_2

and gamified cultural and creative mediums. This allows users to be culturally enriched through interactive experiences. Such an interactive approach to cultural and creative design provides a new methodology for the preservation and transmission of minority cultures.

2 Research on the Cultural Resources of the Guangxi Bronze Drum

The bronze drum is a crystallization of the ancient and splendid culture of China, symbolizing the wisdom of the Chinese ethnic minorities. It embodies a combination of metallurgy, casting, carving, painting, decoration, music, and dance, and is regarded as a "living fossil" of the Zhuang ethnic group's culture, representing one of their significant cultural symbols. The culture of the bronze drum among the Zhuang people has persisted and evolved from the Spring and Autumn and Warring States periods through the Song, Yuan, Ming, and Qing dynasties. Historically, the bronze drum has been closely linked to the lives of the Zhuang people. Originally used as cooking utensils, these drums evolved into percussion instruments and ultimately ceremonial objects, embodying functions such as warding off evil spirits and attracting blessings. Additionally, the bronze drum also symbolized the status, power, and wealth of the nobility among ethnic minorities. Throughout history, the bronze drum has not only been valued for its historical and cultural significance but also for its artistic merit. Particularly noteworthy are its unique design, exquisite decorative patterns, and excellent casting techniques, all of which highlight its enduring artistic charm. The bronze drum is a unique gem within the realm of Chinese ethnic minority art.

2.1 The Design of the Bronze Drum

The bronze drum is a hand-cast bronze artifact, each crafted individually with few repetitions. However, all bronze drums share certain common features: they are entirely made of bronze, with a flat curved waist, a hollow baseless body, and four lugs on the sides. A bronze drum is divided into two main parts: the drumhead and the drum body. The drum body is further subdivided into four sections - the drum chest, drum waist, drum ears, and drum feet. Bronze drums from different periods and regions each have their unique characteristics. For instance, the Shizhaishan-type bronze drum unearthed in Xilin County, Guangxi, has a broad chest that protrudes outward, with the largest diameter positioned higher up, a trapezoidal drum waist, and relatively short drum feet, resulting in a small yet slightly taller overall shape. The Lengshuichong-type bronze drum from Teng County, Guangxi, features a slender and tall body with a larger drum section. Meanwhile, the Lingshan-type bronze drum, popular from the Eastern Han to the Tang dynasty in Guangxi, has a more rounded drum chest with smoother transitions between the drum chest, waist, and feet, presenting a solid, heavy, and delicately shaped appearance.

Originating from cooking utensils, the bronze drum, whether it be the mature Shizhaishan type or the flourishing Lengshuichong, Beiliu, and Lingshan types, still retains the design characteristics of bronze cauldrons. As the bronze drum evolved into a musical instrument and a ceremonial object, the drumhead gradually increased in size.

Its design progressively embraced the concept of 'bigger is better,' leading to a robust and taller physical form.

2.2 Layout and Patterns of Bronze Drum Decorations

The decorative patterns on the bronze drum are a physical representation of the ethnic cultural connotations under specific conditions. Whether it be geometric patterns like sun, cloud and thunder, or sawtooth patterns, or figurative patterns like flying heron, rowing, dancing, and deer patterns, they all represent a refinement, summarization, abstraction, and evolution of natural reality. These patterns reflect the ancient social life of the ancestors of the Guangxi Zhuang ethnic group and their aesthetic pursuits rooted in survival.

Both the drumhead and the drum body of the bronze drum are adorned with unique and exquisite decorative patterns. The arrangement of these patterns exhibits rhythm and rhythmic beauty, serving as a direct carrier of the cultural essence of the bronze drum. The center of the drumhead features a sun pattern, surrounded by multiple layers of halos. Between these halos, various decorative patterns such as cloud and thunder, concentric circles, mat patterns, water wave patterns, and flying crane patterns are used, creating a multi-layered, complex, and splendid drumhead image and pattern. The drum chest, drum waist, and drum feet of the drum body all feature symmetrical decorative patterns. These include realistic patterns like dancing, rowing, deer patterns, and geometric patterns like water wave, dot, and concentric circle patterns. The patterns are arranged in a two-way or four-way continuous style to form decorative scenes. The layout of these decorations is well-ordered, maintaining a high degree of harmony with its structure and design, and is rich in overall aesthetic beauty.

Geometric patterns are the earliest and most consistently present designs on bronze drums, among which the sun pattern is the core pattern on the drumhead. Positioned at the center of the drumhead, it is a simplified representation of the sun, composed of rays and spikes, and is both the earliest and most fundamental decoration on the bronze drum. The cloud and thunder pattern is divided into cloud and thunder parts, representing the reverence and worship of the Zhuang ancestors towards the gods of thunder and rain, as well as their wishes for favorable weather.

The surface of the bronze drum features not only geometric patterns but also many vivid human and animal decorations. These figurative patterns depict scenes of sacrifice, entertainment, production, and life among the Zhuang ancestors, imbued with a strong sense of life and humanity, representing a refinement and simplification of real life. Among these, the feathered-human pattern is a primary human image on the bronze drum. Its distinguishing features include figures adorned with feather decorations and wearing feathered crowns, highlighting the scenes of worship and entertainment being depicted. The content includes boating, sacrifice, herding, dancing, etc., truly reflecting the life of the local ethnic groups. The boat pattern is one of the more complex designs on the bronze drum. Centered around boats and the people on them, it is distributed on the curved surface of the drum chest. It depicts the water activities of boat racing and worship in the southwestern ethnic regions. The boats have upturned ends, are slender and long, and are overall arc-shaped, with characters such as shamans, paddlers, and helmsmen on board. The boat patterns are interconnected and wrap around the drum body in a cyclical pattern, making the entire scene vibrant and rhythmically rich. The flying heron holds auspicious significance for the Zhuang ancestors. In the flying heron pattern, the herons with long beaks, long tails, and outstretched necks, fly around the sun pattern in a counterclockwise direction, forming a ring-like pattern that conveys a sense of dynamic beauty1.

3 Research on the Interaction Design Logic of Guangxi Bronze Drum Cultural and Creative Tourism Products

With the advent of the experience economy, consumers' demand for cultural and creative design has undergone a change. When interacting with cultural and creative products, users are engaged not only in usage but also in aesthetics, interpretation, and ultimately spiritual enjoyment. Contemporary cultural and creative products emphasize the mutual integration of technology, culture, and creativity, where interactive digital cultural and creative products have more competitive strength compared to traditional cultural and creative products. The rapid development of digital technologies such as AR/VR/MR, 3D holographic projection, and motion capture provides technical support for the interactive experience of cultural and creative products. Based on this, the interaction design strategy of the Guangxi Bronze Drum tourism cultural and creative products aims to disseminate the Bronze Drum culture and enrich the sensory experiences of consumers, focusing on technological intervention, cultural innovation, and user experience. This approach makes the ancient Bronze Drum culture more approachable and contemporary, while offering richer and more interesting cultural experiences for the new generation.

The interaction experience logic of Guangxi Bronze Drum tourism cultural and creative products involves the interaction between the user and the product, as well as providing a pleasant, intuitive, and effective user experience. The logic of its interaction design primarily considers the following aspects.

Consumer Demand of Users: Understanding the characteristics, needs, and usage scenarios of target users is fundamental to designing interactive experiences. Firstly, it is crucial to identify the target audience for Bronze Drum cultural and creative products and analyze their emotional needs. The interactivity in the design of Bronze Drum tourism cultural and creative products lies in building a bridge of communication between the product and the user, enabling the user to resonate with the Bronze Drum culture embodied in the product and gain a pleasurable experiential feeling. The primary users of these cultural and creative products are young people. The changing times of consumption and the development of technology and the internet have shaped China's young consumers who are diverse in interests, value individuality, and are concerned with aesthetics. The design of Bronze Drum tourism cultural and creative products should take into account the preferences of young consumers, reinterpreting and creatively expressing the Bronze Drum culture based on their emotional needs.

Emotionalized Experience Content: Expand the content of cultural and creative products to enrich the emotional interaction experience of users. Cultural and creative products represent cultural consumption. When consumers purchase these products, they value not only the functional value of the products but, to a large extent, pay for the artistic and cultural value of the products. Therefore, it is necessary to create an IP image that encapsulates the Bronze Drum culture and possesses contemporary aesthetic appeal, build brand culture, and creatively transform elements of the Bronze Drum culture such as symbolism, color, and design. This approach leads to the derivation of different types of cultural and creative products, extending from everyday items like pillows, water bottles, phone cases, and fridge magnets to other formats such as art picture books, emoticon packs, games, etc., thereby stimulating the consumption desire of cultural and creative consumers who are keen on pursuing personalized consumption and novel experiences.

Immersive Design Approach. Cultural and creative products can provide immersive and narrative experiences, using visual, auditory, and interactive elements to create engaging storytelling experiences. This can make the interaction with Bronze Drum cultural and creative products more convenient and enjoyable. Currently, the cultural industry is showing a trend of development that is predominantly digital, combining both online and offline modes. More and more cultural and creative works are establishing interactive experiences through digitalization, gamification, and intelligent design. However, traditional Bronze Drum tourism cultural and creative products primarily use printed patterns as the main method, with a single product carrier and form, weak interactivity, and insufficient experiential feel, leading to a very limited cultural connotation felt by the users. Therefore, by leveraging modern technological means to expand the forms and carriers of Bronze Drum tourism cultural and creative products, rich interactive experiences can be created through digital and intelligent operations, further stimulating consumers' enthusiasm for purchase and their desire to explore cultural connotations. For example, the use of augmented reality technology in Bronze Drum cultural and creative products can merge the physical products with virtual Bronze Drum scenes, creating an interactive experience that makes these products more interesting2.

4   Feasibility Analysis of Applying AR Technology to Guangxi Bronze Drum Tourism Cultural and Creative Products

4.1   Analysis of the Current Application of AR Technology

Augmented Reality (AR) technology is characterized by the integration of virtual and real environments, real-time interactivity, and the ability to position virtual objects within three-dimensional spaces. AR technology has been widely applied in fields such as cultural tourism, entertainment, education, and commerce. For instance, in the realm of entertainment gaming, AR technology allows players to see virtual scenes and characters within the game and interact with them, thereby enhancing the immersion and fun of the game.

In the context of cultural tourism, AR technology not only provides guided tour services for visitors at cultural heritage tourism sites but also enables them to gain an in-depth understanding of the cultural characteristics and historical background of these sites. In museums, visitors can use AR technology to view virtual exhibits and interactive information or experience digitally reconstructed historical scenes within the real environment, thereby enhancing their visiting experience. In the commercial retail sector, consumers can use AR devices to scan products in stores, seeing virtual product displays and introductions, which enhances their willingness to buy and shopping experience. In the field of education, AR technology enables students to see virtual models and demonstrations while learning, thus aiding in a better understanding of complex concepts and knowledge. The application of AR technology is increasingly penetrating various fields, bringing more convenience and innovation to people's lives and work.

4.2   Analysis of the Value of Applying AR Technology in Cultural and Creative Products

Firstly, it can enhance the fun and educational aspects of cultural and creative products. AR technology offers new ideas and methods for the inheritance and promotion of traditional culture. Cultural and creative products, with their core focus on cultural dissemination, gain a distinct advantage when integrated with AR technology compared to traditional products. The combination of traditional culture and AR technology can innovate the ways traditional culture is communicated and experienced. The use of AR technology not only enhances the educational value of cultural and creative products but also increases their experiential feel and attractiveness, thereby enhancing the added value of these products and making people feel closer to and more affectionate towards traditional culture.

For example, the Zhejiang Natural Museum, focusing on cultural and creative animal IP themes and utilizing its collection of precious resources as product prototypes, has developed cultural and creative products such as the Anshun Dragon AR 3D Paper Model, Parrot-Beaked Dinosaur AR Graffiti Book, Great White Shark AR Plush Pencil Case, and Asian Elephant AR Diamond Blocks. Supported by AR technology, internet technology, and real-time online interactive technologies, these products are not only artistic and fun but also have educational significance in science popularization.

Secondly, it can enhance the participation and immersion of users in cultural and creative products. AR technology, with its characteristics of combining the virtual with the real, real-time interaction, and three-dimensional immersion, brings a strong sense of presence and participation to the experiencer. Through AR technology, virtual cultural information is displayed in the real world, allowing experiencers to interact with this virtual information. Technological means are used to seamlessly integrate reality with virtual information, constructing a three-dimensional scene to display objects that do not exist in reality, which interconnects with real life. This makes the virtual space synchronize with the real space, fostering a consistent and stronger interaction.

For example, the Henan Satellite TV stage play "Night Banquet in Tang Dynasty Palace" utilizes 5G and AR technology to combine virtual scenes with the real stage, creating an immersive experience that makes the audience feel as if they are part of the scene. As the scenes change, the dance and history blend perfectly, and together with the constructed magnificent Tang Dynasty palace scene, it gives the audience the feeling of being in a time tunnel of technology and history.

4.3   Interaction Methods in Cultural and Creative Product Design Using AR Technology

AR technology can provide a variety of interactive methods in the design of cultural and creative products, offering users a more immersive and innovative experience.

It provides real-time interaction for users, enabling object recognition and tracking. By embedding AR recognition markers in cultural and creative products, viewers can scan these markers using smartphones or tablets. Then, utilizing AR technology, they can access virtual content related to the exhibit and interact with virtual elements in real-time. For example, users can view virtual cultural artifacts, alter their appearance, rotate them, or interact with them. They can also view virtual overlays of related cultural content. The application of AR technology assists users in comprehensively understanding the full picture and background knowledge of the cultural and creative products. Furthermore, by adding animation effects to cultural and creative products through AR technology, users can experience the dynamic scenes described by the products in a real-world environment. This makes the products more vivid and enhances users' perception of cultural venues.

Providing Users with Virtual Assembly.   For some complex cultural and creative products, such as models and toys, AR technology can facilitate a virtual assembly process, allowing users to operate and experience these in a real-world setting. Users can see virtual models through AR devices and manipulate them using gestures or touchscreen interactions. This interactive method enhances the product's appeal and interactivity.

Facilitating Social Interaction for Users.   AR technology supports multi-user collaboration, enabling several users to jointly engage with cultural and creative products. In the design of these products, simple interactive gaming elements can be incorporated, realized through shared virtual elements, interactive games, or collaborative creation. Additionally, by integrating AR technology with social media, cultural and creative products can be linked to social platforms. Users can scan AR recognition markers on the products to access related virtual content and engage in social interactions such as sharing, commenting, and liking, thus enhancing the social attributes and communicability of the products.

Offering Users Various Interaction Methods.   For instance, gesture control allows AR technology to capture user gestures through cameras and sensors, turning them into a means to interact with virtual elements. Voice Recognition: Integrating voice recognition technology enables users to interact with AR cultural and creative products through voice commands. Users can inquire about information on artworks, request navigation, or perform other actions3.

4.4   Interaction Content Strategy in Guangxi Bronze Drum Tourism and Cultural Creative Product Design Using AR Technology

The integration of AR technology in the design of Guangxi bronze drum tourism and cultural creative products offers a multisensory, interactive experience that blends virtual experiences with the real world. This approach provides a three-dimensional and immersive sensory experience, making the ancient bronze drum cultural heritage more accessible and engaging.

In terms of interactive carrier design: Designers should consider the psychological needs and emotional experiences of users in the design of Guangxi bronze drum tourism and cultural creative products. They should effectively integrate the traditional cultural element of the bronze drum into modern life. For example, using the unique shape of the bronze drum and its distinct ethnic patterns, designers can create products with bronze drum characteristics such as speakers, bronze drum-themed creative books, decorative items and daily utilities incorporating bronze drum patterns, and bronze drum music education products.

In terms of interactive content: As AR technology can provide rich and engaging interactive content in cultural and creative design, the interactive content for Guangxi bronze drum culture should focus on incorporating AR technology and closely align with the theme of Guangxi bronze drum culture. For instance, users can use AR technology to view virtual markers on the cultural and creative carriers, accessing historical information about the bronze drum culture. Designers can create animations or games featuring virtual bronze drum patterns, the craftsmanship of bronze drum making, and performance scenes to interact with users. By providing an immersive interactive experience, these elements can attract users' interest and attention, thereby enhancing user engagement.

In the design of interaction methods: In the design of Guangxi bronze drum tourism and cultural creative products, appropriate AR interaction methods should be selected based on the product characteristics and user needs. These methods could include smartphone scanning, gesture recognition, touchscreen interactions, and voice control. It is important to consider the compatibility and interoperability of different devices to ensure the stability and reliability of the interaction methods.

5   Practice in Guangxi Bronze Drum Tourism and Cultural Creative Product Design

5.1   Design of Carriers for Bronze Drum Tourism and Cultural Creative Products

The design of Guangxi bronze drum tourism and cultural creative products aims to disseminate the culture of Guangxi bronze drums, integrating AR technology into the creative product design. The physical aspect of this design can be divided into two parts: First, the design of the product's main body. Overall, the physical component of the design uses a mug as the carrier, drawing from the traditional bronze drum's edge lines, appropriately deformed and transformed to enhance visual stability. The handle's inspiration comes from the flying heron patterns found in traditional bronze drum designs, transforming a flat pattern into a three-dimensional form, thereby achieving an organic integration of form and function. Second, the pattern design. The lid pattern of this design retains the basic ornamental layout centered around the drum's sun pattern, using a circular array to orderly arrange patterns like rowing and dancing, presenting symmetrical beauty. The body pattern involves new design pathways for common bronze drum ornaments such as rowing and auspicious heron patterns, modernizing them while retaining their sense of order. The end of the accompanying spoon is decorated with a cute frog head, echoing the three-dimensional sculpture of the squatting frog on the real bronze drum surface. The color scheme uses sober black and white to emphasize the cultural significance (Figs. 1 and 2).

Fig. 1. The evolution of modeling

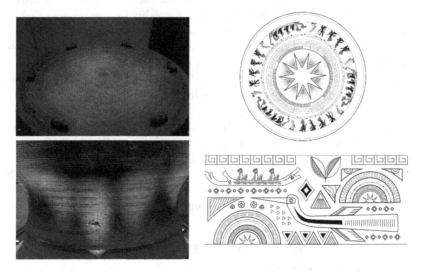

Fig. 2. Patterns inspiration

5.2 Analysis of the Interaction System

Users, through mobile devices equipped with AR technology capabilities such as smartphones or tablets, can gain an in-depth understanding of the product from any location. On these devices, users can touch virtual buttons with their fingers to extensively learn about the culture, historical background, and manufacturing methods of Guangxi bronze drums. Additionally, users can interact with three-dimensional data models on their phones by touching and executing a series of command keys, creating animated effects within the scene, thereby offering a richer perceptual experience.

5.3 AR Cultural and Creative Product Design Practice

Three-Dimensional Model Creation. For the Guangxi bronze drum cultural and creative mug design, a three-dimensional model is created using Rhino 3D software to model the product's appearance. During the modeling process, product details are optimized to ensure the mug's optimal comfort in hand. Considering the common size of mugs in the market, the bottom diameter is set at 110 mm, the mouth diameter at 70 mm, and the height at 110 mm. To meet the requirements of a comfortable grip, a handle with a smooth, curved design is used, more closely resembling the shape of a human hand. The 3D model completed in Rhino software is exported as a 3dm format file, then imported into Keyshot software for rendering the product scene. This step involves giving the product realistic materials, adjusting lighting and camera positions, and creating graphic effects. AI software is used to draw the lid and body patterns of the mug and to design the interactive interface, thereby completing the implementation of the product's interactive functionality (Figs. 3 and 4).

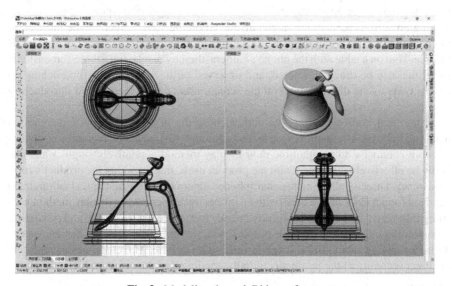

Fig. 3. Modeling through Rhino software

Fig. 4. Visual effect of a mug with traditional patterns

Implementation of AR Interaction. After the completion of the three-dimensional model and the physical production of the cultural and creative product, the practice enters its final stage—integrating AR technology into the design of the cultural and creative product. In terms of application scenarios, to ensure seamless use and deep engagement with this AR interaction by a broad range of users, it's essential first to determine the operating platform. The author selects the widely used smartphones among young people, equipped with camera functionality. Users need only utilize the camera function of the smartphone to recognize real-world objects or images to activate the program.

In selecting the objects of recognition, there are two main concepts. First, the physical body of the cultural and creative product itself is considered as the object for AR recognition. Once the phone's camera captures the outline and shape of the actual object, the system can enter an interactive state. Users can trigger corresponding pop-ups by clicking on various parts of the model displayed on the screen. Second, the more commonly used QR code is employed as the AR recognition object. Users can recognize QR codes laid out on a table with the phone's camera, thereby displaying a three-dimensional model that can be dragged, rotated, and observed on it. Subsequently, by clicking on various parts of the digital model on the screen, users can trigger related introductory pop-ups.

In the final implementation, the author chose the first method of AR recognition mentioned above. The main reason is that although QR codes as recognition objects are more conducive to recognition, their display method is relatively singular and can hardly be effectively integrated with the product itself, thus breaking the product's form consistency. Directly allowing the smartphone camera to recognize the real cultural and creative product can provide users with an immersive experience, a display method with strong interactive properties. This study intends to explore the feasibility and possibility of combining cultural and creative product design with AR interaction design to popularize knowledge about the Guangxi bronze drum culture. Therefore, in this research, the direct scanning of the product is initially attempted as the object of recognition.

Interaction Logic. In terms of interaction logic and process, the author systematically organized the information based on the previously mentioned scenarios and user needs, resulting in a specific plan for the interaction process. Specifically, users trigger the interaction program by using their smartphones to recognize the main body of the mug. Subsequently, the three-dimensional model of the Guangxi bronze drum will be displayed above the mug. At this stage, users can flexibly choose to drag the three-dimensional model of the bronze drum in any direction, allowing for a comprehensive appreciation of its design. Additionally, users can trigger the display of specific introduction pages by clicking certain buttons. Once clicked, the introduction page will float around the three-dimensional model, and if the user clicks the same spot again, the current introduction page will immediately disappear. The design of this interaction process aims to provide a smooth and intuitive interactive experience for users, enabling them to deftly interact with the three-dimensional model of the Guangxi bronze drum cultural and creative mug and obtain related information.

Design Outcome Display. A three-dimensional scan of the actual bronze drum was conducted, endowing it with specific materials and textures to obtain the corresponding three-dimensional model. This model, along with the related interactive interface, was imported into AR generation software, such as Unity or Kivicube, for programming and outputting the interactive program. Ultimately, the use of AR technology to introduce the culture of Guangxi bronze drums was completed, achieving a popular science interactive design that imparts knowledge about the shape and patterns of Guangxi bronze drums. The successful operation on mobile devices and comprehensive testing of the interaction process validated the design's efficacy and feasibility. This process utilized modern technological methods to achieve a technological presentation and knowledge transfer of cultural products (Fig. 5).

Fig. 5. Scanning process

6 Conclusion

The design of Guangxi bronze drum tourism and cultural creative products based on AR technology embodies the organic integration of culture, modern technology, and market forces. By thoroughly sorting through the cultural resources of the Guangxi bronze drum, this approach involves a profound study of the drum's form, color, patterns, and cultural connotations. It systematically extracts elements from the drum and innovatively reinterprets them to align more closely with contemporary aesthetic standards. The creative process aims to produce tourism and cultural creative products that possess both a cultural and artistic atmosphere and practical functionality. The combination of cultural and creative product design with AR interaction is intended to promote knowledge of Guangxi bronze drum culture among modern young people, sparking their interest in actively exploring its underlying meanings. The innovation in this design method lies in blending traditional culture with advanced technology, making the culture of the Guangxi bronze drum more appealing to the younger generation and encouraging them to engage in a deeper study and experience of this rich cultural tradition.

Acknowledgments. This study was funded by Guangxi Philosophy and Social Science Program (grant number 20BMZ016).

References

1. Jie, Z.: Research on the visual language of copper drum decoration Master's Degree Thesis, Kunming Universit y of Science and Technology) (2010). https://kns.cnki.net/kcms2/article/abstract?v=oslmGXurZ-pXPLr1HI_I-HqqzN0ikTJ8PuG5GuTCINzn_p8XRLE8AqQOvQjIDVPLjStU_VR04JnW7YLK47qfptgy_LECAs9q7wdEHp4pPYmUfAtF5PDhuc4vjXIPKX6yB_PjKYWVqXbzLJ5PO7Ilxg==&uniplatform=NZKPT&language=CHS
2. Zhan, Q., Zhao, Y.: Research on interactive integration design of AR technology and traditional paper media. Packag. Eng. **06**, 139–144 (2018). https://doi.org/10.19554/j.cnki.1001-3563.2018.06.027
3. Chu, F.F.F.: Research on developing tourism cultural and creative souvenirs based on AR technology. Wirel. Connected Technol. **18**, 163–164 (2018)

Qianzhan Technology's 5F Perceptual Learning Research Takes VR Wearable Devices as an Example

Yu Di Huang[✉], Po Hsien Lin, and Rungtai Lin

Graduate School of Creative Industry Design, National Taiwan University of Arts, New Taipei City, Taiwan
`artistted@hotmail.com`

Abstract. The purpose of this study is to try to use the timeline of the development of VR wearable device products, distinguish the representative characters of past product designs with English words starting with 5 F as their characteristics, explore the impact of technological evolution on product design features and value, and then explore This article reviews and comments on product design trends from the perspective of "perceptual design" and discusses how perceptual design has become an important design thinking under the influence of human life styles. It is hoped that it can provide some conceptual help in related design fields.

Keywords: 5F · VR wearable devices · perceptual design

1 Research Background and Purpose

1.1 Background

In recent years, due to the advancement of technology, on-site exhibitions can be virtualized and are no longer limited to on-site visits. This virtualization method includes web pages, interactive web pages, online videos and VR. Now, with the development of virtual reality technology, we can look at VR from different design perspectives. At the end of 2021, Mark Zuckerberg proposed that Facebook would strive to create a set of maximized, interconnected experiences directly derived from science fiction—a world called the Metaverse. This sentence is deeply rooted in people's hearts and created VR wearable devices are at the stage where hundreds of schools of thought are contending; until the launch of Apple's first VR wearable device, Vision Pro, in February 2024, VR wearable devices have finally entered the era of humanized and considerate design, so [technology always comes from human nature], or [humanized technology] The concept has always been regarded as the standard for technological products. Technology, humanity and design are closely related.

1.2 The 5 F's of Technologically Evolved Products

The design and aesthetics of the 20th century underwent a transformational journey. Initially, functionalism prevailed with the principle of "form follows function" in the 1930s, considered the paramount guiding principle of design. However, following the end of World War II, people grew tired of design dictated solely by functionality. Thus, in the 1950s, the rise of ergonomics led to a shift towards designs that catered to human needs and comfort, known as "form follows friendly." With the advent of personal computing in the 1980s, the focus shifted towards "user-friendly" designs, emphasizing user-friendliness and convenience, i.e., "form follows friendly." Subsequently, there emerged a trend of playful and personalized designs, advocating for "form follows fun" and "form follows fancy," respectively. Entering the 21st century, the proliferation of digital technology emphasized the importance of "human-centric" design, prioritizing the consideration of users' emotions and experiences, encapsulated in the concept of "form follows feeling." These evolutionary shifts in design philosophies and values reflect the dynamic nature of design thinking throughout different eras. In the world of technology, design based on "humanity" is more important, that is, the so-called perceptual form (form follows feeling) (Lin, 2005).

- (Design for Function)
- (Design for user Friendly)
- (Design for Fun)
- (Design for Fancy)
- (Design for Feeling)

1.3 Research Purpose

The purpose of this study will be to explore VR wearable device products through the five Fs from the perspective of qualitative research on perceptual design.

2 Literature Discussion

2.1 The Evolution of Technology and Its Impact on Products

Design is a longstanding activity that can be traced back to early human civilization. Industrial design emerged in the 1920s and 1930s primarily due to the rise of the Industrial Revolution, which introduced new methods of division of labor. With the advancement of mechanized production, productivity of products increased, while also altering the work environment and leading to the emergence of professional designers. Therefore, whenever there are well-known art and design-related movements in society, certain design movements do indeed have direct relations with the global economy (see Slack Laura, 2008). As shown in Fig. 1, when significant events, movements, and breakthroughs in key technologies occur, representative products are produced. The figure is based on significant events and movements, as well as representative products, from Slack Laura's "What is product design?" and also incorporates the analysis of VR products that will be conducted in this study.

2.2   The 5F Theory Basis of VR Products

Norman. Design is always human-centered. Good design must be built on a partnership between designers and users, fostering a natural inclination for sharing and collaboration, which will help us pursue a good life in a complex world.

Lin, 1996. The design philosophy of "human-centeredness" emphasizes that the purpose of design is people, not products. The consensus on future product design is how to integrate the human lifestyle into the sensory products of technology. Visually appealing products are the most direct and effective way to impress consumers, and culture is also an important criterion for design evaluation.

Maslow. Maslow proposed the Hierarchy of Needs theory in human motivation.

The 5 needs are arranged like a ladder, ascending from high to low, but the order is not fixed and can vary, with various exceptions.

Generally, when one level of needs is relatively satisfied, individuals tend to develop towards higher levels, and the pursuit of higher-level needs becomes the driving force behind behavior.

The 5 needs can be divided into two levels of high and low. Physiological, safety, and belongingness needs belong to the lower level, which can be satisfied through external conditions. Esteem and self-actualization needs are higher-level needs, which can only be satisfied through internal factors, and an individual's pursuit of esteem and self-actualization needs is endless.

The structure of needs for the majority of people in a country is directly related to the country's level of economic development, technological development, culture, and level of education of the people. In underdeveloped countries, a higher proportion of people have lower-level needs, while a lower proportion have higher-level needs. The opposite is true in developed countries.

Qianzhan Design. First of all, the indication when using the product. That is to suggest the use of the product, operational procedure, etc. of this product. It should also show the symbolic of the product. This is mainly reflected in the grade, nature and fun of the product itself. Make full use of the achievements of modern ergonomics and aesthetics, and scientifically increase the emotional factors in product tool design.

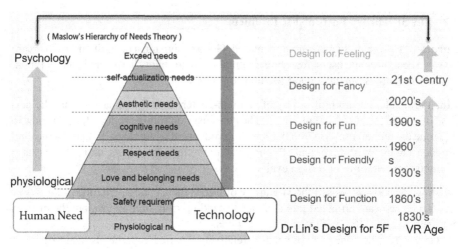

Fig. 1. Maslow's Hierarchy of Needs & Science and technology development

From the perspective of the trend curve representing human physiology to psychological, science and technology as shown in the right half of Fig. 1 will continue to evolve, and human beings cannot break away from humanity like a science and technology leap. The Maslow's Hierarchy of Needs still exists so far. In fact, the five -level demand of 5F product style is echoing each other's five -level needs. As shown in the left half of Fig. 1, from the perspective of human nature and the evolution of technology, the changes in product design trends, product design trends, and finally How will it evolve?

3   Research Methods and Structure

3.1   Research Methods and Processes

This study is a case analysis of qualitative research, using literature and product data to analyze VR wearable device products through 5F of perceptual design.

Analyze the creative and perceptual design analysis results of VR wearable device products through the semantic, effect, and technical aspects of the product.

The overall research process of this study is shown in Figs. 1 and 2:

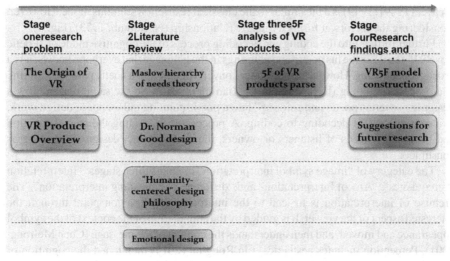

Fig. 2. Overall research process

3.2 Research Structure

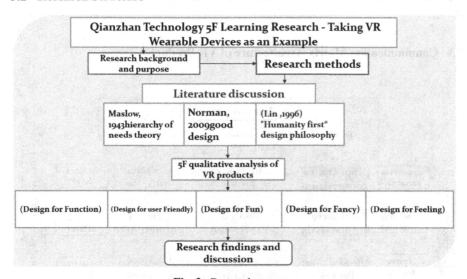

Fig. 3. Research structure

All advertising behaviors can be regarded as the encoding and decoding of symbols. Advertising is essentially a process of encoding messages to transmit messages by the sender, which is transmitted to the audience by various vectors or media to the audience, and the audience will decode after receiving the message. From the perspective of information dissemination, the straight -line communication mode of Shannon and

Weaver (1949) (1949) is a bit similar to the classical restriction stimulus mode. However, Considering the factors, it forms a triangle relationship (Newcomb, 1953) (Fig. 3).

Further further into the coding and decoding process of the cognitive mode of "Poetic Love". If you describe his poetic and paintings in the language that everyone knows, it is a process of decoding. How the same painter converts poetry into a poetic painting painting is a process of coding (Lin Rong tai, Li Xian mei, 2015). So the same reason, how a designer converts "poetic and painting" into a poetic painting indoor space design work, is also a process of decoding to coding. A process of re -coding the spatial function and personality needs of listeners or owners, the same product design is the same as consumers.

The category of "image symbol interpretation" contains three stages: "Interpretation Prerequisites", "Any of Interpretation" and "differences in meaning interpretation". The premise of interpretation is to lead to the interpretation attraction point through the interested aspect of the viewer. It is guided by the connotation of the context of the symbol appearance and moved, and then understands the content of the message (Chen Meirong, 2001). Perception includes aesthetics, Lin Rong tai (2015) mentioned the cognition of three modes in the perception mode of poetic and painting, 1. Style perception (five senses) 2. Septing recognition 3. Expected effect. Perception behavior is an emotional function or emotion, which can be divided into situation (referring to functional function), message (poetic function), contact (social function), rune code (ultra -language function), and finally reached an attempt to be reached (Gao Ya juan, Yan Huiyun, Lin Rong tai, 2017).

3.3   Communication Matrix Architecture of VR Products

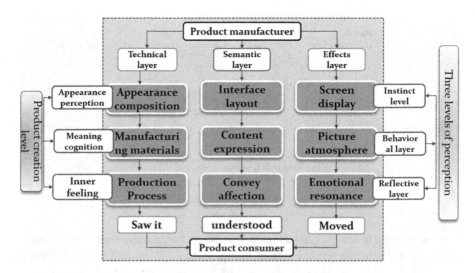

Fig. 4. Communication matrix architecture

The solution of perceptual design is not related to the evolution of the times of the times, but the way of presence of contemporary technology products does not necessarily have to be a so -called sense of rational technology, because there are many human ethnic groups and different culture. The taste style is full of diversified markets, and the model of interaction with products and experience products in recent years is very popular with consumers. From the 5F research and analysis of VR products (as shown in Figs. 4 and 5), you can glimpse this trend; a variety of choices to create a different life of different lives Form, this is also a very important exposition in Maslow's level of demand theory. Moreover, human psychological needs are more complicated and changeable. To achieve the goal of self -realization in your own heart, you must experience it yourself to experience it to affirm your realization. This is also the preciousness of human thinking, because the pursuit of self -realization makes human life and richness. Some researchers have expressed the product experience in the field of user experience and interactive design.

3.4 VR Product Creation and Cognitive Model

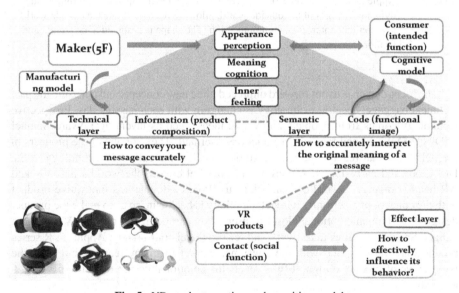

Fig. 5. VR product creation and cognitive model

4 5F Over All Analysis of VR Products

This article focuses on analyzing commonly owned products in daily life, with VR wearable devices as the subject of analysis. VR wearable devices belong to the category of portable mobile display products. In dividing the 5F categories, besides considering the chronological sequence, reference is made to the current (2023) state of technology and design trends as the criteria for assessment. VR products are categorized into five styles corresponding to different user needs.

Table 1. 5F over all analysis

5F	VR wearables
Function	At this time, VR equipment was bulky and had complex functions that required manual operation. The operating interface was a mechanical knob that used lenses and pictures to achieve a three-dimensional effect
Friendly	Enter the curved shape of glasses, improve functions, and integrate interfaces, focusing on military applications and experimental use
Fun	The first commercial VR product, a wearable VR device was launched, which can be worn anywhere without feeling too burdensome. It presents fun and novelty in appearance and interface, and begins to be integrated with mobile phone functions
Fancy	The types of VR wearable devices at this stage can be described as mushrooming, ever-changing, and booming
Feeling	Apple launches Vision Pro. The screen can become transparent according to the dynamic changes of the outside world, allowing the eyes to see the outside world and facilitate interactive communication. The shape is designed to be simple and fashionable like goggles

The focus design is to put forward unprecedented new concepts and put aside the past technical baggage, because technology is changing with each passing day. Prospective technology comes from people's innovative ideas, such as inventing Edward Samuel "ED" CATMULL) and Ivan · Ivan Edward Sutherland: They are one of the pioneers in the field of virtual reality, and they have developed some early VR technology in the late 1960s and early 1970s. Among them, Ivan Sel created the world's first VR and AR headset display "Sword of Damocles" in 1968. Complete this innovative product with the concept of electronics. Great technology is back bun, so as to make the product design more human emotional closer to users. You can be free to close to VR without danger. Space operations make work and leisure travel comfortably. Apple's VR series products are very popular with the consumer market for many reasons, but from the perspective of product design, it fully meets the emotional design model in 5F (Fig. 6 and Table 1).

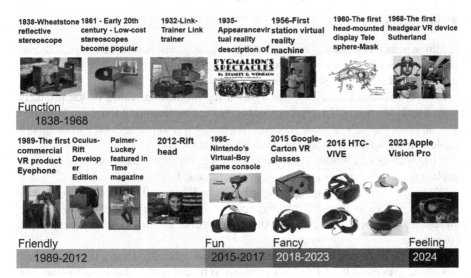

Fig. 6. 5F over all analysis

5 Conclusion and Suggestion

5.1 Conclusion

The conclusions of this study can be summarized as follows:

VR product design must at least be Functional and Friendly, as well as meet people's basic needs. The first generation of products are mainly functional, and then the improvement direction will be based on human considerations to comply with the basic physiology and safety of human nature. need.

When VR products mature and become smaller, lighter and cost-effective, a large number of product styles such as functions, shapes, materials and colors are created to create different tastes. Whether it is Fun or Fancy, they are all Feeling and VR products that satisfy consumers of different ethnic groups. Because of Apple's innovation, the current design style and usage model of VR products are almost the same.

Perceptual design is the trend and thinking of VR product innovation and reform. It must make consumers feel zero distance from technology. VR products must come from perceptual design thinking of humanized use. Product innovation challenges come from changes in consumer lifestyles.

Digital integration improves the thinking of product design, such as the integration of digital cameras and mobile phones. Future products will be Design for Feeling, providing a new lifestyle service chain as an option. VR products must be humane, technological, and timely. The focus on the latest technology and the human level is also the focus of perceptual design.

5.2 Suggestion

In addition to further reflecting on the problems that still exist in the research process and the areas that need improvement during the implementation process, this study further puts forward the following suggestions:

There are several limitations, mainly focusing on the appearance of VR products based on daily life needs. If a larger amount of data can be obtained through random sampling, and then through accurate statistics, the research results presented will definitely be able to more accurately infer the 5F of VR products.

If the number of qualitative research samples is expanded, more oriented attribute correlation analysis and more accurate conclusions can be statistically obtained.

VR image samples are mainly sampled from web pages. If works from web pages from different periods are used, the image composition, shooting and color use may be different, and the display effect in the exhibition environment may be different from that of this study.

In the future, the research team can evaluate the opinions of men, the elderly and other ethnic groups on the 5 Fs of VR products to further understand the differences in opinions of VR5Fs between different subjects.

In-depth discussion of the design and application of VR wearable devices in different periods, and demonstration of practical applications and empirical research.

Finally, I hope to provide VR5 F opinions and suggestions for reference by future researchers.

Acknowledgments. The author would like to thank Professor Lin Rong tai, Professor Lin Po Hsien, and Director Professor Lin Zhi long of the Institute of Cultural and Creative Industries Design at the National Taiwan University of Arts.

Disclosure of Interests. The authors declare no conflicts of interest.

References

1. Shannon, C., Weaver, W.: The Mathematical Theory of Communication. University of Illinois Press, Illinois (1949)
2. Newcomb, T.: An approach to the study of communication acts'. Psychol. Rev. **60**, 393–440 (1953)
3. Tractinsky, N.: Aesthetics and apparent usability: empirically assessing cultural and methodological issues. In: Proceedings of the ACM SIGCHI Conference on Human Factors in Computing Systems, pp. 115–122 (1997). https://doi.org/10.1145/258549.258626
4. Mehrabian, A., Russell, J.A.: An Approach to Environmental Psychology. The MIT Press, Cambridge (1974)
5. Chen, M.R.: Exploring the characteristics of meaning construction and interpretation of image symbols using semiotic theory. Unpublished master's thesis, National Yang-Ming Chiao Tung University, Institute of Applied Arts (2001)
6. Ma, J.W.: Reconstructing the audience. Commun. Sociol. J. **27**(1), 23–25 (2014)

7. Chiu, S.Y.: A study on YouTube True View advertisement viewing behavior (Unpublished master's thesis). National Sun Yat-sen University, Kaohsiung City (2013). https://hdl.handle.net/11296/b4n843

8. Chen, S.J., Yen, H.Y., Lee, S.M., Lin, C.L.: A case study of curatorial design: Poetic Sentiments—Painting Studies of Xian yuu. Des. J. **21**(4), 1–24 (2016)

9. Chang, H.J., Wang, M.X., Chang, C.C.: A study on cognitive fun and immersive experience— Using micro-films as examples (Unpublished master's thesis). Ming dau University, Changhua County (2018). https://hdl.handle.net/11296/8qapk4

10. Yeh, M.L., Lin, P.H., Hsu, C.H.: Application of cultural creativity design in the transformation of poetry and verse imagery. Des. J. **16**(4), 91–105 (2011)

11. Gao, Y.J., Yen, H.Y., Lin, R.T.: A study on transforming artwork into interior design mode: Using the "Poetic Sentiments" series of paintings as an example. Art J. **101**, 107–134 (2017)

12. Lin, R.T., Lee, S.M.: Poetic Sentiments—Experiences in the Study of Beauty, New Taipei City, Yuchen, pp. 17–53 (2015)

13. Hung, P.H., Lin, R.T., Yen, H.Y.: Primary school students' cognition of idiom image design. Des. J. **1**(1), 3–19 (2016)

14. LNCS Homepage: Old Antique in the Yuan Universe: the past and present life of VR (Yahoo.com). Accessed 2 Feb 2024

15. LNCS Homepage: Mark Zuckerberg is betting Facebook's future on the metaverse - The Verge. Accessed 2 Feb 2024

Research on the Application of Virtual Reality Technology in Short Video Production Within the Perspective of Cross-Cultural Arts

Weilong Wu[✉] and Qingli Wang

School of Film Television and Communication, Xiamen University of Technology, Xiamen, China
wu_acedemic@163.com

Abstract. Objectives: With the advancement of globalization and the development of science and technology, cultural exchanges between various countries have become more and more frequent, and cross-cultural communication has become an important phenomenon in today's society, which can help to better understand and appreciate the uniqueness of different cultures, and promote cultural exchanges and integration. Therefore, intercultural communication has become an important research field. However, in the process of cross-cultural communication, due to geographical limitations, people cannot feel the charm of different cultures in their own situation, and their understanding of culture stays on the visual surface, and the experience of watching only through words, pictures and videos will be greatly reduced. The use of virtual reality technology can break this limitation, so that people from different cultural backgrounds can have a more intuitive and in-depth understanding and experience of different cultures, and promote communication and understanding between different cultures. This paper takes "virtual reality technology" as the core of the research, explores the application of virtual reality technology in the process of short video production, analyzes the advantages and shortcomings of virtual reality technology in short video production, and predicts the development trend of virtual reality technology in the future, so as to provide reference experience for the video creators, and to promote the understanding and integration of different cultures.

Virtual reality technology is characterized by interactivity, immersion and multi-sensory, and its development affects our life. In recent years, virtual reality technology has been increasingly used in various fields, not only in film and television, entertainment, education, medical care, military and other fields, but also in short video production. Short videos have become an important part of our lives due to their short duration and the fact that they can be watched in fragmented time. Moreover, its short and concise nature, fast dissemination speed and ease of sharing have also contributed to the rapid dissemination and exchange between different cultures.

Currently, short videos have dominated the social media field, and people commonly use cell phones to watch these video contents. However, on the traditional cell phone screen, there is usually only a fixed perspective, and users can only browse short videos by clicking and sliding, which does not allow for a

---

W. Wu and Q. Wang—These authors contributed equally to this study.

P.-L. P. Rau (Ed.): HCII 2024, LNCS 14702, pp. 44–59, 2024.
https://doi.org/10.1007/978-3-031-60913-8_4

360-degree panoramic view, and the production method is also relatively process-oriented and single shooting method. With the continuous progress of the times, people's demand for media content is constantly upgraded, and the audience is no longer satisfied with traditional print media, but expects to experience more immersive and more realistic media content. Therefore, a new form of media, virtual reality technology is gradually emerging. The perfect integration of virtual reality technology and short video, the user can feel the scene and atmosphere of the video, this new experience will make the user more in-depth understanding and feeling of the content of the short video, so as to enhance its dissemination effect and influence. Virtual reality technology provides new possibilities and opportunities for the production of short videos, and at the same time, the production of virtual reality short videos provides new tools and platforms for cultural communication.

Methods: In this study, 200 questionnaires were distributed to the audience using the questionnaire method, aiming to investigate how much they know about virtual reality technology, their perceptions and attitudes towards virtual reality technology in the production of short videos, and how they perceive the impact of short virtual reality videos on cross-cultural communication. After collecting the data, statistical analysis tools were used to process and analyze the data and produce results.

Results: Through the statistical analysis of the questionnaire data, this study found that most of the audience believes that compared with the traditional sense of the short video, the short video produced using virtual reality technology, the two-dimensional video to 3D imaging expression, the scene experience when watching the feeling of a more realistic, you can experience a more immersive audio-visual effect, improve the video viewing and interactivity. It is believed that virtual reality short videos are more capable of enabling people to experience different cultures and traditional customs across geographical barriers and promote cross-cultural communication.

Conclusions: This study found that by applying virtual reality technology to short video production, short video content can more vividly and imaginatively display the cultural landscape and cultural traditions of different places, and increase the real experience of immersion.

Short videos combined with virtual reality technology create a unique cross-cultural environment, which can help people better experience different cultural characteristics around the world, enhance their interest in and identification with different regional cultures by means of visual and auditory perception, understand the values of other cultures, and reduce the inconvenience of cultural exchanges due to geographical restrictions. This experience helps to enhance people's cross-cultural awareness and be more tolerant of multiculturalism. With the development of science and technology, the future of virtual reality technology in short video production has a wide range of prospects for application, and the way of producing and watching videos will also change, which can provide new ways and means of cultural exchange and dissemination. However, at present, the virtual reality technology innovation is fast, the technical threshold is high, and the popularity of virtual reality technology is low, so how to make better use of virtual reality technology in the production of short videos in the future and how to use VR short videos to promote cross-cultural exchanges still need to be further researched.

Keywords: Cross-cultural Arts · Virtual Reality Technology · Short Video Production

1 Introduction

In recent years, virtual reality technology has been increasingly used in a variety of fields, not only in film and television, entertainment, education, medical care, military and other fields, but also in the production of short videos, which has injected new vitality into the short video industry. VR combined with short video, as a medium of information content dissemination, is more specific and vivid than the previous way of data dissemination, with a larger amount of data and a stronger practical effect [1]. VR environments differ from traditional desktops in that they embed the user in a computer-generated data environment. The creation of a simulated virtual scene that is infinitely close to the real world, simulated through imaging technology, allows for a more holistic perceptual experience [2]. It has the key attributes of presence and immersion, 3D representation and perception, and real-time spatial interaction. Therefore, the integration of virtual reality technology into short video production plays an important role in cross-cultural communication. Through virtual reality technology, people from different cultural backgrounds can communicate and interact in the same virtual space. At present, cross-cultural exchanges and integration are becoming more and more frequent, and virtual reality technology, as an emerging form of artistic expression, provides a brand-new possibility for cross-cultural artistic exchanges. The purpose of this paper is to explore the new creation mode and expression means brought by virtual reality technology for short video production through the research on the application of virtual reality technology in short video, which is of great significance for promoting cross-cultural communication and the development of artistic innovation.

2016 is the first year of the explosion of short videos. Short video has gradually become a window for people to understand the world due to its communication characteristics. However, traditional short videos cannot realize 360° all-round immersive experience, and the way of displaying special cultural content with the help of traditional short videos cannot make the audience experience the charm of culture, which will lead to cross-cultural communication and dissemination effect is greatly reduced. Culture is a crucial factor in communication. With the development of globalization, cross-cultural artistic communication is becoming more and more important [3]. Film and television art does not distinguish between national boundaries, how to use short video art to disseminate regional culture, enhance the sense of participation and identity of culture has become a problem that needs in-depth thinking. The application of virtual reality technology in short video can better complete the cultural communication process from ornamental to experiential transformation, realizing the "zero distance" virtual visit experience. Constructing a virtual reality art space by means of VR can overcome the previous regrets due to the different space for art dissemination. People enter into the virtual video image through practical operation and realize panoramic viewing experience with the help of VR equipment. The development of VR short video provides a new way for the dissemination of culture, through the innovative way of "VR

+ short video" to publicize culture, can give people a strong sense of reality, so that people in the process of accepting the culture of the visual and sensory experience, and at the same time, will increase the people's sense of participation in the culture and a sense of identity.

2 Literature Review

2.1 Cross-Cultural Arts

Cross-cultural arts are a field of study that is receiving increasing attention, which focuses on artistic exchanges, influences and integration in different cultural contexts. Gudykunst William B., a professor at the University of California in the United States of America and a leading international researcher in Cross-cultural communication and interpersonal studies, has defined "Cross-cultural" as a part of cultural anthropology, which focuses on the comparison of cultures and encompasses the presentation of cultures or texts to any degree, as well as interpersonal exchanges of different cultures at any level [4]. Howard McConaughey, professor in the Department of Art Education, examines the role of modern art and artists in expressing unconscious, cross-cultural emotions. It is argued that the expressive focus of modern art, beginning with Post-Impressionism, has been on internal and psychological concerns. "Cross-cultural" is not simply a collision of cultures, but an interaction that occurs when different cultures collide. VR virtual reality technology has gradually become the new favorite of cultural variety shows, and "VR + variety show" is also a more distinctive trend. For example, a Chinese cultural variety show has introduced virtual reality technology to present China's outstanding traditional culture with the help of modern technology. In the stage space design, all kinds of environmental elements are fully utilized to mobilize the audience's senses, creating an immersive and shared environmental atmosphere and historical space for the audience, adding a real three-dimensional immersive viewing effect [5]. While spreading the local culture, it increases the cultural confidence and cultural identity of the nation, so as to achieve the purpose of inheriting Chinese culture and telling a good Chinese story. After the program was broadcasted, it not only gained unanimous praise at home, but also received wide acclaim on overseas platforms.

2.2 Virtual Reality Technology

Virtual Reality is the colloquial name for an engaging, interactive, computer-mediated experience in which a synthetic (simulated) environment is perceived through special human-computer interface devices. It interacts with the simulated objects in that environment as if they were real [6]. The combination of virtual reality technology and the communication effect of short videos highlights its unique advantages in cross-cultural communication. As virtual reality technology is characterized by interactivity, immersion and imagination, in the process of practice, creators will be better able to change the traditional filming method by simulating the real environment.

Due to the development of technology, the use of virtual reality in film and video is becoming more and more common. For example, in the medical field, the use of virtual reality videos has made it easier for participants to make end-of-life decisions and has also helped users to better understand medical scenarios, making it a good decision-making tool for advance care planning. This intervention is generally recognized by participants for its decision-making assistance [7]. Kyunghan Lee's research argues that the development of modern theater technology provides audiences with a more immersive viewing experience, and advances in virtual reality technology have made VR theater possible. The development of this technology is expected to bring greater innovation and flexibility to filmmaking and the theater experience [8]. In addition, virtual reality technology has an important role to play in the experience and learning of culture. Lei Gao's team designed a virtual reality application that allows learners to experience and learn about Western cultures in an immersive environment. This virtual reality application can build immersive learning environments that help participants adapt to foreign cultures at a low cost in terms of time and money, which is of practical value for cultural learning [9].

Under the influence of globalization, the use of virtual reality technology for cultural communication will become an inevitable trend. However, compared with traditional short videos, VR has not yet fully matured technologically, coupled with the need to use a large number of technical equipment in the production of VR short videos, which also greatly increases the production cost of VR short videos. Therefore, virtual reality technology is still not fully utilized in short video production.

2.3 Short Video Production

Short video refers to a new type of video broadcast on network platforms for people to watch, browse and share at any time, ranging from a few seconds to five minutes. According to Zhiqin Lu, short video is mainly produced by stars, internet celebrity, PGC, UGC, and shot, edited and processed on mobile terminals with one click, and disseminated through cell phones and external links, which is characterized by strong social attributes, low threshold of creation, and blurred boundaries between producers and consumers, and so on. It is characterized by strong social attributes, low creation threshold, and blurred boundaries between producers and consumers [10]. The development of short video production can be traced back to 2007, when YouTube has become the most successful Internet site providing a new generation of short video sharing services. Cheng Xu and others conducted an in-depth and systematic measurement study on the characteristics of YouTube videos and found that these videos have strong correlation with each other, and through the Internet platform will effectively deliver the videos to the end-users to realize the dissemination value [11].

In recent years, with the development of new media technology, new ways of short video production have emerged. The emergence of artificial intelligence has revolutionized video production and enabled innovative methods of artistic creation. With the rise of self-media and the demand for user-generated content, AI drives personalized and efficient video production. The study by Yufeng Huang's team evaluates the potential of AI video production through literature integration, revealing the transformative and instructive role of AI in film and video [12].

In terms of application prospects, short video production has become a popular form of social media, such as jittery voice, fast hand and other platforms. Short video production can not only meet users' needs for entertainment, but also be used in various fields such as advertising and marketing, education and training, and news reporting [13]. Therefore, it is undoubtedly a convenient and effective way to disseminate culture with the help of short video production technology. The value of cultural identity that can be pried up by the integrated communication of "culture + short video" in the new media era should not be underestimated, which will bring a new mode of traditional cultural communication.

3   VR Technology in Short Video Production Process

3.1   Applications in Pre-production

The first is scene selection. VR technology allows you to browse different scenes in the virtual environment in advance and choose the most suitable shooting location. Through the use of VR equipment, creators can preview the shooting scenes and make scene layouts in the virtual environment, fine-tune the scene layouts, and simulate the scenes before shooting, allowing creators to better choose the shooting angle, arrange the lighting, etc., to ensure that the shooting effect is optimal. Such scene construction breaks the spatial and geographical limitations, through the 3D technology to show the virtual scene effect in the visual more impactful and three-dimensional sense. Secondly, virtual reality technology plays an equally important role in scriptwriting. Interactive proposals for VR scriptwriting frameworks, created using 360° video technology, present possible plot and extra-plot interactions in a pre-written story with different navigation options. This interactive structure ensures the dramatic tension of the story. Both virtual reality and storytelling have the potential to promote immersion, thus favoring the construction of innovative and effective learning environments [14]. Virtual reality technology is used to simulate the plot in different scenes to help writers better conceptualize the storyline. Finally, during the filming process, VR technology can be used for real-time shooting and scene adjustment. By using VR cameras and related equipment, creators can observe the shooting effect in real time during the shooting process and make real-time adjustments to the scene to ensure that the shooting content is consistent with the expected effect. When shooting short videos, panoramic shooting can be realized through the use of virtual reality technology, and the record of the real scene makes the audience feel immersed when watching the video. In addition, in the shooting process, virtual reality technology can put the virtual background into the actual shooting environment, so that the effect of the short video shot is more realistic.

3.2   Applications in Post-production

The basic goal of post-production in film and television is to put together many shots by using specialized techniques to process the various elements that have been shot, and the post-production aspect is crucial [15]. The application of VR virtual reality in film and television post-production makes the work more colorful. In the late stages of filming, VR technology can be used for editing and post-processing to adjust the images and effects more intuitively. By using VR editing software, creators can edit, splice, adjust colors, add background music and other post-processing of the shooting content to make the short video more vivid, interesting and picture perfect. In addition, VR technology can also be used for the production of special effects during the shooting process, such as virtual backgrounds, virtual characters, etc., to create more three-dimensional and realistic special effects, which can enhance the visual effect of the video and bring the audience a richer visual experience. The application of VR virtual reality technology in the late stage of film and television has promoted the development of diversified creation and the development of film and television post-production. At the same time, the application of VR virtual reality technology improves the efficiency of film and television production and reduces the cost of physical sets [16].

3.3 Specific Applications

Panoramic VR Short Video. Panoramic VR video is a form of video based on virtual reality technology, in which real scenes or fictional situations are filmed or made into 360o panoramic videos by using special cameras and tools. It provides users with the opportunity to experience the video in a fully immersive way [17]. The filmmaker builds a three-dimensional simulated environment through filming, so that the viewer can get a three-dimensional spatial feeling through the network, as if they were there. The viewer can adjust the image, zoom in and out, move the viewer around, and other controls to experience these scenes or situations in an immersive way. Panoramic virtual reality videos are becoming increasingly popular because they offer a truly immersive experience. Increasingly, 360° video covers other applicable areas of content, including education, immersive telepresence, infotainment, documentaries, and sports [18]. On the occasion of the 70th anniversary of the founding of The People's Republic of China, China Central Television released a short VR newsreel titled "Building Blessings", presenting a panoramic view of the country's magnificent 70 years through seven iconic projects (Tabernacle 1959, Subway 1969, Landmark 1979, Desert 1989, Network 1999, Bridge 2009, Airport 2019). In addition, also released "360° panoramic immersion stroll in the Forbidden City" "spectacular! Panoramic VR look at the Three Gorges Dam" and other VR news videos, using a large number of VR footage, 360° panoramic record of China's architecture and mountains and rivers, for the audience to outline a three-dimensional immersive picture of the great beauty of China. While bringing the audience an immersive panoramic experience, it also assumes the important responsibility of culture and knowledge dissemination.

VR Integration into Intangible Cultural Heritage Short Videos. Virtual reality technology plays an important role in the field of culture, virtual reality and traditional desktop media as a medium for displaying intangible heritage environment is significantly different, 360° video presented by virtual reality helps users to immerse themselves in the protection of intangible cultural heritage in the application, [19] more able to help people to experience intangible cultural heritage in a more intuitive, immersive way, immersed in the charm of traditional culture. This significantly improves the audience's interactive experience, and awareness of non-heritage protection. In addition, the application of virtual reality technology in the inheritance and protection of non-heritage culture can inject new vitality into traditional art forms, so that more people can understand, experience and inherit non-heritage culture.

Take the art of paper-cutting as an example, paper-cutting is an intangible cultural heritage in China with a long history. Nick and his team filmed this traditional craft through VR technology, the video shows the 80-year-old paper-cutting master Weizhen Zhu working scene and the process of paper-cutting, the use of virtual reality technology "real" reproduction of intangible cultural heritage paper-cutting techniques, so that users can greatly experience the traditional process and production methods. The audience can see the production process of traditional paper-cutting art in the virtual reality equipment, and closely observe how the non-genetic inheritors use scissors and paper to carefully cut out various exquisite patterns. This immersive experience enables the audience to more intuitively understand the unique charm of the art of paper-cutting. Now, Nick and his team have made a series of VR videos of Chinese intangible cultural heritage bearers, and after spreading these videos of China's excellent traditional culture overseas, they have attracted a great response. Therefore, the innovative exploration of the inheritance and dissemination of intangible cultural heritage can make intangible cultural heritage play a more important role in the development of the country, international social exchanges, and sustainable development of the society, which will further enhance the national cultural self-confidence [20].

4 Experiment Investigation

4.1 Experimental Method

In order to fully study the application of virtual reality technology in the process of short video production, as well as the impact of virtual reality short videos on cross-cultural communication, to achieve the effect of promoting cultural dissemination and communication. A total of 200 questionnaires were distributed to the audience in this study, and the survey data were statistically and analytically analyzed to observe the audience's understanding of virtual reality technology, their perceptions and attitudes towards virtual reality technology in short video production, and their perceptions of the effects of virtual reality short videos on cross-cultural communication.

4.2 Experimental Subjects

The experimental subjects of this study need to have certain experience in Internet use and virtual reality short video viewing to ensure a certain understanding of virtual reality technology. The experimental subjects include college students, educators, enterprise workers, etc. in colleges and universities. The participants cover people of different ages, educational backgrounds and occupational fields to ensure the representativeness and diversity of the experimental results.

4.3 Experimental Process

Questionnaire Design. This questionnaire, on the basis of reference to existing similar questionnaires, has been adjusted and modified accordingly to the differences in the survey respondents, to avoid possible problems, such as irregularities in the formulation of questions, as far as possible, and to improve the accuracy of the questionnaire's formulation. This questionnaire is mainly composed of the following parts:

Part I: Description of the questionnaire. It is intended to introduce the respondents to the purpose of the questionnaire, its use and privacy issues, and to guide the respondents to fill in the questionnaire according to the actual situation.

Part II: Basic Information of Respondents. This part mainly collects the basic information of the respondents, including gender, age, education and so on.

Part III: This part is mainly to understand and grasp the audience's knowledge of virtual reality technology, access to it, and so on.

Part IV: Body part. This part is mainly to examine the cognitive, attitudinal and behavioral aspects of the audience based on the application of virtual reality technology in short videos.

Distribution and Recovery of Questionnaires. A total of 200 questionnaires were distributed to the respondents of this research study mainly through online means, and after screening, 196 valid questionnaires were determined students.

4.4 Experimental Results

Analysis of the Audience Situation. As shown in Table 1, the questionnaire collected a total of 196 valid samples, of which the number of males accounted for 73 people, accounting for 37.24%, and the number of females is 123 people, accounting for 62.76%. The gender distribution of survey respondents is slightly more female than male.

Table 1. Gender distribution

Title	Options	Frequency	Percentages (%).	Cumulative percentages (%)
Gender	Male	73	37.24	37.24
	Female	123	62.76	100.00
Total		196	100.0	100.0

From Table 2, most of the questionnaire fillers are between the ages of 18–35 years old, the number of people accounted for 89.29%, focusing on the least number of people in the age group of more than 40, only 4 people, from the age distribution, filling out the questionnaire is mainly for young and middle-aged people.

Table 2. Age distribution

Title	Options	Frequency	Percentages (%).	Cumulative percentages (%).
Age	< 18	7	3.57	3.57
	18–25	137	69.90	73.47
	26–35	38	19.39	92.86
	36–40	10	5.10	97.96
	> 40	4	2.04	100.00
Total		196	100.0	100.0

As shown in Table 3, the results reflect the distribution of the respondents' education, and the education of the respondents of this questionnaire is mostly concentrated in undergraduate and master's degree and above postgraduate students, totaling 147 people, accounting for as high as 75%. The number of people in high school and below and specialties accounted for a relatively small proportion, totaling 25%.

Table 3. Distribution of education levels

Title	Options	Frequency	Percentages (%).	Cumulative percentages (%)
Education attainment	High school and below	27	13.78	13.78
	Specialized training school	22	11.22	25.00
	Undergraduate	80	40.82	65.82
	Master's degree or above	67	34.18	100.00
Total		196	100.0	100.0

Analysis of the Level and Mode of Understanding of the Audience. From Table 4, it can be seen that most people learn about virtual reality technology through social media platforms and personal experience of related equipment, a total of 57 people learned about virtual reality technology through social media platforms, accounting for 29.08%, and a total of 45 people personally experienced related equipment, accounting for 22.96%. And 23 people chose to learn about virtual reality technology through online video platforms and other people's sharing and recommendation respectively. This shows that using social media to learn new information is now the choice of most people.

Table 4. Ways to understand virtual reality technology

Title	Options	Frequency	Percentages (%)	Cumulative percentages (%)
Ways of knowing	Social media platforms	57	29.08	29.08
	Online video platforms	23	11.73	40.82
	Experience related equipment	45	22.96	63.78
	Shared by others	23	11.73	75.51
	Television programs or media coverage	29	14.80	90.31
	Other	19	9.69	100.00
Total		196	100.0	100.0

As can be seen from Table 5, regarding the analysis of the degree of understanding of virtual reality technology, which has heard of virtual reality technology accounted for the largest proportion, as high as 31.12%, not quite understand and completely unaware of the audience accounted for 25%, very familiar with the virtual reality technology of the crowd only accounted for all the audience of the 19.9%, which can be seen that the public for the degree of understanding of the virtual reality technology is not high, so far, this technology is not yet popularized, the future still has a huge potential for development. This technology has not been popularized, and still has great potential for development in the future.

Table 5. Level of understanding of virtual reality technology

Title	Options	Frequency	Percentages (%)	Cumulative percentages (%)
Knowledge	Very familiar	39	19.90	19.90
	More familiar	47	23.98	43.88
	Heard about it	61	31.12	75.00
	Not familiar	35	17.86	92.86
	Completely unfamiliar	14	7.14	100.00
Total		196	100.0	100.0

Analysis of Audience Attitudes. As shown in Table 6, 16.32% of the respondents indicated that they were neutral or not too supportive of the application of virtual reality technology in short video production, but the overall proportion is relatively small. This may reflect that a part of the respondents still has some doubts about the application of virtual reality technology in the field of short videos. However, 83.67% of the respondents indicated that they supported or very much supported the application of virtual reality technology in short video production, which indicates that virtual reality technology has wide recognition and support in the field of short video and is favored by the audience.

Table 6. Attitude of VR technology applied to short video

Title	Options	Frequency	Percentages (%).	Cumulative percentages (%)
How to see the application of virtual reality technology in short video production	Very supportive	77	39.29	39.29
	Relatively supportive	87	44.39	83.67
	Neutral	23	11.73	95.41
	Unsupported	9	4.59	100.00
Total		196	100.0	100.0

As shown in Table 7, 52.04% of the respondents believe that virtual reality technology can improve the viewing experience of short videos, which indicates that virtual reality technology has considerable attraction and potential in the field of short videos15.82% believe that virtual reality technology has some help to the viewing experience, and 32.14% are skeptical or believe that it is ineffective. This indicates that there are still some respondents who have a conservative attitude towards the application of virtual reality technology in the field of short videos. However, on balance, the audience's attitude towards the VR short video viewing experience is positive.

Table 7. Attitudes toward VR short video viewing experience

Title	Options	Frequency	Percentages (%)	Cumulative percentages (%)
Does virtual reality technology help improve the viewing experience of short videos	Yes	102	52.04	52.04
	There's some help	31	15.82	67.86
	Unsure	40	20.41	88.27
	No	23	11.73	100.00
Total		196	100.0	100.0

As shown in Table 8, 173 respondents indicated that VR short videos are very helpful in understanding other cultures, accounting for 88.27%. This result reflects the positive attitude towards virtual reality technology in facilitating cross-cultural communication.

On the other hand, 18 respondents think that VR short videos are only somewhat helpful, accounting for 9.18%, and 1.53% are not too sure about their effects. This reflects that some of the respondents have some doubts or uncertainty about virtual reality technology in promoting cross-cultural communication. It also reminds us that we need to seriously consider the actual effects of VR short videos when promoting and applying them.

Table 8. Attitudes of VR short video towards cross-cultural communication

Title	Options	Frequency	Percentages (%).	Cumulative percentages (%)
Can short VR videos better facilitate cross-cultural communication and experiences	Yes	173	88.27	88.27
	Some help, but limited effect	18	9.18	97.45
	Not sure	3	1.53	98.98
	No	2	1.02	100.00
Total		196	100.0	100.0

Table 9, as can be seen from the above table, the goodness-of-fit test shows significance (chi = 127.826, $p = 0.000 < 0.05$), which implies that the proportion of choices for each item is significantly different, and the differences can be specifically compared through the response rate or the popularity rate. 19.40% of the respondents believe that it has the effect of breaking down the language barriers, followed by 19.12% who believe

Table 9. The role of short VR videos on cross-cultural communication

Options	Responsive		Penetration rate ($n = 196$)
	n	Response rate	
Breaking the language barrier	136	19.40%	69.39%
Promoting cultural understanding	96	13.69%	48.98%
Providing an interactive experience	124	17.69%	63.27%
Promoting cultural innovation and integration	97	13.84%	49.49%
Expanding avenues of cultural dissemination	134	19.12%	68.37%
Promoting international cooperation	112	15.98%	57.14%
Other	2	0.29%	1.02%
Total	701	100%	357.65%

$x^2 = 127.826 \; p = 0.000$.

that it can expand the cultural communication channels. In terms of the popularity rate, breaking the language barrier and expanding cultural communication channels have the highest recognition, which reflects the unique advantages of virtual reality technology in providing a cross-cultural communication platform and facilitating cross-linguistic communication.

Result. By statistically analyzing the data from the questionnaire, this study found that due to the limitations of the popularity of virtual reality technology, most of the audience still has a low level of understanding of virtual reality technology, and mainly learns about it through social media platforms and experiencing the relevant equipment in person. However, there is a supportive attitude towards the application of virtual reality technology in short video production. It is believed that compared with traditional short videos, virtual reality technology helps to improve the viewing experience of short videos, and the application of virtual reality technology to short videos can better promote cross-cultural communication. The audience has great expectations for the future development of virtual reality technology, and virtual reality technology has a wide range of application prospects in the field of short videos. To sum up, the application of virtual reality technology in short video production is of great significance to cross-cultural communication, which can express two-dimensional video in 3D and bring an immersive viewing experience for the audience. At the same time, with the communication power and influence of short videos, people can experience different cultures and customs across geographical barriers, which will provide more possibilities for the promotion of cross-cultural communication and understanding.

5 Discussion and Analysis

From this study and the findings, we can understand that the combination of short videos and virtual reality technology promotes cross-cultural communication and experience to a great extent. The realistic and three-dimensional scenes and effects created through virtual reality technology allow viewers to understand and experience the cultures of different regions more deeply. This interactive experience allows viewers to participate more actively in cross-cultural communication and improve cultural awareness and cultural sensitivity. At the same time, it can also enrich the content of the short video and bring an immersive and interactive experience to the audience. Virtual reality technology has made great progress in the past few years, but there are still problems of high technical threshold and low popularity. With the development of technology, its development trend will be more expected. In the future, with the continuous updating of virtual reality equipment and the decreasing cost, this technology will become more and more popular, and people may be able to easily use virtual reality equipment at home to enjoy an immersive virtual experience. Virtual reality technology will also be more deeply integrated with other technologies, and this integration will provide more possibilities for the development of virtual reality technology. This study applies virtual reality technology to the production of short videos, realizing a high degree of integration of "virtual reality technology + short videos", breaking through the inconvenience of traditional short videos in cross-cultural communication, and opening up a new way for cross-cultural communication and experience. In addition, when different regions carry out cultural exchanges, with the help of VR short video, it can break the geographical restrictions and improve the efficiency and effect of cultural communication.

Acknowledgments. This work was funded by Social Science Foundation of Fujian Province, China (Funding Number: FJ2022C071). And funded by Xiamen Education Scientific Planning Project: Application of VR in art design courses in the post-epidemic era Innovative Teaching Reform Study (Funding Number: 22002). And funded by High-level Talent Research Project of Xiamen University of Technology (Funding Number: YSK22018R).

References

1. Zhao, X.-Z.: Analysis of VR short video content distribution network based on 5G communication. Electron. Technol. **02**, 120–121 (2022)
2. Blach, R.: Virtual reality technology - an overview. In: Talaba, D., Amditis, A. (eds.) Product Engineering, pp. 21–64. Springer Netherlands, Dordrecht (2008). https://doi.org/10.1007/978-1-4020-8200-9_2
3. Macnamara, J.R.: The crucial role of research in multicultural and cross-cultural communication. J. Commun. Manag. **8**(3), 322–334 (2004)
4. Gudykunst, W.B.: Cross-cultural and Intercultural Communication. Sage (2003)
5. Yikang, G.: Multiple integration and innovation of CCTV cultural programs under new media perspective--taking "Poetry and Painting of China" as an example. West. Radio Telev. **09**, 89–92 (2023). http://mtw.so/5xapZl
6. Mandal, S.: Brief introduction of virtual reality & its challenges. Int. J. Sci. Eng. Res. **4**(4), 304–309 (2013)
7. Hsieh, W.T.: Virtual reality video promotes effectiveness in advance care planning. BMC Palliat. Care **19**(1), 1–10 (2020)
8. Lee, K., Guerrero, G., Cha, S., Kim, Y., Cho, S.: VR theater, a virtual reality based multi-screen movie theater simulator for verifying multi-screen content and environment. In: SMPTE 2017 Annual Technical Conference and Exhibition, pp. 1–13. (2017)SMPTE
9. Gao, L., Wan, B., Liu, G., **e, G., Huang, J., Meng, G.: Investigating the effectiveness of virtual reality for culture learning. Int. J. Hum. Comput. Interact. **37**(18), 1771–1781 (2021)
10. Lu, Z., Nam, I.: Research on the influence of new media technology on internet short video content production under artificial intelligence background. Complexity **2021**, 1–14 (2021)
11. Cheng, X., Dale, C., Liu, J.: Understanding the characteristics of internet short video sharing: YouTube as a case study. ar**v preprint ar**v:0707.3670 (2007)
12. Huang, Y., Lv, S., Tseng, K.K., Tseng, P.J., **e, X., Lin, R.F.Y.: Recent advances in artificial intelligence for video production system. Enterp. Inf. Syst. **17**(11), 2246188 (2023)
13. Wang, Y.H., Gu, T.J., Wang, S.Y.: Causes and characteristics of short video platform internet community taking the TikTok short video application as an example. In: 2019 IEEE International Conference on Consumer Electronics-Taiwan (ICCE-TW), pp. 1–2. IEEE (2019)
14. Reyes, M.C., Zampolli, S.: Screenwriting framework for an interactive virtual reality film. In: 3rd Immersive Research Network Conference iLRN (2017)
15. Ming, X.M.: Post-production of digital film and television with development of virtual reality image technology-advance research analysis. Int. J. Mech. Eng. **7** (2022)
16. Chen, D., Yang, F.: Application of VR virtual reality in film and television post-production. IOP Conf. Ser. Mater. Sci. Eng. **750**(1), 012163 (2020). https://doi.org/10.1088/1757-899X/750/1/012163

17. Pirker, J., Dengel, A.: The potential of 360 virtual reality videos and real VR for education—a literature review. IEEE Comput. Graphics Appl. **41**(4), 76–89 (2021)
18. Westphal, C.: Challenges in networking to support augmented reality and virtual reality. In: Proceedings of the International Conference of Computer Network Communication (ICNC), pp. 26–29 (2017)
19. Selmanović, E., et al.: Improving accessibility to intangible cultural heritage preservation using virtual reality. J. Comput. Cult. Heritage **13**(2), 1–19 (2020)
20. Wulong, X., Sun, X., Pan, S.: Visual dissemination of intangible cultural heritage information based on 3D scanning and virtual reality technology. Scanning **2022**, 1–7 (2022). https://doi.org/10.1155/2022/8762504

Analysis of the Dissemination Effects of VR Audiovisual Arts on Local Culture in Cross-Cultural Contexts: A Case Study of the Broadcasting and Television Industry

Weilong Wu[✉] and Xinyi Yang

School of Film Television and Communication, Xiamen University of
Technology, Xiamen, China
wu_acedemic@163.com

Abstract. Objective: With the advancement of globalization and the progress
of science and technology, communication between people of different cultural
backgrounds has become increasingly frequent. Cross-cultural communication
has become an increasingly common phenomenon in today's world, involving the
collision and intermingling of different cultural backgrounds, values, languages
and customs. In this process, cross-cultural context has become an inevitable part
of people's lives. In this context, people from different cultural backgrounds need
to understand, respect and adapt to each other's cultural differences. These differences include not only language, customs, social etiquette and other aspects, but
also values, ways of thinking, behavioral norms and other aspects. Therefore, in
the cross-cultural context, the dissemination of local cultures across countries is
of great significance. By transmitting native cultures to a wider range of people,
it can enhance people's knowledge and understanding of native cultures in different places, and thus improve their sense of identity and cohesion. At the same
time, the transmission of local culture in the cross-cultural context also helps to
promote the exchange and understanding between different cultures, and promote
the development of the diversity of world culture.

Virtual Reality (VR) technology as a computer simulation system that can
experience the virtual world, through the technology virtual and reality combined
with each other, with immersive, interactive features into the audio-visual arts,
for the dissemination of local culture provides a new way. Audiovisual arts is an
art form that uses sound and picture as the means of expression and visual and
auditory perception. It includes movies, TV dramas, TV variety shows, dances,
dramas and other types. Through the organic combination of picture and sound,
it creates artistic images with a sense of time and space and a sense of dynamics,
which directly affects the audience's visual and auditory senses and thus produces
a unique artistic effect. In the radio and television industry, the innovative integration of VR technology with audiovisual arts brings a new immersive experience
by simulating human audiovisual perception, making users feel as if they were
immersed in a virtual, three-dimensional, audiovisual environment with a sense
of reality. In the meantime, in VR audiovisual arts, the audience can also interact

---

W. Wu and X. Yang—These authors contributed equally to this study.

P.-L. P. Rau (Ed.): HCII 2024, LNCS 14702, pp. 60–73, 2024.
https://doi.org/10.1007/978-3-031-60913-8_5

with the virtual environment, and through their own perception and experience to stimulate unlimited imagination and creativity.

In the figurative presentation of local culture, VR audiovisual arts in the radio and television industry can be delivered to the audience in a more realistic and vivid way, so that the audience can understand and perceive the history, traditions and customs of the local culture in a more in-depth way. Compared with traditional audiovisual arts, this immersive and in-depth experience can enhance the audience's cognition and perception of local culture, and improve their sense of identity and cohesion.

Methods: This experiment adopts the qualitative analysis method to research and analyze the audience effect of VR audiovisual arts in the form of in-depth interviews. The topic of the in-depth interview focuses on the VR cultural variety show "Poetry and Painting of China", which won the "Asia-Pacific Broadcasting Television Union Award", and discusses the communication effect and influence of the program among the audience groups in a specific and in-depth manner. Ten domestic scholars and experts in related fields were selected for the study, and these experts' fields of study include art, culture, media, etc., to ensure that the research results have interdisciplinary depth and breadth. And all of them are audiences who have watched the program and have rich experience and unique insights in cultural communication and artistic expression, providing rich information for the in-depth interviews. The whole interview content centered on the research theme of the communication effect of the VR program "Poetry and Painting of China" on local culture, and five related questions were designed to explore the actual communication effect of local culture through VR audiovisual arts in the audience group.

Results: Through in-depth interviews with ten experts and scholars, it can be found that the VR audiovisual program "Poetry and Painting of China" has achieved a good effect of local culture dissemination among the audience. Specifically, the program brings audiences into an immersive Chinese traditional culture scene through VR technology, which immerses them in the unique charm of Chinese traditional culture. Meanwhile, the program has also made some breakthroughs in cultural inheritance and innovation, allowing the audience not only to be satisfied with the artistic form, but also to gain a rich harvest in terms of cultural knowledge, and to have a deeper understanding and knowledge of the characteristics and connotations of Chinese poetic and pictorial culture, which in turn stimulates the audience's awareness of cultural inheritance and cultural self-confidence. However, VR audiovisual programs still have some deficiencies in the dissemination of local culture, such as the limited level of technology, cross-cultural communication barriers, and limited dissemination channels that still need to be improved. In response to these problems, experts also put forward some specific suggestions, such as increasing R&D efforts on VR technology, expanding the scope of dissemination by utilizing multiple channels, and attracting audiences at different levels in content production, with a view to providing some references and help for VR audiovisual programs in disseminating local culture.

Conclusions: This study finds that VR audiovisual arts is of great significance to the communication effect of local culture in cross-cultural context. Through the integration with local culture, VR audiovisual arts can not only enhance the audience's sense of cultural identity, promote cultural dissemination and inheritance, facilitate cross-cultural communication and understanding, and enhance the national image, but also expand domestic and international cultural communication channels. Therefore, we should fully recognize the potential and role of VR audiovisual arts in the dissemination of local culture. In addition, there are still some existing problems that need to be noticed and improved, such as limited technical level, cross-cultural communication barriers, limited communication channels and other deficiencies in the process of VR audiovisual art's dissemination of local culture in the cross-cultural context. In this regard, this art form will also be actively explored and applied in the future to promote the inheritance and development of local culture, advance global cross-cultural communication and exchange, and contribute to the prosperity and development of world culture.

Keywords: Virtual Reality · Local Culture · Dissemination Effects · Cross-Cultural Contexts

1 Introduction

In the era of high-speed circulation and sharing of information, cross-cultural communication and dissemination has become an important issue that cannot be ignored in today's society. In the age of pluralism, people with different cultural backgrounds need to understand and respect each other's cultures at a deeper level, and all countries and regions need to actively promote their local cultures to the world, so that more people can understand, experience and appreciate the unique charms of different cultures, thus promoting and facilitating the prosperous development of cultural diversity and harmonious coexistence among countries all over the world. Under this social need, virtual reality technology (VR) combined with audiovisual arts has gradually emerged as a striking new art form, and also provides a new way for the dissemination of local culture. VR technology is a kind of interactive technology based on three-dimensional virtual reality environment, which allows users to experience a more realistic scene, mainly through the interactive visual, auditory, tactile and movement sensations to provide users with a realistic experience. Users with interactive visual, auditory, tactile and motion sensations to provide them with a real experience [1]. Its immersive and interactive characteristics give the audience an unprecedented immersive experience, providing a new style of expression for the dissemination of culture and the promotion of cross-cultural understanding. Audiovisual arts, as a form of art that uses sound and picture as language symbols, can realize diverse functions such as education, cognition and entertainment with its intuitive and multi-sensory characteristics. It also has great educational potential in terms of the content and nature of the information it conveys, forming a focal point for personal qualities in terms of spiritual, moral, intellectual and aesthetic self-expression in both individual and collective forms [2].Through the in-depth integration of technology and art, the advantages and characteristics of each can be more extended application and development, which opens up an emerging window for the current cross-cultural context, and also provides a more effective path for the development of cultural prosperity.

As an important platform for information transmission and cultural dissemination, the radio and television industry shoulder the important responsibility of cultural record and inheritance. In the era of digitization, the rapid development of VR audiovisual technology has injected new vitality into the broadcasting and television industry, and also presented an unprecedented cultural feast for the audience.

2 VR Technology and Audiovisual Arts

2.1 Characteristics of VR Technology

VR is an advanced simulation technology that simulates the real world with a computer-generated three-dimensional environment. By simulating the senses of sight, hearing, and touch to create a simulated, virtual sense of reality, users feel as if they are in a fictional environment. VR is uniquely characterized by its immersive and interactive experience, which provides the viewer with a completely new way of perceiving. The immersive experience, through the establishment of virtual scenes and environments, makes the viewer feel as if he or she is actually existing in a fictional world and is completely integrated into it. This feature greatly expands the perceptual boundaries of the audience, and the audience can walk, observe and explore freely in the virtual environment using headgear, controllers and other equipment, as if they were in the real world, and fully immersed in the virtual world to experience the scenes and situations that are beyond the reach of the real world. At the same time, VR technology is also characterized by its compelling interactivity, which refers to the degree to which users can manipulate objects within the simulated environment and the naturalness with which they receive feedback from the environment [3]. Users interact with the virtual environment through interactive devices, and are no longer just passive recipients, but can participate in the virtual scene through the manipulation of devices or interactive interfaces to realize the operation, control, change the virtual environment and other functions. This sense of participation makes the audience become one of the creators, and personalized experience becomes possible, which enhances the sense of immersion and also improves the depth of user participation. Interactivity and immersion are two of the main advantages of VR technology over traditional electronic technology, and VR technology as a powerful tool can be applied to a variety of fields, playing an extremely important role [4]. In the field of art, VR technology can provide art creators with a new way of creation and means of display. The creators can create more immersive and interactive art works through VR technology, which in turn allows the audience to understand and feel the works in an immersive way, and interact and communicate with the works to complete the artistic enjoyment.

2.2 Connotation of Audiovisual Arts

Audiovisual arts is a multifaceted art form that is expressed through visual and auditory means, and it is mainly an art that is conveyed through pictures, sounds and colors to give people enjoyment in the form of art, and it accommodates a variety of art disciplines in the iconic connotation of audiovisual arts [5]. In his book Introduction to Art, scholar Wang Hongjian categorizes the types of art into visual, auditory, audiovisual, and imaginative art based on the way in which the art form is perceived [6]. Audiovisual arts includes a wide range of genres such as theater, film, television drama, documentary, television variety, dance, etc. It integrates visual and sound elements to provide audiences with an all-round sensory experience. This form of art aims to communicate with the audience through audiovisual language, and the artist creates a mesmerizing artistic atmosphere through the careful manipulation of vision and sound, so that the audience can immerse themselves in it and appreciate the infinite charm of art. In this process, audio-visual art is not only a medium for conveying information, but also a conveyor of emotion. Through the perfect fusion of picture and sound, it breaks the singularity of the traditional medium and creates an immersive artistic atmosphere. For example, in movies, the delicate composition of the picture and the harmony of the sound can profoundly convey emotions and stories, and inspire the audience to resonate. This comprehensive art form can break the singularity of the medium and create a more diversified and profound art experience for the audience.

2.3 Innovative Expression of VR Technology Combined with Audiovisual Arts

VR technology, as an emerging technical means, has produced powerful artistic effects and novel experiences in its integration with audiovisual arts. This innovative way of expression not only broadens the creative space of audiovisual arts, but also creates a unique audiovisual experience for the audience. First of all, VR technology presents art works in a three-dimensional and panoramic form in the audience's field of vision through the immersive characteristics, which brings a new viewing experience for the audience. On the basis of visual and auditory language, it fully mobilizes the participation of multiple senses, which enables the audience to wholeheartedly integrate into the artistic creation and feel the real scene and character emotions, thus enhancing emotional empathy. With the help of VR glasses, handles and other equipment, the audience is able to feel the object of the work in close proximity, to draw closer to the distance between the work, to break the time and space limitations in-depth experience of the details of the work and the connotation of the mobilization of audio-visual art to appreciate the enthusiasm. Secondly, VR technology enables audiovisual arts creators to break the limitations of traditional media and create richer and more vivid art works. Through the creation of virtual art space, creators can create the desired environmental space in the virtual environment, comparing and restoring various natural spaces to fit the entire creative work. While giving the audience a multitude of modal spatial experiences, it also achieves the expression of the connotation of the work, making the artistic creation more vital, and creating works with more aesthetic value and inner meaning for the audience. In short, the combination between VR technology and audiovisual arts can play a positive role in enhancing the audience experience, expanding the means of artistic expression, and promoting artistic inheritance and innovation, etc. This fusion brings a broader and more profound development prospect for both the art and technology sectors.

2.4 VR Audiovisual Arts in the Broadcasting Industry

Every revolutionary technology will bring revolutionary changes to human life, and the arrival of virtual reality technology has a great impact on all walks of life, and opportunities come with this impact. For the radio and television industry, this wave of technology has triggered more diversified changes and vitality. In recent years, the generation of VR audiovisual arts has brought the industry many excellent program works that are highly loved and praised, VR movies, VR TV programs, VR commercials, VR concerts, etc. Together, these fields of application demonstrate the diversity of VR audiovisual arts in the broadcasting industry, as well as the new inspiration and creative prospects for the development of the broadcasting industry [7].

1. Virtual studio programs: Radio and television production companies can create a variety of highly ornamental virtual scenes at any time through computer-generated virtual scenes, using VR technology, thus injecting more creative elements into the program, making the production of programs more creative and imaginative, and no longer subject to the physical limitations of the traditional studio [8]. The construction and maintenance costs of virtual studios are also relatively low compared to the traditional construction of live studios. Through virtual technology, the dependence on actual venues and equipment can be reduced, and modifications and adjustments can be made more conveniently during the production process, which improves production efficiency and reduces production costs.
2. Virtual Reality Movies: VR technology provides brand-new possibilities for movie production. Through 3D technology and virtual reality technology, virtual movies can bring a refreshing audio-visual experience, provide the audience with an immersive experience, so that the audience seems to be in the movie plot. Compared with traditional movies, virtual movies provide stronger interactivity, the audience is not just passively accepting the information, through the VR equipment the audience can interact with the virtual content, personal experience to experience the virtual world of the work, and the storyline for a more in-depth interaction, creating a more immersive viewing experience.
3. Virtual Concert: Virtual Concert is a form of music performance based on virtual reality (VR) technology and Internet platform. It enables the audience to participate in music activities immersive through VR equipment or smart terminals, enjoying a highly immersive and unique music feast without the need for real on-site participation. This form of music performance integrates music with advanced technology to provide audiences with a brand new music experience. Performers can create virtual concerts through VR technology, allowing the audience to enjoy music performances in a virtual space, as if they were in the singing scene, and gain the enjoyment of beauty.
4. Virtual commercials: Through virtual 3D animation, TV commercials can present a more vivid and three-dimensional effect, attracting the audience's attention. Advertisers can make full use of virtual reality technology to create more novel and unique presentation effects, so that viewers can experience the products more intuitively through virtual devices, thus enhancing the brand promotion effect [9]. Taking clothing advertisements as an example, virtual reality advertisements can show clothing in a more three-dimensional and vivid effect, allowing viewers to gain a deeper understanding of the design and characteristics of the clothing. This innovative means of advertising not only establishes a unique image for the brand, but also provides a richer experience for the audience, further enhancing the connection between the brand and the consumer.

3 Specific Ways for VR Audiovisual Arts to Spread Local Culture

3.1 Concept, Characteristics and Significance of Dissemination of Local Culture

The Concept of Local Culture. Local culture refers to the unique cultural system formed and developed in a particular region and community, which carries the history, traditions, values and way of life of a particular community and reflects the uniqueness and diversity of that region. The concept of indigenous culture is different from traditional culture, which has been developed and precipitated over a long period of time, while indigenous culture is the crystallization of the habits and ways of thinking of the people, and is a form of culture created uniquely by the local people. It includes not only the classical part, but also the local and vernacular culture, covering all aspects, including language, religion, customs, art, architecture, traditional skills and so on. The formation of native culture is influenced by a variety of factors, such as geographical environment, historical background, and social economy. Different regions and ethnic groups have formed their own unique cultures over a long period of historical development, and these cultures reflect the characteristics of the region's natural and humanistic environments, as well as the wisdom and creativity of the people of the region [10].

The Characteristics of Local Culture. The characteristics of indigenous culture lie mainly in its regional, ethnic, heritage and diversity aspects, which give it a unique charm and value and make it an important part of human civilization. Indigenous cultures are closely related to specific geographical environments, reflecting the characteristics of the region's natural and humanistic environments. Indigenous cultures in different regions show unique regional characteristics in various aspects, including language, food, clothing, art and so on. Indigenous cultures, in turn, are often associated with particular ethnic groups or communities and have a distinct ethnic character. Different ethnic groups have developed their own unique cultural traditions over a long period of historical evolution, which reflect the spiritual outlook and state of life of the ethnic group. In addition, local culture is formed through long-term historical precipitation and is inherited. It is usually passed on from generation to generation through oral transmission, written transmission and ritual transmission, and has a deep historical heritage and a broad mass base. Lastly, diversity is a distinctive feature of indigenous culture, as the cultural traditions of different regions and ethnic groups are distinctive, forming a colorful cultural landscape, and this diversity also reflects the plurality and richness of human civilization.

The Significance of Dissemination of Local Culture. The significance of the dissemination of indigenous cultures lies in the promotion of the protection and transmission of cultural diversity, the enhancement of cultural self-confidence, and the promotion of social progress and economic development. First of all, the dissemination of indigenous cultures contributes to the protection and transmission of cultural diversity. At a time of accelerating globalization and the intermingling of various cultures, the dissemination of indigenous cultures can maintain cultural diversity and uniqueness and avoid cultural homogenization. Through the dissemination of local culture, it can stimulate people's sense of identity and pride in their local culture and promote cultural inheritance and development. Secondly, the dissemination of local culture can help enhance cultural confidence. Local culture is people's common spiritual home, and through the dissemination of local culture, people can understand their own cultural traditions better and enhance their cultural self-confidence. Cultural self-confidence is an important support for individual and social development, and can improve people's overall quality and competitiveness. At the same time, the spread of local culture can also promote social progress and economic development. The spread of local culture can promote the development of cultural industries, drive the development of related industries, and create more employment opportunities and economic benefits. At the same time, the spread of local culture can also promote social harmony and stability and enhance social cohesion.

3.2 Integration of VR Audiovisual Arts and Local Culture Application

VR audiovisual arts, as a new state of art expression, provides audiences with novel landscape worlds. In the dissemination of local culture, technology is also used to support the content, and the deep-rooted culture is expressed in a youthful way, which is highly appreciated and loved by the contemporary audience from the audio-visual level to the cultural content level.

1. Selection of local cultural elements: VR audiovisual arts in the dissemination of local culture, first of all, in the expression of the content of the local culture of the elements, such as carrying a wealth of historical memories of historical events, unique architectural style, as well as full of rhythmic folk customs and so on, as the inspiration for the creation of a rich source of material. Through the innovative expression of technology and the re-creation of form and content, cultural elements are skillfully integrated into the canvas of virtual technology, and the audience is able to fully appreciate the value of local culture in an environment that combines art and technology. For example, the VR TV program "Ancient Books Seeking Journey" takes the four major ancient books, namely Juyan Han bamboo slips, Yin ruins Oracle bones, Dunhuang suicide notes, Ming and Qing archives, as the main content of the program's expression, which, wrapped in the charm of the virtual technology, injects a new vitality into the development of the Chinese civilization and the inheritance and exchange of the local culture.

2. Digital three-dimensional restoration of cultural scenes: through digital three-dimensional modeling technology to build the actual scene into a three-dimensional virtual model, film and television programs can be digitally reconstructed and reproduced for various elements of local culture. This not only restores vanished cultural heritage, but also provides a fine reproduction of existing cultural landscapes, filling in the audience's various visual imaginations of cultural symbols [11]. For example, the program "Chinese Archaeological Conference" uses AI + VR naked-eye 3D studio technology to spatially recreate archaeological sites. Audiences can not only examine and observe the long history and development of Chinese civilization, but also conduct in-depth exploration in the Liangzhu site where virtual and real time and space are interwoven, thereby demonstrating its significant role in "substantiating the 5,000-year history of Chinese civilization."

3. 3D animation show panoramic image: digital 3D animation system can be used in audio-visual art for all-round display of cultural relics details, the audience can be achieved at any angle to observe the viewing effect of cultural relics, to make up for the limitations of space and line of sight [12]. The cultural relics, with the use of 3D animation technology and high-precision reproduction technology, break the constraints of the traditional exhibition, and the texture, color, shape and other details are clearly presented in front of the viewers in a figurative way, so that the viewers can deeply understand the historical and cultural forms and characteristics, and thus deeply feel their historical precipitation. "If the national treasures will talk", "canonical books in China" and other programs through virtual technology, so that cultural relics and ancient books are "alive", not only for the display of cultural relics has brought a higher level of artistic experience, but also for the dissemination of culture has opened up new possibilities.

4. Interaction design and cross-media narrative: In the presentation of local culture by VR audiovisual arts, the integration of interaction design and cross-media narrative, on the one hand, the audience can "break the screen" into the interactive space, Immersive participation in cultural spaces to interact with cultural elements, and feel the culture in an invested way to recognize and cherish the culture and recognize the culture and cherish the emotion. On the other hand, through the integration of various media elements, such as audio, video, images, etc., the elements of local culture can be presented to the viewer in a more multi-dimensional way, thus allowing the viewer to experience and understand the depth of local culture more comprehensively on an interactive basis [13]. The live program "The Fantastic Journey of Sanxingdui" adopts VR interactive technology and cross-media narrative color enhancement, so that the audience can quickly enter the digital interactive space, according to different choices to obtain a unique content experience, and multi-sensory experience to the wonders of the ancient Shu civilization 3,000 years ago.

4   VR Audiovisual Arts Empower the Dissemination Effect of Local Culture

4.1   Enhance the Sense of Cultural Identity

Through VR technology, the audience can understand and feel the charm of local culture more intuitively. This immersive experience is not only impressive, but also can stimulate the audience's deep sense of identity with the local culture. The immersive feeling makes it easier for the audience to resonate with the audience, thus deepening their understanding of the culture, cultivating their unique feelings towards the local culture, and then forming a stronger cultural identity. This not only helps to promote the local culture of the nation, but also inspires a high degree of recognition and self-confidence in the local culture in contemporary society.

4.2   Facilitating the Dissemination and Transmission of Culture

VR technology can provide a new way to preserve and pass on traditional culture that is on the verge of disappearing. By recording and displaying traditional skills and customs,

VR audiovisual arts can not only provide the younger generation with a more compre-hensive understanding of local culture, but also stimulate their keen interest in traditional culture through immersive experiences [14]. This form of cultural dissemination is not subject to geographical constraints and helps to promote traditional culture globally, realizing heritage while attracting a wider audience to participate in the dissemination and development of culture.

4.3 Promoting Cross-Cultural Communication

In the context of globalization, VR audiovisual arts can be a powerful tool for cross-cultural communication. By providing audiences with the opportunity to learn about and experience local cultures around the world, VR technology can break down geographical and linguistic constraints, prompting viewers in different countries and regions to better understand and respect each other's cultural differences [15]. This helps to build bridges of cross-cultural exchanges, enhance mutual trust among countries, promote the common prosperity of cultural diversity, and promote world peace and sustainable development.

4.4 Enhance the National Image

By showing the unique charm and profound heritage of local culture, VR audiovisual arts can effectively enhance the national image. The audience is more likely to feel the coun-try's cultural heritage and creativity through the immersive art experience. This image enhancement helps to deepen the international community's knowledge and understand-ing of the country, thereby increasing its international influence. At the same time, it provides strong support for the country to win more international support, investment and cooperation, and helps to shape a positive national image.

4.5 Broaden Domestic and International Cultural Communication Channels

The novel form and powerful function of VR technology can enable local culture to be pushed to the international stage, expand domestic and international cultural communi-cation channels, and promote the development and promotion of local culture at home and abroad. VR audiovisual arts can break the limitation of time and space, present traditional culture to the global audience, and open a new path for the dissemination of local culture. Such an innovative form can help increase the international audience's understanding and appreciation of local culture, provide a broader market space for the development of the cultural industry, and better integrate local culture into the trend of world culture, thus further broadening the path of cultural dissemination and enhancing the country's international influence.

5 Analysis of the Audience Effect of VR Audiovisual Arts–Taking VR Cultural Variety Show "Poetry and Painting China" as an Example

5.1 Experimental Method

This experiment adopts a qualitative analysis method to research and analyze the audience effect of VR audiovisual arts in the form of in-depth interviews. The subject of the in-depth interview focuses on the VR cultural variety show "Poetry and Painting China", which won the "Asia-Pacific Radio and Television Union Award", and each interview lasts 20 to 30 min, so as to explore the dissemination effect and influence of the program in the audience. The interviews will last for 20 to 30 min each to discuss the program's impact and influence on the audience.

5.2 Experimental Subjects

The in-depth interview design selected 10 domestic scholars and experts in related fields as research subjects (as shown in Table 1 below), whose research fields include art, culture, media, etc., to ensure that the results of the study have interdisciplinary depth and breadth. All of them have watched the program and have rich experience and unique insights in cultural communication and artistic expression, so as to provide effective information for the in-depth interviews.

Table 1. Information on interview subjects

CODE	GENDER	AGE(YEARS)	PROFESSIONAL BACKGROUND
INTERVIEWEE H	FEMALE	39	Cultural Studies
INTERVIEWEE L	MALE	41	Radio and Television Programming
INTERVIEWEE Y	MALE	40	Sociology
INTERVIEWEE S	MALE	38	Culture studies
INTERVIEWEE W	FEMALE	45	Pedagogical
INTERVIEWEE X	MALE	39	Radio and Television Programming
INTERVIEWEE Z	FEMALE	42	Journalism and Communication
INTERVIEWEE F	MALE	43	Radio and Television Programming
INTERVIEWEE G	FEMALE	39	Art Studies
INTERVIEWEE K	FEMALE	38	Radio and Television Programming

5.3 Experimental Content

The content of this interview is centered on the research theme of the dissemination effect of the VR program "Poetry and Painting China" on local culture, and the following five open-ended questions were designed: First, what is your understanding and impression of the program "Poetry and Painting of China"? Secondly, what are the unique features of

"Poetry and Painting of China" in spreading traditional Chinese culture? Third, in what ways does "Poetry and Painting of China" reflect the inheritance and innovation of local culture? Fourth, what are the shortcomings of "Poetry and Painting of China" and the current VR audiovisual arts in spreading local culture? Fifth, what are the suggestions for improvement of VR audiovisual arts in the dissemination of local culture?

5.4 Experimental Results

Through in-depth interviews with ten experts and scholars, it can be found that the VR audiovisual program "Poetry and Painting of China" has achieved a good effect of local culture dissemination among the audience groups. The author made a word frequency table by capturing the results of the verbatim answers of the experts and scholars to the questions and counting the word frequencies. After removing auxiliaries, connectives and other words that have little significance to the study, it can be seen from the following word cloud map of high-frequency keywords (99) of the interviews (Fig. 1) that the experts and scholars coincidentally affirmed the good dissemination effect of the VR audiovisual arts "Poetry and Painting of China" on the local culture as well as gave many positive views on the future development of VR audiovisual arts. Specifically, the program brings audiences into an immersive scene of traditional Chinese culture through VR technology, immersing them in the unique charm of traditional Chinese culture.

At the same time, the program has made certain breakthroughs in cultural inheritance and innovation, allowing the audience not only to be satisfied with the artistic form, but also to gain rich harvests in terms of cultural knowledge, and to have a deeper understanding and awareness of the characteristics and connotations of the Chinese poetic and painterly culture, which in turn stimulates the audience's awareness of cultural inheritance and cultural self-confidence. However, VR audiovisual programs still have

Fig. 1. Word cloud diagram

some deficiencies in the dissemination of local culture, such as limited technical level, cross-cultural communication barriers, and limited dissemination channels, which still need to be improved. In response to these problems, experts have put forward some specific suggestions, such as increasing the R&D of VR technology, expanding the scope of dissemination by utilizing multiple channels, and attracting different levels of audiences in content production, etc., in order to provide some references and help for VR audiovisual programs in the dissemination of local culture.

6   Conclusions

In the face of the challenges brought about by the cross-cultural context, VR audiovisual arts has injected new vitality and breadth into the dissemination of local culture by virtue of its unique technical characteristics. By utilizing the advantageous features of VR technology and the integration of local cultural elements, VR audiovisual arts provides a brand-new expression style for cultural communication with its unique audiovisual effect. Not only are creators able to create richer and more vivid cultural experiences, but audiences are also able to gain a wealth of cultural knowledge in a profoundly visual and innovative way. Through the panoramic presentation of virtual reality and stereo sound, audio-visual art can display all aspects of local culture in a more intuitive and vivid way, and this innovative style of expression transcends the limitations of traditional cultural expression, making the culture itself more attractive and infectious. At the same time, VR audiovisual arts also opens up new ways for the dissemination of local culture to attract a wider audience and also provides a more convenient opportunity for local culture to make its voice heard on the international stage, prompting the dissemination of local culture to become more popular and widespread. In summary, VR audiovisual arts has a profound significance for the dissemination of local culture in cross-cultural contexts. Through the unique technical characteristics and artistic charm, it can not only enhance the audience's sense of cultural identity, promote cultural dissemination and inheritance, facilitate cross-cultural exchanges and understanding, and enhance the image of the country, but also expand the channels of domestic and international cultural communication. Therefore, we should fully recognize the potential of VR audiovisual arts in the dissemination of local culture.

In addition, there are still some existing problems that need to be noticed and improved, such as limited technical level, cross-cultural communication barriers, limited communication channels and other deficiencies in the process of dissemination of VR audiovisual arts to local cultures in the cross-cultural context. In this regard, in the future, it is also necessary to actively improve, explore and apply this art form, effectively integrate cultural contents from various places, in order to promote the inheritance and development of local culture, advance global cross-cultural communication and exchange, and contribute to the prosperity and development of the world's culture, so as to make the VR audio-visual art an advantageous tool for connecting the cultures of various countries, and to deeply promote and realize the flourishing development of global culture.

Acknowledgments. This work was funded by Social Science Foundation of Fujian Province, China (Funding Number: FJ2022C071). And funded by Xiamen Education Scientific Planning

Project: Application of VR in art design courses in the post-epidemic era Innovative Teaching Reform Study (Funding Number: 22002). And funded by High-level Talent Research Project of Xiamen University of Technology (Funding Number: YSK22018R).

References

1. Wang, X.D.: Analysis of innovative application of virtual reality technology in film and television animation production. Cult. Ind. **08**, 58–60 (2023). http://mtw.so/5MbtTl
2. Mengxi, T., Shao Hua, D.: Exploring the connotation and paradigm of audiovisual art in the digital era. Journalism Res. Guide **11**, 7–9 (2022). http://mtw.so/5Usjdn
3. Liao, S.Y.: Characteristics and application of virtual reality technology. Sci. Technol. Commun. **21**, 127–128+135 (2018). https://doi.org/10.16607/j.cnki.1674-6708.2018.21.064
4. Onyesolu, M.O., Eze, F.U.: Understanding virtual reality technology: advances and applications. Adv. Comput. Sci. Eng. 53–70 (2011)
5. Sun, X.: The ideal limit of audiovisual art. Journalism Res. Guide **19**, 106 (2016). http://mtw.so/5UsjhT
6. Hongjian, W.: Introduction to Art, 2010th edn., pp. 85–88. Culture and Art Press, Beijing (2010)
7. Lin, L.: Virtual reality and its application for producing TV programs. Mob. Inf. Syst. **2022**, 1–8 (2022). https://doi.org/10.1155/2022/8018236
8. Fukui, K., Hayashi, M., Yamanouchi, Y.: Virtual studio system for TV program production. In: Advanced Television and Electronic Imaging for Film and Video: SMPTE Advanced Television Imaging Conference, pp. 80–86. SMPTE (1993)
9. Mahmoud, A.A.: Virtual reality technology and its role in advertising field. Int. J. Artif. Intell. Emerg. Technol. **1**(1), 14–38 (2018)
10. Featherstone, M.: Global and local cultures 1. In: Map** the futures, pp. 169–187. Routledge (2012)
11. Pan, Y.: The visualization construction and expression of cultural symbols in cultural and expositional programs--The Chinese archaeological congress as an example. J. Chin. Radio Telev. **03**, 72–74 (2022). http://mtw.so/61Ywn4
12. Bao, Y.: Application of virtual reality technology in film and television animation based on artificial intelligence background. Sci. Program. **2022**, 1–8 (2022)
13. Ursu, M.F., et al.: Interactive TV narratives: opportunities, progress, and challenges. ACM Trans. Multimedia Comput. Commun. Appl. **4**(4), 1–39 (2008). https://doi.org/10.1145/1412196.1412198
14. Limano, F., Piliang, Y.A., Damajanti, I.: Virtual reality as a new reality in the sustainability of cultural heritage. In: Proceeding Conference. p. 151 (2020)
15. Abokhoza, R.R., Sobieh, Y.M.: The role of virtual reality to enhance cultural communication. Int. J. Web Portals **13**(2), 20–35 (2021)

Visual Continuity Revisited: Investigating the Effects of Edited Cuts, Long Take, and Cinematic Virtual Realty on Audience Emotional Response and Perception

Wenbai Xue, Cheng-Hung Lo[✉], and Yong Yue

Xi'an Jiaotong Liverpool University, Suzhou, China
Wenbai.Xue20@student.xjtlu.edu.cn, ChengHung.Lo@xjtlu.edu.cn

Abstract. Since the inception of cinema, narrative continuity has not only served as the backbone of traditional films but has also been at the forefront of exploration in cinematic virtual reality (CVR). Both traditional films and CVR manipulate the visual continuity of shots to engage the audience with intended narrations. In this study, we centered our exploration on visual continuity, investigating its effects in traditional films and CVR on audience emotional responses, as well as spatial and temporal perceptions. We conducted an experiment to compare participants' experiences in viewing continuous edits, One-take, and CVR versions of a sample film. The collected data were statistically analyzed to discern the emotional responses and spatial-temporal perception towards the three viewing conditions. The results demonstrate that CVR shares interesting commonalities with long-take but retain subtle differences brought by its immersive and interactive features. This comparative study enhances our understanding of how manipulating visual continuity in different media can influence audience engagement, laying the groundwork for further exploration of related cinematic practices across traditional and emerging forms of visual storytelling.

Keywords: Visual Continuity · Cinematic Virtual Reality · Emotional Response · Spatial-Temporal Perception

1 Introduction

The art of filmmaking serves as a dynamic narrative exploration canvas, with its influence hinging on seamlessly integrating visual elements to present captivating stories to the audience. The narrative and continuity of films intertwine scenes, time, and emotions, creating a cohesive and immersive storytelling experience. Within this experience, films employ various techniques and skills to become a bridge of communication between the audience and the story, guiding them through the screen's reality and immersing them in a profound experience.

Over the past century since the birth of cinema, from the classic silent era to the emergence of contemporary virtual reality films, narrative continuity has not only been

P.-L. P. Rau (Ed.): HCII 2024, LNCS 14702, pp. 74–85, 2024.
https://doi.org/10.1007/978-3-031-60913-8_6

a pillar of traditional film but also at the forefront of exploration in virtual reality film-making. Traditional films use continuity editing to organically piece together scenes from different times and spaces, creating montage and achieving a visually coherent narrative. Alternatively, employing the technique of the long take, filmmakers guide the audience visually through the river of the story, approaching the "real" by orchestrating camera movements and scene arrangements. Cinematic virtual reality (CVR), while inheriting and innovating traditional methods, presents the flow of space and time in a new way, expanding the emotional and perceptual boundaries of the audience within the storified world. In essence, the purpose of various cinematic techniques is to evoke emotions and engage audience in a resonant narrative. Guided by the principles of narrative continuity, the interaction of visual elements not only facilitates the plot's development but also shapes the audience's emotional trajectories.

The primary objective of most film narratives is to construct a clear and coherent story structure [14]. Traditional filmmaking has long favored the use of cut-editing to achieve the goal of continuous storytelling [19]. This form liberates itself from spatial and temporal constraints, splicing together different frames to maintain a visual illusion of coherence [21]. Research by Joseph et al. [14] confirms the purpose of continuity editing in supporting the audience's understanding of meaningful events and bridging the gaps in visual coherence. The use of continuity editing not only maintains narrative coherence but also influences the audience's emotional responses. Filmmakers control the visual rhythm of narrative continuity through editing, allowing the audience to "sync" with the images, time, and emotions in the film [20]. Bordwell and Thompson [3] emphasize the importance of temporal and spatial coherence in the continuity of narratives in traditional filmmaking. Adams and Venkatesh [1] introduce the concept of "Aesthetic Structuralizer" in their research, stating that continuity editing can increase or decrease the consistency of spatial and temporal representations, effectively eliminating ambiguity.

CVR places films in a unique medium – immersive virtual reality. When maintaining narrative continuity, directors can still use techniques such as editing, gaze matching, and the "180-degree rule" to preserve the continuity of narrative space and time. Although these traditional visual narrative techniques are still in the experimental stage in CVR [6], studies show their effective application in practical contexts [28]. However, some argue that the audience's excessive "freedom" in exploring VR environments deprives directors of absolute control over the camera [2]. Therefore, the rules of traditional filmmaking may not directly apply to VR viewing contents [8, 15], e.g., excessive editing in continuous storytelling may induce dizziness in the audience. While Kjaer et al. [12] later confirmed through experimentation that an increase in editing frequency did not significantly affect narrative continuity, their study utilized a relatively slow narrative pace and fixed camera positions in simple scenes.

To ensure narrative continuity and not disrupt the immersion in VR, many CVR videos adopt the "One-take" approach [22]. This "One-take" method bears a strong resemblance to the long take technique in traditional films. To some extent, "One-take" can be understood as an extended version of the long take, both involving continuous shooting from a single position over a continuous period. Like long takes, "One-take" directly influences the audience's emotions in continuous storytelling. For example, in the film "Children of Men" [24], the director uses the long take to make the audience believe they are witnessing events "in real-time," intensifying the narrative's emotional impact [9].

Our research aims to examine the commonalities and differences between traditional filmmaking and CVR from the perspective of visual narrative continuity. We believe that whether shooting a scene using traditional 2D film techniques or CVR methods, the goal is to achieve narrative storytelling. This raises the question: when filming the same content and maintaining visual continuity for a consistent narrative, do traditional films and CVR elicit aligned emotional impacts and spatial-temporal perceptions among audiences? In this study, we will focus on the differences and similarities among continuity editing and the long take (One-take) in traditional cinematography, as well as the continuous shooting from a single position in CVR.

We hypothesize that CVR and One-take would produce similar effects on the audience. Consequently, the long-standing differences between continuity editing and the long take in traditional films [17] suggests that there would be differences between continuity editing and CVR's one-take approach. Our research thus formulates the null hypothesis that, under the conditions of viewing the same filmed content, there is no significant difference in the audience's emotional responses among the three production methods. The alternative hypotheses are, therefore, that there is no significant difference between continuity editing and the other two methods, while there is a significant difference between long-take and CVR.

2 Methodology

The experiment included experiences with three independent video clip versions: first, the 2D raw edit version (referred to as "Cut"); second, the 2D long-take version, adjusted based on segments of the original edit (referred to as "One-take"); and finally, the CVR formatted version adjusted from the original edit (referred to as "CVR"). All participants viewed these three versions of video clips. To mitigate potential learning effects due to repeated viewing and ensure the comparability of results, we controlled the order of participants' viewing through a computer-generated random index. For measuring emotional responses, we employed a pre/post-design and used the changes in emotional states as the measurement data for further analysis. While the order of presenting the three video clips was randomized across participants, considerations were taken in having equal distributions of each video being the first, second, and third to present. This allowed us to gather spatial and temporal estimates from participants after viewing the "first" videos, which contained equal number of samples experiencing each of the three conditions. So, participants reported the estimates based only on the first video viewed (cut, one-take, or CVR), instead of accumulated insights after watching all three.

2.1 Materials and Apparatus

The tests were conducted in a quiet, isolated setting, with each participant seated in a chair allowing 360° rotation. To prevent interference between participants, there was a spacing of over two meters between each other. To minimize variations caused by viewing devices, we choose to use the HTC VIVE Pro Eye as experimental equipment. Participants were instructed to wear this HMD to watch all three versions of video clips.

To ensure the consistency of the test videos and make them more authentic as a cinematic experience, we opted not to use scenes constructed with simple geometric shapes. Instead, we chose the first 90 s of the demo "Infiltrator" [11], created in Unreal Engine 4 (UE4) and showcased at the GDC2013 conference, as the prototype for the test video. The project files, including all video scene designs, character animations, Mise-en-scéne, and camera movements, are downloadable and freely available for use (see Fig. 1).

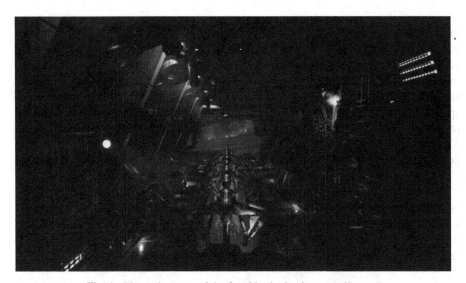

Fig. 1. The main scene of the first 90 s in the demo "Infiltrator"

The Cut represented the first 90 s of the original Infiltrator film. The One-take, while retaining the original design, used the Cinecamera Actor component in UE4 to smoothly connect the content switching between original camera shots and produce a visually continuous long shot, maintaining the original camera's position, angle, and lens parameters. In the HMD's virtual scape, both 2D versions' viewing environments were set up in a dark virtual space, with a 1920x1080 movie screen placed at an equal distance, presenting contents of the two 2D versions for participants to view without external interference in the HMD. CVR, based on the processed long-take, added a VR Pawn component controlled by blueprint programming, maintaining the same motion path, speed, and other parameters as the Cinecamera Actor in the One-take while ensuring participants could view the video clip in 360° within the HMD (see Fig. 2).

2.2 Data Collection

We incorporated a questionnaire to collect data on participants' emotional measurement, spatial and temporal perception measurements. For emotional measurement, we used

Fig. 2. Participants viewed in two different modes while put on the HMD.

the Self-Assessment Manikin (SAM) applied widely in emotional evaluations across various contexts and events. To assess spatial and temporal perception, we designed two additional sections in the questionnaire, each containing nine descriptions of varying magnitudes of time or space, scored on a 9-point scale. In the options describing spatial size and time length, a score of 1 indicated that participants did not notice the size of space or the passage of time during the viewing process or were unable to estimate. The remaining scores of 2–9 corresponded to eight increasing intervals of time and space. The space intervals started from less than or equal to $10\,\mathrm{m}^3$, with each point representing an additional $100\,\mathrm{m}^3$. Time intervals started from less than or equal to 10 s, increasing by 15 s for each scoring interval.

We used pre/post testing approach to eliminate initial differences in emotional self-assessment, participants filled out the SAM questionnaire before watching the video, with the results serving as the baseline. After experiencing each version of the video, participants completed the SAM again for measuring changes in emotional state and reported the perceived space size and time duration.

2.3 Participants and Procedures

Participants were recruited through voluntary enrollment and random selection. Ultimately, 45 university students, with an average age of 19.7 years, were included. Prior to the tests, all participants were thoroughly briefed on the testing requirements and asked to sign the informed consent forms. All participants reported no potential impairments in visual, auditory, emotional, or other cognitive functions before the experiment. They were also requested to fill out the SAM scale to record their initial emotional states. During the experiment, participants viewed all three versions of video clips in a random order. To alleviate the occurrence of motion sickness, participants had a 3 to 5-min rest period after each experience.

3   Results

For statistical analysis purposes, our experiment design consists of three independent variables (Cut, One-take, and CVR) and three sets of dependent variables, which are self-reported emotional changes (Valence, Arousal, and Dominance), participant ratings of spatial and temporal perception. Corresponding methods were then employed to analyze the data obtained during the experiment.

3.1   Emotional Responses

We calculated the differences between the pre and post experiments – "SAM" scores. Figure 3 illustrates the mean fluctuations in participants' emotional responses after viewing different versions of clips. Overall, while the two 2D versions exhibited some differences in the level of emotional response, they displayed a similar trend, whereas CVR showed significant distinctions.

As depicted in Fig. 3, participants exhibited a similar decreasing trend in pleasure levels after viewing both 2D versions, whereas the emotional response to pleasure after viewing CVR was more intense. The pleasure level showed a noticeable increase compared to the baseline.

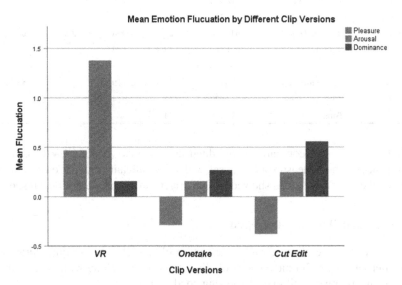

Fig. 3. Mean Emotional Fluctuation by Different Clip Versions

Furthermore, it is evident from the figure that all three versions of the clips increased participants' arousal levels. The two 2D versions showed similar trends in arousal with pleasure, maintaining a close relationship. However, CVR clearly induced a higher level of arousal. In comparison to the other two versions, CVR magnified substantially the extent of emotional arousal.

Additionally, all three versions of video clips generated relatively low dominance levels. Although the differences were not as pronounced as in pleasure and arousal, it is noticeable that the CVR version triggered a relatively higher dominance level. The feedback on dominance levels after watching the Cut version was the lowest, significantly lower than both CVR and One-take versions.

To validate the statistical significance of the impact of different versions of video clips on emotional responses and identify differences among versions, ANOVA with post hoc tests were applied. Our analysis adhered to the conventions of statistical analysis, using probability measures (p-values $= 0.05$) to determine statistical significance [7].

Table 1 presents the impact of different clip versions on all three emotional responses. The results indicate significant differences only in pleasure and arousal (p < 0.05). To further clarify whether the significant influences among the three versions align with the null hypothesis, LSD post hoc analysis was conducted.

Table 1. The results of a one-way ANOVA, investigating the effects of versions

		Sum of Squares	df	Mean Square	F	Sig.
Pleasure	Between Groups	19.378	2	9.689	3.485	.034
	Within Groups	367.022	132	2.780		
	Total	386.400	134			
Arousal	Between Groups	41.793	2	20.896	6.650	.002
	Within Groups	414.800	132	3.142		
	Total	456.593	134			
Dominance	Between Groups	3.837	2	1.919	.637	.531
	Within Groups	397.822	132	3.014		
	Total	401.659	134			

As shown in Table 2, compared to the edited and One-take versions, CVR has significant influences on both pleasure and arousal, with no significant influence on dominance. Moreover, the two 2D versions showed similar effects on all three emotional responses.

3.2 Spatial and Temporal Perception

Figures 4 and 5 present participants' perception of spatial size and time duration of scenes after viewing different versions of clips, respectively, along with the proportion of participants relative to all in each viewing condition.

As illustrated in Fig. 4, it is evident that when watching CVR, participants' perception of the same spatial size is relatively greater than when viewing the two 2D versions. While participants' perceptions of spatial size were relatively similar when experiencing the two 2D clips, the proportion of people perceiving larger scene spaces for One-take was slightly more than that for the edited version. Therefore, participants' perception of the same spatial size was slightly greater when watching One-take compared to the edited version.

Figure 5 displays participants' perception of the duration of videos of the same length in three different versions. From the distribution proportion, it is observed that when watching CVR, the perceived scene duration is slightly longer than when viewing the two 2D versions. If using the actual video length as the benchmark, the proportion of participants perceiving the duration close to the actual length reached 42% for CVR, relatively higher than the other two versions. The two 2D versions had the same proportion of people approaching the actual length, only with slight differences in the proportions of the remaining distributions.

Table 2. The result of a post- hoc test, determine which version has significant difference between.

LSD

Dependent Variable	(I) Versions	(J) Versions	Mean Differenc e (I-J)	Std. Error	Sig.
Pleasure	VR	Onetake	.756*	.352	.033
		Cut Edit	.844*	.352	.018
	Onetake	VR	-.756*	.352	.033
		Cut Edit	.089	.352	.801
	Cut Edit	VR	-.844*	.352	.018
		Onetake	-.089	.352	.801
Arousal	VR	Onetake	1.222*	.374	.001
		Cut Edit	1.133*	.374	.003
	Onetake	VR	-1.222*	.374	.001
		Cut Edit	-.089	.374	.812
	Cut Edit	VR	-1.133*	.374	.003
		Onetake	.089	.374	.812
Dominance	VR	Onetake	-.111	.366	.762
		Cut Edit	-.400	.366	.276
	Onetake	VR	.111	.366	.762
		Cut Edit	-.289	.366	.431
	Cut Edit	VR	.400	.366	.276
		Onetake	.289	.366	.431

*. The mean difference is significant at the 0.05 level.

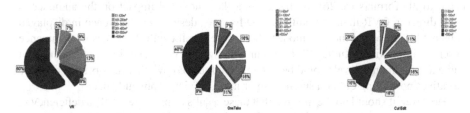

Fig. 4. The number distribution of each version on spatial perception

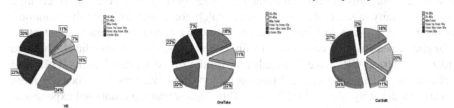

Fig. 5. The number distribution of each version on temporal perception

Furthermore, non-parametric tests were conducted to explore statistical significances in spatial and temporal perception for the three versions of video clips to. We chose Friedman as the non-parametric test method and employed Wilcoxon for post hoc comparisons between data pairs. The results showed statistically significant differences among the three versions in spatial and temporal perception, and significant differences existed between each pair ($p < 0.05$).

In summary, the results indicate that while there are some differences in emotional responses to video clips of different versions, there is no significant difference in the impact on dominance levels among the three versions. Overall, the effects of the two 2D versions on all three dimensions are relatively similar. CVR demonstrates a positively directed trend in pleasure and possesses a high level of arousal. Furthermore, in terms of spatial and temporal perception, CVR outperforms the two 2D versions, particularly in spatial perception. Although the distributions of the two 2D versions in the overall data are similar, One-take performs slightly better than the edited version. The test results also indicate significant differences among the three versions of clips.

4 Discussion

Our research explores the commonalities and differences between traditional film and CVR from the perspective of visual continuity in film narrative. Taking into account audience emotional responses, as well as perceptions of space and time, we aim to examine the nuances that distinguish these two cinematic formats.

Through our comparative analysis, we observed differences in emotions invoked by videos with varied visual continuities resulted from traditional cinematic methods and VR approaches. Some of our findings echoed previous studies with the observed heightened emotional effects demonstrated by audiences under VR format (CVR) compared to 2D formats [5, 26]. It appears that the emotional impact on the audience is more direct in CVR than in traditional 2D formats, despite the difference in displayed contents [4]. Between the two modes, there were significant differences in dominance observed in previous studies [27] but our experiment. We argue that the influence on audience dominance levels could be strongly confounded by other factors such as scene narratives portraying either a submissive or majestic view from audience.

However, it should not be inferred that these results imply necessarily a deficiency in conveying pleasure and arousal level to the audience in traditional 2D films. Regardless of whether continuity is achieved through montage or long takes, the core of creating visual continuity in screen-based films is not solely for transmitting positive emotions. Its primary purpose is to convey intended emotions within the narrative context by arranging a sequence of continuous or discontinuous shots in a specific rhythm and order. In contrast, CVR, due to its inherent feature of "Voluntary Framing" [25] and embodiment in an immersive environment [16], prevents viewers from focusing more directly on the story plot as in 2D films. This implies that the emotional experiences gained by viewers in CVR are partially derived from the interaction and immersion in VR, rather than the narrative itself.

Furthermore, the unique immersive experience in VR environments enhance the cognitive performance of the audiences [10], while continuous editing in traditional film sometimes hinders or diminishes the audience's psychological experience of spatial integration [22]. Although the long take technique in traditional film achieves the integrity of narrative space [13] and allows viewers to experience the continuity of the visual environment [23], the freedom of viewing and the depth perception of 3D images presented in CVR contribute to enhancing the audience's perception of space.

In terms of time perception, when using the actual duration as a reference to compare the time perception results, CVR's performance was found to be slightly better to 2D. However, the higher accuracy in the perception of video length does not directly serve narrative purposes. For instance, in 2D editing, most traditional films contain deliberately arranged edits by directors, aiming to provide audiences with a specific perception of time flow through continuous shots [9]. This often leads to a certain degree of deviation in the audience's perception of the passage of time in the film. In contrast, the single camera, continuous shooting approach commonly attached to CVR presents viewers with an almost real-time experience. With the primary purpose of simulating a real experience, the continuity of real-time CVR makes it naturally incompatible with approaches of distorting time perception in a non-realistic experience [18].

Finally, it is worth mentioning that, despite the visual continuity shared between the traditional one-take approach and single camera continuous shooting CVR, there are evident distinctions in terms of audience emotional feedback and the perception of space and time. The comparison of the two reveals pronounced disparities. Conversely, when compared to continuous editing, which exhibits noticeable distinctions in immediate sensory experiences, there emerge informative similarities in the outcomes. This implies that while film cutting or montage inherently disrupts the visual continuity, the application of long takes should not be treated back forth as an integration of montage [29]. As indicated in our study, long takes maintain an overarching narrative coherence but still retain subtle differences in the conveyed emotions and perceived spatial-temporal characteristics.

5 Conclusion

This comparative study investigates the commonalities and differences between traditional film and CVR from the perspective of visual continuity in film narration. By examining the impact of continuous editing, One-take, and CVR, three versions of videos depicting the same content on audience emotions and spatial-temporal perception, we demonstrate significant advantages of CVR over traditional film in influencing audience emotional responses and spatial-temporal perception. Our findings indicate that, across the three dimensions of emotion, CVR elicits stronger emotional responses in terms of pleasure and arousal compared to traditional film. However, no significant difference is observed in dominance level between CVR and traditional film. Furthermore, audiences perceive larger spatial dimensions and more accurate durations when watching CVR compared to traditional film. This implies that, when emphasizing emotional continuity, and providing an authentic spatial-temporal experience is crucial, employing CVR for filming the same content becomes a favorable choice. While revealing important findings, this study represents an initial investigation into the visual continuities manipulated with traditional cinematographic techniques and CVR. Our results are valid for the specific materials used, providing us a foundation to build upon. Future work should systematically investigate additional factors, such as genre and narrative style, to deepen knowledge of how medium impacts audience engagement.

References

1. Adams, B., Venkatesh, S.: Weaving stories in digital media: when Spielberg makes home movies. In: International Multimedia Conference: Proceedings of the Eleventh ACM International Conference on Multimedia, 02–08 November 2003, pp. 207–210 (2003)
2. Aylett, R., Louchart, S.: Towards a narrative theory of virtual reality. Virtual Real. J. Virtual Real. Soc. 7(1), 2–9 (2003)
3. Bordwell, D., Thompson, K., Smith, J.: Film Art an Introduction, 11th edn. McGraw-Hill Education, New York (2016)
4. Carpio, R., Baumann, O., Birt, J.: Evaluating the viewer experience of interactive virtual reality movies. Virt. Real. J. Virt. Real. Soc. 27(4), 3181–3190 (2023)
5. Ding, N., Zhou, W., Fung, A.Y.H.: Emotional effect of cinematic VR compared with traditional 2D film. Telematics Inf. 35(6), 1572–1579 (2018)
6. Fearghail, C.O., Ozcinar, C., Knorr, S., Smolic, A.: Director's cut - analysis of VR film cuts for interactive storytelling. In: 2018 International Conference on 3D Immersion (IC3D), pp. 1–8 (2018)
7. Field, A.: Disscovering Statistics Using SPSS, 2nd edn. Sage Publications Ltd, Thousands Oaks (2005)
8. Gödde, M., Gabler, F., Siegmund, D., Braun, A.: Cinematic narration in VR – rethinking film conventions for 360 degrees. In: Chen, J.Y.C., Fragomeni, G. (eds.) VAMR 2018. LNCS, vol. 10910, pp. 184–201. Springer, Cham (2018). https://doi.org/10.1007/978-3-319-91584-5_15
9. Ghosh, A.: Analysis of Single-Shot and Long-Take Filmmaking: Its Evolution, Technique, Mise-en-scène, and Impact on the Viewer (2022). https://doi.org/10.54105/ijmcj.b1023. 122222
10. Huang, K., Li, J., Sousa, M., Grossman, T.: Immersive pov: filming how-to videos with a head-mounted 360° action camera. In: Proceedings of the 2022 CHI Conference on Human Factors in Computing Systems. pp. 1–13 (2022)
11. Ivey, C.: Infiltrator Released for Free!. Unreal Engine (2015). https://www.unrealengine.com/en-US/blog/infiltrator-released-for-free
12. Kjær, T., Lillelund, C.B., Moth-Poulsen, M., Nilsson, N.C., Nordahl, R., Serafin, S.: Can you cut it? an exploration of the effects of editing in cinematic virtual reality. In: Proceedings of the 23rd ACM Symposium on Virtual Reality Software and Technology, pp. 1–4 (2017)
13. Gao, L.: Enrichment and development of film aesthetics by digital long take. In: Proceedings of the International Conference on Education, Language, Art and Intercultural Communication (2014)
14. Magliano, J.P., Zacks, J.M.: The impact of continuity editing in narrative film on event segmentation. Cogn. Sci. 35(8), 1489–1517 (2011)
15. Maranes, C., Gutierrez, D., Serrano, A.: Exploring the impact of 360° movie cuts in users' attention. In: 2020 IEEE Conference on Virtual Reality and 3D User Interfaces (VR), pp. 73–82 (2020)
16. Mateer, J.: Directing for Cinematic Virtual Reality: how the traditional film director's craft applies to immersive environments and notions of presence. J. Media Pract. 18(1), 14–25 (2017)
17. Menard, D.G.: Toward a synthesis of cinema -a theory of the long take moving camera, part 1. Offscreen 7(8) (2003)

18. Lescop, L.: Narrative grammar in 360. In: 2017 IEEE International Symposium on Mixed and Augmented Reality (ISMAR-Adjunct), pp. 254–257 (2017)
19. O'steen, B.: The invisible cut: how editors make movie magic (2009)
20. Pearlman, K.: On rhythm in film editing. In: Carroll, N., Di Summa, L.T., Loht, S. (eds.) The Palgrave Handbook of the Philosophy of Film and Motion Pictures, pp. 143–163. Springer, Cham (2019). https://doi.org/10.1007/978-3-030-19601-1_7
21. Serrano, A., Sitzmann, V., Ruiz-Borau, J., Wetzstein, G., Gutierrez, D., Masia, B.: Movie editing and cognitive event segmentation in virtual reality video. ACM Trans. Graph. **36**(4), 1–12 (2018)
22. Tian, F., Hua, M., Zhang, T., Zhang, W.: Spatio-temporal editing method and application in virtual reality video. In: 2020 IEEE 4th Information Technology, Networking, Electronic and Automation Control Conference (ITNEC), vol. 1, pp. 2290–2294. IEEE (2020)
23. Troiani, I., Campbell, H.: Orchestrating spatial continuity in the urban realm. Arch. Cult. **3**(1), 7–16 (2015)
24. Universal Pictures (through Toho-Towa in Japan). Children of men [VHS]. United Kingdom and United States (2006)
25. Xue, W., Lo, C.H.: Sound-guided framing in cinematic virtual reality–an eye-tracking study. In: International Conference on Human-Computer Interaction, pp. 520–535. Springer, Cham (2022). https://doi.org/10.1007/978-3-031-06047-2_39
26. Yeo, N.L., et al.: What is the best way of delivering virtual nature for improving mood? an experimental comparison of high definition TV, 360° video, and computer generated virtual reality. J. Environ. Psychol. **72**, 101500 (2020)
27. Yu, Z., Lo, C.H., Niu, M., Liang, H.N.: Comparing cinematic conventions through emotional responses in cinematic VR and traditional mediums. In: SIGGRAPH Asia 2023 Technical Communications, pp. 1–4 (2023)
28. Zhang, Y., Weber, I.: Adapting, modifying and applying cinematography and editing concepts and techniques to cinematic virtual reality film production. Media Int. Aust. Incorporat. Cult. Policy **186**(1), 115–135 (2023)
29. Zhipeng, Y.: The dialectic of realism and surrealism in long take films. Front. Art Res. **5**(15) (2023)

Rethinking Defaults: Examining the Effects of Default Camera Height and Angle on Embodied Presence in Cinematic Virtual Reality

Zhiyuan Yu🅐, Cheng-Hung Lo^(✉)🅐, Ganlin Yang🅐, and Hai-Ning Liang🅐

Xi'an Jiaotong-Liverpool University, 111 Renai Road, Suzhou, China
Cheng-Hung.Lo@xjtlu.edu.cn

Abstract. This study investigates the avatar-less embodiment experienced by viewers in cinematic virtual reality (CVR), with a focus on comparing grounded and aerial camera perspectives. We conducted an experiment using a between-subjects design with 63 participants across nine viewing scenarios in a virtual Hogwarts environment. The scenarios systematically manipulated camera height (Grounded or Aerial) and angle (High, Eye level, Low). Participants completed adapted questionnaires measuring embodiment and discomfort. Our analysis reveals pronounced effects of camera positioning on embodiment, with aerial heights eliciting higher embodiment than grounded positions across angles. Low aerial angles further enhanced embodied sensation. Interestingly, adding virtual grounding elements at aerial heights balanced increased stability with slightly reduced embodiment. These empirical findings provide insights to help CVR practitioners optimize default camera settings for crafting appropriately immersive, comfortable VR narrative experiences aligned to specific narrative goals.

Keywords: Default camera · Cinematic virtual reality · Embodiment

1 Introduction

Cinematic virtual reality (CVR) offers audiences the unique experience of being 'inside' films, representing a new form of immersive storytelling [10]. This transformation is shaped by embodiment in VR, which enhances users' sense of presence and identification [8]. As storytelling in CVR format requires much more user-centered engagement, it is thus essential for researchers to define into the effect of embodiment during the content creation process to optimize the immersive experience [2]. To render a virtual scene, a default virtual camera is always needed so that 3D-modeled scene elements can be projected onto a displayable 2D visual field. In VR, there are two horizontally displaced virtual cameras to enable stereoscopic projection. The head-mounted display fuses these projections to facilitate stereoscopic viewing. VR also allows for non-stereoscopic, 360-degree panoramic images. The need for a single default virtual camera still applies in scene rendering for both stereoscopic and non-stereoscopic cases. We can generalize both cases as using a default virtual camera, which functions as the vantage point in VR experiences. The positioning of this default camera, particularly its height and angle, is instrumental in shaping viewers' engagement, emotional responses, and the sense of presence experienced within a virtual environment [7]. However, research on default camera settings in CVR remains limited. We aim to address this gap by examining how camera height and angle impact avatar-less embodiment and discomfort, with a focus on comparing grounded and aerial perspectives. The finding may inform CVR practitioners to appropriately adjust default camera setups and construct scenes that effectively align with the intended narratives.

In this paper, we present an experiment taking place in a virtual environment modeled after the iconic Hogwarts Castle from the Harry Potter series. This realism-oriented setting supports a feeling of authentic narrative immersion, while also providing sufficient space to explore different camera perspectives. Specifically, we systematically vary camera height between Grounded and Aerial positions, as well as camera angle among High, Low, and Eye level views. As illustrated in Fig. 1, this experimental design enables us to examine how different visual framings of the highly familiar Hogwarts landscape influence users' sense of experience.

Fig. 1. Experimental viewing scenarios: default camera settings overview

Unlike traditional cinema, CVR introduces the dimension of embodiment, which raises important questions around the use of aerial camera perspectives.

While we manipulate camera heights as an experimental factor, the elevated, aerial shots may impact viewer immersion, embodiment, and potential discomfort in CVR. Though aerial and establishing shots are commonplace and crucial storytelling devices in conventional films [1], their effects may differ in embodied CVR experiences. Therefore, we also integrate a novel grounding element in our aerial scenarios. This visual flooring applied at aerial heights is designed to test its influence on viewers' sense of embodiment and discomfort mitigation. By incorporating this grounding cue, we can systematically assess its effectiveness in enhancing embodied presence and reducing unease during aerial CVR footage.

2   Related Works

In the evolving field of CVR, the role of camera height, viewer position, camera distance, shot size, and field of view has been a subject of extensive research. These elements are critical in determining the viewers' experience, influencing factors such as presence, embodiment, and emotional response. Keskinen et al. [7] investigated the impact of camera height and viewer position on the viewer experience, identifying a more natural and comfortable camera height around 1.5 m for both seated and standing viewers. Rothe et al. examined how camera positioning and field of view affects presence, sickness, and overall experience in CVR, seeking to provide guidance on optimal camera placement for enhanced immersion, also highlighted the acceptance of camera heights lower than the viewer's own height [13,14,16]. Pope et al. [11] contrasted staging techniques between 360° cameras and traditional positioning, noting the importance of proxemics in narrative performances. Rothe et al. [15] further explored the application of traditional shot sizes in CVR, categorizing them based on proxemic distances. Dooley [3] suggested that Edward T. Hall's proxemics theories could inform spatial screen grammar in 360° CVR and also aid 2D filmmakers in considering character spatial relationships. This was supported by Dooley's later findings that factors such as proximity and gaze direction influence viewer empathy [4]. Probst et al. [12] discussed how various camera distances in CVR elicit emotional responses akin to shot sizes in traditional films. Zhiyuan et al. [18] suggest CVR's embodied, interactive qualities altered the impact of cinematic techniques, which enhances engagement through heightened arousal and lowered dominance.

These insights are important for understanding the spatial cognition in CVR. However, research specifically addressing default camera settings in CVR production remains limited. Our research aims to fill this gap, offering a comprehensive understanding of how various default camera settings can enhance or alter the embodiment level in CVR. This assists CVR practitioners in their production process and provides a guideline on how various cinematic techniques can be effectively adapted and optimized for immersive VR experiences across different storytelling contexts.

3   Methodology

This study investigates the effects of default camera angles and heights on the avatar-less embodiment level in CVR, with an additional focus on examining the influence of grounding in aerial height scenarios. To evaluate the impact on embodiment, our study employed a between-subjects design with 63 participants. They experienced nine viewing scenarios, each utilizing VR headsets to deliver diverse perspectives within the virtual environment. Viewer experiences were evaluated through questions adapted to align with our experimental context from the selected questionnaires. These adapted questions were specifically chosen to reflect the unique conditions of our study, enabling an accurate measurement of avatar-less embodiment levels and any associated discomfort.

3.1   Materials and Apparatus

The experimental viewing scenarios were generated using Unreal Engine 5 due to its advanced graphical rendering capabilities, which are crucial for creating realistic and detailed virtual environments. The Pico 4 Pro VR headset was selected for the experiment to ensure a high-quality visual experience, allowing for an accurate representation of different camera heights and angles as experienced by the user.

Fig. 2. 9 viewing scenarios in different default camera settings

Figure 2 illustrates the nine different viewing scenarios, each representing a unique combination of default camera settings. These scenarios were designed to systematically vary in camera height (Grounded or Aerial) and camera angle (High angle, Eye level, Low angle), with the additional variable of a virtual floor providing grounding in aerial height.

3.2   Measurements

To assess the embodiment levels and discomfort experienced by participants, our methodology incorporated a combination of three widely-used questionnaires, including Igroup Presence Questionnaires (IPQ) [17] and Embodiment Questionnaires (EQ) [5], in conjunction with the Simulator Sickness Questionnaire (SSQ) [6]. The IPQ was utilized to measure the sense of spatial presence, involvement, and experienced realism within the VR environment. Specific questions selected from the IPQ focused on aspects like the sense of 'being there' in the computer-generated world and feeling surrounded by the virtual environment. In addition to the IPQ, we adapted questions from the EQ to specifically gauge the embodiment level, which included perceptions of body changes in response to camera height and angle. These questions were carefully chosen to align with the context of our CVR study, ensuring the relevance and accuracy of our findings.

- IPQ Questions for Sense of Presence:
  - *In the computer-generated world, I had a sense of "being there". (−3: fully dis-agree, 3: fully agree) - Somehow, I felt that the virtual world surrounded me. (−3: fully disagree, 3: fully agree) - I felt present in the virtual space. (−3: fully disagree, 3: fully agree) - I was completely captivated by the virtual world. (−3: fully disagree, 3: fully agree)*
- EQ Questions for Embodiment:
  - *I felt out of my body. (−3: fully disagree - 3: fully agree) - I felt that my own body could be affected by camera height. (−3: fully disagree - 3: fully agree) - I felt that my own body could be affected by camera angle. (−3: fully disagree - 3: fully agree)*

The SSQ was used to measure symptoms of simulator sickness, including general discomfort, eyestrain, difficulty focusing, nausea, difficulty concentrating, and dizziness. This comprehensive questionnaire approach aimed to provide an understanding of the technical aspects of CVR and their embodiment impact on the viewer's immersive experience.

3.3   Participants and Grouping

A total of 63 individuals were recruited to participate in the study, with a wide age distribution ranging from 20 to 50 years and a balanced gender ratio of 33 males and 30 females. Most were in their twenties and had little to no previous experience with VR. Participants were evenly distributed into the nine VR viewing scenarios, seven per scenario, to ensure diverse responses across different default camera setting.

3.4 Procedures

Before the commencement of the experiment, a thorough briefing was conducted with participants to ensure they were well-informed about the process and any potential health concerns, such as motion sickness or physical discomfort. Participants had the option to halt the experiment at any time should they feel uneasy.

The experiment was conducted in a controlled, quiet environment where the objectives and procedures were clearly articulated. Participants were acquainted with the IPQ, EQ, and SSQ questionnaires and their relevance to the study. Upon viewing, each participant was in standing position and wearing the Pico 4 Pro headset, which was adjusted to their individual interpupillary distance to achieve the clearest virtual imagery possible. Upon successful calibration, participants were immersed in the predefined default camera settings.

To ensure the accuracy of responses and to capture the immediacy of the participants' reactions, researchers verbally administered each questionnaire item during the viewing scenario. Participants responded to a series of thirteen questions, with the entire session lasting approximately 3–4 min. Throughout this process, re-searchers recorded each response and observed the participants' physical and emotional reactions, providing a rich dataset for subsequent analysis. This detailed procedure was designed to obtain a genuine first-hand account of the participants' experiences, reflecting the true impact of the default camera settings on their sense of presence, embodiment, and comfort within the virtual environment.

Participants' responses to the questionnaires were quantified based on a scoring system where higher scores correlated with greater immersion, embodiment, and discomfort. Specifically, the IPQ-EQ included items such as 'sense of being there', 'feeling surrounded', 'being captivated', and 'perception of camera height and angle affecting the body'. These items were designed to cumulatively represent the degree of embodiment experienced by the participants.

4 Result

We computed the mean scores for each of the nine groups, with seven participants in each group, to establish average indices for embodiment and discomfort. This approach allowed us to evaluate the overall impact of camera settings on the participants' virtual experience. The sum of scores from each item within the questionnaires provided a composite measure of embodiment level and the degree of discomfort, with the intention of reflecting the participants' immersive experience in the CVR environment.

The evaluation concentrates on discerning the influence of diverse default camera heights and angles, and the implementation of grounding with aerial heights, on participants' perceived level of embodiment and discomfort. The results reveals associations between various default camera settings and their impact on the sense of avatar-less embodiment, as well as the extent of discomfort experienced by viewers.

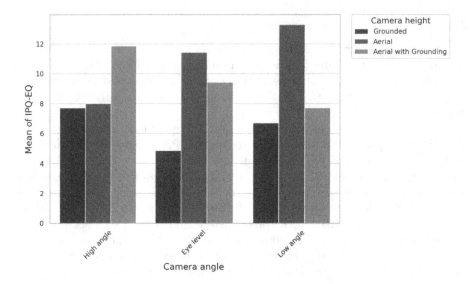

Fig. 3. IPQ-EQ Mean Scores Bar Chart

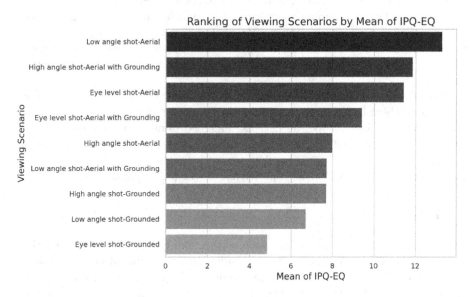

Fig. 4. Ranking of Viewing Scenarios by IPQ-EQ Scores

Figure 3 displays a bar chart illustrating the mean IPQ-EQ scores across various default camera settings in our viewing scenarios. It is apparent that camera height invokes different levels of embodiment within the same camera angles, as reflected by the IPQ-EQ scores. This suggests that camera height plays a role in influencing the viewer's sense of embodiment.

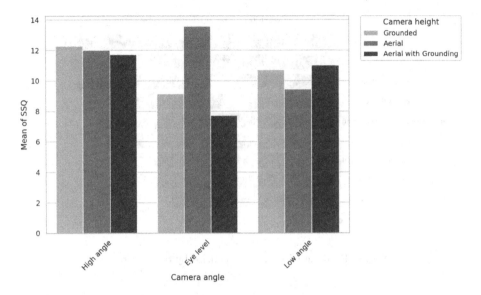

Fig. 5. SSQ Mean Scores Bar Chart

The mean IPQ-EQ scores were ranked, providing a comparative measure of immersion across different experimental conditions (see Fig. 4). This ranking offers valuable insights into which specific default camera settings contribute the most to the sense of embodiment in CVR environments. The aerial low-angle garnered the highest mean IPQ-EQ score, suggesting an amplified sense of embodiment in comparison to the other conditions, while the grounded eye-level angle recorded the lowest score.

The SSQ score bar chart (Fig. 5) illustrates the mean SSQ scores across different camera perspectives, focusing primarily on comparing aerial heights with and without grounding. The SSQ scores for the high-angle shot in both aerial height scenarios were nearly identical, while the low-angle shot showed slight changes with grounding. However, the eye-level view demonstrated an apparent reduction in discomfort when a virtual floor was added at the aerial height.

We then ranked the mean level of the SSQ (Fig. 6), which indicates that the eye-level shot in the aerial height scenario led to the highest level of discomfort among viewers, as denoted by the red bar reaching the furthest on the scale. Conversely, the eye-level shot in the aerial height with the grounding scenario showed the least discomfort. The variation in bar lengths across different scenarios suggests a correlation between camera angles, heights, and grounding and the intensity of discomfort experienced by viewers.

These findings are pivotal for crafting CVR experiences that aim to understand avatar-less embodiment and offer a potential solution to minimize discomfort at aerial heights. The insights gathered from the analysis of these visualizations are beneficial in refining default camera settings for a suitable content

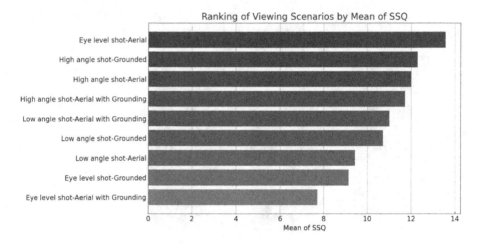

Fig. 6. Ranking of Viewing Scenarios by SSQ Scores

user experience in CVR, providing a foundation for further research on the interplay between default camera settings and viewer embodiment level in immersive narratives.

5   Discussion

Our study results demonstrate that across nine viewing scenarios, in comparison to grounded height perspectives, all aerial height perspectives elicited a heightened level of avatar-less embodiment. The embodiment experience in CVR is indeed influenced by the camera's position relative to the virtual environment. The aerial low angle shot exhibited the highest level of embodiment, whereas the grounded-eye-level shot scored the lowest. Thus, the high embodiment level observed in the aerial low-angle shot established its uniqueness within the CVR, eliciting stronger user engagement and substantial physiological stimulation owing to its height difference from the ground and a fixed upward viewing angle. The lowest embodiment performance might be because the grounded eye-level camera position aligns more closely with the everyday physiological state of individuals. These findings highlight the impact of camera placement within the virtual environment and default camera tilt on the viewer's sense of embodiment and immersion.

Furthermore, the SSQ indicates that the grounding elements in aerial scenarios can influence and potentially alleviate viewer discomfort. The aerial eye level with grounding effectively reduced viewer discomfort compared with the aerial height eye level. This aspect of our research is especially relevant to CVR practitioners, who emphasize the importance of grounding elements in mitigating discomfort while maintaining a strong sense of embodiment.

In traditional filmmaking, established shots are often composed of extremely long shots combined with various camera angles, serving to orient the audience within the geographical context of the narrative and establish character relationships. These shots are typically utilized at both ground and aerial heights, without the need to account for the viewer's physical experience, as the audience is not a physical part of the environment in conventional cinema. In contrast, the embodiment approach in CVR dramatically alters the audience's spatial perception. Because of the 360-degree immersion in CVR, as opposed to traditional film and television, there is enhanced spatial cognition [9], especially in distinguishing the differences in embodiment between aerial and ground perspectives. The sense of presence brought about by CVR implies that the default camera settings for establishing shots become a critical element of storytelling.

6   Conclusion

Our findings reveal a pronounced effect of camera perspective on embodiment, with the default camera height clearly impacting the sense of embodiment. All aerial heights led to higher embodiment than grounded camera positions across different angles, with low-angle aerial shots particularly enhancing embodied sensation. Interestingly, adding a virtual floor at aerial heights appeared to balance increased stability with a slightly reduced feeling of embodiment, especially for eye-level shots.

However, there are some limitations to this initial study. While diverse, our relatively small sample size may limit generalizability of the results to a broader population. Moreover, as just one technique in the cinematic toolkit, established shots require further exploration within full narratives.

To look ahead, a clear need exists to investigate emotional impacts of default camera positions and subconscious viewer behaviors in CVR. More extensive studies could recruit larger, more varied samples to enable robust statistical analysis. Additionally, examining a broader range of camera manipulations and their specific effects on emotions and instincts could reveal the underlying explanations for these reflexive reactions, leading to a more comprehensive understanding of the embodied CVR experience.

References

1. Barsam, R., Monahan, D.: Looking at Movies. WW Norton (2015)
2. Dooley, K.: Storytelling with virtual reality in 360-degrees: a new screen grammar. Stud. Australas. Cinema 11(3), 161–171 (2017)
3. Dooley, K.: A question of proximity: exploring a new screen grammar for 360-degree cinematic virtual reality. Media Pract. Educ. 21(2), 81–96 (2020)
4. Dooley, K.: Spatial relationships in 360-degree space: proximity, body orientation and the gaze. In: Cinematic Virtual Reality, pp. 97–110. Springer, Cham (2021). https://doi.org/10.1007/978-3-030-72147-3_6
5. Gonzalez-Franco, M., Peck, T.C.: Avatar embodiment. Towards a standardized questionnaire. Front. Robot. AI 5, 74 (2018)

6. Kennedy, R.S., Lane, N.E., Berbaum, K.S., Lilienthal, M.G.: Simulator sickness questionnaire: an enhanced method for quantifying simulator sickness. Int. J. Aviat. Psychol. **3**(3), 203–220 (1993)

7. Keskinen, T., et al.: The effect of camera height, actor behavior, and viewer position on the user experience of 360 videos. In: 2019 IEEE Conference on Virtual Reality and 3D User Interfaces (VR), pp. 423–430. IEEE (2019)

8. Kilteni, K., Groten, R., Slater, M.: The sense of embodiment in virtual reality. Presence Teleoper. Virtual Environ. **21**(4), 373–387 (2012)

9. MacQuarrie, A., Steed, A.: Cinematic virtual reality: evaluating the effect of display type on the viewing experience for panoramic video. In: 2017 IEEE Virtual Reality (VR), pp. 45–54. IEEE (2017)

10. Mateer, J.: Directing for cinematic virtual reality: how the traditional film director's craft applies to immersive environments and notions of presence. J. Media Pract. **18**(1), 14–25 (2017)

11. Pope, V.C., Dawes, R., Schweiger, F., Sheikh, A.: The geometry of storytelling: theatrical use of space for 360-degree videos and virtual reality. In: Proceedings of the 2017 CHI Conference on Human Factors in Computing Systems, pp. 4468–4478 (2017)

12. Probst, P.C., Rothe, S., Hussmann, H.: Camera distances and shot sizes in cinematic virtual reality. In: ACM International Conference on Interactive Media Experiences, pp. 178–186 (2021)

13. Rothe, S., Kegeles, B., Allary, M., Hußmann, H.: The impact of camera height in cinematic virtual reality. In: Proceedings of the 24th ACM Symposium on Virtual Reality Software and Technology, pp. 1–2 (2018)

14. Rothe, S., Kegeles, B., Hussmann, H.: Camera heights in cinematic virtual reality: how viewers perceive mismatches between camera and eye height. In: Proceedings of the 2019 ACM International Conference on Interactive Experiences for TV and Online Video, pp. 25–34 (2019)

15. Rothe, S., Sarakiotis, V., Hussmann, H.: Where to place the camera. In: Proceedings of the 25th ACM Symposium on Virtual Reality Software and Technology, pp. 1–2 (2019)

16. Rothe, S., Zhao, L., Fahrenwalde, A., Hußmann, H.: How to reduce the effort: comfortable watching techniques for cinematic virtual reality. In: De Paolis, L.T., Bourdot, P. (eds.) AVR 2020, Part I. LNCS, vol. 12242, pp. 3–21. Springer, Cham (2020). https://doi.org/10.1007/978-3-030-58465-8_1

17. Schwind, V., Knierim, P., Haas, N., Henze, N.: Using presence questionnaires in virtual reality. In: Proceedings of the 2019 CHI Conference on Human Factors in Computing Systems, pp. 1–12 (2019)

18. Yu, Z., Lo, C.H., Niu, M., Liang, H.N.: Comparing cinematic conventions through emotional responses in cinematic VR and traditional mediums. In: SIGGRAPH Asia 2023 Technical Communications, pp. 1–4 (2023)

Cross-Cultural Design in Aviation and Transportation

Exploring the Impact of Interpretable Information Types on Driver's Situational Awareness and Performance During Driving Take-Over

Xi Fu[⊠], Yiming Zou, and Hao Tan

Hunan University, Changsha 41006, Hunan, China
Fuxi@hnu.edu.cn

Abstract. In Level 3 (L3) autonomous driving, the system issues a take-over request to the driver if the Automated Driving System (ADS) fails or operates outside its design domain. The driver must takeover control and resume vehicle operation. This study demonstrates that in Level 3 (L3) autonomous vehicles, varied information presentation strategies—namely no explanation, reason explanation (Why), outcome explanation (What), and both reason and outcome explanation (What + Why)—significantly affect drivers' situational awareness and take-over performance. The "What + Why" strategy yields the most significant improvements. Furthermore, the research highlights differences in the effectiveness of these strategies among less experienced drivers and a gender disparity in responses to the "Why" explanation, with males showing more favorable outcomes. In conclusion, effective information presentation is crucial in autonomous vehicle human-machine interfaces, particularly for L3 systems. This underscores the need for user-centered, interpretable AI that customizes information delivery according to driver-specific characteristics, optimizing performance and safety.

Keywords: Automated vehicles · Driving take-over · XAI · Situational Awareness

1 First Section

1.1 A Subsection Sample

In recent years, autonomous driving technology has rapidly advanced, continuously increasing the level of vehicle automation [1]. The development and adoption of autonomous vehicles are expected to enhance traffic efficiency [2], reduce environmental pollution [3], and decrease traffic accidents by approximately 90%, potentially saving about one million lives annually when fully implemented [4].

According to the classification standards set by the Society of Automotive Engineers (SAE), autonomous driving is divided into six levels: no automation (L0), driver assistance (L1), partial automation (L2), conditional automation (L3), high automation (L4), and full automation (L5) [5]. In 2021, the SAE updated and refined the classification

P.-L. P. Rau (Ed.): HCII 2024, LNCS 14702, pp. 99–114, 2024.
https://doi.org/10.1007/978-3-031-60913-8_8

standards for driving automation, further clarifying the functions of Automated Driving Systems (ADS) at different levels of automation and the corresponding human-machine allocation issues. Level 3 conditional autonomous driving can perform all dynamic driving tasks (DDT) within its Operational Design Domain (ODD), without the need for driver supervision of the L3 ADS. However, when the ADS fails or the driving environment exceeds the system's operational design domain and cannot support the continuation of ADS, the system will issue a takeover request (TOR) to the driver. The driver needs to respond promptly and take control of the vehicle to resume dynamic driving tasks [6]. Therefore, when the L3 ADS is operating normally, drivers can engage in non-driving-related tasks (NDRT), such as using a phone, reading, or watching videos. Studies have shown that engaging in NDRT can diminish a driver's ability to understand the surrounding road environment, and this negative impact can persist following a takeover request.

From the perspective of human-machine interface design, the interface and medium for interaction between humans and machines within the autonomous driving system play a crucial role. How the information is presented during the takeover process is vital for enhancing the driver's takeover performance. From the perspective of explainable artificial intelligence, autonomous vehicles, as a quintessential product of AI, can focus on technology, developing new or improved machine learning techniques to enhance the transparency and interpretability of autonomous driving systems' decisions [7]. Alternatively, it can adopt a user-centered approach, investigating how the content, manner, and timing of information display affect users' understanding of autonomous vehicles' decision-making behaviors [8, 9].

This study aims to explore the impact of four information presentation strategies— no explanation, explaining the reason, explaining the outcome, and explaining both the reason and the outcome—on drivers' situational awareness and takeover performance in L3 automated vehicles when the autonomous driving system issues a takeover request.

2 Related Work

2.1 Autonomous Driving Takeover

In the context of autonomous driving, the most prominent change compared to traditional manual driving is the emergence of takeover tasks by autonomous driving systems [10]. Takeover refers to a new task that traditional drivers need to perform during the autonomous driving process, either due to system malfunctions or simply based on subjective desire [11, 12]. When the system encounters situations it cannot handle, such as limitations in sensors or actuators, unclear environmental observations, etc., reaching the system's capability boundaries, drivers are required to intervene and take control within a reasonable transition time to avoid collisions [10]. Failure to take over a malfunctioning system within the allowed time may lead to accidents involving autonomous vehicles. The takeover performance of drivers is crucial for road safety in the context of autonomous driving, and thus, takeover failures or poor performance may pose potential risks to future road safety.

Previous research has indicated a close correlation between warning system design in autonomous driving systems and drivers' situational awareness and takeover performance. Specifically, the design of takeover request (TOR) in the warning system is closely related to these factors [13]. Zhang et al. investigated the design of available time before automation system reaches its limits, known as prelude time design [14]. Ma et al. studied the impact of progressive and hierarchical warning stage designs on human takeover performance [15]. Qu et al. explored the relationship between different ways of presenting warning information in autonomous driving systems and driver trust [16]. Bazilinskyy et al. studied the effects of different channels of warning methods on human perception of warning information and system takeover [17]. Therefore, in the context of autonomous driving takeover scenarios, the impact of different warning takeover designs on drivers' situational awareness and takeover performance has been explored in previous research. However, previous studies have mainly focused on the effects of takeover system designs under specific conditions, and there is still insufficient research on the effectiveness and differences of multimodal takeover prompts.

Hence, the primary objective of this study is to elucidate the influence of explainable information types (multimodal) and explanation structures during the initiation of takeover requests by intelligent autonomous driving systems on drivers' situational awareness and takeover performance in emergency situations. This research aims to provide design recommendations for the development of takeover warning systems in autonomous vehicles and to expand the application of explainable artificial intelligence in diverse scenarios.

2.2 Explanations in Autonomous Vehicles

Currently, deep learning (DL) and artificial intelligence (AI) models play a crucial role in autonomous vehicles (AV) or connected autonomous vehicles [18–20]. Deep learning models exhibit excellent high representation and generalization capabilities but are known for their inherent black-box characteristics, making them challenging to interpret. This opacity hinders the ability to demonstrate the fundamental principles behind the decisions made by intelligent systems. Moreover, due to the system's opaqueness, system failures are often unpredictable and challenging to diagnose, significantly impacting user trust in the system. However, research has shown that trust is a key factor influencing user acceptance and support for autonomous driving systems [21, 22]. Therefore, providing explanations for the decisions made by automated systems is effective, if not essential, in enhancing user trust. This capability not only improves the transparency and accountability of decision-making in autonomous driving but also aids in evaluating the role of autonomous vehicles in pre- and post-critical events (e.g., collisions or near misses).

Research on explanations for autonomous driving systems can be approached from two perspectives: a technical-centric view and a user-centric view [23]. From a technical-centric perspective, efforts focus on studying how to generate effective explanations in dynamic traffic situations. Despite significant progress in this field, explanations for autonomous driving vehicles are far from perfect. The impact of these explanations on human drivers in autonomous vehicles has sparked extensive research.

User-centric explainability research has explored how to interpret content, form, and timing of explanations in autonomous driving systems. Koo et al. investigated the different impact patterns of information explanation structures on driver performance and experience [24]. Rezvani et al. found that the content of explanations for autonomous driving systems must be limited, requiring appropriate information explanation content to optimize system performance [25]. Yan et al. discovered that the perception of environmental information by autonomous driving systems contributes to enhancing driver situational awareness and trust [26]. Wang et al. developed a system using 3D auditory prompts to present advisory information, contributing to driver performance and situational awareness [27].

2.3 Measures of Situational Awareness in AV

The dynamic decision-making of human drivers is closely associated with Situational Awareness (SA), encompassing three cognitive levels: perception, comprehension, and projection [28]. Methods for measuring SA in automated vehicles include freeze-frame techniques, post-trial methods, and question probes, which can be employed to understand drivers' decision-making processes [29].

Simultaneously, the level of trust that drivers place in autonomous driving systems is a critical factor influencing the safety of autonomous vehicle operation. Miscalibration of trust in the autonomous system can lead to adverse (even fatal) consequences [30]. In prior research, Muir developed a scale for assessing automation trust [31], which was subsequently adapted for the context of autonomous driving by Du et al. [32]. However, this scale can only measure the drivers' general trust (GT) throughout the entire driving process. Although general trust is paramount, situational trust (ST) is equally crucial in the field of autonomous driving (AV), as it may vary across different driving scenarios [33]. Holthausen et al. developed a Situational Trust Scale for Automated Driving (STS-AD) and conducted preliminary validations in the AV context [34]. Both general trust and situational trust are included as measurement indicators in this study.

Research on the assessment of situational awareness in autonomous driving also involves studies on emotional experience measures, such as drivers' preferences and anxiety as dependent variables. Drivers' preferences for autonomous vehicles are often investigated when exploring specific technologies or features, which is also applicable to the study of explanations [35, 36]. Additionally, anxiety is another attitude indicator negatively correlated with the effectiveness of explanations [35, 37]. In our study, we concurrently include these subjective measurement indicators to assess drivers' subjective attitudes throughout the entire driving process under specific explanation conditions.

3   Method

3.1 Participants

Totally, 20 participants (8 males and 12 females) aged from 22 to 29 (M = 24.7years old; SD = 2.13 years old) were recruited for this experiment. Each one needs to test four different HMI conditions (see Sect. 3.3). All the participants held valid driver's licenses, and the mean of years obtaining the driver's license was 4.7 (SD = 2.105).

3.2   Apparatus and AD System

Logitech G29 Driving Force Driving Simulator was used in this study (see Fig. 1). The physical system included a steering wheel with input buttons and force feedback, a turn signal lever, brake and gas pedals and a shift lever. We created a simulation environment of urban roads and scripts of different driving takeover scenarios. We used an iPad to simulate the central control screen to display driving takeover prompts.

Fig. 1. Experiment apparatus

3.3   Experiment Design

Totally, 20 participants (8 males and 12 females) aged from 22 to 29 (M = 24.7years old; SD = 2.13 years old) were recruited for this experiment. Each one needs to test four different HMI conditions (see Sect. 3.3). All the participants held valid driver's licenses, and the mean of years obtaining the driver's license was 4.7 (SD = 2.105).

HMI Setting. This study aims to explore the impact of four information presentation strategies on driver takeover in L3 automated vehicles when the autonomous driving system issues a takeover request: no explanation, explaining the reason, explaining the outcome, and explaining both the reason and the outcome. We selected a scenario with a high probability of human intervention in autonomous driving, where the autonomous vehicle requires human control due to hardware sensor failures (such as LIDAR, cameras) that lead to issues in environmental perception or positioning. Based on this scenario, our four HMI strategies are set as follows:

Group I (None): Displays "Take over" without any explanation.
Group II (Why): Displays the takeover icon and explains the reason for the autonomous driving system's error.
Group III (What): Displays the takeover icon and explains the outcome of the autonomous driving system's error.
Group IV (What + WHY): Displays the takeover icon and explains both the reason for and the outcome of the autonomous driving system's error (Figs. 2 and 3).

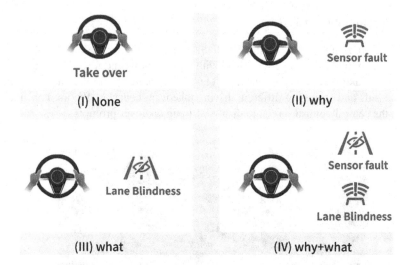

Fig. 2. HMI design with four conditions (examples in perceived failure)

Fig. 3. The display effects of the HMI design on the central control screen

Experiment Environment. In the simulation environment, a city road scenario measuring 5000 m in length and 50 m in width was constructed. Before a takeover request was issued, the Level 3 (L3) autonomous driving system operated the vehicle at 50 km/h in an urban road environment, which included a four-lane, two-way road. As the vehicle approached an intersection, the autonomous driving system initiated a takeover request. Participants were required to respond timely and take control of the vehicle to resume dynamic driving tasks. The criterion for successful takeover was whether the participant followed the navigation route displayed on the central control screen. A takeover was considered successful if the turning direction matched the navigation instruction; otherwise, it was deemed a failure. The experiment had three possible turning directions: (1) turn left, (2) go straight, (3) turn right (as shown in Fig. 4). In the four trials, the direction of the navigation route was randomly selected, and the sequence of the four HMI explanation strategies was also random to minimize the interference caused by learning effects.

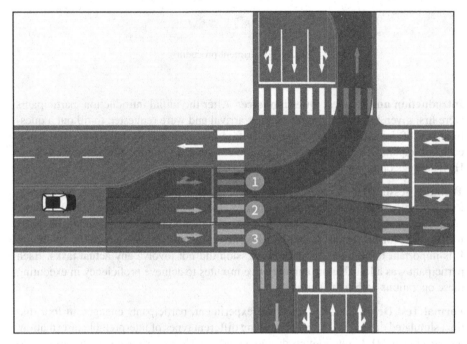

Fig. 4. Steering Task for Determining Successful Takeover

Measurements. SART method is one of the self-rating techniques that can be used easily and quickly which was made by Taylor in 1990 [38]. This method uses 10 dimensions as a parameter for calculating the SA value with low to high categories. Of the 10 dimensions, it can be grouped into 3 main parts which are commonly called 3D SART. The measure comprised the following dimensions: Demand—demands on attentional resources, Supply—supply of attentional resources, and Understanding—understanding of the situation. Participants will be asked about a scale from 1 to 7, namely 1 for low to 7 for the highest which is used as a scale that can represent the results to be achieved. After participants answer according to the existing scale, SA will be calculated using the formula: $SA = U - (D - S)$.

3.4 Procedure

The whole study was mainly divided into four sessions, including pre-test questionnaires, a training session, a formal test drive, and post-drive questionnaires and interviews (see Fig. 5).

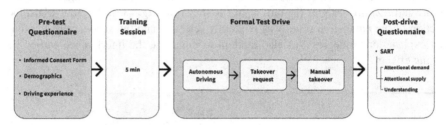

Fig. 5. Experiment procedure.

Introduction and Pre-test Questionnaire. After the initial introduction, participants were first given informed consent on their arrival and were requested to fill out a questionnaire of demographic information. Before being guided to the driving simulator, each participant was given a brief explanation of the AD system condition as well as the HMI settings on the screen.

Training Session. In the initial phase, participants were acquainted with the simulator's operations, Human-Machine Interface (HMI) elements, and Automated Driving (AD) system settings. To align their understanding with the objectives and tasks of the forthcoming formal test drive, participants traversed an identical route in the simulator. It is important to note that the training session did not involve any actual tasks. Each participant was allotted approximately five minutes to achieve proficiency in executing these operations within the simulator.

Formal Test Drive. During the formal experiment, participants engaged in four distinct simulated driving tasks, each involving different types of interpretable information, within a Level 3 (L3) autonomous driving simulator. The experiment was structured into three stages:

L3 Autonomous Driving Phase (30–60 s): Here, participants were involved in non-driving related tasks while the vehicle operated under L3 autonomy.

Takeover Request (100–150 m before an intersection): In this stage, the simulator replicated a scenario where the autonomous vehicle failed to detect lane lines, necessitating an urgent manual takeover by the participant. The vehicle's display provided interpretable information alongside auxiliary decision-making data to assist in this process.

Manual Takeover and Navigation Stage: Participants were required to manually take control of the vehicle, using the provided interpretable and decision-making information to navigate the planned route.

Across the four simulation trials, the location and timing of the takeover event varied slightly. Additionally, the sequence of presentation for interpretable information, auxiliary decision-making data, and the planned route was randomized. After each trial, participants took a brief rest of 1–2 min. Meanwhile, the experimenter documented and saved the data, and prepared the simulator for the next scenario.

Post-test Questionnaires and Interviews. After the formal test drive, participants filled out questionnaires regarding situation awareness. Then we conducted interviews to explore their underlying thoughts about how they made decisions and how they felt in different scenarios. Finally, valid participants were rewarded with gifts and discharged. The whole study lasted for about 30 min.

4 Result

We obtained a total of 20 sets of valid experimental data, including 12 sets from drivers with extensive driving experience and 8 sets from drivers with limited experience; 12 sets were from female drivers, and 8 sets were from male drivers. The analysis that follows will focus on two dimensions: situational awareness and takeover performance.

4.1 Driver Situational Awareness

The comparison of participants' SA scores under different explanation methods is shown in Fig. 6. Shapiro-Wilk tests for normality indicated that the data for all groups were normally distributed (p values were 0.686, 0.478, 0.486, and 0.381, all > 0.05). The differences in SA scores among the explanation methods were statistically significant (one-way ANOVA, $F = 6.557$, $P = 0.001 < 0.01**$). Post-hoc tests revealed that the SA score for "Why" was 3.750 points higher than for "None" (95% CI: 0.96–6.54), a difference that was statistically significant ($P = 0.009 < 0.01**$); "What" was 5.050 points higher than "None" (95% CI: 2.26–7.84), also statistically significant ($P = 0.001 < = 0.001***$); and "Why + What" was 5.650 points higher than "None" (95% CI: 0.96–6.54), with statistical significance ($P = 0.000 < 0.001***$).

Figure 7 shows the distribution of SA scores among participants with different driving experiences under various explanation methods. There were no significant differences in SA scores among participants of different driving experience levels across the four explanation methods (independent samples t-test, p values were 0.494, 0.413, 0.400, and 0.345, respectively). Among participants with extensive driving experience, there were no significant differences in SA scores across the explanation methods (one-way ANOVA, $F = 2.160$, $P = 0.112 > 0.05$). However, among participants with limited driving experience, significant differences were observed in SA scores across explanation methods (one-way ANOVA, $F = 4.398$, $P = 0.009 < 0.01**$).

Figure 8 also presents the distribution of SA scores among participants of different genders under various explanation methods. There were no significant differences in SA scores between genders under the "None," "What," and "Why + What" explanation methods (independent samples t-test, p values were 0.739, 0.555, and 0.667, respectively). However, under the "Why" explanation method, a significant difference was observed, with males scoring higher (M = 19.13, SD = 3.00) than females (M = 15.00, SD = 4.65; t = 2.210, p = 0.04 < 0.05).

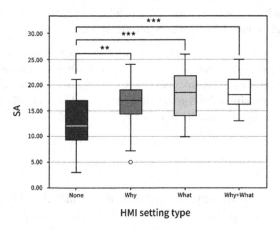

Fig. 6. Distribution of SA overall scores for four HMI setting types

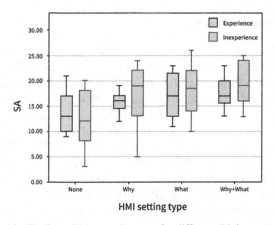

Fig. 7. Distribution of SA overall scores for different driving experiences

4.2 Driver Situational Awareness

This paper assesses drivers' takeover performance by determining whether the driver successfully took over control. The criterion for successful takeover is whether participants turned according to the navigation route displayed on the central control screen. A takeover is considered successful if the turning direction matches the navigation direction; otherwise, it is deemed a failure (Table 1).

As shown in the table above, using the chi-square test to investigate the relationship between different explanatory schemes and performance, it is evident that different

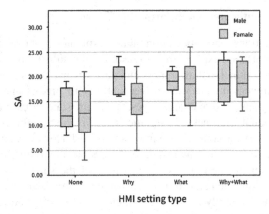

Fig. 8. Distribution of SA overall scores for different genders

Table 1. Chi-square test of takeover performance overall scores for four HMI setting types

Chi-square test							
HMI Setting type				Total	χ^2	p	
None	Why	What	Why + What				
S	4(20.00)	7(35.00)	14(70.00)	18(90.00)	43(53.75)	24.689	0.000***
F	16(80.00)	13(65.00)	6(30.00)	2(10.00)	37(46.25)		
Total	20	20	20	20	80		

explanatory schemes significantly affect performance (p < 0.05). The schemes show a level of significance at 0.001 (X2 = 24.689, p = 0.000 < 0.01). A comparison of percentage differences reveals that the "Why + What" scheme has a 90.00% success rate in completing the takeover driving task, significantly above the average of 53.75%. The "What" scheme has a success rate of 70.00%, also significantly above the average of 53.75%. The success rates for the "None" and "Why" explanatory schemes are 20% and 35%, respectively, both below the average of 53.75%.

5 Discussion

In this study, we looked into the impact of four options on the driver's takeover performance: no explanation (none), explanation of reasons (why), explanation of results (what), and explanation of reasons and results (why + what) when the autonomous driving system issues a takeover request to the driver in L3 automated vehicles. Combining the results above with subjective statements from the interviews, we attempted to discuss and develop implications for presenting explanations in driving takeover situations. Also, the limitations of this study and prospects for future work were clarified in this section.

5.1   The Impact of Interpretable Information Types

Four types of explanations—no explanation (none), explanation of reasons (why), explanation of results (what), and explanation of reasons and results (why + what)—significantly impact drivers' situational awareness and performance during takeover.

Situational awareness includes the driver's ability to predict and understand the surrounding environment, its dynamic changes, and future states. Research indicates that a high level of situational awareness can significantly improve the efficiency and safety of drivers taking over from autonomous driving systems [39]. However, long-term reliance on autonomous driving systems may reduce drivers' level of situational awareness, thereby diminishing their attention to and alertness of the surrounding environment. Without any explanation when an autonomous driving system issues a takeover request, drivers are unable to promptly assess the vehicle's status or formulate future action plans. The no explanation scenario (None), serving as a baseline condition, reveals the challenges drivers face in taking over tasks without sufficient information.

The low takeover performance and situational awareness scores in this scenario emphasize the importance of information presentation for drivers to make quick and accurate decisions in emergency takeover scenarios. Explaining the reasons for an autonomous driving system's failure (Why) enables drivers to understand the root cause of the failure and why the car is requesting takeover, significantly improving situational awareness and takeover performance over providing no explanation.

Explaining the results of an autonomous driving failure (what) directly addresses the capability deficits caused by the vehicle's malfunction. Drivers can use these deficits to predict and understand the vehicle's own status and the road environment outside, thus significantly improving situational awareness and takeover performance compared to no explanation. This study posits that directly explaining the results (what) better assists drivers in assessing the vehicle's status without needing to deduce the limitations from the root cause of the failure. In terms of takeover performance, the success rate of explaining the results (what) is significantly higher than that of explaining the reasons (why).

Finally, explaining both the reasons and results (Why + What) clearly offers the best outcomes in terms of situational awareness and takeover performance. However, this study suggests that the cognitive load for drivers with (Why + What) is the highest. In more complex and urgent scenarios, the performance of the explanation scheme that includes both reasons and results (Why + What) warrants further in-depth investigation.

5.2   The Impact of Driving Experience and Gender

Experienced drivers showed no significant differences in situational awareness across various explanation methods, suggesting that adaptability or familiarity with driving tasks may reduce the need for detailed explanations. In contrast, drivers with less experience exhibited significant differences in situational awareness based on the explanation method, indicating that the type and depth of information provided can be crucial in supporting their understanding and performance.

In the "Why" explanation method, gender differences were particularly pronounced, with male drivers scoring higher in situational awareness than female drivers. This finding suggests that men and women may process and utilize explanatory information differently, possibly due to differences in information processing or cognitive preferences. Of course, more experiments are needed to further investigate this.

5.3 Limitations and Future Work

In this section, we present some limitations to better interpret our findings. First, most of the participants recruited in this study are university students. So our findings are based on a relatively young and less experienced sample. For more representative results, further experiments are to be arranged with participants from a more general population of drivers.

Second, this experiment was executed in a fixed-base driving simulator with light traffic. Although most participants highly rated its immersive experience and near-real physical simulation, some of them also claimed that they were less cautious due to the nature that they were free of dangers in the simulator. And lack of physical movement might influence their awareness in lane-changing scenarios. The future study should involve more traffic.

Finally, we assessed drivers' takeover performance solely based on whether they successfully took over control. In the future, we will employ more measurement methods to evaluate drivers' takeover performance, such as gaze movement, takeover time, and the number of gazes.

6 Conclusion

This research highlights the importance of effective information presentation in autonomous vehicle human-machine interfaces, particularly in L3 systems. The study indicates that in L3 autonomous driving systems, simply displaying a takeover request with icons and text is insufficient. It is also necessary to explain the reasons for and outcome of errors in the autonomous driving system. Compared with explaining (why), explaining reasons (What) does not significantly affect situational awareness recovery, but significantly enhances takeover performance. Optimal takeover performance, without increasing driver cognitive load, occurs when both reasons and outcomes (Why + What) are explained. Our findings show that gender differences also play a role in the effectiveness of these strategies, with "Why" explanations being more beneficial for male drivers. This research not only is crucial for designing human-machine interaction interfaces in L3 autonomous vehicle takeovers but also underscores the necessity of tailoring information delivery to driver-specific characteristics for optimal performance and safety.

Acknowledgments. This study was supported by the Natural Science Foundation of Hunan Province of China (No. 2023JJ30149).

References

1. Badue, C., et al.: Self-driving cars: a survey. Expert Syst. Appl. **165**, 113816 (2021)
2. Lai, J., et al.: A generic simulation platform for cooperative adaptive cruise control under partially connected and automated environment. Transport. Res. Part C: Emerg. Technol. **121**, 102874 (2020)
3. Hu, J., Zhang, Z.H., Xiong, L., et al.: Cut through traffic to catch green light: eco approach with overtaking capability. Transport. Res. Part C: Emerg. Technol. **123**, 102927 (2021)
4. Bonnefon, J.F., Shariff, A., Rahwan, I.: The social dilemma of autonomous vehicles. Science **352**, 1573 (2016)
5. SAE J 3016–2014, Taxonomy and definitions for terms related to on-road motor vehicle automated driving systems (2014)
6. SAE International. Taxonomy and definitions for terms related to driving automation systems for on-road motor vehicles. SAE International, New York (2021)
7. Atakishiyev, S., Salameh, M., Yao, H., Goebel, R.: Explainable artificial intelligence for autonomous driving: a comprehensive overview and field guide for future research directions (2021). arXiv pre-print arXiv:2112.11561
8. Koo, J., Kwac, J., Ju, W., Steinert, M., Leifer, L., Nass, C.: Why did my car just do that? explaining semi-autonomous driving actions to improve driver understanding, trust, and performance. Int. J. Interact. Des. Manuf. **9**(4), 269–275 (2015). https://doi.org/10.1007/s12008-014-0227-2
9. Rezvani, T., Driggs-Campbell, K., Bajcsy, R.: Optimizing interaction between humans and autonomy via information con-straints on interface design [Paper presentation]. In: 2017 IEEE 20th International Conference on Intelligent Transportation Systems (ITSC), pp. 1–6. IEEE (2017). https://doi.org/10.1109/itsc.2017.8317686
10. SAE International. Taxonomy and Definitions for Terms Related to Driving Automation Systems for On-Road Motor Vehicles (2021). https://doi.org/10.4271/J3016_202104
11. Techer, F., et al.: Anger and highly automated driving in urban areas: The role of time pressure. Transport. Res. Part F: Traffic Psychol. Behav. **64**, 353–360 (2019)
12. Xing, Y., et al.: Toward human-vehicle collaboration: review and perspectives on human-centered collaborative automated driving. Transport. Res. Part C: Emerg. Technol. **128**, 103199 (2021)
13. Zhang, W., et al.: Optimal time intervals in two-stage takeover warning systems with insight into the drivers' neuroticism personality. Front. Psychol. **12**, 601536 (2021)
14. Zhang, B., et al.: Determinants of take-over time from automated driving: a meta-analysis of 129 studies. Transport. Res. Part F: Traffic Psychol. Behav. **64**, 285–307 (2019)
15. Ma, S., et al.: Take over gradually in conditional automated driving: the effect of two-stage warning systems on situation awareness, driving stress, takeover performance, and acceptance. Int. J. Hum.-Comput. Interact. **37**(4), 352–362 (2021)
16. Qu, J., et al.: Understanding trust calibration in automated driving: the effect of time, personality, and system warning design. Ergonomics 1–17 (2023)
17. Bazilinskyy, P., Petermeijer, S.M., Petrovych, V., et al.: Take-over requests in highly automated driving: a crowdsourcing survey on auditory, vibrotactile, and visual displays. Transport. Res. F: Traffic Psychol. Behav. **56**, 82–98 (2018)
18. Chen, S., Leng, Y., Labi, S.: A deep learning algorithm for simulating autonomous driving considering prior knowledge and temporal information. Comput.-Aided Civil Infrastruct. Eng. **35**(4), 305–321 (2020)
19. Di, X., Shi, R.: A survey on autonomous vehicle control in the era of mixed-autonomy: from physics-based to AI-guided driving policy learning. Transport. Res. Part C: Emerg. Technol. **125**, 103008 (2021)

20. Dong, J., et al.: Space-weighted information fusion using deep reinforcement learning: the context of tactical control of lane-changing autonomous vehicles and connectivity range assessment. Transport. Res. Part C: Emerg. Technol. **128**, 103192 (2021)
21. Hulse, L.M., Xie, H., Galea, E.R.: Perceptions of autonomous vehicles: relationships with road users, risk, gender and age. Saf. Sci. **102**, 1–13 (2018)
22. Omeiza, D., et al.: Explanations in autonomous driving: a survey. IEEE Trans. Intell. Transport. Syst. **23**(8), 10142–10162 (2021)
23. Atakishiyev, S., et al.: Explainable artificial intelligence for autonomous driving: a comprehensive overview and field guide for future research directions. arXiv preprint arXiv:2112. 11561 (2021)
24. Koo, J., et al.: Why did my car just do that? explaining semi-autonomous driving actions to improve driver understanding, trust, and performance. Int. J. Interact. Des. Manuf. (IJIDeM) **9**, 269–275 (2015)
25. Rezvani, T., Driggs-Campbell, K., Bajcsy, R.: Optimizing interaction between humans and autonomy via information constraints on interface design. In: 2017 IEEE 20th International Conference on Intelligent Transportation Systems (ITSC). IEEE (2017)
26. Yan, F., et al.: Spatial visualization of sensor information for automated vehicles. In: Proceedings of the 11th International Conference on Automotive User Interfaces and Interactive Vehicular Applications: Adjunct Proceedings (2019)
27. Wang, M.J., et al.: Using advisory 3D sound cues to improve drivers' performance and situation awareness. In: Proceedings of the 2017 CHI Conference on Human Factors in Computing Systems (2017)
28. Endsley, M.R.: Situation awareness in future autonomous vehicles: beware of the unexpected. In: Bagnara, S., Tartaglia, R., Albolino, S., Alexander, T., Fujita, Y. (eds.) IEA 2018. AISC, vol. 824, pp. 303–309. Springer, Cham (2019). https://doi.org/10.1007/978-3-319-96071-5_32
29. Sirkin, D., et al.: Toward measurement of situation awareness in autonomous vehicles. In: Proceedings of the 2017 CHI Conference on Human Factors in Computing Systems (2017)
30. Banks, V.A., Plant, K.L., Stanton, N.A.: Driver error or designer error: using the perceptual cycle Model to explore the circumstances surrounding the fatal Tesla crash on 7th May 2016. Saf. Sci. **108**, 278–285 (2018)
31. Muir, B.M.: Trust between humans and machines, and the design of decision aids. Int. J. Man Mach. Stud. **27**(5–6), 527–539 (1987)
32. Du, N., et al.: Look who's talking now: Implications of AV's explanations on driver's trust, AV preference, anxiety and mental workload. Transpor. Res. Part C: Emerg. Technol. **104**, 428–442 (2019)
33. Frison, A.-K., et al.: Why do you like to drive automated? a context-dependent analysis of highly automated driving to elaborate requirements for intelligent user interfaces. In: Proceedings of the 24th International Conference on Intelligent User Interfaces (2019)
34. Holthausen, B.E., et al.: Situational trust scale for automated driving (STS-AD): development and initial validation. In: 12th International Conference on Automotive User Interfaces and Interactive Vehicular Applications (2020)
35. Abraham, H., et al.: Autonomous vehicles and alternatives to driving: trust, preferences, and effects of age. In: Proceedings of the Transportation Research Board 96th Annual Meeting. Transportation Research Board, Washington, DC (2017)
36. Koo, J., et al.: Understanding driver responses to voice alerts of autonomous car operations. Int. J. Veh. Des. **70**(4), 377–392 (2016)
37. Shabanpour, R., et al.: Eliciting preferences for adoption of fully automated vehicles using best-worst analysis. Transport. Res. Part C: Emerg. Technol. **93**, 463–478 (2018)

38. Taylor, R.M.: Situational awareness rating technique (SART): The development of a tool for aircrew systems design. Situational Awareness in Aerospace Operations (AGARD-CP-478). Neuilly Sur Seine, France: NATO-AGARD (1990)
39. Cooper, D.: Effective safety leadership: Understanding types & styles that improve safety performance. Prof. Saf. **60**(02), 49–53 (2015)

The Priority of Information for Crew Members in Various Flight Scenarios: An Eye-Tracking Study

Xiaohui Hao[1], Haochun Zhang[2] (ID), and Hao Tan[2](✉) (ID)

[1] Shanghai Aircraft Design and Research Institute, COMAC, Shanghai 201210, China
[2] School of Design, Hunan University, Changsha 410000, China
htan@hnu.edu.cn

Abstract. The cockpit of modern commercial aircraft has a complex interface layout and the complex human-machine interaction interfaces can impose a cognitive load on the flight crew. A cockpit interface that meets human factors engineering requirements can reduce pilot cognitive load, enhance operational efficiency, and improve flight safety. In order to summarize the interaction mechanisms between flight crew members and cockpit interfaces, this research employs the methodology of eye-tracking to investigate the level of attention and salience that crew members pay to different areas of the cockpit in different flight scenarios. These two aspects are respectively reflected through the pilot's total duration of fixation and number of visits to specific areas. The eye-tracking experiments involved the participation of two experienced professional pilots in a flight simulator that accurately replicates the cockpit of mainstream aircraft in proportion. The flight crew, consisting of the pilot flying (PF) and the pilot monitoring (PM), was tasked with executing flight procedures at eight stages during normal flight operations. These eight stages include cockpit preparing, engine starting, taxiing, taking-off, approaching, landing, after-landing, and shutdown. By dividing the aircraft cockpit into 18 areas of interest, we found that the crew members' focus areas within the cockpit interface dynamically change at different stages of the flight. Through eye-tracking analysis, we summarized and prioritized the focus areas for the PF and the PM in eight different flight scenarios. The results can help designers of human-machine interfaces in aircraft cockpits to capture design requirements and provide guidance for future aircraft cockpit human-machine interaction design.

Keywords: Aircraft Cockpit · Eye-Tracking · Human-Machine Interaction Design

1 Introduction

In modern commercial aircraft, cockpit design significantly emphasizes human-machine interaction research. The intricate architecture of aircraft cockpits necessitates that pilots retrieve essential information quickly and accurately, performing correct actions under altitude pressure. Improperly designed cockpit interfaces can escalate the mental load on

P.-L. P. Rau (Ed.): HCII 2024, LNCS 14702, pp. 115–129, 2024.
https://doi.org/10.1007/978-3-031-60913-8_9

pilots, potentially leading to impaired situational awareness due to difficulties in handling pertinent information [1]. Thus, human-machine interaction within the cockpit is vital for the overall system operation and functionality [2]. Aircraft cockpits are organized based on varied scenarios and task flows encountered by pilots, and divided into distinct interactive interface modules. These modules encompass functionalities like display, control, and alert systems. Common display interfaces include the Primary Flight Display (PFD) and Navigation Display (ND), while control interfaces comprise the central console and overhead panel. Moreover, the alert functions are managed by interfaces such as the Engine/Warning Display (E/WD). The areas of the interface that pilots focus on vary across different flight scenarios. Consequently, a thoughtfully constructed cockpit interface layout is key to enhancing pilots' situational awareness, thereby improving operational efficiency and safety in flight missions.

Visual attention marks the onset of attention allocation, situational analysis, and cognitive decision-making processes [3]. The trajectory of visual attention elucidates the cognitive process of human-machine interaction between operators and machines [4], revealing how operators process information and the impact of interface designs on their performance. Eye-tracking technology, with its extensive application in evaluating human-machine interaction interfaces [5], plays a crucial role in aviation research. It is instrumental in exploring pilots' scanning behavior and associated performance, expertise, cognitive load, and vigilance, as well as in assessing display interfaces and cockpit setups [6]. Therefore, employing eye-tracking technology, this study analyzes the interface areas pilots predominantly focus on during different flight scenarios, aiding cockpit human-machine interface designers to capture design requirements and offer guidance for optimizing the aircraft cockpit's human-machine interface.

Modern commercial aircraft typically operate with two pilots: the Pilot Flying (PF) and the Pilot Monitoring (PM). The PF primarily takes charge of the aircraft's control, while the PM handles auxiliary flight tasks, monitoring, and confirming the PF's maneuvers. Owing to their distinct roles, the PF and PM focus on different cockpit interface areas while executing flight tasks. This research aims to delve into the focused information analysis for these two disparate flight roles.

2 Methodology

2.1 Participants

For this study, two professional pilots with substantial flight experience were recruited. Both participants had previously piloted and were familiar with the aircraft model used for the experiment. During the experiment, the two pilots alternately played the roles of PF and PM. The role switches midway through the experiment aimed to reduce potential biases stemming from their personal flying habits.

2.2 Apparatus

Flight Simulator. The experiment was conducted using a flight simulator of a popular aircraft model, depicted in Fig. 1. This simulator boasts a fully enclosed and authentic cockpit with sophisticated flight control software, image data fusion technology, and a distributed anti-collision system. It utilizes flight and maintenance data packages licensed by the aircraft's manufacturer, ensuring highly precise flight simulations. Capable of simulating real-time weather conditions, malfunctions, and emergency flight scenarios, it offers a 180-degree panoramic projection system, providing an exceptionally immersive experience for users. Additionally, the flight simulator includes a six-degrees-of-freedom motion platform, capable of replicating various in-flight sensations such as turbulence, air disturbances, and overload.

Fig. 1. Interior of the Flight Simulator

Eye-Tracking Device. Both the pilot and co-pilot stations in the flight simulator were equipped with eye-tracking devices to record the visual activity of the PF and PM throughout the experiment. Both devices were Tobii Pro Glasses 3, mounted on the pilots' head. The eye trackers are capable of recording the pilots' total duration of fixation as well as their number of visits. Additionally, their integrated recording feature can capture the cockpit's audio information during flights.

2.3   Research Design

Flight Scenarios.   In the experiment, flight scenarios were meticulously selected from the standard operating procedures outlined in the flight crew's operating manual. These scenarios encapsulated eight critical stages of a typical flight process, aligning with conventional flight routines. The stages encompassed: cockpit preparing, engine starting, taxiing, taking-off, approaching, landing, after-landing, and parking. Participating pilots, conforming to their respective flight roles, were required to execute flight tasks under standard conditions. Each pilot undertook both PF and PM roles across the eight stages, cumulatively participating in 16 trials. The sequence of these trials for each pilot was randomized through a lottery draw.

Areas of Interest and Key Areas. The study segmented the aircraft cockpit into 18 distinct areas of interest, as illustrated in Fig. 2. These areas included the central control pedestal, left and right multi-function control display units (MCDU-L, MCDU-R), PF and PM checklists, engine/warning display (E/WD), system display (SD), left and right instrument control panels, left and right primary flight displays (PFD-L, PFD-R), left and right navigation displays (ND-L, ND-R), backup dashboard, landing gear lever control and display, flight control unit, exterior view, and overhead panel. The PFDs, NDs, MCDUs on both sides and the E/WD and SD in the center constituted the experiment's focal points. These key areas were further dissected for more granular analysis. The eye-tracking data were employed to scrutinize both the broad areas of interest and the key areas, aiming to dissect the crew's focus on cockpit information across diverse flight scenarios.

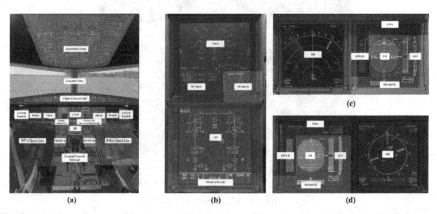

Fig. 2. Division of Areas of Interest and Subdivision of Key Areas in the Cockpit. (a) division of areas of interest. (b) subdivision of key areas

Experimental Procedure. The entire study was executed within a flight simulator, under rigorously controlled lighting conditions to guarantee eye-tracking data accuracy. Initially, participants were briefed on the experiment and provided informed consent. The experimenter then detailed the procedural flow and the eight involved flight scenarios. Two experimenters assisted the PF and PM in appropriately fitting and calibrating the eye-tracking devices. The eye-tracking data was monitored and documented throughout the whole experiment. Crew assignments for each flight scenario were determined by a random draw before each trial. After completing the initial task in each scenario, participants switched roles for a repeat trial. Once all scenarios were concluded, data were meticulously verified for accuracy and completeness, then compiled and preserved. The entire experiment spanned approximately eight hours.

Data Processing and Analysis.   Upon completion of the experiment, the eye-tracking data was preliminarily organized. Analysts used the "Automatic Mapping" function in Tobii Pro Lab software to map the recorded experimental videos from the eye trackers to the panoramic cockpit view of the aircraft simulator. Manual corrections were made to this mapping to achieve an accuracy rate exceeding 90% for the experimental videos relative to the panoramic snapshots used in the analysis. This meticulous approach ensured the reliability of the data exportation and visualization process.

After mapping the experimental videos to the cockpit panoramas, the analysts utilized the "AOI Tool" in Tobii Pro Lab to delineate areas of interest within these panoramas. This step facilitated a comprehensive study of the crew's focal points across different flight scenarios and roles.

3 Results and Discussion

The experimental findings are categorized into eye-tracking visualization results and eye-tracking metric data. The visualization includes heat maps and trajectory maps, vividly showcasing the pilots' focused areas of interest. The eye-tracking metrics comprise total duration of fixation, number of visits, time to first fixation, and number of fixations. The study primarily analyzed total duration of fixation and number of visits, where total duration of fixation reveals the degree of pilots' attention to specific cockpit areas, and number of visits reflects the level of importance assigned by pilots to these areas. To depict the prominence of focus across various areas of interest, a two-dimensional chart was employed, plotting number of visits on the x-axis against total duration of fixation on the y-axis, with the size of each point indicating the relative weight of importance.

During the data analysis phase, statistical analysis and graphical representation were performed using tools like Excel and SPSS.

3.1 Participant Characteristics

The two professional pilots participating in the eye-tracking study each amassed 12,000 h of flight experience, with rich expertise to the aircraft used for the experiment. Both pilots were 180 cm in height. They formed a crew, comprising a PF and a PM, to conduct the eye-tracking experiment within the flight simulator.

3.2 Analysis of Attention Significance Across Different Flight Scenarios and Roles

Cockpit Preparing.   Figures 3 and 4 illustrate the visualization results and eye-tracking metric data during cockpit preparing stage. The findings show that the PF's primary focus was on the E/WD, MCDU-L, central control pedestal, overhead panel, SD, and flight control unit. The PM, on the other hand, primarily concentrated on the PM checklist, E/WD, MCDU-R, central control pedestal, landing gear lever control and display, and overhead panel, with the PM checklist receiving substantially greater attention and importance than other areas.

During this stage, the PF was engaged in performing safety checks and inputting flight management data as part of cockpit preparing. The PM's role involved monitoring activities, audibly reading out the checklist to prompt the PF's procedural actions, and cross-verifying the flight management data entered by the PF.

For key areas, both PF and PM paid attention to the PFD interfaces on either side. However, the PF's focus on the right PFD was considerably less compared to the left PFD, while the PM exhibited the opposite trend. Furthermore, the PF showed increased attention and importance to the ALT area within the left PFD relative to other areas within the PFD. Additionally, both PF and PM demonstrated notably higher levels of attention and importance to the EWD and SD compared to other areas.

Fig. 3. Eye-tracking Visualization Results During Cockpit Preparing Stage. (a) heatmap and gaze plot for PF. (b) heatmap and gaze plot for PM.

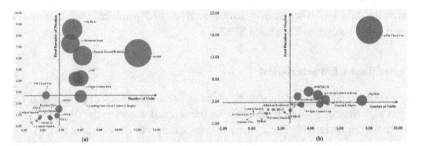

Fig. 4. Eye-tracking Data Presentation for Cockpit preparing Stage. (a) eye-tracking data for PF. (b) eye-tracking data for PM.

Engine Starting. Figures 5 and 6 showcase the eye-tracking visualization results and metric data during engine starting stage. The findings reveal that the PF primarily focused on the Engine/Warning Display (E/WD), System Display (SD), central control pedestal, and overhead panel, with the E/WD and SD receiving significantly greater combined attention and emphasis compared to other areas. The PM's focal areas were the E/WD, SD, PM checklist, and central control pedestal, with a particularly high level of combined focus and importance on the E/WD.

During this stage, the PF was engaged in the engine start procedure, necessitating scrutiny of key parameters in the E/WD such as low-pressure rotor speed, exhaust temperature, and fuel flow. Meanwhile, the PM, tasked with overseeing the engine start process, also concentrated on relevant parameters in the E/WD.

For key areas, both PF and PM exhibited a relatively lower focus on the Primary Flight Display (PFD) during this stage. Their attention and importance given to the EWD and SD were markedly higher than to other areas, especially the EWD.

Fig. 5. Eye-tracking Visualization Results During Engine Starting Stage. (a) heatmap and gaze plot for PF. (b) heatmap and gaze plot for PM.

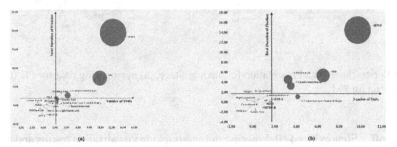

Fig. 6. Eye-tracking Data Presentation for Engine Starting Stage. (a) eye-tracking data for PF. (b) eye-tracking data for PM.

Taxiing. The taxiing phase's eye-tracking visualization and metric data are illustrated in Figs. 7 and 8. The results indicate that the PF's main areas of focus were exterior view and E/WD, with a notably higher combined level of attention and importance on the exterior view. The PM, on the other hand, concentrated mainly on the PM checklist, exterior view, E/WD, SD, and central control pedestal, with the PM checklist and exterior view receiving the most significant combined focus and emphasis.

In this stage, the PF's primary task was executing the taxiing procedure, requiring both PF and PM to maintain vigilance on the external environment through the exterior view and to monitor the engine parameters on the E/WD. Additionally, the PM, due to monitoring duties, also needed to focus attentively on the PM checklist.

For key areas, the PF paid attention to the left PFD interface, though overall the focus was moderate. Both PF and PM showed notably higher attention and emphasis on the EWD and SD, particularly the SD area.

Fig. 7. Eye-tracking Visualization Results During Taxiing Stage. (a) heatmap and gaze plot for PF. (b) heatmap and gaze plot for PM.

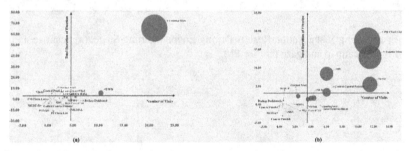

Fig. 8. Eye-tracking Data Presentation for Taxiing Stage. (a) eye-tracking data for PF. (b) eye-tracking data for PM.

Taking-off. Figures 9 and 10 showcase the eye-tracking visualization results and metric data during the taking-off stage. The results show that the PF's primary areas of focus were the PFD-L, exterior view, ND-L, and E/WD, with notably higher attention and importance given to the PFD-L and the exterior view. The PM, in contrast, focused mainly on the PFD-R, exterior view, E/WD, and ND-R, with the PFD-R and exterior view receiving significantly greater attention and emphasis.

In this stage, the PF was primarily responsible for executing the takeoff procedure, focusing on the aircraft's takeoff attitude and speeds (V1, VR, V2). The PM, tasked with overseeing the takeoff and climb procedures, was mainly attentive to standard callouts (takeoff speeds V1/VR/V2), leading to both roles placing a heightened focus on the PFD area.

For key areas, the PF concentrated on the left PFD interface, while the PM focused on the right PFD interface. Both the PF and PM mainly paid attention to the FD, SPEED, and ALT areas on the right or left PFD interface. During the takeoff procedure, both the PF and PM monitored the flight direction and track, the aircraft's climb speed, and the rate of ascent, all of which are displayed on the PFD.

Fig. 9. Eye-tracking Visualization Results During Taking-off Stage. (a) heatmap and gaze plot for PF. (b) heatmap and gaze plot for PM.

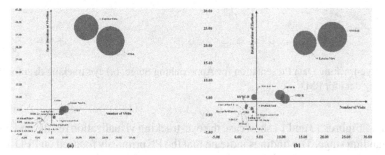

Fig. 10. Eye-tracking Data Presentation for Taking-off Stage. (a) eye-tracking data for PF. (b) eye-tracking data for PM.

Approaching. Figures 11 and 12 present the eye-tracking visualization and metric data during approaching stage. The findings indicate that the PF's primary focus areas were the PFD-L, ND-L, MCDU-L, and flight control unit, with a particularly high level of attention and importance on the PFD-L, ND-L, and MCDU-L. The PM's main focus areas were the PM checklist, ND-R, PFD-R, exterior view, and flight control unit, with the PM checklist, ND-R, and PFD-R receiving the most significant combined attention and emphasis.

During this stage, the PF was primarily engaged in executing the approaching procedure, necessitating the precise input of flight management data such as landing runway, approaching method, ILS frequency, approaching route, and decision altitude. The PM's role involved monitoring the approaching procedure, performing checklist duties, and confirming parameters like the aircraft's trajectory and approaching speed.

For key areas during this phase, the PF concentrated on the left PFD interface, while the PM focused on the right PFD interface. Both the PF and PM mainly directed their attention to the FD, SPEED, and ALT areas on their respective sides of the PFD interface.

Fig. 11. Eye-tracking Visualization Results During Approaching Stage. (a) heatmap and gaze plot for PF. (b) heatmap and gaze plot for PM.

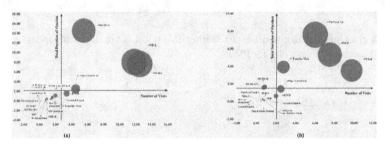

Fig. 12. Eye-tracking Data Presentation for Approaching Stage. (a) eye-tracking data for PF. (b) eye-tracking data for PM.

Landing. Figures 13 and 14 showcase the eye-tracking visualization results and metrics during landing stage. The findings indicate that the PF primarily focused on PFD-L, ND-L, and exterior view, with a notably high level of attention and emphasis placed on the PFD-L. Conversely, the PM focused mainly on PFD-R, ND-R, PM checklist, and exterior view, with a particularly significant focus on the PFD-R.

In this stage, the PF was engaged in executing landing procedures, paying close attention to the aircraft's configuration, such as approaching speed, descent rate at low altitude, localizer, glide path, and monitoring the glide slope ratio. The PM, responsible for monitoring the landing procedures, focused on checklist duties and ensuring the aircraft's trajectory and approaching method aligned with air traffic control instructions.

For key areas, the PF concentrated on the left PFD interface, particularly the ALT and FD areas of the left PFD. This is because the PF, during the landing procedure, primarily focuses on aircraft configuration management, where controlling the aircraft's attitude and glide slope ratio is crucial. The PM, on the other hand, focused on the right PFD interface, particularly the FD, ALT, and SPEED areas of the left PFD. This is because, for the PM, the most critical monitoring data during landing are the aircraft's attitude, glide slope ratio, and approaching speed.

After-landing. The after-landing stage eye-tracking visualization and metrics are illustrated in Figs. 15 and 16. These results show that the PF's main focus was on exterior view and PFD-L, with the exterior view receiving substantially more combined attention

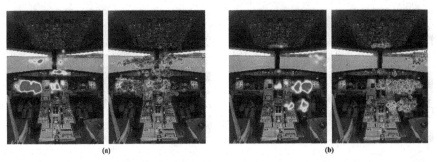

Fig. 13. Eye-tracking Visualization Results During Landing Stage. (a) heatmap and gaze plot for PF. (b) heatmap and gaze plot for PM.

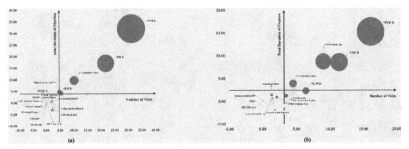

Fig. 14. Eye-tracking Data Presentation for Landing Stage. (a) eye-tracking data for PF. (b) eye-tracking data for PM.

and importance. The PM's focal areas were exterior view, PFD-R, PM checklist, and E/WD, with the highest level of attention and importance placed on the exterior view.

In this stage, the PF's primary task involved vacating the runway and navigating taxiways according to air traffic control directives. The PM was tasked with monitoring the aircraft, identifying taxiways based on control instructions, and confirming the absence of runway obstructions. Thus, both the PF and PM placed a significant emphasis on the window-side exterior view, outweighing other areas in terms of focus.

For key areas, the PF intensely focused on the left PFD interface, particularly concentrating on FD area within the left PFD. Meanwhile, the PM devoted attention to the right PFD interface, E/WD and SD, with the most significant focus being on the FD area of the left PFD.

Parking. The eye-tracking visualization results and metric data during parking stage are depicted in Figs. 17 and 18. These results highlight that the PF primarily focus on E/WD, overhead panel, landing gear lever control and display, SD, and exterior view. Of these, the E/WD and overhead panel garnered significantly more attention and importance. The PM's focal points were sequentially the E/WD, PM checklist, overhead panel, and SD, with the E/WD, PM checklist, and overhead panel notably receiving the highest combined levels of attention and importance.

In this stage, both PF and PM were engaged in executing parking stage procedures, mainly centering on the monitoring of engine parking parameters after the aircraft had

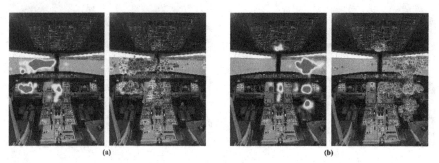

Fig. 15. Eye-tracking Visualization Results During After-landing Stage. (a) heatmap and gaze plot for PF. (b) heatmap and gaze plot for PM.

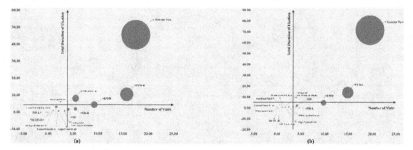

Fig. 16. Eye-tracking Data Presentation for After-landing Stage. (a) eye-tracking data for PF. (b) eye-tracking data for PM.

ceased movement. Additionally, the PM also had duties concerning actions related to the overhead panel and checklist tasks during the parking.

For key areas, both PF and PM primarily focused on E/WD and SD interfaces, with their attention significantly more concentrated on the EWD area. This heightened focus is attributed to the necessity for both PF and PM to monitor the relevant parameters associated with engine parking during the parking procedures.

Fig. 17. Eye-tracking Visualization Results During Parking Stage. (a) heatmap and gaze plot for PF. (b) heatmap and gaze plot for PM.

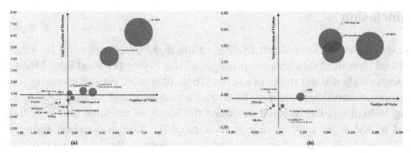

Fig. 18. Eye-tracking Data Presentation for Parking Stage. (a) eye-tracking data for PF. (b) eye-tracking data for PM.

3.3 Future Directions in Aircraft Cockpit Technology

Based on eye-tracking analysis, primary flight tasks and focus areas on the cockpit interface vary across different flight stages. Pilots need to quickly gather information from the complex cockpit interface during flight, a significant source of crew workload. Designing cockpit display controls task-specifically and presenting varied interfaces for different flight stages could reduce this workload. For example, in the parking phase, shifting focus between the E/WD and overhead panel for verification is common. Introducing the necessary controls from the overhead panel into the display interface during this phase could facilitate information access under a lower workload.

Moreover, customizing display control interfaces for different flight roles could be advantageous. For instance, digitizing checklists in the PM's display control interface, with electronic reminders and touch-based controls, could alert pilots to procedural oversights and enable prompt actions.

Lastly, the Flight Management System's (FMS) input interface could be redesigned based on flight tasks, using more user-friendly methods like non-natural language recognition or touch input. For example, if air traffic control instructs a SASAN 2A approaching, the FMS could automatically recognize and require only pilot confirmation.

3.4 Limitations and Future Research Directions

Firstly, this study involved only two expert users in the eye-tracking experiment. Although their extensive flight experience and strict adherence to standard operating procedures lend some universality to the findings, there could still be potential biases. Future research could involve a larger pool of pilots to achieve more universally applicable results, categorizing findings based on pilots' experience levels.

Secondly, the research was conducted using only one mainstream aircraft model. Future studies could incorporate various models to explore the potential impacts.

Lastly, the current study focused solely on normal flight conditions and did not encompass emergency scenarios like fires, depressurization, or stalls. Future studies could simulate such conditions in flight simulators to derive insights relevant to these emergency scenarios.

4 Conclusion

This study conducted an in-depth analysis of the flight tasks performed by a modern commercial aircraft flight crew, comprising the Pilot Flying (PF) and Pilot Monitoring (PM), across eight distinct stages of a normal flight operation: cockpit preparing, engine start, taxiing, takeoff, approaching, landing, after-landing, and parking. Utilizing eye-tracking technology, the research identified the levels of attention and prioritization afforded by the flight crew to various sections of the cockpit interface during these stages. The study also proposed potential future directions for the development of cockpit human-machine interfaces.

The aircraft cockpit was categorized into 18 areas of interest for this study, including the central control pedestal, MCDU-L, MCDU-R, PF checklist, PM checklist, E/WD, SD, left and right instrument control panels, PFD-L, PFD-R, ND-L, ND-R, appendage stand-by instrument, landing gear handle controls and display, flight control unit, window-side external view, and overhead panel. Eye-tracking analysis was employed to ascertain the crew's focal points within these areas.

The findings revealed that during the cockpit preparing phase, the PF primarily focused on the E/WD, MCDU-L, central control pedestal, overhead panel, SD, and flight control unit. Conversely, the PM's attention was mainly on the PM checklist, E/WD, MCDU-R, central control pedestal, landing gear handle controls and display, and overhead panel. In the engine start phase, the PF's focus areas included E/WD, SD, the central control pedestal, and overhead panel, while the PM paid particular attention to the E/WD, SD, PM checklist, and central control pedestal. During the taxiing phase, the PF predominantly focused on the exterior view and E/WD, whereas the PM's attention was directed toward the PM checklist, exterior view, E/WD, SD, and central control pedestal. In the takeoff phase, the PF's key focus areas were PFD-L, the exterior view, ND-L, and E/WD, while the PM's attention was on PFD-R, the exterior view, E/WD, and ND-R. The approaching phase saw the PF and PM focusing on different specific areas. During landing, the PF's primary focus was on PFD-L, ND-L, MCDU-L, and flight control unit, with the PM concentrating on the PM checklist, ND-R, PFD-R, the exterior view, and flight control unit. In the after-landing phase, the PF mainly focused on PFD-L, ND-L, and the exterior view, while the PM's attention was on PFD-R, ND-R, PM checklist, and the exterior view. During the parking phase, the PF primarily focused on the exterior view and PFD-L, whereas the PM's key attention areas were the exterior view, PFD-R, PM checklist, and E/WD.

In addition to the analysis of key attention areas within the identified interest zones, the study conducted a granular examination of PFD-L, PFD-R, E/WD, and SD, offering further insight into the crew's attention distribution within these critical areas.

Through this analysis of cockpit interface information across various flight scenarios, the findings of this study can assist cockpit HMI designers in capturing pertinent design requirements and providing guidance for interface design efforts.

Disclosure of Interests. The authors have no competing interests to declare that are relevant to the content of this article.

References

1. Ahlstrom, U., Friedman-Berg, F.J.: Using eye movement activity as a correlate of cognitive workload. Int. J. Ind. Ergon. **36**(7), 623–636 (2006)
2. Li, W.C., Zhang, J., Le Minh, T., Cao, J., Wang, L.: Visual scan patterns reflect to human-computer interactions on processing different types of messages in the flight deck. Int. J. Ind. Ergon. **72**, 54–60 (2019)
3. LAvE, R.A., SIERT, J.L., GokuR, M.: Eye-tracking measures and human performance in a vigilance task (2002)
4. Allsop, J., Gray, R.: Flying under pressure: Effects of anxiety on attention and gaze behavior in aviation. J. Appl. Res. Mem. Cogn. **3**(2), 63–71 (2014)
5. Goldberg, J.H., Kotval, X.P.: Computer interface evaluation using eye movements: methods and constructs. Int. J. Ind. Ergon. **24**(6), 631–645 (1999)
6. Rudi, D., Kiefer, P., Giannopoulos, I., Raubal, M.: Gaze-based interactions in the cockpit of the future: a survey. J. Multimodal User Interfaces **14**, 25–48 (2020)

Tangible Narrative - An Intelligent Cockpit Design Methodology for Designers to Experience

Mingyu Li[1], Danhua Zhao[1,2], Zijiang Yang[1,3(✉)], and Tao Wang[3]

[1] School of Design, Hunan University, Lushan Road (S), Yuelu District, Changsha, Hunan, China
{Lmy00559,zhaodanhua}@hnu.edu.cn

[2] State Key Laboratory of Advanced Design and Manufacturing for Vehicle Body, Lushan Road (S), Yuelu District, Changsha, Hunan, China

[3] Huizhou Desay SV Automotive Company, Limited, Huizhou, China
{Zijiang.Yang,Tao.Wang}@desaysv.com

Abstract. Intelligent cockpit is a complicated spatial scenario merging technology and design, with more complex scenarios and interactions that set it apart from typical automobiles. With the electrification and intellectualization of automobiles, user experience is more important than styling design and interaction interface design. In this regard, we have established a research framework for intelligent cockpit based on scene space, and introduced the concept of tangible narrative, which strengthens the authenticity of the design content in the dimension of time and space through the realistic restoration of the situation, so that the designers can be more in the shoes of the user's perspective in the design of the experience. This paper describes the positive experience of tangible narratives and their value for the process of design testing and optimization. The use of tangible narratives provides tangible and timely feedback for the testing and optimization of intelligent cockpit creative concepts.

Keywords: Intelligent Cockpit · Tangible Narrative Interaction · Design Methodology · Scenario Building

1 Introduction

The autonomous driving revolution is transforming automotive user interface research by emphasizing productivity and entertainment within the in-cockpit space scenario [1]. Designers are now giving more weight to user experience in the development of intelligent cockpits. Establishing a connection between the vehicle and the user is deemed crucial in every imaginable scenario [2]. The substantial changes brought about by the autonomous driving revolution create challenges for designers who encounter resistance during the design process. As user scenarios become more diverse, the dimensions of user experience in the cockpit grow increasingly complex. The absence of a clear framework to guide the design and development of complex products, such as cockpits, underscores the need for tools and methods to simulate human and machine behavior

P.-L. P. Rau (Ed.): HCII 2024, LNCS 14702, pp. 130–146, 2024.
https://doi.org/10.1007/978-3-031-60913-8_10

feedback platforms in the early stages of design. This approach enables real-world testing to enhance the viability of design solutions and user acceptance [3]. Given the limited investigation and study on intelligent cockpit objects in academia thus far, our aim is to explore how user experience, interaction design, and styling design can be integrated in a comprehensive study.

Recent research on cockpit simulation has predominantly followed a technological route [4–6]. However, as scenarios continue to evolve, designers must rapidly test various scenario experiences, necessitating a heightened awareness of the user experience pathway. In our review of existing interaction design approaches to intelligent cockpits, we found that methods such as enactment, contextual inquiry, scale scenarios, Wizard of Oz, and field experience all emphasize the construction of user experience scenarios. These approaches also incorporate narrative expression, providing a scenario for the experience. They also have narrative expression, which provides a scenario for the experience. Humans inherently gravitate towards narrative [7]. Narrative can link imagination and creativity [8]. Within the narrative, designers can generate new ideas and thoughts for the design of the cockpit experience. Design is essentially the process of creating a more vivid future by constructing prospective futures. The combination of narrative, 3D design, and physical prototyping allows the mind of the design participant to engage in abductive thinking [9]. According to Featherstone, the automotive experience is an embodied experience, as individuals respond to the thrum of the engine, the scent of the cockpit, and the feel of the car seat [10]. The spectrum of experiences available ranges from scenario-based experiences like in-car audio and video to subtle movements such as raising a hand or turning around.

Tangible narrative is a metaphorical representation of an experience, and its applicability extends seamlessly to the context of the cockpit. Particularly in discussions about user experience, the cockpit experience for users is a blend of temporality and spatiality. Our objective is to utilize tangible narrative as the foundation for a design methodology that accentuates the user's embodied experience in the cockpit. We anticipate that tangible narrative will empower designers by providing them with the user's experiential perspective through the storytelling of future scenarios. We aim for tangible narrative to contribute to the design of intelligent cockpits in the following ways:

1. Establish a connection between technology and design, enabling designers to test the logic of incorporating technology into the program during the design process.
2. Enable the representation of complex concepts in real space intuitively, aiming for a more suitable layout for intelligent cockpits, human-machine scale, and interaction design schemes.
3. Provide designers with a user's perspective during the creation of potential future experiences. Establish authentic user interaction experiences and feedback during the cockpit design phase to identify issues and make necessary modifications to existing conceptual solutions.

2 Literature Review

2.1 From Automotive to Intelligent Cockpit

User experience has become more important. The intelligent cockpit, as a space reflecting technological advancements, is designed to meet the evolving needs of user experience. The evaluation of user experience plays a pivotal role in determining whether in-vehicle gadgets meet or surpass user expectations [11]. Specifically in the context of Autonomous Vehicles (AVs), creating positive experiences requires designers to adopt an experience-oriented perspective on automotive Human-Machine Interaction (HMI) [12]. As autonomy levels increase, drivers can also engage in non-driving functions within the cockpit, adding versatility to various scenarios. The cockpit scenario is richer and more diversified. The car, being a unique time-space, is shaped by the varied journeys and preferences of both the driver and passengers [13], Even before the advent of autonomous driving, occupants could partake in a myriad of activities within it. As Featherstone aptly states, 'the automobile becomes a new form of communications platform with a complex set of possibilities' [10]. The interaction dimension becomes more complex. Engagement within the automobile now extends beyond the screen to encompass the entire cockpit. This has led to the emergence of a five-sense design, gradually enhancing experiences such as multi-screen interaction, car-computer ecology, and other interactive elements [14]. A shift in the relationship between people and vehicles. The driver transitions from full control of the vehicle to sharing control with the machine, ultimately evolving towards the future of machine self-control [15]. The car is no longer merely a vehicle driven by the user; instead, the relationship between the user and the car has expanded.

2.2 Traditional Automotive Design Workflow

With the aforementioned shifts in automotive design and interaction design, the cockpit is evolving into a more intricate spatial interaction vehicle. As autonomous driving and other interaction technologies advance, the potential for diverse user scenarios within the car increases. Consequently, a systematic and effective design methodology must evolve to address the complexity of this changing object. This methodology will allow designers to pace their creations, ensuring that the experiences and scenarios align with user preferences. Designers must approach the development of intelligent cockpits by seamlessly integrating both interaction and style.

Comparing the styling design process of traditional automotive [16] and the automotive Human-Machine Interface (HMI) Design Process [17] (see Fig. 1), it is evident that the process involves a substantial amount of iteration. This iterative nature is characterized by concept generation, validation, and continuous refinement.

We believe that the design trajectory for the intelligent cockpit will undergo a shift in the context of the aforementioned transition from traditional automotive to intelligent cockpits. We envision tangible narrative as a design activity encompassing the enhanced experience facilitated by technological innovations.

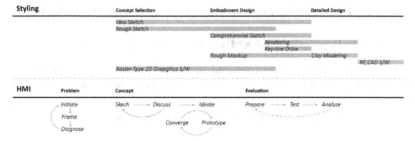

Fig. 1. Design process for traditional automotive style and interaction.

2.3 Creating Real Experiences

For the study of driving behavior, Bellet et al. developed the simulation modeler COSMO-SIVIC to investigate driving distractions [3]. This model involves both physical simulation of the driving space and digital simulation of the vehicle's driving environment. To ensure an accurate representation of the operator's driving environment, real driving proportions and dimensions are incorporated, creating realistic experiential environments for human-machine data studies, resulting in more authentic test data [18]. When interpreting research findings, it is crucial to consider the creation of genuine experience spaces and the utilization of experiential testing techniques, especially when these results strongly correlate with user experience [19]. In the realm of intelligent cockpit design, the arrangement of the cockpit, interaction points for feedback, and the user's experience in various cockpit scenarios are pivotal elements in crafting realistic environments.

2.4 Tangible Narrative Design

Tangible interaction is characterized by figurative interaction, tangible manipulation, physical representation of data, and embedding in real space [20]. Harley et al. argue that tangible interactive technologies are a necessary component of narrative or narrative construction [21]. Bruner [22] demonstrates the significant role physical objects play in bridging the abstract and the concrete. When designers conceptualize the intelligent cockpit, they are essentially constructing a plausible vision of the future. Interactive narratives can employ diegetic Tangible User Interfaces (TUIs) to bridge the gap between real-world and future scenarios. Tversky and Lee [23] argue that language can effectively communicate space, bringing us closer to the spatial experience that designers aim to create through more realistic in-cockpit activities. As stated [24], 'Scenarios give people a 'memory' of the future.' Tangible narrative interactions in real scenarios translate future possibilities into experiences, allowing for a more profound analysis of participants' actions. This analysis, in turn, contributes to a better understanding and iterative refinement of the intelligent cockpit concept solution.

3 Framing Tangible Narrative Design of Intelligent Cockpit

3.1 Elements in Intelligent Cockpit Design

We present a theoretical concept map and framework to guide our work in tangible narrative interactions. Developing a theoretical framework enhances the comprehension of intelligent cockpit components for design participants. Moreover, it establishes a well-defined connection between design participants and the user experience within the cockpit.

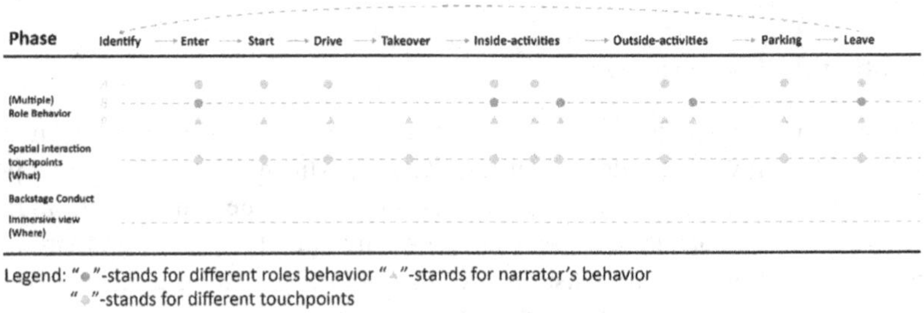

Legend: "●"-stands for different roles behavior "▲"-stands for narrator's behavior
"○"-stands for different touchpoints

Fig. 2. Intelligent cockpit experience process and roles, technical elements.

1. Storyline:
   Storytelling is a crucial narrative technique that has the power to provide, engage, and compel stakeholders, fostering change in the present moment [25]. In the realm of cockpit design research, the in-cockpit experience is comprised of a collection of stories across multiple phases. Traditionally, we categorize the cockpit experience into phases such as identity, enter, start, drive, takeover, inside-activities, outside-activities, parking, leave, and departing (see Fig. 2). Depending on the specific design or research focus, tailored stories for different stages can be targeted.

2. Narrator (Narrative position):
   Ryan distinguishes four narrative positions through two dimensions, positional and exploratory [26]. In the tangible narrative, where the existence of contingency is acknowledged, both external-exploratory and internal-exploratory roles are essential. The pacing of a story is crucial, and its development must align with actual circumstances to 'recreate' the story in future scenarios. The narrator controls the story's progression in the tangible narrative, indicated by triangle markers (see Fig. 2). These markers enable participants to advance the story development alongside them at the appropriate time, taking the next action.

3. Character:
   Characters play a crucial role in the plot, and we prefer to have characters involved in the actual space story rather than study participants. Depending on the specific design study concept, the story's protagonist may be a designer or a user, and the number of people in the cockpit can vary. In the given context, the character also possesses a unique identity, such as a parent, a child, a race car driver, a gamer, a business owner, etc. In future-focused scenarios, obtaining more authentic user feedback during the

cockpit experience is possible when the participant's identity aligns closely with the role played or when the participant immerses themselves more deeply into the performed role, as indicated by circular markers (see Fig. 2)

4. Behavior:

A behavior consists of a group of acts. With the advent of new technologies and emerging interaction techniques, the future cockpit experience will predominantly hinge on how users engage with all interactable devices in the cabin. Designers can identify issues by observing how users behave when confronted with new interaction mediums. Tangible narrative enables users to manipulate objects representing story components, offering an engaging exploration of the narrative [21]. It is crucial to provide users with a sense of how these actions would genuinely feel for real users. Users are more immersed in interacting with the cockpit and receiving feedback in the physical context we design. Inferring user interactions and perceptions from 2D drawings or 3D digital models can be challenging.

5. Boundary Space:

As cockpits are fundamentally spatial products, specifying the location and emphasizing the veracity of the user experience is crucial in design research. Combining elements of light, sound, and music can create a more immersive ambient space for the experience. In interactive storytelling, physical spaces can transform the reader's physical environment, making them feel integral to the story world [27].

There is a finite interaction distance between characters seated differently. Characters in various seats may possess distinct identity traits and interact with the cockpit differently based on the design scheme. In the parent-child gaming cockpit concept, for instance, parents and kids sit in separate sections of the cockpit, facilitating interaction and feedback between them.

6. Tangible Object:

The needs and experiences of the user inside the cabin must be closely replicated throughout the creation of the conceptual scenario for the intelligent cockpit. An alternative to placing the user's interactions outside the story world is dynamic tangibles [21]. The needs and experiences of the user inside the cockpit must be closely replicated throughout the creation of the conceptual scenario for the intelligent cockpit.

3.2 Techniques of Automotive Interaction Design

These design approaches are constructed and evaluated using context-specific prototypes, with distinct design strategies positioned at various stages of the design process. The iterative nature of technology, especially in the case of the intelligent cockpit, a complex interaction space, poses challenges and complexities for the design process. Design teams must leverage current values and desires to envision a better and more plausible future [28] (Table 1).

Table 1. Design approaches used in automotive design.

	Phases	Brief	Cases
Drawing and Collaging	Concept	Have participants describe, collage, and draw their visions of autonomous cars, including types of cars and cityscapes	Understand the expected impacts of autonomous vehicles on society and infrastructure through drawing, collaging, and interviewing [29]
Enactment	Concept Evaluation	Gesturing and expressing the actions of humans and systems	gain a more grounded experience in self-driving car design for design teams [29]
Contextual Inquiry	Concept Evaluation	Observing and interviewing in context allows designers more tacit knowledge of the scenario	Users imagine they are riding in a self-driving vehicle and explore the new situations that automation brings to passengers through interviews [30]
Scale Scenarios	Problem Concept Evaluation	3-D mock-ups have been employed as a participatory design technique to explore future interactions	enable discussion and analysis of the actions tactics, particularly in less-typical situations [31]
Wizard of Oz	Concept Evaluation	In real-time Collaborative design. it can inform system engineering and be used with built-in evaluation systems	An efficient system design process provides vital information [32]
Field Experiments	Problem Concept Evaluation	Taking the interactions from the lab or studio into the real-world setting to understand the impacts of tech	Interaction between people and vehicles [33]
Video Prototyping	Evaluation	Designers can more easily develop multiple alternatives to compare reflect, classify, categorize, and refine	Further evaluation and analysis by recordings based on previous methods

(continued)

Table 1. (*continued*)

	Phases	Brief	Cases
Animation Prototyping	Evaluation		Demonstration to understand the user's emotional feedback for different interactions
Design Metaphors	Concept Evaluation	Are used to frame design problems, create meaningful product experiences, and guide interaction	Helps to understand the concrete properties of abstract concepts [34]

Characteristics		Drawing and Collaging	Enactment	Contextual Inquiry	Scale Scenarios	Field Experiments	Wizard of Oz	Video Prototyping	Animation Prototyping	Design Metaphors
Story	Storyline	O	O	O	●	O	O			
Story	Narrator (Narrative position)				O		●			
Story	Character		●	●		●	●	●	●	O
Story	Behavior(Interaction)	O	●	●	●		●	●	O	O
Space	Tangible object(Touchpoint)		O	O	O		●			
Space	Boundary space		●	●						

Legend: "●"-the criterion is fully covered by the corresponding technique
"O"-the criterion is only partly covered

Fig. 3. The characteristics contained in different techniques.

The chart above illustrates those methods like Enactment, Contextual Inquiry, and Wizard of Oz focus on the interaction context within the space when exploring the potential of future cars. We posit that the process of constructing the context can be primarily divided into two parts: story and space. The former is utilized to enhance the construction of the narrative and the behaviors of the characters, while the latter clarifies the composition of elements in the scene.

However, most cases primarily discuss the methods used and the ensuing outcomes, with a focus on studying user behavior and machine feedback in specific areas of the cockpit. None of these approaches genuinely consider the value of the cockpit in the user experience process, nor do they delve into contextualization through a framing format (see Fig. 3). In our pursuit of providing designers with more precise tools for guiding their work in the forthcoming intelligent cockpit era, we aim to create a tangible narrative framework.

3.3 Framework of Tangible Narrative Interaction

Tangible narrative has the potential to enhance the contextualization of spatial encounters. Establishing a theoretical framework allows design participants to gain a profound understanding of the features of the intelligent cockpit and the factors involved in tangible narrative interaction. The three processes of tangible narrative interaction include story generation, space setting, and tangible narrative validation (see Fig. 4).

We can test the tangible narrative throughout the design process, from concept to evaluation, starting with identifying the problem. The primary goal of story generation is to clarify how user behavior, the system backend, and interactive touchpoints relate to the experience story flow. This information forms the basis of the narrative script used in tangible narrative testing.

After resolving the plot, the space setting aims to reestablish the area and interactive tangible elements, allowing users to engage with the real space. Following the creation of the story, we construct a 1:1 scale model of the cockpit within the experimental setting, incorporating effective techniques to recreate all interaction points, such as movable interaction devices, switchable interaction interfaces, sound effects, light effects, etc. To generate the most realistic experience environment, participants can manually operate the program if needed.

The next step involves recruiting participants to validate the tangible narrative, documenting validation content, and gathering suggestions for enhancements. Once adjustments are made, the process continues until the product development stage.

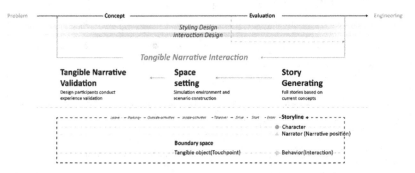

Fig. 4. Framework of tangible narrative and the relationship with the design process.

4 Case Study

The project aims to create a one-to-one real cockpit displayed at the exhibition, providing the public with a comprehensive experience. This involves designing the whole-process intelligent cockpit from the perspectives of scene, technology, function, and medium. After initial investigation and analysis, we integrated three entertainment, office, and leisure scenes into the design of the intelligent cockpit. Cutting-edge interaction technologies, including L3 auto-pilot, were also incorporated to enhance in-cabin interaction within the intelligent cockpit's dimensions. The use of tangible narrative in the development of interaction modeling is a primary focus of this article. This is because the project's progression from conception to execution relies on the collaborative development of interaction and styling once the scenario is established. To gain a deeper understanding of the user experience in a potential future cockpit, this study intends to leverage tangible narrative.

4.1 Participants

Ten people are involved in the project's tangible narrative process, comprising one intelligent mobility direction instructor, two professional designers, four interaction designers, and three interior designers. To regulate the rhythm and advance the process, one interaction designer served as the narrator, three individuals were tasked with switching display materials and regulating environmental changes based on the user's operation, and one person was responsible for recording the entire process.

4.2 Story Generating

In addition to designing interactive interfaces, we are crafting narratives that connect through shared experiences. To replicate real-world interaction between the user and the intelligent cockpit, a story is created. The simulation story paradigm we developed is based on a real user's interaction with the intelligent cockpit at the exhibition site. In this scenario, the character user navigates around the booth, visits the intelligent cockpit to experience it, and exits the intelligent cockpit after going through the full interaction flow under the guidance of a guide. This aligns with the design definition from the project's inception, serving as an exhibit at the exhibition site where the entire experience flow is showcased. (see Fig. 5).

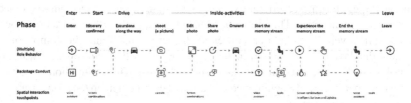

Fig. 5. Entire experience flow of the design case.

4.3 Space Setting

Spatial interaction serves as the foundation for styling design, and its design should be functional. The scenario is crafted to enhance the previously established story and create a more realistic setting for the experiencer. The approach involves adapting the cockpit layout to match the state required for the scenario and physically placing changing interaction touchpoints in the correct spots within the area. This process was executed on a simulated driving pedestal in the university's laboratory. The original condition of our simulated ride stands replicates the arrangement of a typical automobile inside and includes customary interaction touchpoints. (see Fig. 6).

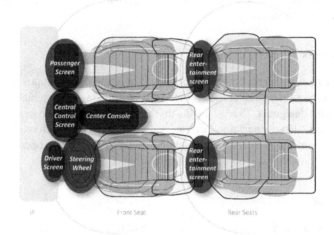

Fig. 6. Traditional car interior interaction contact location.

We opted for an unconventional cockpit space configuration, featuring one driver seat and two back passenger seats. Figure 7 illustrates the major interaction sites in the solution, with touchpoints differing significantly from the typical car interior (see Fig. 7 right). To create the human-machine verification 3D model, we adjusted the seat to match the solution's location and used laboratory equipment to position the screen accordingly. We printed high-fidelity information displayed on the screen to scale and incorporated page-turning functionality, making the screen function as tangible objects with interactive capabilities. This allows users to better experience the interaction process in the cockpit, given the unique properties of the screen itself and the complexity of the content displayed. The program includes a rear screen that can move forward and backward, as well as a front seat that can rotate and move. These alterations result in a distinct user experience and a heightened sensation of engagement in the space compared to conventional interior setups.

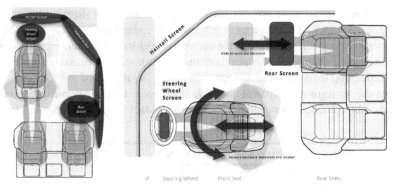

Fig. 7. Case interaction contact location (left). Laboratory simulation of cockpit layout and components (right).

4.4 Tangible Narrative Experience Process

In the starting page on screen, the selection of different mode orders can be carried out, here is one of the complete processes as an example, experience the process as shown in Fig. 9.

The experiencer is positioned in the last row behind the screen as soon as the narrator leads them into the cockpit. The narrator guides the user in the back row into travel photography mode, enabling them to take pictures of the outside scenery or group photos inside the cockpit using gripping gestures and photograph sound effects on a mobile device. The user can then crop, adjust, and add stickers and text to the photos displayed on the back screen through a picture operation interface.

Next, the narrator instructs the user to drag the adjusted image to the hairtail screen using the rear screen. The photo album screen replaces the hairtail screen. On the memory image page, the front seats rotate 90 degrees to the right, bringing the front and back rows of users together to watch the memory animation on the hairtail screen. Once completed, the rear screen switches to the mode selection page, and the seats are reset.

The experiencer is guided into the parent-child mode by the narrator, who assumes the role of parents in the driver's seat, waving to the right. A ball appears from the left side of the hairtail screen, and the interface displaying the ball's movement is shown on the hairtail screen. Seated behind the back screen as the child, the child rotates the virtual knob on the screen to catch the ball corresponding to its color. The catch wheel interface is displayed on the back screen.

The final experience is the office mode. The experiencer uses gestures to drag contacts from the back screen into the video conference. The rear screen switches to the contact interface when the front seat turns 90 degrees to the right, and the rear screen moves forward. The Hairtail screen displays the meeting document screen.

Mimicking file editing activity, the back screen switches to the file page when a file on the Hairtail screen is gestured to the back screen. On the back screen, the user chooses the recipient of the file and then drags it into the file library with their finger. At the end of the procedure, the seat is reset.

In the tangible narrative process, we utilize a behavior log sheet to document the experience (see Fig. 8). Gaining a more macroscopic understanding of the flow and logic of the user's experience operating in the cockpit proves useful for subsequent iterations of design problem discovery and optimization. Throughout the process, we meticulously recorded detailed behaviors and dialogues to assess the impact of this tool on tangible narrative during testing. Simultaneously, we documented the relationship between the location of different behaviors and the location of contact points in multi-user scenarios.

PHASE	Narrator	Character A		Character B		Character n	Position
	Lines	Behavior	Lines	Behavior	Lines		
Phase 1	lines for narrator	Behaviors for character A	lines for character A	Behaviors for character B	lines for character B		
Phase 2							
Phase 3	⋮	⋮	⋮	⋮	⋮		
......							
Phase n							

Fig. 8. Behavior Log Sheet.

After the tangible narrative experience, the challenges identified throughout the entire process, including story development, interaction logic, interface content, etc., were incorporated into interviews with the participants. The focus was on asking participants to assess any issues they encountered during their interactions in the real cockpit environment. Participants were encouraged to actively voice suggestions for improving the experience. This information was then shared with the design team, recorded, and considered for future enhancements to the solution.

Fig. 9. Process of tangible narrative interaction.

4.5 Results

The main component of our approach is the creation of future scenarios. The cockpit was created using a variety of scenarios, multidimensional interactions, and human-vehicle interactions. We linked the story, fundamental technology, cockpit design, and user interaction with the tangible narrative framework to provide a user perspective for designers (see Fig. 10).

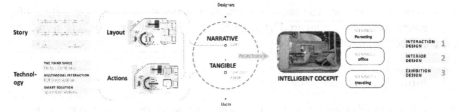

Fig. 10. The example of tangible narrative use.

The tangible narrative interaction addresses the human-machine relationship, spatial scale, and accessibility of interaction. We actively participated in the interaction process on a real physical scale, confirming the connection between the user and the interaction touchpoints in the solution. We observed that the positioning of the new sensors and cameras in the cockpit closely matched the user's motions within the cockpit space, providing a clearer understanding of where to place the sensors in the real-scale space to better align with the user's natural interaction patterns.

This approach also provides insights into how information is displayed on screens, evaluating whether buttons and other screen elements are positioned in user-friendly locations and sizes, and assessing whether the content is presented straightforwardly. Post-interview feedback from participants highlighted that while tangible narrative interaction could be a fundamental improvement, challenges arise from the unpredictability of the unrealistic setting and the lack of realism in the experience during the design implementation process.

5   Discussion

The approaches and case studies discussed in this paper lay the groundwork for the user experience design of the intelligent cockpit. While the optimization part was not conducted in a systematic quantitative manner, practical experiences guided iterative optimization recommendations, steering the design concept through the full-scale cockpit project. We explore the following, beginning with the concept of the intelligent cockpit as a blend of interactivity and spatial styling:

5.1   New Technology Used

Two- and three-dimensional drawings can no longer easily provide an interactive experience with the use of new technologies. Users now demand an interactive experience tailored to their natural interaction style. The tangible narrative framework, through the creation of scenarios, facilitates designers in more intuitively considering how new technologies will be utilized in cabins.

5.2   Full Flow Experience

Most of the time, scenario and storytelling are the levels at which we work when creating an intelligent cockpit concept. However, this doesn't mean we can't consider the user's comfort and ease of use. The tangible narrative framework proves particularly useful when connecting to the actual product development stage, as it aids designers in creating the entire cockpit interaction process.

5.3 Future Scenario Building

The impressions of designers and users of a product are based on current products and prior experiences. We believe that creating future scenarios can assist users in getting a glimpse of future interaction experiences and more thoroughly investigating the issues with current designs in future scenarios. The Tangible narrative framework can help establish future experience scenarios more clearly.

6 Conclusions

As technology rapidly advances, having a deeper understanding of how to engage in the intelligent cockpit area allows us to more effectively address the problems of in-cockpit interaction design. The tangible narrative holds enormous potential for the development of intelligent cockpits, even intervening before the scenario is finalized to assess the viability and development potential of the direction through a straightforward storyline and tangible objects, according to an analysis of the case study's findings.

Tangible narrative establishes a connection between technology and design, enabling designers to better comprehend the characteristics of a scenario and harness the significant impact that new interactive technologies have on the user experience. It also facilitates a more intuitive analysis of fundamental human-machine interaction and cockpit information presentation. Users can immerse themselves more fully in the cockpit experience through this approach. When the experiencer is truly in the scenario, they can gain a genuine sense of what the potential future might be like, identifying issues with the experience and making adjustments as interactive activities unfold in the environment.

A highly effective design approach for creating intelligent cockpits is tangible narrative interaction. It is crucial to analyze the interaction between the experiencer and the cockpit in the space for optimizing and iterating the design solution, creating a realistic experience environment and a cockpit space with feedback. This approach accurately reflects the changes brought about by technology, more realistically builds the experience of future scenarios, and improves design participants' awareness and understanding of the user's perspective in the intelligent cockpit solution.

There are still many aspects of this approach that we have not thoroughly investigated. For instance, we have not compared and examined the effects of various interaction media approaches on the validation process in our case, or determined whether physical versus virtual environments are more effective for interaction validation. However, this initial investigation of the approach provides crucial information about how designers can enhance upcoming design iterations from the viewpoint of the user.

Acknowledgments. This research is supported by Paradigm Construction and Theoretical Boundary of Design Research, National Social Science Foundation (20BG103).

References

1. Kun, A.L., Boll, S., Schmidt, A.: Shifting gears: user interfaces in the age of autonomous driving [J/OL]. IEEE Pervasive Comput. **15**(1), 32–38 (2016)
2. Flemisch, F., Heesen, M., Hesse, T., et al.: Towards a dynamic balance between humans and automation: authority, ability, responsibility and control in shared and cooperative control situations [J/OL]. Cogn. Technol. Work **14**(1), 3–18 (2012)
3. Bellet, T., Mayenobe, P., Bornard, J.C., et al.: A computational model of the car driver interfaced with a simulation platform for future virtual human centred design applications: COSMO-SIVIC [J/OL]. Eng. Appl. Artif. Intell. **25**(7), 1488–1504 (2012)
4. Rosique, F., Navarro, P.J., Fernández, C., Padilla, A.: A systematic review of perception system and simulators for autonomous vehicles research [J/OL]. Sensors **19**(3), 648 (2019)
5. He, D., Ai, B., Guan, K., et al.: The design and applications of high-performance ray-tracing simulation platform for 5G and beyond wireless communications: a tutorial [J/OL]. IEEE Commun. Surv. Tutorials. **21**(1), 10–27 (2019)
6. Fathy, H.K., Filipi, Z.S., Hagena, J., et al.: Review of hardware-in-the-loop simulation and its prospects in the automotive area [C/OL]. In: Modeling and Simulation for Military Applications, pp. 117–136 (2006)
7. Mcneil, L.D.: Homo inventans: the evolution of narrativity [J/OL]. Lang. Commun. **16**(4), 331–360 (1996)
8. Tully, R.: Narrative imagination: a design imperative [J/OL]. Irish J. Acad. Pract. **1**(1) (2012)
9. Childs, P., Zhao, Y., Grigg, J.: Narrative in design development. In: DS 76: Proceedings of E&PDE 2013, pp. 108–113 (2013)
10. Featherstone, M.: Automobilities: an introduction [J/OL]. Theor. Culture Soc. **21**(4–5), 1–24 (2004)
11. Koerber, M., Eichinger, A., Bengler, K., et al.: User experience evaluation in an automotive context. In: 2013 IEEE Intelligent Vehicles Symposium Workshops (IV Workshops), pp. 13–18 (2013)
12. Wintersberger, P., Dmitrenko, D., Schartmüller, C., et al.: S(C)ENTINEL: monitoring automated vehicles with olfactory reliability displays[C/OL]. In: Proceedings of the 24th International Conference on Intelligent User Interfaces, pp. 538–546 (2019)
13. Cycil, C., Perry, M., Laurier, E.: Designing for frustration and disputes in the family car. Int. J. Mob. Hum. Comput. Interact. **6**(2), 46 (2014)
14. Tan, H., Sun, J., Guan, D., et al.: Research on the development trend of human-computer interaction in intelligent vehicles [J/OL]. Packagin Eng. **40**(20), 32–42 (2019)
15. Sheridan, T., Parasuraman, R.: Human-automation interaction [J/OL]. Rev. Hum. Factors Ergon. **1**, 89–129 (2005)
16. Bae, S.H., Kijima, R.: Digital styling for designers: in prospective automotive design. Proc. Virt. Syst. Multi Media **1**, 546–553 (2003).
17. Bavendiek, J., Oliveira, E., Eckstein, L.: A novel method for designing metaphor-based driver-vehicle interaction concepts in automated vehicles[C/OL]. In: Stanton. N. (ed) Advances in Human Factors of Transportation, pp. 15–26 (2020). https://doi.org/10.1007/978-3-030-205 03-4_2
18. Wang, X., Chevalot, N., Monnier, G., et al.: From motion capture to motion simulation: an in-vehicle reach motion database for car design. SAE Trans. **115**, 1124–1130 (2006)
19. Gkouskos, D., Pettersson, I., Karlsson, M., et al.: Exploring user experience in the wild: facets of the modern car [C/OL]. In: Marcus, A. (ed.) Design, User Experience, and Usability: Interactive Experience Design (Duxu 2015), pp. 450–461 (2015)
20. Hornecker, E., Buur, J.: Getting a grip on tangible interaction: a framework on physical space and social interaction. In: Proceedings of the SIGCHI Conference on Human Factors in Computing Systems, pp. 437–446 (2006)

21. Harley, D., Chu, J.H., Kwan, J., et al.: Towards a framework for tangible narratives. In: Proceedings of the TEI 2016: Tenth International Conference on Tangible, Embedded, and Embodied Interaction, pp. 62–69 (2016)

22. Bruner, J.: Studies in cognitive growth : a collaboration at the center for cognitive studies [C/OL] (1966)

23. Tversky, B., Lee, P.U.: How space structures language [M/OL], pp. 157–175 (1998)

24. Julie, A., Gerard, F., Barbara, H.: The power of the tale: using narratives for organisational success (2002)

25. Rasmussen, L.B.: The narrative aspect of scenario building - How story telling may give people a memory of the future [J/OL]. AI & Soc. **19**(3), 229–249 (2005)

26. Ryan, M.L.: Beyond myth and metaphor: narrative in digital media [J/OL]. Poetics Today. **23**, 581–609 (2002)

27. Gupta, S., Tanenbaum, T.J., Tanenbaum, K.: Shiva's Rangoli: tangible storytelling through diegetic interfaces in ambient environments [C/OL]. pp. 65–75 (2019)

28. Odom, W., Zimmerman, J., Davidoff, S. et al.: A fieldwork of the future with user enactments[C/OL]. 338–347 (2012)

29. Pettersson, I., Karlsson, I.C.M.: Setting the stage for autonomous cars: a pilot study of future autonomous driving experiences [J/OL]. IET Intel. Transp. Syst. **9**(7), 694–701 (2015)

30. Ive, H.P., Sirkin, D., Miller, D., et al.: "Don't make me turn this seat around!": driver and passenger activities and positions in autonomous cars [C/OL]. pp. 50–55 (2015)

31. Pettersson, I. Ju, W.: Design techniques for exploring automotive interaction in the drive towards automation [C/OL]. pp. 147–160 (2017)

32. Geutner, P., Steffens, F., Manstetten, D.: Design of the VICO spoken dialogue system: evaluation of user expectations by wizard-of-OZ experiments [C/OL] (2002)

33. Pettersson, I., Rydström, A., Strömberg, H., et al.: Living room on the move: autonomous vehicles and social experiences [J/OL]. pp. 1–3 (2016)

34. Stromberg, H., Pettersson, I., Andersson, J., et al.: Designing for social experiences with and within autonomous vehicles - exploring methodological directions [J/OL]. Des. Sci. **4**, 13 (2018)

Research on the Efficiency of Continuous Warning Sound Time Interval in Perceiving Hazards of eVTOL Low Altitude Flight Obstacles

Yanxin Shu, Bingxi Wang[✉], Daiquan Bian, Mingyang Gao, and Ning Xin

The Second Reserach Institue of Civil Aviation Administration of China, Chengdu, SiChuan, China
yanxin.shu@foxmail.com, wangbingxi@caacsri.com

Abstract. The scale of China's general aviation industry is developing rapidly, Various new types of passenger short-distance air transportation vehicles are continuously emerging, among which the rise of electric vertical takeoff and landing aircraft (eVTOL) provides a new means of low-altitude flight. The pilotability of passenger aircraft is a necessary condition for flight. In low-visibility environments, when an eVTOL encounters obstacles during flight, how the onboard warning sounds efficiently alert the pilot is an important means to assist in improving flight safety. This paper starts by considering the time intervals between warning sounds. By designing multiple experimental groups with different warning sound time intervals, experiments were conducted in a simulated flight environment, and data was collected. The analysis of the subjects warning recognition efficiency and subjective evaluation scales in different experimental groups, The conclusion was drawn that shorter time intervals between warning sounds are more effective in perceiving danger, providing suggestions for the design of the warning sound module in the obstacle avoidance alarm system for future eVTOL pilot flights.

Keywords: Aviation safety · General aviation · Human-computer interaction · Warning sounds · Danger perception

1 Introduction

In recent years, the scale of general aviation has developed rapidly. In 2016, the General Office of the State Council of China issued the "Guiding Opinions on Promoting the Development of General Aviation Industry," proposing to expand the opening of low-altitude airspace, leading the domestic general aviation aircraft industry into a path of rapid development. Looking at policies both domestically and internationally, Countries around the world are promoting the rapid development of eVTOLs (Electric Vertical Take-Off and Landing), the Federal Aviation Administration (FAA) in the United States and the European Union Aviation Safety Agency (EASA) respectively supported the development of eVTOL by amending airworthiness certification regulations in 2016 and 2019. The Civil Aviation Administration of China (CAAC) began implementation of the "Airworthiness Regulations for Normal Category Aircraft" (CCAR-23-R4) in 2022, promoting the rapid application of new technologies on aircraft covered by Part 23 and reducing the certification cost for eVTOLs, with their compact size, high safety, low noise, minimal pollution, low manufacturing and operational costs, and small space requirements for takeoff and landing [1], have become an important solution for developing future Urban Air Mobility(UAM), alleviating urban commuting congestion, and improving the efficiency of short-distance travel. The transition from carrying objects to carrying people is an inevitable outcome of the development of urban air transportation. In April 2022, the airworthiness certification process for the largest domestic class of eVTOL, the AE200 model by AEROFUGIA, was officially launched. In February 2023, the XPENG Motors' Traveler X2 officially obtained a Special Flight Certificate issued by the Civil Aviation Administration of China's Central and Southern Region, making the Traveler X2 the first manned eVTOL product approved in China.

On July 18, 2023, the Federal Aviation Administration (FAA) released a detailed implementation plan for Advanced Air Mobility (AAM), titled "Advanced Air Mobility (AAM) Implementation Plan V1.0." The operational section of the plan mentions that pilots will be able to fly new advanced mobility aircraft between multiple locations, following predetermined flight plans, with pilots on board.

The arrival of the AAM era will see eVTOL aircraft redefine the structure of cities, suburbs, and towns, greatly expanding the scope of people's living and production activities. The efficient operation of eVTOL aircraft in the air not only avoids the congestion of ground transportation but also significantly reduces passengers' travel time, thereby enhancing the efficiency of time utilization and further stimulating and strengthening human creative potential. As a result, the three-dimensional transportation model is gradually becoming a new trend and norm in social development. The development of eVTOL involves continuous exploration in many aspects. Among them, low-altitude obstacles are a major factor affecting flight safety. The risk of flying into obstacles is higher in conditions of low visibility [2]. Generally, warning markers are set for obstacles to improve the warning efficiency. It is also important to enhance the pilot's awareness of danger during flight. In the urban backgrounds with clusters of towering and dense supertall buildings, obstacles become more concealed in the pilot's field of view. Therefore, it is crucial to find ways to enable pilots to perceive obstacles more effectively during the eVTOL flight process. This article conducts experiments and discussions from the perspective of improving the perception of pilots during eVTOL flights.

2   Aviation Safety Based on Sound Perception

Currently, during the flight process, pilots primarily detect obstacles through visual means, with the source of information coming from warning sign devices installed on the obstacles. The International Civil Aviation Organization's (ICAO) Annex 14, "International Standards and Recommended Practices", as well as China's "Civil Aviation Law of the People's Republic of China" and the "Technical Standards for Airfield Area of Civil Airports" (MH5001–2021) all provide comprehensive regulations for the installation of warning signs on tall buildings. In the densely built-up urban environment, pilots need to allocate greater visual attention to the identification and anticipation of obstacles, and to the execution of evasive flight maneuvers, which leads to an increase in psychological stress for pilots. Studies have shown that sound is a primary influence on human peripheral attention and represents an effective supplementary means of information acquisition in addition to visual channels [3, 4]. Throughout the cognitive process, the auditory pathway is the shortest and most direct route of cognition, and it persists throughout the entire process [5, 6]. Among the three modes of information perception—visual, auditory, and tactile—changes in sound signals have a more pronounced effect on human attention [7]. For ground transportation vehicles, researchers have found that when image and sound information are presented simultaneously, drivers respond more rapidly [8].

Warning sounds can assist pilots in perceiving danger, and the sound warning systems on aircraft are constantly being developed and improved. In recent years, the continuous development and widespread installation of the Terrain Awareness and Warning System (TAWS) have significantly reduced the rate of Controlled Flight Into Terrain (CFIT) accidents due to a lack of awareness of the surrounding terrain. The Helicopter Terrain Awareness and Warning System (HTWAS) is an improved version of TAWS [9, 10]. Its principle involves collecting data from the aircraft's sensor system, processing it through algorithms such as the Ground Proximity Warning System (GPWS), altitude reporting, terrain lookahead, and display algorithms, as well as wind shear alarm algorithms. The system then outputs the results, which are communicated to the pilot through aural warnings via the speaker system, visual warnings via alarm lights, and the Electronic Flight Information System (EFIS).Obstacles that are not easily detectable from a flight perspective, such as transmission cables between utility poles and the connecting parts between tall buildings, are difficult to update and identify in real-time within terrain databases due to their rapid changes and small physical size. Research and development of more complex terrain awareness and warning systems are currently being explored and validated both domestically and internationally [11–13]. eVTOL share many similarities with traditional helicopters in terms of takeoff, landing, and flight operations, thus there is much content available for reference in the research and application of flight warning sounds. Obstacles that are not easily detectable from a flight perspective, such as High voltage power lines between towers and the connecting parts between tall buildings, are difficult to update and identify in real-time within terrain databases due to their rapid changes and small physical size. During the driving process, warning sounds can affect the emotions and psychology of drivers [14]. Experiments have shown that in a noisy driving environment, high-frequency warning sounds are more effective in conveying information [15]. The eVTOL aircraft share many similarities with traditional helicopters in terms of takeoff, landing, and flight operations, thus there is much content available for reference in the research and application of flight warning sound.

Aircraft warning sound are typically categorized into four levels: emergency (level 3), abnormal (level 2), advisory (level 1), and information (level 0). The higher the number, the higher the priority for alerting. For example, Enhanced Ground Proximity Warning System (EGPWS), Traffic Alert and Collision Avoidance System (TCAS), fire, main warning, landing gear, cabin altitude, and unable to take off (wing flaps or slats in an incorrect position/rudder trim in an incorrect position/brakes in an incorrect position/

spoilers in an incorrect position), and the autopilot (normal or abnormal) are all classified as level 3 alerts. The warning sounds for these alerts also vary, such as a fire alarm which is a bell, and an overspeed alert which is a "HIGH SPEED" voice message. The warning sound for encountering and avoiding obstacles during flight is of the highest priority and requires an immediate signal to inform the pilot. This method is also applicable to eVTOL. The warning and alerting system is a comprehensive system. This article aims to explore the impact of changes in the duration of continuous warning sounds on the alerting efficiency and psychological response of pilots flying eVTOLs. It also aims to investigate additional visual aids to enhance the possibility of improving flight safety, and to provide recommendations for the design and development of future flight warning system sound alarms.

3 Simulation Experiment of Obstacle Avoidance for eVTOL Low-Altitude Flight

This experiment aims to simulate a visual flight scene at night with low visibility over an urban area, where an aircraft is flying at a constant speed along a set route. There is a tall building obstacle on the flight path that may pose a risk to flight safety. As the aircraft approaches the obstacle, a warning sound is triggered to alert the pilot, prompting evasive action. Multiple sets of identical flight experiments are designed with the variable being the time intervals between the warning sounds with the same timbre heard by the subjects. The objective is to explore the changes in reaction time and subjective judgments of the subjects after hearing the warning sounds.

3.1 Experimental Design

The experimental environment is shown in Fig. 1, where flat ground is set at 0 m. The simulated urban terrain is 3600 m long and 3600 m wide, with a total flying distance across the city of 3600 m. The simulation for eVTOL perspective is from a viewpoint with a field of view of 120°. The cruising altitude for domestic eVTOL products is approximately 300 m to 600 m, hence the flight altitude is set at a fixed 350 m. The flight attitude is horizontal forward, with a cruising speed of 60 m/s and an aircraft climb speed of 10 m/s. The total duration of the entire flight is 60 s.

On a clear and cloudless night, with the average height of ground buildings at 180 m, the aviation obstacle lights on the rooftops are functioning normally. At a distance of 2400 m from the flight origin, there is a twin-tower connected structure building, standing at a height of 380 m. The twin towers are spaced 100 m apart and connected by a bridge structure at a height of 360 m at the top and 350 m at the bottom. The eVTOL is set to approach and fly through the twin-tower connected structure. The aural warning system on the aircraft is programmed to initiate warnings when the aircraft is 600 m away from the bridge structure obstacle, and the warnings will continue until the aircraft reaches a distance of 0 from the bridge structure obstacle, with a total alert duration of 10 s.

To simplify the obstacle avoidance flight operation, it is established that upon hearing the warning sound, the test subject will press the obstacle avoidance button. The aircraft will then automatically climb to a height of 400 m and continue to fly forward at a constant speed of 60 m/s to navigate over the twin-tower structure. As depicted in Fig. 2, the warning sound is stereo, with a fixed frequency of 2000 Hz and a duration of 200 ms. To investigate the effect of the warning sound on humans, the flight simulation environment is designed to simulate not only the warning sound but also the engine noise experienced during the aircraft's flight.

3.2 Experimental Content

Five sets of comparative experiments are to be established. In Experiment 1, the aircraft does not emit any warning sounds throughout the entire flight. In Experiments 2, 3, 4, and 5, the aircraft begins emitting warning sounds when it approaches structural obstacles of bridge connections at a distance of 600 m. The duration of the warning sounds is set at 10 s. The specific intervals for the warning sounds in each experiment are as follows: Experiment 2 emits warning sounds at intervals of 100 ms, Experiment 3 at intervals of 300 ms, Experiment 4 at intervals of 600 ms, and Experiment 5 at intervals of 1000 ms.

The experiment was conducted in a closed room, inviting 30 participants with normal hearing, intelligence, and judgment. The simulation of the flight process was displayed on a 27-inch 4k monitor. The participants were asked to sit upright next to the monitor, with their line of sight parallel to the monitor and their glasses 80cm away from the screen. An alarm speaker was used with left and right stereo sound. In front of the monitor, there was a simulated flight obstacle avoidance button, which, when pressed, would cause the aircraft to climb. The participants were informed that the simulation task involved flying an aircraft at a constant speed and fixed altitude. There might be obstacles ahead that could affect the flight. They were instructed to try to maintain a safe distance from obstacles in front or below while ensuring flight safety. The climbing opportunity was limited to once. Each participant sat quietly for 30 s before the experiment to ensure a calm state of mind. The experiments were randomized and divided into 5 groups, with each participant performing only once per group. The timing of the experiment was recorded in seconds, accurate to 0.01s.

The flight scoring was established as follows: when the aircraft reaches the same horizontal position as the tower, if the vertical distance of the aircraft exceeds the total height of the tower by 380 m, it is deemed to have successfully avoided the obstacle and considered a safe flight, scoring 2 points. If the vertical distance of the aircraft is between 360 and 380 m, and it flies through the gap between the twin towers, it is considered a dangerous flight, scoring 1 point. If the participant does not press the climb button, or if the vertical distance of the aircraft is at 350 m, the aircraft will collide with the connecting bridge structure, which is deemed a failed flight, scoring 0 points. During the experiment, the time at which the participant presses the obstacle avoidance button is recorded, as well as whether each trial results in a successful or failed obstacle avoidance. Please translate this paragraph into English without grammatical or lexical errors, and ensure that the translation is related to the civil aviation field.

The experiment recorded the time for each participant from the start of the experiment to the moment they pressed the button. To facilitate the recording of whether any participants pressed the button before the warning sound was emitted, a button response time difference (c) was established. The time from the start of the experiment to the emission of the warning sound was recorded as point a, and the time when the button was pressed was recorded as point (b). The equation (c = b - a) was used, where a negative value of (c) indicated that the button was pressed before the warning sound was emitted. A positive value of (c) that approaches 0 indicates a faster reaction. For the experimental groups where no warning sound was recorded, only the time at point (b) was recorded. Please translate this paragraph into English without grammatical or lexical errors, ensuring that the translation is related to the civil aviation field.

Each participant is scored using a subjective scale after each set of experiments. First, an evaluation scale for the intuitive feeling of flying is established, with scores ranging from 1 to 9. The evaluation is conducted from two dimensions, as follows:

1. The degree of attention attracted by obstacles ahead during the entire flight is scored, with 1 point indicating no attention at all, and 9 points being the full score, indicating that it very clearly attracted my attention.
2. The extent to which visual attention concentration improved during the entire flight is scored, with 1 point indicating no improvement in attention, and 9 points being the full score, indicating that the participant maintained a very high level of attention in the subsequent flight process.

The comparative experiment can be understood as a comparison of user usage on the same operating system, with the addition of warning sounds and changes in the intervals between warning sounds. To facilitate comparison, a flight attefntion intuitive feeling scale System Usability Scale (SUS) were established, each comprising 10 items for on-site scoring. This scale consists of 10 questions, with odd numbered items as positive statements and even numbered items as negative statements. It evaluates the experience of the warning sound system added to groups 2–5 in the entire flight simulation operation process. The 4th, 5th, and 10th evaluation scales are related to effectiveness and ease of learning; The evaluation scales 2, 3, 7, and 8 are related to usage efficiency and usability; The 1st, 6th, and 9th evaluation scales are related to satisfaction.

After all the experiments are concluded, the survey questionnaire results will be statistically analyzed (Fig. 3).

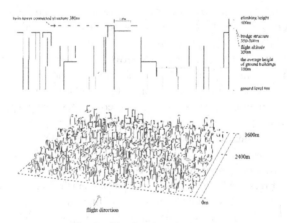

Fig. 1. Simulated environment

Fig. 2. Acoustic spectrum of warning sound

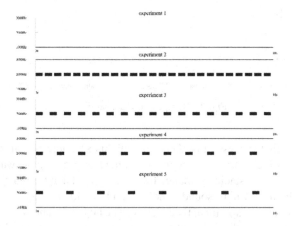

Fig. 3. Spectrogram of the time interval of the warning sound

4   Experimental Results

To facilitate the display of the overall reaction times of each participant in the 5 experimental groups and for comparison of the distribution characteristics of multiple datasets, as shown in Fig. 4, a boxplot of reaction times was created. It can be observed that the group without an auditory warning had the largest range of values, indicating a higher degree of data dispersion compared to the groups with auditory warnings. The interquartile range (IQR) values of the groups with auditory warnings were generally not significantly different from each other, with the 100 ms interval and 300 ms interval groups showing similar values, as did the 600 ms interval and 1000 ms interval groups. This suggests that the experimental groups with auditory warnings had more concentrated overall results. The 100 ms interval group had reaction times in a lower range, indicating an overall faster response speed.

The statistical analysis of the flight scores, as shown in Fig. 5, reveals that the flight scores of the experimental group without warning sounds are generally lower compared to the group with warning sounds. The experimental group without warning sounds exhibited more dangerous flights and failed flights during the testing process. The accumulated total scores and average scores of the group with warning sounds are generally

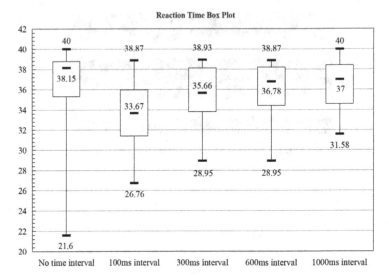

Fig. 4. Box plot of reaction time

higher, indicating that successful or dangerous flights are more prevalent. When combined with Fig. 6, which represents the reaction time from hearing the warning sound to pressing the button for obstacle avoidance flight, it is found that the reaction time differences between the no-warning-sound condition and the 300 ms, 600 ms, and 1000 ms interval conditions are not significantly different. The larger variance for the no-warning-sound condition suggests that without the warning sound, participants' reaction times varied widely. Some individuals were able to judge the distance of obstacles through sight almost equally quickly, while others may not have been able to assess whether the obstacles posed a flight risk, resulting in premature risk avoidance and larger sample variability. The mean reaction time for the 100 ms interval is the lowest. According to the interviews conducted after the experiment, some participants felt anxious with a short, insistent warning sound, prompting them to press the button for danger avoidance quickly. The results for the 300 ms, 600 ms, and 1000 ms intervals do not differ significantly, showing a slight trend of longer reaction times with greater interval spacing. Whether this trend is statistically significant would require further analysis.

The flight performance scores from five experimental groups were compiled and integrated, as depicted in Fig. 7. A scoring graph was constructed with the degree of attention attraction as the horizontal axis and the degree of improvement in attention focus as the vertical axis. To facilitate the concentrated display of score distributions for each group, a heat map representation was utilized to highlight areas with a higher concentration of scores. The size of each point corresponds to the number of participants who assigned that particular score.

In reviewing the aggregate data from all experimental sessions, the distribution of scores was observed to be predominantly symmetrical, with the central axis of symmetry located at the point where both the horizontal and vertical axes intersect at the 5-point score. This symmetry is characterized by a gradient of decreasing score frequency as

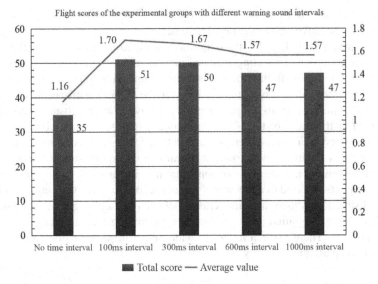

Fig. 5. Flight scores of the experimental groups with different warning sound intervals.

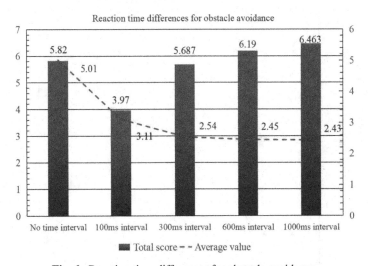

Fig. 6. Reaction time differences for obstacle avoidance.

one moves away from the central point towards the lower left and upper right quadrants of the rating scale.

The scores are distributed towards the lower left and upper right quadrants. The scores scattered in the lower left quadrant predominantly reflect the evaluations from the group without auditory warnings. Some participants opined that although the use of aviation lights facilitates the visualization of architectural obstacles at night, the absence of auditory warnings during flight does not provide sufficient alertness, resulting in a predominantly negative bias in their evaluations.

For the groups 2, 3, 4, and 5, the majority of evaluations cluster above the 5-point threshold on both axes, indicating that auditory warnings have a positive impact on obstacle detection during flight. Specifically, the groups with 100 ms, 300 ms, and 600 ms interval warnings are more commonly found in the higher positive evaluation zones, suggesting that these intervals are perceived as effective in aiding obstacle recognition.

The data distribution for the 1000 ms interval group is more variable. During the trials, as illustrated in Fig. 6, the average reaction time for obstacle avoidance was notably longer. In a noisy environment, participants heard a non-urgent, steady warning sound that may have induced a sense of confusion, unfamiliarity, or other emotional responses. Some participants reported that this sound was not recognized as a warning, leading to a potential distraction of their attention. Others believed that although the sound was not urgent, it may have signified impending danger, prompting them to prepare avoidance plans in advance. There exists a relatively wide range of interpretations regarding the efficacy of this particular auditory cue.

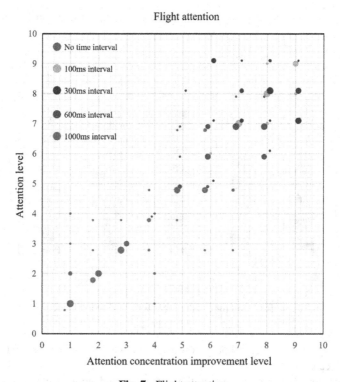

Fig. 7. Flight attention

To evaluate the usability of the warning sound system across four different time intervals in experimental groups, Fig. 7 was manipulated to overlay the cumulative ratings of all participants, thereby creating a flight attention map. The data from the

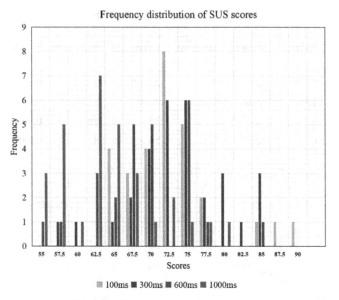

Fig. 8. SUS Score Frequency Distribution

five experimental groups exhibit an approximate symmetrical distribution around the central point where both the horizontal and vertical axes intersect at the 5-point score. In comparison to the flown conditions with auditory warnings, the subjective evaluations of flight attention without auditory warnings are consistently located in the lower scoring regions. The distribution of subjective evaluations for the 1000 ms group generally falls below the scoring regions of the other groups equipped with auditory warnings.

The SUS scale scores were statistically analyzed, and the frequency distribution of SUS ratings was plotted, as shown in Fig. 8. It was observed that the scores with a 1000 ms interval were generally lower, with the majority of scores in the 100 ms, 300 ms, and 600 ms groups falling between 65 and 75. Due to the variability in scoring results among individuals, the Shapiro-Wilk test was employed to ascertain whether the data adhered to a normal distribution, with a significance level set at $p = 0.05$, the calculated P-values were predominantly greater than 0.05,as shown in Table 1. To further validate the assumption of normal distribution, Q-Q plots were constructed, as shown in Fig. 9, which compared the distribution of each experimental group to the normal distribution. The plots reveal that most data points cluster around the red line, suggesting that the assumption of normal distribution for the experimental data is reasonable. However, there are also some points that deviate from the line, which may indicate the presence of outliers or skewness within the data, although the overall distribution is consistent with a normal distribution.

To confirm whether the duration of time intervals was the cause of these differences, Welch's ANOVA method was employed for the test. The null hypothesis proposed was that the means of the groups were equal, while the alternative hypothesis was that the means of the groups were not all equal. The calculations yielded an F-statistic of 11.9 with a p-value less than 0.01. Since the p-value is much smaller than the commonly used

Table 1. Shapiro Wilk test results

Experimental Group	Average	Median	Standard Deviation	Maximum	minimum	W value	P value
100 ms	72.3	72.5	7.17	52.5	90	0.915	0.020
300 ms	73.8	73.8	6.65	57.5	85	0.957	0.264
600 ms	69.8	70	6.14	55	85	0.960	0.306
1000 ms	64.2	62.5	6.61	55	80	0.936	0.073

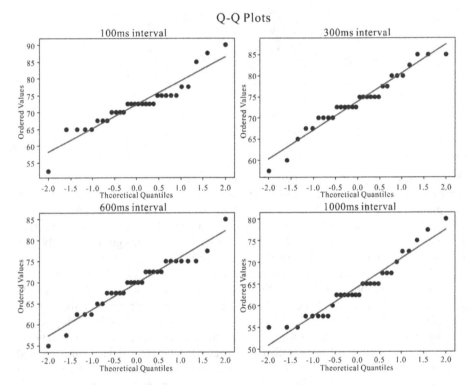

Fig. 9. Quantitative Plot of SUS Score

significance level, we can reject the null hypothesis. This implies that, based on our data, there is sufficient evidence to indicate that the duration of time intervals has a significant impact on subjective ratings.

Combining the comprehensive analysis of Figs. 4, 5, 6, 7 and 8, although the scores of all four experimental groups fall within the critical value and acceptable evaluation range, there are still some differences in the overall results. The total scores of the 1000 ms experimental group are mostly around 62.5 points, with the scores for effectiveness, learnability, efficiency, usability, and satisfaction being generally lower compared to the other three experimental groups. The longer duration intervals of the warning sounds make them less comprehensible to the participants, resulting in lower efficiency in assisting with the recognition of obstacles and an less than ideal auditory experience. The distribution of the scores for the 100 ms and 300 ms groups is similar, indicating that warning sounds with shorter time intervals are easier to understand and recognize, and they can better focus and enhance attention. During the experiment, some participants' scores fell within the critical value evaluation area, suggesting that subjective scale evaluations vary from person to person and may also be influenced by emotions or usage experiences outside of the test. Therefore, it is believed that most people have a better auditory experience and higher 辅助 warning efficiency with warning sound intervals of 100 ms and 300 ms.

5 Conclusion

This experiment approaches the topic from a very fine angle, exploring the impact of warning sounds on the driving experience through the perspective of acoustic intervals. By constructing an eTVOL simulated flight environment, different duration intervals of warning sounds were set, and the analysis was conducted from two perspectives: objective reaction data and subjective scale evaluations. The study analyzed the physiological and cognitive responses of participants to different warning sounds from three aspects: reaction time difference, subjective flight evaluation, and SUS system usability evaluation. It was found that in low-visibility environments, the presence of warning sounds can enhance the perception of low-altitude obstacle danger during flight. Among these, fixed-frequency warning sounds with shorter time intervals demonstrated better usability, assisting in improving flight attention and enhancing the efficiency of avoiding obstacles while flying. The overall evaluation of the flight experience was positive. Auditory assistance in judging low-altitude obstacles showed a certain positive effect, providing a reference for the design of sound modules in future flight warning systems.

Although the sample size of the experiment was small, and the selection of participants was limited, the results are somewhat representative and may vary from person to person. For the emotional types produced by different warning sounds in the experiment and the optimal duration intervals of warning sounds in various environments, future studies will conduct in-depth exploration and refinement.

References

1. Kawamoto, H.: Development trends and prospects for eVTOL: a new mode of air mobility. Mitsui & Co. Global Strategic Studies Institute Monthly Report, pp. 1–8 (2018)
2. Shu, Y.X., Gao, M.Y., Yan, F.S., et al.: Analysis and prospect of early warning technology for low AltitudeFlying obstacles in general aviation. In: Proceedings of the 10th China Aerospace Society Young Scientists Forum, pp. 584–588. Science Popularization Publishing House (2022)
3. Rocchesso, D., Serafin, S.: Sonic interaction design. Int. J. Hum. Comput. Stud. **67**(11), 905–906 (2009)
4. Favalli, S., Skov, T., Spence, C., Byrne, D.V.: Do you say it like you eat it? The sound symbolism of food names and its role in the multisensory product experience. Food Res. Int. **54**(1), 760–771 (2013)

5. Pressnitzer, D., Sayles, M., Micheyl, C., Winter, I.M.: Perceptual organization of sound begins in the auditory periphery. Curr. Biol. **18**(15), 1124–1128 (2008). https://doi.org/10.1016/j.cub.2008.06.053
6. Sussman, E., Wong, R., Horvath, J., Winkler, I., Wang, W.: The development of the perceptual organization of sound by frequency separation in 5–11-year-old children. Hear. Res. **225**(1–2), 117–127 (2007)
7. Stevens, M.N., Barbour, D.L., Gronski, M.P., Hullar, T.E.: Auditory contributions to maintaining balance. J. Vestib. Res. Equilibr. Orient. **26**(5–6), 433–438 (2016)
8. Geng, L.X., Liu, S.N., Liu, D.X.: Research on reaction time of driver. Energy Conser. Environ. Protect. Transp. **11**(2), 5 (2015). https://doi.org/10.3969/j.issn.1673-6478.2015.02.005
9. Kuchar, J.K.: Markov model of terrain for the evaluation of ground proximity warning system thresholds. J. Guid. Control. Dyn. **24**(3), 428–435 (2001)
10. Honeywell International Inc. MK VI and MK VIII Enhanced Ground Proximity Warning System pilot's guide (060-4314-000 Rev B). Honeywell International Inc. (2002)
11. Liu, Y. F.: Research on helicopter terrain alert warning simulation platform. Master's thesis, Nanjing University of Aeronautics and Astronautics (2017)
12. Zhang, Y.: Research and Imlemention of Portable TerrainAwareness System Based on Digital ElevationMap (DEM). Master's thesis, Civil Aviation Flight University of China (2016)
13. Li, S.Y., He, F., Zhao, C.L., Xiao, G.: Design of TAWS simulator. Electron. Sci. Technol. (11), 93–95+98 (2013). https://doi.org/10.16180/j.cnki.issn1007-7820.2013.11.006
14. Tong, Q., Jinrong, Y.: Relationship between sound perception and acoustics of seat-belt warning sound. Hum. Factors Ergon. Manuf. Serv. Ind. **31**(6), 693-705 (2021)
15. Hsu, M.C., Chen, H.J., Tsai, M.L., et al.: Effect of environmental noise, distance and warning sound on pedestrians' auditory detectability of electric vehicles. Int. J. Environ. Res. Public Health **18**(17), 9290 (2021)

User Experience Evaluation Indicators for Automotive Autonomous Driving Takeover System

Lei Wu[1], Qinqin Sheng[1], Yu Wu[2(✉)], and Banben He[3]

[1] School of Mechanical Science and Engineering, Huazhong University of Science and Technology, Wuhan 430074, People's Republic of China
[2] School of Art and Design, Wuhan University of Technology, Wuhan 430074, People's Republic of China
51434769@qq.com
[3] Dongfeng Motor Corporation Research & Development Institute, Wuhan 430058, People's Republic of China

Abstract. Automotive automation technology reduces the burden on humans, it also introduces new human factors and difficulties such as low or excessive cognitive load, lack of attention, and so on. However, the user experience review of the automotive autonomous driving takeover system has yet to establish a consistent standard. In this study, we use user research to better understand users' real needs, behavioral habits, and experience feelings, to clarify current problems in the user experience of the automotive autonomous driving takeover system, and to obtain and analyze user experience indexes to build a more comprehensive evaluation system with practical significance. In this study, we initially obtain the indicator dimensions through qualitative research methods and analyze and categorize them accordingly, apply the user experience evaluation method and model construction method, use the grounded theory to interpret the semi-structured interview materials in a bottom-up progressive description, refine the concepts and cluster categories, and construct the relevant evaluation indicator system by analyzing the logical relationship. This study systematically constructed user experience evaluation indicators for autonomous driving takeover systems in automobiles, which has corresponding guiding significance for relevant researchers.

Keywords: Intelligent vehicles · User experience evaluation · Automotive autonomous driving takeover system · Grounded theory

1 Introduction

Intelligent vehicles are a new generation of vehicles that are gradually transitioning from simple transportation instruments to intelligent mobile spaces equipped with partial or full autonomous driving capabilities [1]. Society of Automotive Engineers International (SAE) has proposed a six-level automation classification scheme [2], with L0 indicating no autonomous driving function, L1 and L2 indicating mostly driver assistance, and L3,

P.-L. P. Rau (Ed.): HCII 2024, LNCS 14702, pp. 161–177, 2024.
https://doi.org/10.1007/978-3-031-60913-8_12

L4, and L5 indicating high-level and fully autonomous driving capability [3]. This study focuses on L3-level autonomous driving, in which the system can do specific driving tasks under certain conditions while also recognizing problems it cannot manage and prompting the driver to take back control within a set time limit.

When the conditional self-driving car is unable to deal with the current working conditions, it will send a takeover request to the driver, and the driver must make a decision and respond to the takeover request as soon as possible, which is known as the self-driving takeover process [4]. While automation technology reduces human strain, it also adds new human factors difficulties, such as inattention, low or high cognitive load, and a lack of situational awareness [5]. Research in automobile interaction experience design focuses on interactive technologies and tools [6], user satisfaction, integrated touch panel studies, multi-channel interaction modes, and feedback [7]. The Automobile Autonomous Driving Takeover System's user experience is not currently standardized, however, several research has looked into models and evaluation methods. To investigate the quantitative indicators of takeover performance influencing elements and develop a high-precision takeover performance prediction model, Wang, W.J. [8] provided a thorough evaluation technique based on subjective assessment from the driver population. Summarizing the developments in user experience research in the field of intelligent vehicles from the perspectives of evaluation subjects, evaluation indicators, and evaluation methods, Tan H [9] examined the effects of the trend toward digitalization and intelligence of automobiles on the design and evaluation of automotive interaction interfaces. An upgraded Delphi approach and expert subjective assessment were utilized by Zhang X.J [10] of the China National Institute of Standardization to create an ergonomic design evaluation index system for automobile display interfaces. To create a more logical evaluation technique for the design of automobile all-LCD instrument interfaces, Jiang C.J. [11] from Jilin University conducted studies employing eye-tracking technology and applied the method of semantic differential method for subjective evaluation. This paper use user experience evaluation and model construction methods to collect and encode automotive autonomous driving takeover system user experience evaluation indicators using semi-structured interviews and grounded theory, and then summarize and determine the indicator dimensions, to provide a reference for improving the user experience of the automotive autonomous driving takeover system for drivers.

2 Methods

2.1 Research Methodology

Understanding how users initially obtain assessment indicators and analyzing and generalizing indicator dimensions make up the two key components of the research method. Understanding user acquisition metrics is the first step. The research content is conducted methodically using the user interview method, allowing for a more thorough collection and comprehension of the user's overall experience from the user's basic information, assisted driving information, and take-over evaluation information of the three clue dimensions. The study gathers as much information as it can about user experience, including knowledge, demand, sentiment, and feedback regarding the automotive autonomous driving takeover system. The indicator dimensions are analyzed and summarized in the second section. The indicators gathered from the insight portion of the study were coded, arranged, and separated using grounded theory. To broaden and synthesize ideas, as well as to innovate research, indicators with comparable properties are grouped based on the content relevance of the collected indicators.

As shown in Fig. 1, grounded theory is a research methodology whereby the investigator conducts a process- and interaction-driven bottom-up progressive descriptive interpretation of empirical materials, refines concepts, clusters categories, and builds pertinent theories by examining the logical relationship between core categories [12]. The concepts of the dimensional evaluation indicators division are gathered from a substantial quantity of intricate research factual data using the grounded theory method, which is also utilized to analyze and summarize the indicator dimensions stage in this study. The establishment of the system framework is effectively promoted by the dimension evaluation index division ideas.

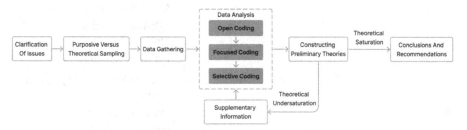

Fig. 1. Steps in grounded theory research

2.2 Preparation for Interview Research

There is a large selection of smart car products on the market, and the brands that sell most of them include Tesla, Huawei, XPENG motors, NIO, and so on. Thus, from October 2023 to December 2023, purposive sampling was employed in this study to interview owners of Tesla, Huawei, XPENG motors, and NIO. Twelve interview subjects were chosen after the information saturation concept was used to calculate the sample size. Based on their skill level and comprehension of the autonomous driving system, users are divided into novice users, regular users, and power users, which defines the study's scope in the context of L3 conditional autonomous driving. Novice users are those who have driven before and have used assisted or autonomous driving features; they are less skilled at autonomous driving and have a lesser comprehension of the autonomous driving takeover system. Regular users are individuals who have a greater degree of driving experience as well as more expertise with automated driving; these individuals are better knowledgeable about autonomous driving and are accustomed to its features and modes of operation; Power users are individuals who possess extensive driving experience, are professionals in automotive design, and are experts in their field. They are well-versed in the autonomous driving vehicle's human-computer interaction system and have conducted extensive research and have more experience designing automotive interfaces and human-computer interactions design.

Semi-structured interviews—that is, unstructured conversations carried out in line with a loose framework—allow for the abstraction of pertinent concepts and categories using grounded theory as well as the understanding of the interviewees' feelings and perceptions. They also yield rich, vivid, and detailed textual information in a relatively informal setting [13]. As shown in Table 1, the interview plan is primarily divided into three sections: basic user information, aided driving information and takeover evaluation information.

Table 1. Semi-structured interviews

No.	Level 1	Level 2	Questions
1	Basic user information	Basic information	Q1: How old are you?
2			Q2: What gender are you?
3			Q3: Your current place of residence?
4			Q4: What is your line of work?
5		Driving habits	Q5: At what point did you start driving?
6			Q6: In what situation do you drive most often?
7			Q7: What is your typical frequency of vehicle use?
8	Aided driving information	Driver assistance habits	Q8: To what extent are you familiar with driver assistance, or autonomous driving?
9			Q9: What autopilot setup do you often use? How long have you been using it?
10			Q10: In your daily driving, how frequently do you utilize autopilot features such as automated cruise control? How often do you use it?
11			Q11: What kinds of driving technology support services are most frequently used?
12			Q12: What are some scenarios where the driving assistance features are activated?

(continued)

Table 1. (*continued*)

No.	Level 1	Level 2	Questions
13		Evaluation of driver assistance	Q13: Why is the driver aid feature activated in this case, or why is it off?
14			Q14: What is your impression of the driver-aid feature? Does the system suddenly flashback when you're driving? Will there be an unforeseen circumstance involving a withdrawal?
15			Q15: Are there any aspects of driver assistance that you believe ought to be offered but aren't at the moment?
16			Q16: Which aspects of the driver assistance features require improvement?
17	Takeover evaluation information	Driver status	Q17: Do you know how the current in-car takeover system works? Is it utilized frequently?
18			Q18: When using automated cruise control, what is your usual course of action?
19			Q19: When your car is operating on autopilot, do you still keep an eye on the road?
20		Taking over	Q20: How does the system typically notify you when it's time to resume driving?
21		Taking over evaluation	Q21: After engaging in non-driving chores, what is the typical timeframe for you to resume driving?
22			Q22: What sort of alerts about a takeover would you notice initially?
23			Q23: How do you feel about takeover alarms in general? How many times, on a scale of 1 to 10, would you think about rating a widely utilized system?
24			Q24: What sort of takeover are you anticipating?

(*continued*)

Table 1. (*continued*)

No.	Level 1	Level 2	Questions
25			Q25: Are you happy with the driver takeover system's visual cueing interface? Do you find the vibration of the sound satisfactory? Do you think the light effects are satisfactory?
26			Q26: Do you believe that taking control of the car carries any risk?

In this study, one-on-one interviews were conducted with the interviewees based on the interview outline and recorded throughout the entire interview, which lasted 40~80 min/times, and the interviewees were given an honorarium of RMB 100 yuan. After each interview, the interviewer organized the content of the interview into textual information and provided timely feedback to the respondents to further supplement and improve the relevant information. Before the interview, the interviewer explains the main purpose and content of the interview, and then proceed with the interview after obtaining the interviewee's consent, and the interviewer should pay attention to recording the interviewee's expression, tone of voice, and movement during the interview.

2.3　The Process of Interview Research

In-depth interviews were conducted through both online and offline channels, and in light of the current resource situation, a total of 12 sample subjects were recruited for this research, of which the sample capacity for online interviews was 9, and the sample capacity for offline household interviews was 3. The recruited sample subjects were in the range of young and middle-aged white-collar workers aged between 20–40 years old, and all of them had experience in using at least one automotive self-driving system, to avoid homologous errors and to ensure the quality and validity of the research results as much as possible. To avoid homologation errors and maximize the quality and validity of the research results, the sample covers users of different genders, ages, and product usage backgrounds. The numbers and information of the sample are summarized in Table 2.

Table 2. Summary of information about respondents

No.	Type	Name	Age	Experience	Area	Autonomous driving system
1	Novice user	Ms. Wu	24	1 year	Nanjing	NIO
2	Novice user	Ms. Xiao	39	10 years	Wuhan	Tesla
3	Regular user	Ms. Zou	24	1 year	Hangzhou	Tesla
4	Power user	Mr. Qian	32	10 years	Hangzhou	Tesla
5	Power user	Ms. Zuo	28	10 years	Shanghai	Mercedes-Benz
6	Power user	Mr. He	35	10 years	Wuhan	Dongfeng
7	Power user	Mr. Wang	35	5 years	Beijing	XPENG
8	Power user	Ms. Li	37	5 years	Shanghai	Huawei
9	Regular user	Mr. Huang	26	6 years	Hangzhou	NIO
10	Regular user	Mr. Jiang	32	13 years	Shenzhen	NIO
11	Novice user	Mr. Jiang	27	5 years	Shanghai	XPENG
12	Regular user	Mr. Liu	31	5 years	Wuhan	NIO

The sample selected for this study had an equitable distribution of male-to-female proportions, with 42% of the sample being female and 58% of the sample being male. As shown in Fig. 2, the age distribution of the sample subjects was 17% in the 20–25 age range, 25% in the 26–30 age range, 41% in the 30–35 age range, and 17% in the 36–40 age range. As shown in Fig. 3, different user types are involved in the distribution of sample objects, with a generally even distribution of each type of user: 25% of novice users, 33% of senior users, and 42% of expert users.

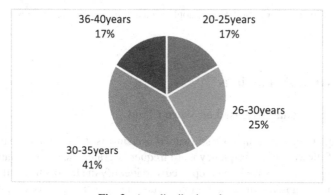

Fig. 2. Age distribution chart

As shown in Fig. 4, NIO, Tesla, XPENG, Huawei, and Dongfeng Motor are among the car brands whose autopilot systems are most frequently used by the sample subjects. NIO, Tesla, and XPENG have a higher number of sample subjects than the other brands,

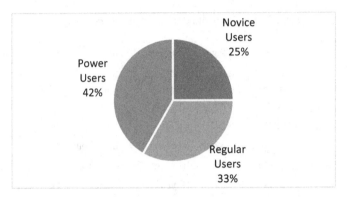

Fig. 3. Type distribution percentage chart

which is consistent with the current situation where Tesla, NIO, XPENG, and other brands are leading the competition for intelligent electric vehicles in China.

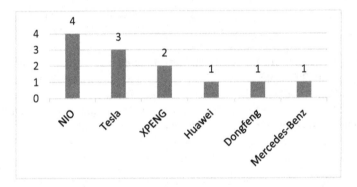

Fig. 4. Distribution of commonly used automated driving systems

3 Results and Discussions

3.1 Preliminary Analysis Based on Word Cloud

NVivo 11.0 qualitative data analysis software is used in this study for data analysis. First, to create the following high-frequency word frequency graph, the original data of the 11 interview sample subjects were read repeatedly to identify the factors that influenced the user experience evaluation of the automotive autonomous driving takeover system. The words that had the highest rankings were driving, automation, functionality, assisting, problem, reminding, taking over, needing, using, experience, system, prompting, etc., as shown in Fig. 5.

Fig. 5. High-frequency word cloud map

3.2 Open Coding

Open coding, also known as initial coding, is a research process in which textual materials are sorted and interpreted according to certain principles. Firstly, the long paragraphs in the original data are streamlined and turned into short concepts, and secondly, the subordinate categories between the concepts are explored in depth. In the coding process, it is necessary to try to avoid the researcher's subjective ideas and inherent thinking about things, restore the original connotation of the text to the greatest extent possible, and summarize the formation of the initial concept, as shown in Table 3.

Table 3. Open Coding

Original representative statement (partial)	Concept tags	Initial category
It's all there, the whole transparency of information is higher, and then it leads you to the status of the car, the status of the takeover, and the status of the road conditions are very clear	Distinct messages in a clear manner	Details openness
Linkage is the best way because now it is also linked, will steering wheel will vibrate, like lane departure, and the steering wheel will vibrate, it will not voice prompts, but the pilot-assisted driving exit, is the dashboard will display, and then voice notification, but the steering wheel will not vibrate, that is to see it should be out of the function of its needs	Clarity of takeover information	
As for him saying that the LIDAR is abnormal or which abnormalities I can know, but because I understand where the LIDAR is, but a lot of users he does not know what the LIDAR is. He knows that this information may not be of much use to him, that is, anyway, can be said to be able to remind him in time to take over, I think he has realized his meaning, to achieve his purpose	Interaction of touch, aural, and visual information	Combinations of multiple modes

(continued)

Table 3. (*continued*)

Original representative statement (partial)	Concept tags	Initial category
A driver who feels the steering wheel move is certainly obvious, a normal driver would be an immediate reaction to such a situation	Operation prompt for the next step	Instructional clarity
He now has seatbelt vibration and many different kinds of alerts. I think that is a bit redundant, but overall acceptable, and visual alerts	Quick reaction to alarms	Alarm timeliness
The key is that this will not scare the driver, or he may still have a gradual process, let's say I transitioned from voice to alarm and then transitioned to vibration, I think there is such a transition will be relatively better	Redundant prompts	Alarm redundancy
For example, the simplest, you overtake at high speed, there is a large truck on the right, and you oversize trucks, it the car system to determine my lateral distance from it is enough. But, the human driver sitting inside, his human perspective to see his words, this distance feels very close, very dangerous. Then in that case we humans might panic and take over on our own	Gives people anxiety	Alarm irritation
When we are on autopilot, I may be relatively more relaxed. But he has a reminder, if my eyes are out of the road for a long time, or I have twisted my head, attention drift, there will be a reminder	Adheres to the customs and expectations of human drivers	Compliance with expectations for driving
Because he has a feature that may prevent you from fatigue if you have been out on the road for a long time, the screen will show that you have to turn the steering wheel, but the angle at which it turns the steering wheel is only a little bit	Constraints on non-driving tasks	Tracking of driver conduct

3.3 Focused Coding

Through open coding, the concepts and initial categories of the original information were established, and to find out how the different categories and concepts are related to each other in open coding, this stage will link the severed information again and try to find out the cause and effect relationship between the different variables according to the process of focused coding in grounded theory, as shown in Table 4.

Table 4. Focused coding

Secondary nodes	Tertiary nodes	Amount
Alarm safety	Details openness	10
	Combinations of multiple modes	16
	Instructional clarity	18
	Alarm timeliness	6
	Alarm redundancy	5
	Alarm irritation	13
Driving safety	Compliance with expectations for driving	14
	Tracking of driver conduct	8
	Anti-fatigue alert	6
	Safety distance limit	6
	Human-computer interaction safety	3
Technical safety	Iteration timeliness	11
	Technology maturity	10
	Data perfection	9
	Clarity of responsibility	12
System reliability	Road compatibility	5
	Risk controllability	4
	Frequency of accidents	16
	System misjudgment rate	8
Predictability	Vehicle status alert	4
	Road condition prediction	8
	Hierarchical takeover warning	13
	Flexible real-time feedback	1
Integrity	Function richness	5
	Failure response	7
	Emergency road condition handling	11
	Exit compensation program	7
Efficiency	Takeover completion	4
	Takeover completion time	9
	Passing efficiency	2
Driver status	Safety awareness	10
	Fatigue level	2

(*continued*)

Table 4. (*continued*)

Secondary nodes	Tertiary nodes	Amount
	Stress management	3
	Concentration	12
Perceived complexity	Road environment judgment	23
	System interaction complexity	8
	Driving state judgment	11
Satisfaction	Personalization	16
	Comfort	26
	Trust	17
	Intelligence	23
Experience load	Smoothness	4
	Usability	10

3.4 Selective Coding

Selective coding is an in-depth and systematic analysis of the main categories based on the internal logic of each category. From the summarized categories, we extract and mine the core categories and storylines of a summarized nature. The core categories

Table 5. Selective coding

Main scope	Selective coding	Amount
Security	Alarm safety	55
	Driving safety	39
	Technical safety	44
	System reliability	33
Completeness	Predictability	26
	Integrity	30
Efficiency	Takeover completion	4
	Takeover completion efficiency	9
	Passage efficiency	2
Situational awareness	Driver capability	3
	Driver status	36
	Perceived complexity	42
Subjective experience	Satisfaction	82
	Experience load	14

have the role and significance of a high degree of condensation of the theory, which can integrate the relationship between the categories to form a relatively complete theoretical interpretation structure, as shown in Table 5.

3.5 Theoretical Sampling and Saturation

Sampling was stopped when the core category reached saturation. A saturation test was performed on the one set aside and found that no new information on the core category emerged, as shown in Table 6.

Table 6. Theoretical sampling and saturation

Selected source materials	Open coding
There are also sounds, some of which are based on the intensity of the sound, the volume of the sound, and the frequency of the sound, reflecting different emergencies, all of which can serve as effective reminders. If a single visual reminder is not enough	Details openness
Interference is there. Sometimes it's also annoying, I know I won't play all the time, but he still reminds me, but he's sure it's not like he can read minds, and it's not like he knows what I'm thinking at the time. This is a very normal reminder, and it's necessary to have it. But, understandably, this one doesn't work	Alarm redundancy
The vast majority of them are put in his pipe, just sometimes is to meet some very large truck, when he drove a little bit, bias a little bit off the lane of that kind of situation, this kind of scenario may be triggered to take over my own	Compliance with expectations for driving
Including that seat belt, I use I think it is better. I was chewing gum, and then my mouth was wide open, he thought I was yawning, so subconsciously he would pull you	System misjudgment rate
For example, when I was driving myself, one of the features of the Tesla that was better was the anti-tailgating feature, that is, for example, if I suddenly got too close to the car in front of me, he would drop. That's very good, and then I subconsciously put my foot on the brake, and that's very good	Function richness

(continued)

Table 6. (*continued*)

Selected source materials	Open coding
Just that I'm in this kind of assisted driving scenario, I may be able to be more relaxed mentally, the posture I can be more relaxed if I have to go to do something extra, then maybe drink water, then I may briefly leave the steering wheel, this I think is the most appear a practical scenario, less likely to go to play the phone, or go to play the game, or to take a nap	Concentration
I have more confidence in the car, but not so much in our road conditions	Road environment judgment
It will display the surrounding vehicle situation, around what people, cars, the display the surrounding realities, I will stare at the screen to compare, for example, people close to me, but the reality is that people have been close to me for a second, the screen has a delay	System interaction complexity
In my daily driving state, I can play my vehicle very strong perception of this ability to identify the surrounding driving risks, and then help me to make a better judgment of the vehicle driving state	Driving state judgment
This may be related to personal preference the design can be done in the car machine inside an option, that is, the driver can choose what voice reminders	Personalization

3.6 Integration and Establishment of Indicators

In summary, through the collection of primary data and coding process, the framework of the overall departmental expenditure performance evaluation index system is summarized into five main dimensions: security, completeness, efficiency, situational awareness, and subjective experience. A total of 40 open codes and 14 spindle codes were obtained to form 14 secondary indicators and 40 initial indicators of the autonomous driving takeover system user experience evaluation indicator system at the third level, as shown in Table 7.

Table 7. User experience evaluation indicator system

Primary indicators	Secondary indicators	Tertiary indicators
A1 Security	B1 Alarm safety	C1 Details openness
		C2 Combinations of multiple modes
		C3 Instructional clarity
		C4 Alarm timeliness
		C5 Alarm redundancy
		C6 Alarm irritation
	B2 Driving safety	C7 Compliance with expectations for driving
		C8 Tracking of driver conduct
		C9 Anti-fatigue alert
		C10 Safety distance limit
		C11 Human-computer interaction safety
	B3 Technical safety	C12 Iteration timeliness
		C13 Technology maturity
		C14 Data perfection
		C15 Clarity of responsibility
	B4 System reliability	C16 Road compatibility
		C17 Risk controllability
		C18 Frequency of accidents
		C19 System misjudgment rate
A2 Completeness	B5 Predictability	C20 Vehicle status alert
		C21 Road condition prediction
		C22 Hierarchical takeover warning
		C23 Flexible real-time feedback
	B6 Integrity	C24 Function richness
		C25 Failure response
		C26 Emergency road condition handling
		C27 Exit compensation Program

(*continued*)

Table 7. (*continued*)

Primary indicators	Secondary indicators	Tertiary indicators
A3 Efficiency	B7 Takeover completion	/
	B8 Takeover completion time	/
	B9 Passing efficiency	/
A4 Situational awareness	B10 Driver competence	/
	B11 Driver status	C28 Safety awareness
		C29 Fatigue level
		C30 Stress management
		C31 Concentration
	B12 Perceived complexity	C32 Road environment judgment
		C33 System interaction complexity
		C34 Driving state judgment
A5 Subjective experience	B13 Satisfaction	C35 Personalization
		C36 Comfort
		C37 Trust
		C38 Intelligence
	B14 Experience load	C39 Smoothness
		C40 Usability

4 Conclusion

In summary, five factors make up the automotive autonomous driving takeover system's user experience evaluation: security, completeness, efficiency, situational awareness, and subjective experience. This study uses a grounded theory approach, takes into account the driver's actual demands and feelings, and develops the automotive autonomous driving takeover system's user experience evaluation index system. An assessment of the automotive autonomous driving takeover system's user experience. Through anchored theory coding, which forms a comprehensive and systematic theoretical framework in the research process, the indicator system's indicators are obtained. This approach yields indicators that are clear, highly relevant, and reliable.

The user experience evaluation of the automotive autonomous driving takeover system was collected in this study by semi-structured interviews; nevertheless, there are limitations because of certain objective factors: Firstly, a large-sample investigation is required to confirm the findings of the qualitative research based on the rooted theory. It is envisaged that an empirical study would help to further develop and validate the findings of this study. It is intended to conduct a large-sample questionnaire survey, improve the user experience evaluation measurement tool, and use empirical research to confirm the validity and scientific integrity of the study's findings. Secondly, the evaluation index system does not give the specific weights of the indexes, which needs to be improved in the future research.

Acknowledgments. This work was supported by the Key Research and Development Project of Hubei Province (2022BAA071).

References

1. Popovich, V.: Space theory for intelligent GIS. In: Information Fusion and Intelligent Geographic Information Systems, pp. 3–13. Springer, Cham (2018). https://doi.org/10.1007/978-3-319-59539-9_1
2. Zhou, Y., Zhu, L.J.: Research on the development trend of HMI design in smart cockpit. Auto Time **18**(10), 113–114+117 (2021)
3. Tan, H., Sun, J.H., Guan, D.S et al.: Development trend of human-computer interaction in intelligent vehicles. Packag. Eng. **40**(20), 32–42 (2019)
4. Lin, J.H.: Design research on HMI of conditional autonomous vehicle based on situational awareness. Jiangnan University (2023)
5. Wu, C.Z., Wu, H.R., Lyu, N.C.: Review of control switch and safety of human computer driving intelligent vehicle. J. Traffic Transp. Eng. **18**(06), 131–141 (2018)
6. Schmidt, A., Spiessl, W., Kern, D.: Driving automotive user interface research. IEEE Educ. Activit. **9**, 85–88 (2010)
7. Zen, Q.S.: A Integrated design study of automotive soft and hard human-machine interface. Hunan University, Hunan (2016)
8. Wang, W.J., Li, Q.K., Zen, C., et al.: Review of take-over performance of automated driving: influencing factors, models, and evaluation methods. China J. Highway Transp. **36**(09), 202–224 (2023)
9. Tan, H., Tang, S.Y.: User experience evaluation methodology of interactive interface in intelligent vehicle. Packag. Eng. **44**(06), 12–24+469 (2023)
10. Zhang, X.R., Yin, Y., Feng, Y.Q., et al.: Study on ergonomics evaluation index system for display and control interface of automobile. Transp. Energy Conser. Environ. Protect. **12**(04), 12–16 (2016)
11. Jiang, C.J.: Research on automotive instrument interface evaluation based on eye movement information and semantic difference. Jilin University, Changchun (2016)
12. Charmaz, K.: Constructing Grounded Theory, 2nd edn. Sage, Thousand Oaks (2014)
13. Shen, J.J., Wang, Z.Y., Dai, J.W et al.: Analysis of demand and influencing factors of scientific research data based on the grounded theory. J. Intell. **38**(4), 175–180 (2019)

Exploration of Narrative Design Method and Tool on Intelligent Cockpit Experience Design

Zhongjie Xue[1], Danhua Zhao[2], Zijiang Yang[3(✉)], and Tao Wang[3]

[1] School of Design, Hunan University, Lushan Road (S), Yuelu District,
Changsha, Hunan, China
zjxue622@hnu.edu.cn

[2] State Key Laboratory of Advanced Design and Manufacturing for Vehicle Body, Lushan Road (S), Yuelu District, Changsha, Hunan, China
zhaodanhua@hnu.edu.cn

[3] Huizhou Desay SV Automotive Company, Limited, Huizhou, China
Zijiang.Yang@desaysv.com

Abstract. Technological innovation has a profound impact on people's work and daily lives, introducing unprecedented challenges for societal development. Initially focused on meeting life's necessities, design now encompasses the orchestration of relationships across various domains, including human-object, human-human, human-environment, and human-future interactions. As problems become increasingly complex, the required knowledge becomes more diverse and interdisciplinary. Design has evolved from a mere focus on "innovation" to a deeper emphasis on "collaboration," with research guiding theoretical methodologies toward practical implementation.

This paper introduces the ICMA toolkit, specifically designed for intelligent cockpit designs, and addresses integrating emerging technologies within interdisciplinary, multi-role stakeholder environments. The toolkit hierarchically organizes elements within the cockpit based on experiential frameworks, facilitating the translation of technologies into contextual experiences to foster mutual understanding. Over three years, application cases have not only showcased but also substantiated the development of intelligent cockpit designs tailored to meet the diverse needs of stakeholders. The ICMA tool enables nuanced comprehension of information and its practical application, effectively managing complex systems and transforming traditional information transmission across disciplines. It plays a crucial role in fostering consensus and facilitating joint decisions for interdisciplinary teams grappling with multifaceted challenges, particularly in understanding and implementing novel technologies, while also discerning the future experiential value embedded in intelligent cockpits.

Keywords: Intelligent cockpit · Design Method · Card-based design tools · Experience Design

P.-L. P. Rau (Ed.): HCII 2024, LNCS 14702, pp. 178–191, 2024.
https://doi.org/10.1007/978-3-031-60913-8_13

1   Introduction

Design often confronts complex and wicked problems [1]. Technological innovations lead to societal shifts and environmental transitions, intensifying and profoundly affecting people's work and lives. These changes pose unprecedented challenges to the future development of human society. Developing an intelligent cockpit design blends many technologies, culminating in an intelligent cockpit concept that synergizes various disciplines into a sophisticated system [2, 3]. The co-creation design powerfully addresses the complex, interdisciplinary system challenges associated with intelligent cockpit design formation.

Traditional cockpit design requires extensive testing and long iterative phases to finalize designs [4]. Collaborative creation helps stakeholders from various fields address design challenges efficiently [5], seek consensus, and develop tools for collaborative solutions in complex systems [6]. In this approach, designers use synergy tools for collaborative exploration, expressing solutions through visual thinking focused on product design involving using visual elements [7].

This study explored the situational theory and the ICMA toolkit's impact on collaborative cockpit system design, emphasizing how 'constructing contextual experiences and scenarios' fosters multidisciplinary co-creation, better adaptation, and diversity of ideas. The toolkit's application in workshops enhanced interdisciplinary understanding, resolved conflicts, and set common goals. Finally, we discussed how to evaluate the ICMA toolkit in interdisciplinary co-creation, noting that the ICMA tool aids designers in reflecting and capturing group dynamics. Using such tools improves understanding of complex issues and promotes cross-disciplinary negotiation.

2   Literature Review

2.1   Technological Transformation Leads to Interdisciplinary Co-creation Design

Technological innovation has fostered interdisciplinary integration, transforming products from their original simple forms into complex and diverse structures [8]. Technology is divided into two categories: experiential technology and high-tech technology. [9]. Experiential technology emerges directly from daily life, embodying ingrained habits. High-tech technology now profoundly impacts societal life, leading to a comprehensive transformation in the overall structure of traditional technological networks and even bringing about fundamental changes in entire industrial systems. However, the development of this technological form still has a dual impact on individuals. High-tech technologies often emerge rapidly, primarily from laboratories, characterized by pure rationality, futurism, and high permeability. The accelerating pace and shortened cycles of technological iteration in contemporary times add complexity to high-tech technology, making it challenging for individuals to adapt, resulting users in unfamiliarity and fear and creating specific cognitive and transitional barriers.

The technology establishes a Gestell framework structure involving humans and entities. Only when human factors permeate scientific and technological realms can the instrumental characteristics of technology have a clear direction and purpose. Design serves as a blueprint for creating a healthier and more beautiful world for people. The fundamental principle of design is human centricity, which aims to transform technological designs into humanized ones as much as possible.

Amid global pushes for dual circulation and strong Chinese policy support for energy and sustainable development, the automotive industry is rapidly transitioning towards autonomous driving. This shift in intelligent cockpit design emphasizes digital integration with collaborative human-machine technologies, turning the cockpit into a "third space" for decentralized activities and fluid resources [10]. However, the rapid rise of In-Vehicle Information Systems (IVIS) enhances user experience but introduces multitasking risks [11, 12]. As cockpit interactions become increasingly intricate, designers encounter the challenge of seamlessly integrating diverse functions to enhance user interaction.

Consequently, the design's emphasis has shifted from "Innovation" to "Collaborative design" [13], and the research focus has elevated from problem-solving capabilities to the examination and implementation of theoretical approaches guiding practical applications [14, 15]. Interdisciplinary co-creation is a primary driver and solution for tackling intricate and diverse issues, amalgamating insights from various technological sectors [16, 17].

2.2   User Experience and Narrative Design

Norman divides design into three levels: the behavioral level, the visceral level, and the reflective level [18]. Based on Norman's theory and contextual system within the cockpit, combined with user behavior theory, intelligent cockpit attributes can be classified into three levels: the explicit level (content), the behavioral level (context), and the experience level (imaginary). The explicit level of the cockpit corresponds to the physical environment within the cockpit, encompassing elements such as cockpit form, spatial layout of interactive entities, and specific functional features of technology. When the content level interacts with the user, it represents the primary stage of experience, namely, the experience of 'The perception of an object.' The behavioral level corresponds to the users within the cockpit and their specific actions, constituting the intermediate stage of experience, the contextual experience. The advanced level, namely the experience level, is for imagination and refers to the user's experience of specific ideas, values, and spiritual needs within the cockpit.

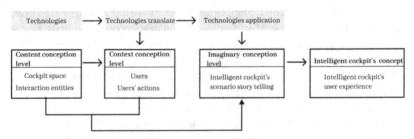

Fig. 1. Intelligent cockpit's user's experience and narrative design

Per Phelan's definition, narration represents events occurring in a specific time and space through a medium [19]. From an informational perspective, narration and inter-action require simultaneous support from time and space to be actualized. They both demand involvement from factors such as individuals, behaviors, and events, sharing structural and elemental similarities. From an experiential perspective, narrative explo-ration at the levels of experience and meaning exhibits intrinsic characteristics that can infuse a human element into human-computer interaction design, emphasizing rational task flows. The uniformity in information structure establishes narrative intervention as the cornerstone of cockpit experience design, whereas the differentiation in functional purposes enables narrative intervention in interactive experience design to engender novel possibilities. Narrative in the research process contributes to a better understanding of technology, translates user experiences, and fosters consensus among team members.

As Fig. 1 shows, the narrative is not just a form of expression but also a mode of content presentation. Through compelling scenario stories, designers can convey information in visual, dynamic, and spatial design, evoke emotions in the audience, and play a crucial role in narrating the interaction processes and user experiences. Therefore, narrative is vital in guiding users to perceive and understand the design [20]. Designers can concretize abstract technological concepts through narrative, making them more tangible and vibrant. This helps eliminate communication barriers among team members, promoting mutual understanding. In designing prototypes, the narrative provides a shared framework for the team, aiding them in collaborating effectively to achieve design goals.

2.3 Participatory Design for Complex Systems and Design Tools

At present, intelligent cockpits integrate various high-tech technologies, forming a complex system. With continuous iterative upgrades in technology, the complexity of intelligent cockpits is constantly increasing.

In 1984, Norman first defined "co-creation": in co-creation, customers complete some tasks that should initially be provided by the service company [21]. In previous studies, co-creation design methods, processes, and tools have facilitated a better mutual understanding of complex problems faced by design personnel from different disciplines, promoting the generation of design thinking creativity and managing complexity in systems [22]. Participatory design has been widely applied in various fields, such as mechanical design, computer design, product design, and sustainable development [23].

In the multidisciplinary context of intelligent cockpits, the concurrent engagement of multiple stakeholders in the design process is essential for the swift development of cockpit systems. However, there is currently limited research on collaborative design specifically focused on the conceptual stage of intelligent cockpit design. In this study, we integrated narrative design theory to investigate intelligent cockpit design methodologies when multiple stakeholders collaborate within the context of complex systems.

In the design field, tools such as storyboards, experience maps, and blueprints, com-monly used in interaction, service, and experience design, possess characteristics of co-creation design. These tools can serve as a method to gain insights into problems, identify points of opportunity, and develop design concepts.

Narrative methods involve incorporating events into a story, finding corresponding emotions in time and space, and forming the foundation for guiding multiple stakeholders in structuring complex problems and constructing experiences. Simultaneously, narrative design is based on concepts from semiotics and semantics, and its core integrates storytelling elements and distinctive design features to form the narrative process. Hence, within cockpit scenario narration, the "storytelling" approach necessitates the systematic organization and arrangement of numerous design elements to craft a coherent structure for conveying the narrative theme effectively. Nevertheless, when addressing the cockpit as a multi-layered and multi-element complex system, traditional tools such as storyboard, experience map, and blueprint may translate technical narratives and organize elements within a limited timeframe. Therefore, there is a necessity for a novel tool to streamline the translation of advanced technologies, foster the engagement of multiple stakeholders in design endeavors, aid in organizing elements across various experiential levels within the cockpit, generate scene concepts, and foster a shared understanding, ultimately leading to consensus in decision-making.

3 Development and Practice of Narrative Design Tools Based on Cockpit Experience

From July 2020 to September 2023, 14 design researchers participated in creating the ICMA toolkit. The ICMA toolkit plays a pivotal role in facilitating the development of intelligent cockpit design. It offers inspiration through experiential levels and narrative methods, aiding in organizing complex elements of intelligent cockpit scenarios and user experience. This toolkit development aims to foster co-creation among multidisciplinary stakeholders by providing comprehensive support. Based on Schön's proposition sign practice and reflection [24], during the development process, we invited design researchers from other universities to use the ICMA toolkit and try to generate intelligent cockpit scenario concepts in each iterative stage. The reflections from each round of testing, including common feedback regarding the incomplete scenario information on the cards during the initial stage and feedback regarding the overly scattered and difficult-to-organize scenario information in the subsequent stage, served as inspirations for refining the tool. Finally, the ICMA toolkit underwent three iterations, incorporated expert opinions, and consulted other card-based design information sources to continually enhance the form and usage of the ICMA toolkit, thus facilitating design exploration. (as detailed in Sect. 4.1). In response to the global pandemic's effects in 2020, we engaged with stakeholders beyond the organization through online workshops, utilizing the ICMA toolkit to conduct its initial validation. Through this initial practice, we preliminarily determined the efficacy of this tool in idea generation and collaboration with diverse stakeholders, thereby facilitating the establishment of consensus on interests.

We begin by outlining the iterative development of the tool, identifying the fundamental elements crucial for fostering consensus among multiple stakeholders, and detailing the structure and utilization methods of the co-creation ICMA toolkit. Following this, we delve into the application and outcomes of the tool through two sub-workshops involving multidisciplinary stakeholders within distinct corporate settings.

3.1 Format and the Elements of the ICMA Toolkit

The ICMA toolkit comprises two categories of cards: mission-actions cards and spatial-layout cards. We drew inspiration from the approaches of Vera and Mueller, who used context pictures in their designs to enhance participants' understanding of the cards. [25, 26]. Most card design tools combine graphics and text, except for a few like Oblique Strategies Cards and The House of Cards, which are text or image-based. Cardoso believes text stimuli during idea generation could limit cognitive flexibility [27], while Bougienages that images promote broader conceptual exploration [28], enhancing flexibility. Text stimuli lead to more ideas, whereas images increase idea uniqueness without affecting their quantity, quality, or novelty. As Fig. 2 shows, Mission-action cards measure 15 cm x 12 cm and are provided in paper format, featuring a concise cockpit scenario narrative and interactive tasks for the user to complete within the scenario. Each card includes a title, a description of the scenario story, and a series of actions for the user to follow over time, accompanied by pertinent visual representations of the scenario and the user's profile picture. To facilitate swift card sorting by creators, we suggested categorizing these cards thematically and assigning distinct front border and back colors corresponding to five predefined categories.

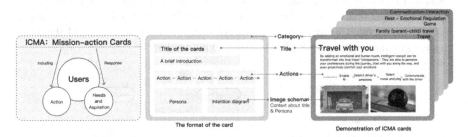

Fig. 2. ICMA-mission and action cards and the five categories.

The cockpit spatial-layout card draws inspiration from architectural concepts. As Fig. 3 shows, the cards include a three-dimensional perspective layout of the cockpit. It aids participants in comprehending the spatial layout within the intelligent cockpit. Leveraging the existing spatial arrangement, participants can endeavor to annotate elements of the Content Conception Level and Context Conception Level by using this cockpit spatial-layout card. For example, participants can use spatial-layout cards to mark ICMA cards' touch points and connect them with path lines, providing explicit spatial references for users' actions, systematic actions, the cockpit layout, and the form of entities. We identified 12 basic spatial-layout cards to help participants understand the specific actions in using the cards to design the cockpit.

3.2 ICMA Toolkit's Technique

The ICMA toolkit be utilized in the co-creation design workshop to facilitate rapid ideation for intelligent cockpit design. The workshop involves participants taking on roles as either facilitators or participants, divided into small groups. As depicted in

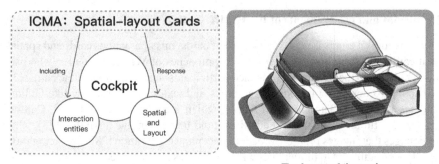

The format of the card

Fig. 3. ICMA: spatial-layout card format.

Fig. 4, the workshop follows a four-stage ICMA toolkit technique. Participants leverage their multidisciplinary knowledge, construct a scenario narrative using various cards, and engage in discussions to refine and reach consensus on design matters. They select a theme and organize pertinent cards on a large sheet to track the evolution of concepts, thereby nurturing creativity. During the idea selection phase, participants select a cockpit spatial layout card from the ICMA cards, marking connections and sketching corresponding spaces. Subsequently, they present the scenario narrative and assess the concepts generated, ensuring that spatial considerations are duly acknowledged and considered in the development of intelligent cockpit design.

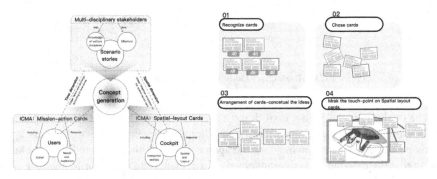

Fig. 4. The four stages of usage process of the ICMA toolkit in the workshop.

4 Design Workshop - ICMA Toolkit's Practice

This extensive project, conducted amidst the global pandemic, employed a combination of online and in-person workshops, utilizing diverse recording methods, such as audio and video, throughout the process to capture participants' ethnographic perspectives. [29]. The lead and corresponding authors played crucial roles in designing the toolkit and coordinating the workshops, acting as facilitators to address conflicts and cultivate the 'experience' among stakeholders. We conducted analyses of each workshop's procedures and outcomes to investigate how stakeholders from diverse disciplines interacted with the scenario story methodology and deliberated on the results throughout the workshops.

4.1 The First Practical Case

In January 2021, participants were invited to a three-day online workshop to employ and validate the ICMA toolkits, addressing the situation in which offline gatherings are not feasible due to the pandemic. 20 students and educators from various disciplines (5 in interaction design and 3 in product design), and the remaining 12 participants are teachers from various colleges and universities across China (7 in mechanical design and 5 in automotive electronics). They were divided into four teams to use the card tool to refine the concept of an Intelligent cockpit. Guided through the process, teams familiarized themselves with the card components, generated new cards, and crafted conceptual scenario narratives using the ICMA toolkit.

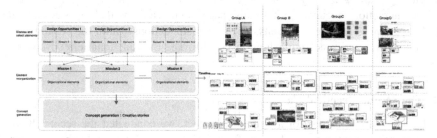

Fig. 5. During the first practice, Participants selected cards and combined them to create a cohesive narrative for the intelligent cockpit scenario design.

As depicted in Fig. 5, the empirical findings suggest that participants from diverse disciplines can generate ideas for intelligent cockpit concepts by integrating ICMA cards and constructing scenarios. They effectively address different temporal features and missions by leveraging ICMA cards as a basis for their designs.

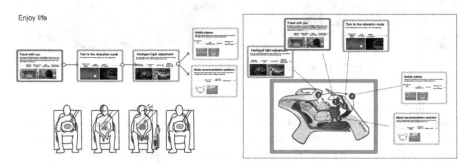

Fig. 6. Group A's ideation: Enjoy life.

Group A is an illustrative example, comprising 3 mechanical design professors, 1 automotive electronics professor, and 1 interaction design student. Group A's work depicts the cockpit as a mobile office and relaxation area on a physical level. Consequently, on a situational level, the user is perceived as a young professional in an office setting. Participants conducted a detailed analysis of user actions and identified specific user needs. For instance, considering potential user fatigue, they proposed incorporating sensor and lighting adjustment technology into the vehicle to address these needs.

As illustrated in Fig. 6, participants from Group A suggested leveraging spare time within the cockpit to accomplish basic office tasks while simultaneously transforming the intelligent driving space into a personalized, soothing third space. The narrative unfolds across three levels: situational experience, experiential context, and artistic ambiance, skillfully combining the cards. Each level aligns with specific behavioral and emotional settings, with corresponding technological transformations and applications delineated at each stage's technical interface.

The participants' ideas and narratives underscore the concept of experience as they collaboratively construct a shared understanding of the user's experience within the cockpit. By crafting a story depicting the user's journey in the cockpit, they delve into the interactions occurring within this space, acknowledging that users accumulate travel experiences at different points. The systematic actions within the cockpit assist or facilitate the user in accomplishing tasks, affirming the functional effectiveness of ICMA.

4.2   The Second Practical Case

In September 2021, as part of a corporate project, we conducted the second ICMA toolkit exercise, engaging stakeholders from various disciplines, including designers, engineers, product managers, and marketing personnel. Over two days, forty participants were organized into nine multidisciplinary teams. Each group comprised four or five members, representing at least three disciplines.

Fig. 7. Photo documentation from the second practice.

As illustrated in Fig. 7, we examined the design concept named "A Cloud-Piercing Arrow" proposed by Group A."A Cloud-Piercing Arrow", documenting the process through photos, audio recordings, and video files. This group focused on depicting a family vacation involving Mrs.Han and her son Xiao Ming. Participants incorporated five mission-action cards: "Travel Plan Recommendations," "One-Click Contact," "Mobile Viewing Platform," "In-Car Photography," and "Automatic VLOG Editing." The narrative unfolds with Mrs.Han plans the journey via the car's AI and notifies Xiao Ming with a one-click feature, on the trip, the car provides a 360° scenic view of the scenery, then Xiao Ming captures photos by using gestures. At the end of their trip, the car system automatically generates a VLOG upon the trip's conclusion.

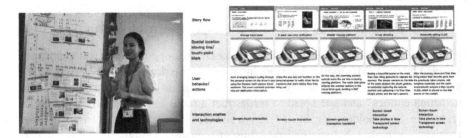

Fig. 8. Left: Team members of "A Cloud-Piercing Arrow" are narrating the concept story; Right: The story flow is organized by the author based on the concept storyboard.

As depicted in Fig. 8, participants utilized the ICMA cards to construct their scenario narrative. Throughout the design process, participants use the ICMA toolkit to interpret a variety of high-tech technologies within the intelligent cockpit into a narrative story of a travel journey. They consider the user experience throughout the travel journey. These experiences are subsequently integrated into the design to establish different functional aspects within the intelligent cockpit. The interconnection of these functional aspects culminates in a comprehensive cockpit scenario design experience.The story encompasses contextual conception, detailing user actions, descriptions of users' actions, interaction entities, and elements such as cockpit space and applied technologies within the narrative content. The "scenario theme" encapsulates a high-level overview of the story setting within the cockpit, while "user actions," drawn from ICMA's cards, delineate the user's actions at various stages of the story. "User action descriptions" provide specific interpretations of these actions, with participants modifying or enhancing card content, such as incorporating scenarios like "gesture photo-taking" and "real-time uploading" into the "in-car shooting" action. The arrangement of user action cards reflects the flow of usage, offering a tangible depiction of the scenario. "Spatial movement" is indicated and organized by participants on form cards, outlining user positions or interaction points with cockpit components during each action, such as marking the screen on the driver's seat for route planning by the mother. "Applied Technology" signifies the technical capabilities necessary for cockpit functions during user actions, representing engineers' technical expertise and functional constraints in designing the intelligent cockpit, documented textually alongside corresponding actions.

The practical results demonstrate that participants effectively leverage narrative experience design methods and tools. Through the utilization of cards, they translate technology into personalized scenario narratives. By emphasizing content and context conception, they redirect the spotlight from technology within the cockpit towards the planning of user behavior, thereby crafting a distinctive experience centered around the user within the cockpit. Participants emphasize the emotional attributes and experiential significance of this journey. This approach delves into how experiences evolve into emotional memories and evolve into compelling stories worth sharing.

5 Discussion

5.1 Narrative Methods and Tools Facilitate Experience Achievement

During the workshop, participants identified innovative opportunities and challenges presented by the ICMA toolkit, categorizing them as "missions," such as gesture-based photo-taking or real-time uploading. They selected scenario elements like "user, action, interaction entities" and attempted to reconstruct a scenario narrative from the user's perspective. Stakeholders contributed design and technological insights based on these narratives, fostering a holistic understanding of scenarios. Designers typically supervised the tool's usage, managing event flows and crafting initial concept stories. Engineers assessed technical feasibility, while product managers evaluated market and user receptivity.

By utilizing the ICMA toolkit, multidisciplinary teams could collaboratively explore possibilities for cockpit design, establish shared goals. They amalgamated expertise to craft valuable design narratives, using cards to interpret cockpit scenarios and indicate user positions with action touchpoints. This process culminated in developing a comprehensive design concept encompassing scenario elements.

However, this method and tools will encounter new challenges in the future. With the ongoing advancement of AI technology and big data models, the structure of narratives and the methods of story generation may transform. This aspect of emerging technological changes has not been extensively discussed in this paper, representing a limitation. In future research, we intend to delve deeper into narrative methods and tools related to AI technology within the context of intelligent cockpit design.

5.2 Multiple Stakeholders Reached Co-Experience Through a Co-creation Toolkit

When confronted with continually evolving and increasingly unfamiliar high-tech technologies, users may feel apprehension regarding "how to use these technologies?" and "high-tech might be more unsafe than they are worth?" In the design process of intelligent cockpits, it is crucial to contemplate the application transformation of high-tech technologies and user adaptability. Narrative methods empower stakeholders to translate high technology collaboratively and promptly into a story of user experience, seamlessly integrating high technology into people's daily lives. As illustrated in Fig. 9, we leverage narrative methods and tools to encourage the involvement of multidisciplinary stakeholders, enabling them to grasp the technological transformations and conceptual designs within the cockpit. Through the storytelling structure, we engage participants to comprehend the specific experiences of users within, immersing them in the narrative backdrop. In real-time, they employ technologies into scenarios, articulating their perspectives cohesively with the central user experiences depicted in the story. This

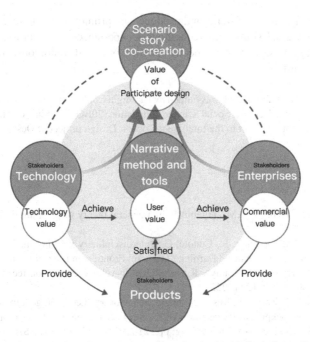

Fig. 9. Narrative method: A Co-Experience Creation by Multi-disciplinary Stakeholders

storytelling approach enhances mutual understanding among participants. While our approach has initiated a value transformation, it's important to note that in this study, we have not thoroughly explored whether other emerging technologies could potentially expedite or provide additional applications for technological transformations. This represents a minor limitation in our ability to develop enhanced user experience designs within the cockpit.

6 Conclusion

This study explored the application of narrative design methods and tools to aid multidisciplinary participants in navigating complex design challenges amidst rapid technological transformations.

Narrative design represents a novel approach to addressing complex systems and user experiences, shifting the design focus from mere "things" to dynamic "events." It entails a user-centric exploration of requirements to infuse experiences with deeper, fundamental meaning. This paper introduces the concept of experience level in intelligent cockpit design and proposes the ICMA toolkit to elucidate narrative design elements, steps, and methodologies. As a storytelling tool for scenario development, the ICMA toolkit facilitates interdisciplinary collaboration in tackling complex challenges.

The research findings suggest that the ICMA toolkit assists multidisciplinary stakeholders in addressing complex system issues by systematically organizing and reconstructing elements within the system hierarchy. The toolkit offers valuable insights for its application in complex systems and products and promotes stakeholder engagement in the design process. Using narrative methods in experience design harnesses the power of storytelling, provides a fresh perspective on the world, and continuously drives design innovation forward.

Acknowledgments. This research was funded by Paradigm Construction and Theoretical Boundary of Design Research, National Social Science Foundation (20BG103). Sincerely thanks to those who provide enormous support to the Intelligent Cockpit Design project of Desay SV.

References

1. Rittel, H.W.J., Webber, M.M.: Dilemmas in a general theory of planning. Policy Sci. **4**(2), 155–169 (1973)
2. Scanlon, E., Anastopoulou, S., Conole, G.: Interdisciplinary working methods: reflections based on technology-enhanced learning (TEL). In: Frontiers in Education, vol. 4 (2019)
3. Murali, P.K., Kaboli, M., Dahiya, R.: Intelligent in-vehicle interaction technologies. Adv. Intell. Syst. **4**(2), 2100122 (2022)
4. Guo, X., Yang, J., Zhang, J.: Research on user behavior oriented intelligent interactive design of automobile cockpit. In: Proceedings of the 5th International Conference on Information Technologies and Electrical Engineering, pp 521–525. New York, NY, USA, Association for Computing Machinery (2023)
5. Wang, J., Yue, T., Liu, Y.: Design of proactive interaction for in-vehicle robots based on transparency. Sensors **22**(10), 3875 (2022)
6. Ayoub, J., Zhou, F., Bao, S., 等.: From manual driving to automated driving: a review of 10 years of AutoUI. In: Proceedings of the 11th International Conference on Automotive User Interfaces and Interactive Vehicular Applications, pp. 70–90. Association for Computing Machinery, New York, NY, USA (2019)
7. Altinger, H., Wotawa, F., Schurius, M.: Testing methods used in the automotive industry: results from a survey (2014)
8. Dindler, C., Iversen, O.S.: Fictional inquiry—design collaboration in a shared narrative space. CoDesign **3**(4), 213–234 (2007)
9. Hengchun, X.: Design Finding Place between Hight-tec and low-tec. Zhuangshi **08**(1), 13–17 (2009)
10. GuoMing, Y., Hui, M.: The new power paradigm in the internet age: "Relationship empowerment." Int. News **38**(10), 6–27 (2016)
11. Orr, R.J., Abowd, G.D.: The smart floor: a mechanism for natural user identification and tracking. In: CHI 2000 Extended Abstracts on Human Factors in Computing Systems (CHI EA 2000), pp. 275–276, Association for Computing Machinery, New York, NY, USA (2000)
12. Qian, G., Zhang, J., Kidané, A.: People identification using gait via floor pressure sensing and analysis. In: Roggen, D., Lombriser, C., Tröster, G. (eds.) pp. 83–98. Smart Sensing and Context. Springer, Berlin (2008). 10.1007/978-3-540-88793-5_7
13. Skorb, E.V., Möhwald, H.: "Smart" surface capsules for delivery devices. Adv. Mater. Interf. **1**(6), 1400237 (2014)
14. Smith, R.C., Bossen, C., Kanstrup, A.M.: Participatory design in an era of participation. CoDesign **13**(2), 65–69 (2017)
15. Sanders, E.B.N., Stappers, P.J.: Co-creation and the new landscapes of design [J/OL]. CoDesign **4**(1), 5–18 (2008). https://doi.org/10.1080/15710880701875068

16. Li, B., Chen, S., Larivière, V.: Interdisciplinarity affects the technological impact of scientific research. Scientometrics **128**, 6527–6559 (2023)
17. Klaassen, R.G.: Interdisciplinary education: a case study. Eur. J. Eng. Educ. **43**(6), 842–859 (2018)
18. Norman, D.: Emotional Design: Why We Love (or Hate) Everyday Things. 1st Basic Books, New York (2007)
19. Dan, S.: Rhetorical narratology: a keyword in critical theory. Foreign Lit. **1**(1), 80–95 (2020)
20. Hunsucker, A., Siegel, M., Siegel, M.: Once upon a time: storytelling in the design process (2015)
21. Normann, R.: Service Management: Strategy and Leadership in Service Business, 3rd edn. Wiley, NewYork (2008)
22. Scariot, C., Heemann, A., Padovani, S.: Understanding the collaborative-participatory design. Work **41**, 2701–2705 (2012)
23. Lähteenoja, S., Marttila, T., Gaziulusoy, İ.: Transition co-design dynamics in high level policy processes. Des. Stud. **88**, 101207(2023)
24. Schön, D.: The Reflective Practitioner: How Professionals Think In Action. 1st. Basic Books, New York (1984)
25. Lucero Vera, A.A.: Co-designing interactive spaces for and with designers: supporting mood-board making. Eindhoven: Technische Universiteit Eindhoven (2009)
26. Mueller, F., Gibbs, M., Vetere, F.: Supporting the creative game design process with exertion cards. In: CHI (2014)
27. Cardoso, C., Gonçalves, M., Badke-Schaub, P.: Searching for inspiration during idea generation: pictures or words? In: Proceedings of International Design Conference, DESIGN, pp. 1831–1840 (2012)
28. Borgianni, Y., Maccioni, L., Fiorineschi, L.: Forms of stimuli and their effects on idea generation in terms of creativity metrics and non-obviousness. Int. J. Des. Creativity Innov. **8**, 1–18 (2020)
29. Blomberg, J., Burrell, M., Guest, G.: An ethnographic approach to design. 3rd, CRC Press, Boca Raton, Florida (2002)

Artificial Intelligence
from a Cross-Cultural Perspective

Multidisciplinary Review of Artificial Empathy: From Theory to Technical Implementation and Design

Chiju Chao, Zhiyong Fu$^{(\boxtimes)}$, and Yu Chen

Department of Information Art and Design, Tsinghua University, Beijing 100084, China
{zjr21,chenyu21}@mails.tsinghua.edu.cn,
fuzhiyong@tsinghua.edu.cn

Abstract. Collaboration between humans and intelligent agents has become an integral component of everyday life due to advancements in intelligent technologies. Emotional communication plays a particularly important role in this human-computer relationship. In addition to enhancing experiences, emotional communication facilitates decision-making, improves efficiency, and serves various other beneficial purposes. Current research is focused on human-computer empathy, which enables intelligent agents to seamlessly integrate into human societies by simulating empathic emotions. This research draws upon knowledge from psychology, computer science, design, sociology, and other relevant disciplines. This paper provides an overview of human-computer empathy, covering definitions, principles, technical implementations, and design aspects to illuminate the complex landscape of knowledge in this area. Two specific areas are given detailed attention: technical implementation and empathy design. In the technical implementation section, the paper delves into the psychological theoretical foundations for developing artificial empathy models, techniques of affective computing, and related artificial empathy models. In the design section, it discusses methods for implementing empathic responses, analyzing designs using social psychology, and outlines various design principles and evaluation methods. Finally, the paper addresses ethical considerations, design challenges, and other pertinent topics.

Keywords: Artificial Empathy · Human-Computer Empathy · Affective Design · Design theory

1 Introduction

In the realm of Artificial Intelligence (AI) research, virtual agents have seamlessly integrated into our daily lives, serving not only as tools but also as assistants and even partners [1]. HCI researchers envision the next generation of robots capable of engaging with people in human-centered environments and assisting them in their daily activities [2]. Studies have shown that humans interact with computers in ways akin to interpersonal interactions [3]. Given the emotional nature of human societies, it is imperative to consider the emotional connection established between users and AI when designing agents, emphasizing the importance of empathy in this process [4].

P.-L. P. Rau (Ed.): HCII 2024, LNCS 14702, pp. 195–209, 2024.
https://doi.org/10.1007/978-3-031-60913-8_14

However, striving to make computers as human-like as possible is not necessarily the optimal approach for intelligent systems, despite their level of intelligence. Computers inherently lack the ability to genuinely convey real emotions, but they can offer support and assistance in various contexts where human intervention is needed. By incorporating the positive aspects of empathy into our systems while mitigating the negative aspects, we can enhance their effectiveness [5].

In the domains of computer technology, human-computer interaction design, and psychology, numerous researchers have explored the design and implementation of human-machine empathy. Although machines cannot experience and express empathy authentically, various research endeavors have aimed to develop robots capable of displaying empathy [6]. Researchers in computer science draw upon empathy theory from social psychology to construct artificial empathy models [1, 7, 8]. Moreover, HCI design researchers devise diverse expressions to address emotional responses from a user experience standpoint [9–11].

A multidisciplinary approach, spanning psychology, design, and computer science, is essential for researchers to develop a comprehensive understanding of human-computer empathy. This paper aims to offer a comprehensive overview of this subject from various angles, covering definitions, principles, technical implementation, and design. By exploring these aspects, researchers can gain insights into various facets of human-computer empathy, enabling them to pursue research endeavors aligned with their interests in this domain.

2 About Empathy

2.1 What is Empathy

The concept of empathy was first introduced by humanist Carl Rogers in 1975, defining it as the ability to perceive another person's inner world [12]. It encompasses any reaction triggered by observing another individual's emotional state and subsequently activating one's own emotions [13]. Empathy research is broadly divided into two systems: affective empathy and cognitive empathy [14]. Affective empathy involves individuals directly and unconsciously experiencing the emotional state of another person, leading to a similar emotional response [15]. On the other hand, cognitive empathy, also known as higher-level empathy, entails imagining how the other person feels, activating emotions, evoking empathy, and engaging in corresponding behavioral responses [16].

Psychological research on empathy typically involves three components. Firstly, the empathizer's intention and emotional state towards themselves or the target, along with their understanding of the current situation, serve as prerequisites. Secondly, a comprehensive assessment of the preconditions is conducted. Finally, empathic outcomes are expressed through behavior, such as expressing concern [17]. These components allow researchers to formulate process models of empathy, conceptualizing empathy as a superordinate category that encompasses all phenomena with similar mechanisms. Artificial Empathy leverages these process models to develop a theory of empathic interaction for intelligent products in this study.

2.2 The Role of Empathy in Human Society

Empathy is widely recognized as a crucial element in interpersonal interactions, encompassing various aspects such as ethical considerations, pro-social behavior, and cooperation [18, 19]. Consequently, its significance in social interactions is on the rise. Empathy enables individuals to continuously assess each other's situational contexts, adjust their emotional states accordingly, and exhibit empathetic behavior in response to these dynamics [20]. In fact, empathy often serves as the driving force behind altruistic behavior in human interactions. Recent psychological research has shown that individuals tend to be more helpful and generous when they experience empathy [21].

In collaborative settings, empathy yields numerous positive effects on individuals' attitudes and behaviors towards one another. Depending on the nature of interaction, individuals may vary in their willingness to express their emotions. Criticism or lack of interest may discourage further expression, leading to withdrawal. Empathy can mitigate such negative outcomes and foster open communication [5]. Moreover, empathetic responses aid in resolving conflicts among team members, facilitating smooth decision-making processes [22]. Furthermore, studies suggest that empathy helps individuals comprehend vital environmental cues about others and anticipate their future behavior [8] Psychologists have also confirmed that emotions play a significant role in rational thinking, influencing behavior and decision-making processes [23, 24]. In essence, empathy in teamwork not only supports positive emotional communication but also enables individuals to gather information about others' environments, understand their behaviors, and make informed decisions.

2.3 The Positive Effects of Empathy on HCI

Numerous studies have highlighted the significant positive impact of empathic emotions on users' perceptions of intelligent systems, thereby enhancing the overall user-computer interaction experience [25, 26]. Users tend to view AI systems that display empathy as more sympathetic, likable, and trustworthy compared to those devoid of empathic responses [5, 27]. Consequently, empathetic AI systems are not only more appealing but also more likely to retain user engagement [28].

Furthermore, empathy plays a pivotal role in enhancing the efficiency of human-robot collaborations. For instance, intelligent products can utilize emotional expression to aid humans in understanding their capabilities, enabling users to discern tasks that the robot can perform effectively and optimize its utilization [29]. Studies have demonstrated that teams making decisions based on empathy tend to perform better, underscoring empathy as a mechanism that enhances the effectiveness of AI agent teams [30].

The impact of empathic responses by intelligent agents varies depending on the user and the scenario. Therefore, empathic responses constitute one of the most crucial elements in the design of human-computer interaction, significantly influencing user experience and operational efficiency. For instance, research on AI interviewers revealed that users preferred systems they could empathize with during high-stakes job interviews, indicating a preference for a serious approach [31]. Similarly, in studies on AI teaching, it was observed that providing students with positivity and affirmation could significantly enhance classroom quality [5].

3   About Artificial Empathy

Social science research on human relationships serves as a foundational framework for constructing human-computer relationships [32]. Asada conducted an extensive review of psychological models pertaining to empathy mechanisms and processes, laying the groundwork for the development of artificial empathy [7]. To effectively incorporate artificial empathy into design, HCI designers must first grasp its implementation. Artificial empathy has emerged from established psychological theories of empathy and the advancements in affective computing technology. Affective computing has enabled the simulation of empathy processes within human society.

3.1   Research on Empathy in Psychology

There are two types of empathy: emotional empathy and cognitive empathy. Asada examines the logical relationships between these two types of empathy in psychology. The concept of emotional empathy refers to the matching of an emotional response to the emotional state of another person by directly feeling that person's emotions. Comparatively, cognitive empathy refers to the ability to think differently in order to activate emotional or affective empathy through imagination. Emotional contagion coincides more closely with physiological instinct than emotional empathy because it is automatic, unconscious, and is the basis for a higher level of empathy. Comparatively, sympathy is more closely aligned with rational judgment than cognitive empathy since it refers to emotions that are not necessarily shared and primarily effected by the self's view of the emotions of others (Asada, 2015). In comparison to these theory [7]. In comparison to these theories of empathy, emotional contagion/emotional empathy is more closely related to human physiology and consciousness and is less likely to be employed to construct artificial empathy, while sympathy/cognitive empathy is more commonly used to conduct artificial empathy research.

It is suggested by cognitive empathy theory that empathy involves understanding or knowing a particular object's state, its environment, its emotions, or its exposure to a particular event [6] According to cognitive empathy theory, researchers have dismantled these elements and proposed a variety of alternative models. According to [33] Rodrigues proposed a model of artificial empathy evaluating responses, which includes multiple elements such as events, emotional cues, similarities, links, moods, dispositions, behavioral responses, etc. de Vignemont also analysed four categories of factors that can modulate empathic responses in the artificial empathy model: characteristics of the emotion, the subject and the target relationship, situational context, and characteristics of the subject [8]. Understanding the psychological research on empathy can help us better understand the principles and elements of artificial empathy in which to design human-computer interaction (Fig. 1).

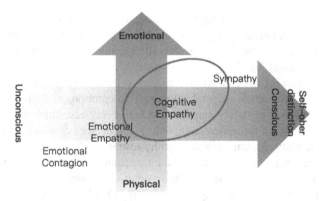

Fig. 1. Different Types of Empathy.

3.2 About Affective Computing

Artificial empathy is rooted in the concept of affective computing, which involves the ability to comprehend and respond to emotional cues conveyed by communication partners. Conversational agents, as discussed by Ochs, are equipped to calculate and identify empathetic emotions appropriate for a given conversational context [31, 34]. Through affective computing techniques, AI systems can learn about users' emotions by collecting physiological data via computer vision, skin conductance, and electromyography. This data can then be computationally interpreted into various affective states, allowing the system to deliver empathetic responses to users [35]. Hegel characterize empathy responses as non-verbal displays of emotions and a means of empathetic engagement, encompassing facial expressions and motor mimicry.[36].

Affective computing was initially proposed by Picard in 1997 following Minsky's 1986 identification of the challenge of emotion recognition in intelligent machines [37]. Presently, research in emotion computing technology is mainly bifurcated into two streams: emotion-based affective computing (Emotional Analysis) and viewpoint-based affective computing (Sentiment Analysis). Professor Picard leads the field of emotion-based affective computing, which focuses on gathering emotional data, recognizing and analyzing emotions, understanding emotions and cognitions, and expressing emotional information. This approach aims to categorize emotional traits and quantify their intensity [38]. On the other hand, sentiment analysis based on viewpoint, as proposed by Professor Liu, involves analyzing perspectives, inclinations, attitudes, and positions of the target. This method allows for sentiment calculations regarding specific issues, events, themes, as well as users, organizations, and products [39].

3.3 Build Artificial Empathy

Various approaches to modeling empathy have been developed in psychology over the past few decades [40]. However, due to differences in purposes and application contexts, computational approaches to artificial empathy vary in their modeling strategies [1]. Integrating a range of cognitive and behavioral skills into these approaches has been suggested by several researchers to develop comprehensive computational models of empathy. To achieve this, they propose dividing the components of artificial empathy into emotional communication, emotion regulation, and cognitive mechanisms, which can be manipulated synthetically and structurally to enhance understanding of emotional development processes [7].

Rodrigues, drawing from cognitive empathy theory, proposes an active empathy model where individuals respond selectively to emotions and situations based on assessment rather than passively empathizing with every encounter. In contrast to De Vignemont and Singer's theoretical approach [8], Rodrigues divides empathy into two main stages: empathy assessment and empathy response. During the assessment stage, intelligence infers the emotional state of the target and generates empathic emotions, which are modulated by factors like similarity, emotional connection, mood, and personality. These empathic emotions trigger specific empathic behaviors, such as expressing concern [27]. Smith and Lazarus's Cognitive-Motivational-Emotive psychological theory also focuses on evaluating cognitive empathy and response as fundamental processes in organizing empathy models [41].

While much research has concentrated on the evaluation and reaction phases of empathy, moderating factors also play a crucial role between these phases. Boukricha's computational model divides empathy into three phases: evaluation, moderation, and reaction [42]. Researchers have developed mechanisms for regulating emotions by utilizing personality traits, emotional and social bonding parameters, and situation assessment to reflect empathy's degree [34, 42]. Empathy is further influenced and moderated by assessing the value, intensity, and salience of emotions, social relationships, situations, and the agent's mood, personality, gender, age, and affect.[43].

While there's been significant research on computational models for assessing emotions [44, 45], little attention has been paid to how intelligences respond to these models. In McQuiggan's CARE empathy framework, agents respond to the target's emotions or specific attributes gathered from the target, thus displaying empathy [20]. The design of such intelligent agent responses has become a focal point of HCI research since technicians developing empathy models may lack expertise in interaction design. Designers play a crucial role in shaping artificial empathy by considering factors like voice tone, movement, language, expression, user similarity, personality, and role within the intelligent body design.

4   Design of Artificial Empathy

4.1   Implementation of Artificial Empathy Design

Designers play a pivotal role in creating empathic experiences for users by crafting the responses of intelligences [36]. This is primarily achieved through visual appearances, speech, voice features, facial expressions, and movements [11]. Visual appearance has been identified as a major factor influencing initial impressions, shaping people's expectations during interactions with AI [46] Adjusting visual appearance can reveal different dimensions of emotional expression, as suggested by Broadbent [47]. Furthermore, linguistic style can significantly impact how people perceive a robot, with a friendly demeanor often resulting in a positive user experience, while an insistent attitude may lead to negative perceptions [48, 49]. Vocal characteristics, such as volume, speech speed, pitch, and intonation, also contribute to the empathic quality of interactions. Extroversion tends to be associated with higher volume, faster speech speed, varied intonation, and increased speech volume, whereas introversion is characterized by lower volume, slower speech, monotonous intonation, and reduced speech volume [50–52]. Despite the diverse forms of products, there are discernible patterns in locomotion. For instance, Meerbeek designed the iCat robot with two personality versions: the introverted, polite, and responsible version exhibited slower, less frequent head movements and conservative nods, while the extroverted, friendly, and somewhat careless version engaged in more frequent head movements, playful movements, and nods during conversations [10]. In current research, visual appearance and movement are the most commonly utilized design elements, followed by speech, vocal features, facial expressions, and movement [11].

4.2 Design Analysis with Social Psychology

Despite the multitude of approaches to design, the question remains: how should analysis be conducted? Design researchers, such as B. J. Fogg, often regard products as social actors [53]. Consequently, theories from human societies are employed to explain users' emotional perceptions of products, attributing human-like characteristics to computers to foster more intuitive and engaging interactions [54]. Cliff Nass's research indicates that people typically interact with computers in a social manner, attributing human-like qualities such as personality to them. It's important to recognize that these emotional aspects aren't merely superficial behaviors but can also be considered essential components of an organization's structure, facilitating the integration of various computing modules. The interplay between emotion, cognition, and coping behaviors in psychological research can serve as a central organizing principle for human-like autonomous agent behavior [40]. Studies highlighting the influence of social interaction and socially perceived expectations, as emphasized by social psychology [55], apply to human-computer interaction as well [56].

Social psychology proposes an integration of personality psychology with social roles. An individual's personality dictates the stable characteristics, needs, motivations, and attitudes manifested in their social behavior. For instance, when interacting with a product, users may attribute a specific personality to it based on how it elicits emotions [57]. The process of personifying products, assigning various personality traits, and envisioning their interaction with users serves as a generative approach for designers [58]. Conversely, roles emphasize the significance of relationships, occupations, social categories, and the impact of norms [59]. For instance, there have been efforts to design smart products with 'character' archetypes using role conceptualization, such as policeman, butler, or friend [9], and to examine products in terms of masculinity and femininity, leading to different user expectations [60]. Through the lens of human-computer interaction, elements of social psychology can aid designers in analyzing how products should be designed to engage in empathic interactions with users (Fig. 2).

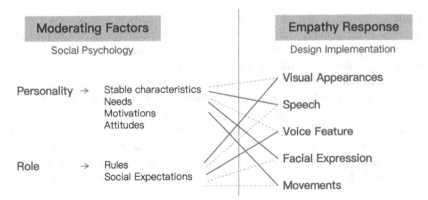

Fig. 2. The Analysis and Implementation of Artificial Empathy Design.

4.3 Concept of Design

While we aim to design empathic human-computer experiences to cultivate empathic relationships within human societies, the design processes diverge due to the fundamentally different nature of the interacting entities. Numerous studies have explored the philosophy of conducting human-computer empathic design, examining aspects of logic, realism, and influencing factors.

Firstly, human-computer empathy doesn't necessarily adhere strictly to perfect logic. Empathy involves understanding another's emotions without always eliciting emotional feedback, or even triggering unexpected emotions [34]. For instance, a study on smart speakers revealed that users often abandon new features quickly if the system fails to provide answers to unexpected questions. Offering unexpected yet relevant responses can prolong user engagement [61].

Secondly, it's crucial not to design human-computer empathy overly realistically. Just as in all realms of human-computer interaction, managing user expectations is paramount. AI inherently lacks the capacity for true empathy; it merely simulates, projects, and imitates empathy through recognition and expression. If an AI's empathic response is overly realistic, it may fail to meet users' expectations [62]. Therefore, empathy should be designed to be credible while still retaining a "human-like" quality.

Lastly, various factors influence the design approach to empathy. User personality, task or interaction context, cultural background, and demographic information all shape perceptions of a product's performance [11]. Researchers have identified two types of attraction in human-robot interactions: similarity attraction and complementary attraction. Participants often prefer interacting with robots possessing similar personality traits, but they also show interest in collaborating with complementary robots [63, 64].

4.4 Assessment for Artificial Empathy

Continuous evaluation of the empathic impact and iterative program adjustments are essential in human-computer empathic interaction design. Presently, psychological evaluation scales are predominantly employed to measure and assess users' empathic experiences. The most prevalent assessment concept revolves around evaluating the perceived personality of the product. "Product personality" encompasses a set of characteristics used to delineate a specific product and differentiate it from others [65]. Both user interaction and product evaluation are influenced by product personality, aiding users in anticipating how to engage with the product. Hence, designing products with predefined personalities during the design phase may be desirable [66]. Research has shown that a set of 20 items can determine a product's personality based on its appearance during the design process [66].

Another method of assessing empathy involves evaluating the relationship between the user and the intelligence. This is because the user's own personality traits, such as extroversion, influence their perception and behavior towards the AI interface [31]. Consequently, an alternative approach argues that the emphasis should not solely be on evaluating the perceived personality of the product but also on assessing the user's social relationship with the intelligent product. Examples include the Interpersonal Reactivity Index (IRI) [67] and the Barrett-Lennard Relationship Inventory (BLRI) [68].

5 Potential Issues

5.1 Regarding Technical and Design Issues

Advancements in AI technology have sparked concerns regarding the societal impact of intelligent machines, often overlooking moral and ethical considerations. Trust, as a fundamental element of successful cooperation, poses the primary challenge. For robots to effectively function within society, they must be designed to inspire trust. Societies foster trust among members through morals, ethics, and social norms. Hence, artificial intelligences must be designed to adhere to these norms, ensuring acceptance and societal benefits [69].

Another critical issue is the perception of threat. Research indicates that humans perceive robots with higher thinking abilities as more competent in serving them [3]. However, people may also perceive threats, including real ones like unemployment and resource loss, as well as symbolic threats like the loss of human uniqueness. Future research may focus on mitigating user threat perceptions through empathic interaction during the design phase.

While robots with greater intelligence capabilities may evoke ambivalent attitudes [70] the expression of empathic emotions by anthropomorphic agents can also have adverse effects [71]. For instance, virtual agents expressing emotions in inappropriate contexts may yield more negative outcomes than those that do not [34]. Therefore, the expression of empathic emotions must always be contextualized within human societal norms, especially when the product impacts users' emotional experiences on a large scale. Designers must proceed cautiously in such scenarios.

5.2 The Difficulty of AI Design

HCI designers often struggle with conceptualizing and prototyping AI systems. Many researchers find machine learning particularly challenging to design for due to the complex technical principles underlying it and the high uncertainty associated with its outputs. While machine learning has expanded design possibilities, collaboration between engineers and software developers still tilts heavily towards technological engineering innovations, with design-led innovations lagging behind [72]. Moreover, without adequate prototyping, AI systems may produce reasoning errors when not tailored to diverse users and environments, potentially violating established usability guidelines for traditional user interface design [73, 74].

Researchers in Human-Computer Interaction have delved into AI system design. Extensive research has led to the proposal and validation of 18 guidelines for AI interaction design [73] Some studies have also devised simple rule-based simulators as AI prototyping tools, linking rule-based interaction features to AI design complexity [75, 76]. While these studies offer valuable insights into designing more fluid AI systems, we believe that, given the rapid evolution of artificial intelligence, the crux of designing empathic human-computer interactions lies in establishing an intrinsic logic relationship between them. By integrating this understanding with the current context of AI technology, we can enhance the cognitive, regulatory, and reactive capabilities of intelligences.

6   Conclusion

The aim of this paper is to explore various aspects of human-computer empathy construction from diverse perspectives. To initiate the discussion, we provide a definition of empathy and examine its impact on human society. We then delve into both implementation and design aspects of empathy, with a focus on technical implementation, given the predominant role of technology in driving human-computer empathy interactions currently. Drawing from cognitive empathy theory in psychology, computer researchers have developed a model for human-computer empathy. Leveraging advancements in emotion computing technology, a model of artificial empathy can be established through three key steps: emotion assessment, mediation, and response. Subsequently, we delve into the design implementation phase. Despite significant research on models and algorithms in computer technology, designers must consider regulating factors such as personality, similarity, and context in the emotion regulation phase. Furthermore, providing emotional feedback to users through language, expression, and actions is crucial in the emotion response section.

Additionally, this paper addresses potential challenges and obstacles in this research direction, enabling readers to anticipate and navigate them effectively. By providing a comprehensive overview of human-computer empathy, we aim to facilitate a deeper understanding of this complex research area for technicians and designers interested in this field. While this paper strives to ensure high-quality literature citations, we encourage readers to conduct independent research, as there is no standardized search and filtering of papers. Instead, the integration and collection of core information are subjective. We recommend exploring the referenced literature further to gain a deeper understanding of the topic.

References

1. Yalçın, Ö.N., DiPaola, S.: Modeling empathy: building a link between affective and cognitive processes. Artif. Intell. Rev. **53**(4), 2983–3006 (2020). https://doi.org/10.1007/s10462-019-09753-0
2. Tapus, A.: Socially assistive robots: the link between personality, empathy, physiological signals, and task performance. In: Emotion, Personality, and Social Behavior, Papers from the 2008 AAAI Spring Symposium, Technical Report SS-08-04, Stanford, California, USA, p. 8 (2008)
3. Nass, C., Moon, Y.: Machines and mindlessness: social responses to computers. J. Soc. Issues **56**(1), 81–103 (2000). https://doi.org/10.1111/0022-4537.00153
4. Paiva, A., et al.: Caring for agents and agents that care: building empathic relations with synthetic agents. In: AAMAS '04: Proceedings of the Third International Joint Conference on Autonomous Agents and Multiagent Systems, New York, p. 8 (2004)
5. Cooper, B., Brna, P., Martins, A.: Effective affective in intelligent systems – building on evidence of empathy in teaching and learning. In: Paiva, A. (ed.) IWAI 1999. LNCS (LNAI), vol. 1814, pp. 21–34. Springer, Heidelberg (2000). https://doi.org/10.1007/10720296_3
6. Tapus, A.: Emulating empathy in socially assistive robotics. In: Multidisciplinary Collaboration for Socially Assistive Robotics, Papers from the 2007 AAAI Spring Symposium, Technical Report SS-07-07, Stanford, California, USA, p. 4 (2007)
7. Asada, M.: Towards artificial empathy. Int. J. Soc. Robot. **7**(1), 19–33 (2014). https://doi.org/10.1007/s12369-014-0253-z
8. de Vignemont, F., Singer, T.: The empathic brain: how, when and why? Trends Cogn. Sci. **10**(10), 435–441 (2006). https://doi.org/10.1016/j.tics.2006.08.008
9. ShiJian, L.: Design of Intelligent Product. Publishing House of Electronics Industry (2017). https://tsinghua-primo.hosted.exlibrisgroup.com.cn/permalink/f/1secrdm/86THU_ALMA_CN21465934010003966
10. Meerbeek, B., Hoonhout, J., Bingley, P., Terken, J.M.B.: The influence of robot personality on perceived and preferred level of user control. Interact. Stud. **9**(2), 204–229 (2008). https://doi.org/10.1075/is.9.2.04mee
11. Mou, Y., Shi, C., Shen, T., Xu, K.: A systematic review of the personality of robot: mapping its conceptualization, operationalization, contextualization and effects. Int. J. Hum. Comput. Interact. **36**(6), 591–605 (2020). https://doi.org/10.1080/10447318.2019.1663008
12. Rogers, C.R.: Empathic: an unappreciated way of being. Couns. Psychol. **5**(2), 2 (1975). https://doi.org/10.1177/001100007500500202
13. de Waal, F.B.M., Preston, S.D.: Mammalian empathy: behavioural manifestations and neural basis. Nat. Rev. Neurosci. **18**(8), 498–509 (2017). https://doi.org/10.1038/nrn.2017.72
14. Lim, A., Okuno, H.G.: A recipe for empathy. Int. J. Soc. Rob. **7**(1), 35–49 (2014). https://doi.org/10.1007/s12369-014-0262-y
15. De Waal, F.B.M.: Putting the altruism back into altruism: the evolution of empathy. Annu. Rev. Psychol. **59**, 279–300 (2008)
16. Daniel Batson, C.: These things called empathy: eight related but distinct phenomena. In: Decety, J., Ickes, W. (eds.) The social neuroscience of empathy, pp. 3–16. The MIT Press (2009). https://doi.org/10.7551/mitpress/9780262012973.003.0002
17. Davis, M.H.: Empathy: A Social Psychological Approach. Westview Press, Boulder (1996)
18. Hoffman, M.L.: Empathy and Moral Development: Implications for Caring and Justice. Cambridge University Press (2000). https://doi.org/10.1017/CBO9780511805851
19. Frijda, N.H., Manstead, A.S.R., Bem, S. (eds.): Emotions and Beliefs: How Feelings Influence Thoughts. Cambridge University Press (2000). https://doi.org/10.1017/CBO9780511659904

20. McQuiggan, S.W., Lester, J.C.: Modeling and evaluating empathy in embodied companion agents. Int. J. Hum. Comput. Stud. **65**(4), 348–360 (2007). https://doi.org/10.1016/j.ijhcs. 2006.11.015

21. Singer, T., Lamm, C.: The social neuroscience of empathy. Ann. N. Y. Acad. Sci. **1156**(1), 81–96 (2009). https://doi.org/10.1111/j.1749-6632.2009.04418.x

22. Stephan, W.G., Finlay, K.: The role of empathy in improving intergroup relations. J. Soc. Issues **55**(4), 729–743 (1999). https://doi.org/10.1111/0022-4537.00144

23. Dalvandi, B.: A Model of Empathy for Artificial Agent Teamwork. Doctoral dissertation, University of Northern British Columbia, Prince George (2013). https://doi.org/10.24124/2013/bpgub878

24. Marg, E.: Descartes' Error: emotion, reason, and the human brain. Optometry Vis. Sci. **72**(11), 847–848 (1995). https://doi.org/10.1097/00006324-199511000-00013

25. Dehn, D.M., van Mulken, S.: The impact of animated interface agents: a review of empirical research. Int. J. Hum. Comput. Stud. **52**(1), 1–22 (2000). https://doi.org/10.1006/ijhc.1999. 0325

26. Brave, S., Nass, C., Hutchinson, K.: Computers that care: investigating the effects of orientation of emotion exhibited by an embodied computer agent. Int. J. Hum. Comput. Stud. **62**(2), 161–178 (2005). https://doi.org/10.1016/j.ijhcs.2004.11.002

27. Rodrigues, S.H., Mascarenhas, S., Dias, J., Paiva, A.: A process model of empathy for virtual agents. Interact. Comput. **27**(4), 371–391 (2015). https://doi.org/10.1093/iwc/iwu001

28. Lisetti, C., Amini, R., Yasavur, U., Rishe, N.: I can help you change! An empathic virtual agent delivers behavior change health interventions. ACM Trans. Manage. Inf. Syst. **4**(4), 1–28 (2013). https://doi.org/10.1145/2544103

29. Norman, D.A.: Emotional Design: Why We Love (or Hate) Everyday Things. Basic Books, New York (2004)

30. Dalvandi, B.: A model of empathy for artificial agent teamwork. Master of Science, University of Northern British Columbia (2013). https://doi.org/10.24124/2013/bpgub878

31. Zhou, M.X., Mark, G., Li, J., Yang, H.: Trusting virtual agents: the effect of personality. ACM Trans. Interact. Intell. Syst. **9**(2–3), 1–36 (2019). https://doi.org/10.1145/3232077

32. Bickmore, T.W., Picard, R.W.: Establishing and maintaining long-term human-computer relationships. ACM Trans. Comput. Hum. Interact. **12**(2), 293–327 (2005). https://doi.org/10. 1145/1067860.1067867

33. Rodrigues, S.H., Mascarenhas, S.F., Dias, J., Paiva, A.: I can feel it too!: Emergent empathic reactions between synthetic characters, In: 2009 3rd International Conference on Affective Computing and Intelligent Interaction and Workshops, pp. 1–7. IEEE, Amsterdam (2009). https://doi.org/10.1109/ACII.2009.5349570

34. Ochs, M., Sadek, D., Pelachaud, C.: A formal model of emotions for an empathic rational dialog agent. Auton. Agent. Multi-Agent Syst. **24**(3), 410–440 (2012). https://doi.org/10. 1007/s10458-010-9156-z

35. Prendinger, H., Ishizuka, M.: The empathic companion: a character-based interface that addresses users. Appl. Artif. Intell. **19**(3–4), 267–285 (2005). https://doi.org/10.1080/088 39510590910174

36. Hegel, F., Spexard, T., Wrede, B., Horstmann, G., Vogt, T.: Playing a different imitation game: interaction with an empathic android robot. In: 2006 6th IEEE-RAS International Conference on Humanoid Robots, University of Genova, Genova, Italy, pp. 56–61. IEEE (2006). https:// doi.org/10.1109/ICHR.2006.321363

37. Minsky, M.: The Society of Mind. Simon & Schuster, New York (1988)

38. Taylor, S., Jaques, N., Nosakhare, E., Sano, A., Picard, R.: Personalized multitask learning for predicting tomorrow's mood, stress, and health. IEEE Trans. Affective Comput. **11**(2), 200–213 (2020). https://doi.org/10.1109/TAFFC.2017.2784832

39. Liu, B.: Sentiment Analysis and Opinion Mining. Springer International Publishing, Cham (2012). https://doi.org/10.1007/978-3-031-02145-9

40. Marsella, S., Gratch, J.: Modeling coping behavior in virtual humans: don't worry, be happy. In: Proceedings of the Second International Joint Conference on Autonomous Agents and Multiagent Systems - AAMAS 2003, Melbourne, Australia, pp. 313. ACM Press (2003). https://doi.org/10.1145/860575.860626

41. Lazarus, R.S.: Emotion and Adaptation. Oxford University Press, Oxford (1991)

42. Boukricha, H., Wachsmuth, I., Carminati, M N., Knoeferle, P.: A computational model of empathy: empirical evaluation. In: 2013 Humaine Association Conference on Affective Computing and Intelligent Interaction, Geneva, Switzerland, pp. 1–6. IEEE (2013) https://doi.org/10.1109/ACII.2013.7

43. Paiva, A., Leite, I., Boukricha, H., Wachsmuth, I.: Empathy in virtual agents and robots: a survey. ACM Trans. Interact. Intell. Syst. 7(3), 1–40 (2017). https://doi.org/10.1145/2912150

44. El-Nasr, M.S.: FLAME—Fuzzy Logic Adaptive Model of Emotions (2000)

45. Reilly, W.S.N.: Believable Social and Emotional Agents (1996)

46. Woods, S.: Exploring the design space of robots: children's perspectives. Interact. Comput. 18(6), 1390–1418 (2006). https://doi.org/10.1016/j.intcom.2006.05.001

47. Broadbent, E., et al.: Robots with display screens: a robot with a more humanlike face display is perceived to have more mind and a better personality. PLoS ONE 8(8), e72589 (2013). https://doi.org/10.1371/journal.pone.0072589

48. Kim, Y., Kwak, S.S., Kim, M.: Am i acceptable to you? Effect of a robot's verbal language forms on people's social distance from robots. Comput. Hum. Behav. 29(3), 1091–1101 (2013). https://doi.org/10.1016/j.chb.2012.10.001

49. Bertelli, J.A., Peruchi, F.M., Rost, J.R., Tacca, C.P.: Treatment of scaphoid non-unions by a palmar approach with vascularised bone graft harvested from the thumb. J. Hand. Surg. Eur. 32(2), 217–223 (2007). https://doi.org/10.1016/J.JHSB.2006.10.014

50. Gu, J., Kim, T., Kwon, Y.: Am i have to extrovert personality? An empirical investigation of robot's personality on the two contexts, INDJST. 8(26), 1–11 (2015) https://doi.org/10.17485/ijst/2015/v8i26/87065

51. Celiktutan, O., Gunes, H.: Computational analysis of human-robot interactions through first-person vision: personality and interaction experience. In: 2015 24th IEEE International Symposium on Robot and Human Interactive Communication (RO-MAN), Kobe, Japan, pp. 815–820. IEEE (2015). https://doi.org/10.1109/ROMAN.2015.7333602

52. Chang, R.C.-S., Lu, H.-P., Yang, P.: Stereotypes or golden rules? exploring likable voice traits of social robots as active aging companions for tech-savvy baby boomers in Taiwan. Comput. Hum. Behav. 84, 194–210 (2018). https://doi.org/10.1016/j.chb.2018.02.025

53. Fogg, B.J.: Persuasive technology: using computers to change what we think and do. Ubiquity 5, 32 (2002). https://doi.org/10.1145/764008.763957

54. Shi, Y.: The application of psychology in human-computer interaction, DEStech transactions on social science. Educ. Hum. Sci. (2017). https://doi.org/10.12783/DTSSEHS/MSIE2017/15429

55. Zhang, L.: Social Psychology (2022).https://doi.org/10.31219/osf.io/3w5tr

56. Reeves, B., Nass, C.: The Media Equation: how people treat computers, television, and new media like real people and Pla, Bibliovault OAI Repository, the University of Chicago Press (1996)

57. Sepahpour, G., Blackler, A., Chamorro-Koc, M.I.: Love for inanimate objects: a model to understand relationships between people and products. In: Bruyns, G., Wei, H. (eds.) With Design: Reinventing Design Modes: Proceedings of the 9th Congress of the International Association of Societies of Design Research (IASDR 2021), pp. 291–310. Springer Nature Singapore, Singapore (2022). https://doi.org/10.1007/978-981-19-4472-7_20

58. Park, S., Nam, T.-J.: Product-personification method for generating interaction ideas. Int. J. Interact. Des. Manuf. **9**(2), 97–105 (2015). https://doi.org/10.1007/s12008-013-0196-x

59. Ickes, W., Knowles, E.S. (eds.): Personality, Roles, and Social Behavior. Springer New York, New York, NY (1982). https://doi.org/10.1007/978-1-4613-9469-3

60. Iyer, E.S., Debevec, K.: Gender stereotyping of products: are products like people? In: Malhotra, N.K. (ed.) Proceedings of the 1986 Academy of Marketing Science (AMS) Annual Conference, pp. 40–45. Springer International Publishing, Cham (2015). https://doi.org/10.1007/978-3-319-11101-8_9

61. Cho, J., Rader, E.: The role of conversational grounding in supporting symbiosis between people and digital assistants. ACM Hum. Comput. Interact. **4**(CSCW1), 1–28 (2020). https://doi.org/10.1145/3392838

62. Mori, M., MacDorman, K.F., Kageki, N.: The uncanny valley [from the field]. IEEE Robot. Autom. Mag. **19**(2), 98–100 (2012). https://doi.org/10.1109/MRA.2012.2192811

63. Craenen, B.G.W., Deshmukh, A., Foster, M.E., Vinciarelli, A.: Shaping gestures to shape personality: big-five traits, godspeed scores and the similarity-attraction effect (2018)

64. Joosse, M., Lohse, M., Perez, J. G., Evers, V.: What you do is who you are: the role of task context in perceived social robot personality. In: 2013 IEEE International Conference on Robotics and Automation, Karlsruhe, Germany. pp. 2134–2139. IEEE (2013). https://doi.org/10.1109/ICRA.2013.6630863

65. Govers, P.C.M., Schoormans, J.P.L.: Product personality and its influence on consumer preference. J. Consum. Mark. **22**(4), 189–197 (2005). https://doi.org/10.1108/07363760510605308

66. Mugge, R., Govers, P.C.M., Schoormans, J.P.L.: The development and testing of a product personality scale. Des. Stud. **30**(3), 287–302 (2009). https://doi.org/10.1016/j.destud.2008.10.002

67. Davis, M.H.: Measuring individual differences in empathy: evidence for a multidimensional approach. J. Pers. Soc. Psychol. **44**(1), 113–126 (1983). https://doi.org/10.1037/0022-3514.44.1.113

68. Barrett-Lennard, G.T.: The relationship inventory now: issues and advances in theory, method and use. In: The Psychotherapeutic Process: A Research Handbook, Greenberg, L. S., Pinsof, W. M., Greenberg, L. S., Pinsof, W. M., Eds., Guilford Press, pp. 439–476 (1986)

69. Kuipers, B.: How can we trust a robot? Commun. ACM **61**(3), 86–95 (2018). https://doi.org/10.1145/3173087

70. Dang, J., Liu, L.: Robots are friends as well as foes: ambivalent attitudes toward mindful and mindless AI robots in the United States and China. Comput. Hum. Behav. **115**, 106612 (2021). https://doi.org/10.1016/j.chb.2020.106612

71. Becker, C., Prendinger, H., Ishizuka, M., Wachsmuth, I.: Evaluating affective feedback of the 3D agent max in a competitive cards game. In: Tao, J., Tan, T., Picard, R.W. (eds.) ACII 2005. LNCS, vol. 3784, pp. 466–473. Springer, Heidelberg (2005). https://doi.org/10.1007/11573548_60

72. Dove, G., Halskov, K., Forlizzi, J., Zimmerman, J.: UX design innovation: challenges for working with machine learning as a design material. In: Proceedings of the 2017 CHI Conference on Human Factors in Computing Systems, Denver Colorado USA, pp. 278–288. ACM (2017) https://doi.org/10.1145/3025453.3025739

73. Amershi, S., et al.: Guidelines for human-AI interaction. In: Proceedings of the 2019 CHI Conference on Human Factors in Computing Systems, New York, NY, USA, pp. 1–13. Association for Computing Machinery (2019). https://doi.org/10.1145/3290605.3300233

74. Yang, Q., Steinfeld, A., Rosé, C., Zimmerman, J.: Re-examining whether, why, and how human-AI interaction is uniquely difficult to design. In: Proceedings of the 2020 CHI Conference on Human Factors in Computing Systems, Honolulu HI USA, pp.1–13. ACM (2020). https://doi.org/10.1145/3313831.3376301

75. van Allen, P.: Prototyping ways of prototyping AI. Interactions **25**(6), 46–51 (2018)
76. Bogers, S., Frens, J., van Kollenburg, J., Deckers, E., Hummels, C.: Connected baby bottle: a design case study towards a framework for data-enabled design. In: Proceedings of the 2016 ACM Conference on Designing Interactive Systems, New York, NY, USA, pp. 301–311. Association for Computing Machinery (2016). https://doi.org/10.1145/2901790.2901855

Using Artificial Intelligence in Music Creation? a Survey Based on Copyright Consciousness

Pin-Hsuan Chen and Pei-Luen Patrick Rau

Department of Industrial Engineering, Tsinghua University, Beijing, China
rpl@tsinghua.edu.cn

Abstract. Artificial intelligence (AI) hits music creation. With the assistance of AI, the threshold of music generation decreases. Users are capable of generating high-quality music for entertainment and business purposes. As the increasing number of music generated by either AI algorithms or musicians, who should be responsible for or benefit from the music? Whether the music is public property or private property is widely argued. This study focuses on copyright consciousness of music created by AI algorithms. To understand copyright consciousness, this study investigated five copyright determinants (economic incentive, independence, creativity, intelligence effort, and tool property) and identified eight music creation scenarios based on stakeholders (programmers, music producers and end-users) and the degree of AI involvement (fully autonomous, partially autonomous, and automatic) through survey research. This study ended up with 137 valid responses via online survey platforms. Kruskal-Wallis test and logistic regression were used for data analysis. According to the results, this study indicated that creativity and tool property were important for programmers' copyright consciousness; economic incentive mattered end-users' copyright consciousness; economic incentive, independence, and creativity were critical for music producers' copyright consciousness. Moreover, tool property influenced overall copyright consciousness in AI creative spaces, while intelligence effort was increasingly important as the growth of the degree of AI involvement. Gathering the results, this study proposed a copyright consciousness framework for suggesting critical copyright determinants for recognizing AI music as personal or public property from the perspective of different stakeholders. As the increasing use of AI in music creation, this study believes that the results and proposed framework could help understand copyright consciousness from various aspects, which should be foundations for developing future human-centered AI-related copyright.

Keywords: Artificial intelligence · Copyright · AI music · Music creation

1 Introduction

Artificial intelligence (AI) reduces the threshold of music creation and facilitates music production processes. Everyone may be a creator with the assistance of AI. For example, users can generate soundtracks with inputting genres, moods and instruments to AI machine; musicians can facilitate the songwriting process with AI collaboration;

manufactures can produce perfect music pieces for commercialization by developing powerful AI algorithms. While debates about the copyright of the work created with AI are ongoing, there are legal grey areas of the copyright to computer-generated work, including arts, music, and articles.

The scope of copyright has expanded to encompass anyone who uses AI machines. Discussions about the copyright of AI-generated work (AI work) suggest that individuals such as users, musicians, manufacturers, and programmers all contribute to the creation process to varying degrees, which raises questions about who has rightful ownership of the work. However, the current copyright practices in most countries define "work" as a form of presenting ideas and require human authors for copyrightable work. This definition is not applicable to AI work since the originality and human involvement are uncertain in AI-based creation.

It is true in creative spaces where rules about AI work are ambiguous and immature. This leads to negative impacts on human beings due to the lack of passion on work, the loss of employment, and even disordered market [1]. To safeguard humanity, a complete understanding of copyright is necessary as it is a formal way to protect human values from being threatened by AI. Investigating public copyright consciousness is a starting point to achieve this goal. This study aims to focus on the copyright consciousness of AI-generated music and propose a copyright framework for stakeholders involved in AI music creation. Given the blooming applications of AI, this study believes that understanding people's attitudes towards AI work can provide prospective insights for the future of AI copyright.

2 Related Work

2.1 Computer-Generated Work and AI Work

Computer-generated work has been widely mentioned in several court judgments and legal discussions. Computer scientists have argued the necessity for copyright protection of computer-generated work since the early stages of AI. Although the first submission of the registration for computer-generated work was before 1965, two reasons have made it difficult to manage (Copyright Office Library of Congress, 1966) [2]. One argued that the computer was merely a tool, and the other was the human prerequisite of copyright [3].

AI has significantly advanced computer-generated work as it can approximate human intelligence and collaborate with humans to complete tasks [4]. For example, with the assistance of AI, video creators can quickly find out and regenerate suitable music for fitting their videos [5]. Thus, AI is somewhat autonomous and unpredictable, making AI work an extending definition of computer-generated work [6].

Nevertheless, the lack of transparency of AI presents new challenges for the copyright of AI work since it impedes the ability to determine the contributions of programmers and users to the AI work [7]. While AI is highly autonomous, humans are still required to manipulate the AI machine. In the creation process of AI work, programmers have to develop and tune the algorithms, while users execute AI machine for creation. This study argued that both roles do put intelligence efforts on creating an AI work, making them eligible for rights over the AI work. Therefore, in addition to consider the tool property and human prerequisite in copyright domain following with the traditional regulations, this study suggested that intelligence efforts should be crucial factor for clarifying the responsibility between AI machines and humans, which is associated with copyright concerns, legal and ethical problems [8, 9].

2.2 Divergent Copyright of AI Work

Copyright ensures authorship of the original work, which is established for two primary purposes: 1) to contribute to public welfare and 2) to encourage continuous creation [10]. The first purpose is to attract more attention and increase public accessibility, which builds mutual communication between the public and the authors, and develop a good connection. The second purpose shows that copyright serves as an incentive for authors to keep innovation [11]. In other words, copyright protection can affirm efforts of specified authors and ensure their rights over the work.

However, whether AI work can be applicable to the current copyright remains unclear and varies across countries. Civil law countries generally employ natural right justification, while common law countries adopt utilitarianism, resulting in different copyright perspectives on AI work [12–14]. Common law countries such as the United Kingdom (UK) explicitly mention computer-generated work, while civil law countries like Japan do not [15, 16]. The UK Act s 178 states the copyright of computer-generated work protected those work generated by an original program and *"the work generated by a computer in circumstances such that there is no human author of the work"*. Similarly, the Irish Copyright and Related Rights Act 2000 protects that the work *"the work is generated by computer in circumstances where the author of the work is not an individual"*. Nonetheless, the copyrightability of AI work was still debated based on factors like originality, creativity, and algorithmic adaptation [17], with creativity being the most significant concern [16].

McCutcheon [18] identified three different authorship types undertaken across the following countries: the UK, the United States, Germany, Italy, and Australia. The first type was the UK, stating that the authorship belonged to the person who performed the work's necessary arrangements. The second type was the US, Germany, and Italy. Their rule of thumbs was to give authorship to works that satisfy human prerequisites and personal intellectual creation. Hence, creative individuals are required for authorship. The third type was Australia, which prohibited the protection of computer-generated work unless it could benefit the public and originated through intelligence effort. Benefitting the public was another concern for authorship in the third implementation type, in addition to human requirements. Hoesl and Butz [19] reported that various authorships were emerging, and the degree of work experience might be a sense of authorship in AI applications. Nevertheless, recognizing authorship in AI work is still an open problem, and there is no ground truth to follow. Erdélyi and Goldsmith [20] suggested that proactive action internationally helped regulate wide-scale AI applications.

While many studies have examined copyright laws related to AI work, few have focused on relevant laws in Asian countries. Two notable cases in China in 2019 shed light on the issue of copyright protection for AI work. In *Beijing Film Law Firm v Beijing Baidu Netcom Science & Technology Co Ltd (Film)*, the court concluded that natural persons were required for copyright protection; thus, the work was not copyrightable

[21]. Additionally, in *Shenzhen Tencent Computer System Co Ltd v Shanghai Yingxun Technology Co Ltd (Tencent)*, the court presented that the output of the intelligent writing computer met the requirements of written work; thus, the work was copyrightable [22]. In addition to justifying the copyrightability of AI work, both cases highlighted the importance of considering the key action for the output and originality for determining authorship in AI creative spaces. This study argued that these issues must be discussed to address the copyrightability of AI work.

2.3 Research Model

AI music is a form of computer-generated works, and it is a work of cognitive non-consciousness with few personalities. The gap between the artist and the audience have been enlarged because of the engagement of programmers. Daniele and Song [23] reported that it was difficult to examine the value of creativity and the role of AI in art-creation procedures. Identifying human intelligence input and ensuring predictable and duplicable expressions are two challenges for AI copyright. In fact, AI relies heavily on abundant datasets and algorithms. Artists' and programmers' input makes ambiguous in responsibility among artists, programmers, and even machines [24, 25].

Based on AI music creation processes, this study proposes a research model (See Fig. 1) to understand AI copyright consciousness with copyright determinants. Three copyright stakeholders of AI music, including programmers, end-users of AI machine, and music producers, were considered in the research model. This study constructed eight music creation scenarios on the basis of hybrid situations of human and machine intelligence, which clearly divided different human-machine collaboration scenarios by decision preparation and decision [26]. In this way, this study could figure out copyright consciousness that AI music in the personal domain or in the public domain in different hybrid AI music creation scenarios. Meanwhile, the critical copyright determinants for stakeholders in AI music creation in these scenarios were pointed out.

There are five determinants identified for AI copyright in the research model, including economic incentive (of work), independence (of work), the creativity (of work), intelligence effort (whether the human effort is involved during creation?), and tool property (what role does the AI play as?). First, economic incentive encourages artists to maintain their creation and motivation because of copyright. Second, originality and creativity contribute to the independent work, while it is difficult to determine in deep learning methods, such as a generative adversarial network (GAN). It enhances performance by self-generated noises and reduces the originality and creativity of human beings at the same time. Third, a minimal degree of creativity is essential for copyrightable work [27]. The prior visual examination of creativity is insufficient and no longer adaptable to distinguish between human and computer creativity. Fourth, whether or not human intelligence is involved in the work is difficult to evaluate [28]. Personality and human intelligence may be excluded once the neural network can generate without human interruption. Fifth, the role of a computer is a tool or an autonomous machine during creation. This is because a lower autonomous level is likely to be a support for artists and relevant to clarifying a work's copyrightability [29].

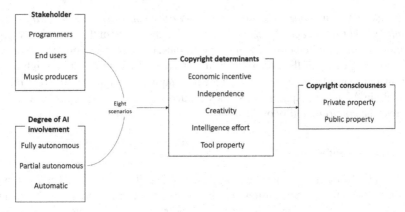

Fig. 1. Research model of this study

3 Methodology

3.1 Questionnaire Design

There are three parts of the survey questionnaire, including demographic characteristics, the understanding of AI music, and scenarios for measuring copyright consciousness. First, the demographic characteristics and participants' previous music learning experiences, such as age and instruments, were collected. The understanding of AI music revealed participants' knowledge of AI, music, and law. Subsequently, eight scenarios were designed for investigation.

Although AI machine is complex, programmers might be the ones who have the best understanding of the mechanism for maintaining and developing the machine. By contrast, it is like a black box for end-users and music producers. Thus, the studied scenarios were designed according to three stakeholders' perspectives with different degrees of AI involvement. Table 1 presents eight scenarios in this study.

Table 1. Perspective and degree of AI involvement in eight scenarios

Scenario	Perspective	Degree of AI involvement	Description
S1	Programmers	Fully autonomic	Feed data directly
S2	Programmers	Partially autonomic	Gather rules beforehand
S3	End-users	Fully autonomic	With end-users input, unpredictable results
S4	End-users	Partially autonomic	Selection of unpredictable results
S5	Music producers	Fully autonomic	No input, unpredictable results

(continued)

Table 1. (*continued*)

Scenario	Perspective	Degree of AI involvement	Description
S6	Music producers	Partially autonomic	Machine evaluation
S7	Music producers	Partially autonomic	Human-machine collaboration
S8	Music producers	Automatic	

S1 and S2 were designed to examine the copyright when programmers applied AI for developing purposes. S3 and S4 were proposed to investigate copyright consciousness when AI was released to the market for entertainment purposes. S5, S6, S7, and S8 were described to evaluate the copyright consciousness of music producers who are likely to use AI for work. Table 2 describes the eight scenarios in detail.

Table 2. Description of eight scenarios

Scenario	Scenario description
S1	To create a track with your styles through a machine, programmers directly input a large number of your works to generate music of your styles by the program
S2	To create a track with your styles through a machine, programmers analyse a large number of your works and conclude your styles (scales, modes, arrangement, etc.) as rules. Then they can generate music of your styles by the program under the condition of rules
S3	There is a music generation software, and it is a product for users. Users would do only two steps: one is to input someone's music, and the other is to click the "Start" button. After that, they could obtain a piece of music with someone's style
S4	There is a music generation software, and it is a product for users. After inputting someone's music, users then click the "Start" button. They could obtain a piece of music with someone's style. Furthermore, users can evaluate the music based on their preferences and choose to keep it or not
S5	Artificial Intelligence can generate music with originality. Thus, we can complete the whole creation process simply with an AI machine. The only we should do is to click a button and motivate the program
S6	To generate a suite, we input several music pieces to a machine. After machine evaluating the quality and performance of a different combination of music, it will output the optimal suite
S7	You summarize someone's styles into rules and create some part of music as conditions. Then you could generate a music piece from your collaboration with the machine
S8	You can make music with the assistance of AI by entering your ideas to the machine. Then, a piece of music can be generated accordingly

In the questionnaire, every respondent was assigned four random scenarios and completed the following questions regarding the five copyright characteristics (economic incentive, independence, creativity, intelligence effort, and tool property). In addition, the copyright consciousness indicating the work generated from the scenario was in public or personal domain should be answered. A seven-point Likert scale was applied to participants to indicate their agreement with the corresponding statements. A score of 1 represented completely disagree, while a score of 7 meant completely agree. The questions are presented in the Appendix.

This study ensured response quality via controlling the questionnaire in a short version, indicating respondents could finish within 15 to 30 min [30]. Meanwhile, this study provided small prizes to appreciate their participant for each valid response.

3.2 Reliability Analysis

According to the rule of Cronbach's alpha coefficients in the exploratory analysis, it is acceptable when the value is greater than 0.5. Therefore, to test the internal consistency, this study calculated the Cronbach's alpha for each determinant of scenarios in the questionnaire. Results indicated that reliability of this study was acceptable (Table 3).

Table 3. Cronbach's alpha for the investigation of copyright consciousness

Determinant					
Scenario	EI	ID	CR	IE	TP
S1	0.91	0.79	0.87	0.72	0.88
S2	0.89	0.78	0.88	0.69	0.81
S3	0.94	0.85	0.86	0.79	0.86
S4	0.96	0.91	0.93	0.79	0.92
S5	0.97	0.91	0.87	0.87	0.85
S6	0.96	0.87	0.86	0.81	0.92
S7	0.93	0.89	0.86	0.70	0.94
S8	0.94	0.87	0.87	0.72	0.90

*EI = Economic incentive; ID = Independence; CR = Creativity; IE = Intelligence effort; TP = Tool property

3.3 Participants

This study received 137 valid questionnaires. The age of the 137 respondents ranged from 19 to 64 (mean = 25.37, SD = 7.96). Those who had learned music for at least one year were eligible to participate in this investigation as they should reflect the needs of people and be potential users of AI machine for music creation. Nearly 70% of respondents (95 out of 137) had learned music for more than five years, while over 40% of respondents (57 out of 137) had more than ten years of learning experience.

Since most AI and electronic music were based on Western music elements, this study also noted the instruments that respondents had learned. Respondents had to recall the instruments they had learned as much as possible. Among all respondents, 73 respondents learned piano (53%), which was the most popular instrument mentioned in the questionnaires. On the other hand, Guzheng was reported as the most favoured Chinese instrument.

Additionally, this study asked participants to report their experiences for making music in the past year, which indicated their familiarity with the music creation process. Twenty respondents disclosed that they participated in music creation, including, but not limited to, composing, arranging, and recording. On average, they were involved in the music creation process 3.7 times (SD = 3.21) in the past year.

4 Results and Discussion

Results overviewed participants' understanding of AI music and relevant legal knowledge. Nonparametric test was applied in this analysis because the data did not follow the normal distribution. Hence, this study used Kruskal-Wallis Test and post-hoc test for the Kruskal-Wallis Test with R to conclude the results. In addition, this study conducted logistic regression to predict the overall copyright consciousness, which refers to personal or public property. Five copyright determinants served as independent variables, and overall copyright consciousness was the dependent variable.

4.1 Understanding of AI Music

This study collected the participants' understanding of the relevant issues in AI music before the main questionnaire. Figure 2 shows the overall understanding levels. With the comparison of AI + music (mean = 3.33, SD = 1.47) and AI + music + law (mean = 2.23, SD = 1.23), participants were more familiar with AI + music. Nevertheless, over half of the participants scored 1 to 4 in AI + music, which indicated that the understanding of AI music was limited. On the other hand, most respondents scored 1 to 4 in AI + music + law (129 out of 137, 93%), which meant that nearly all of them were unfamiliar with the legal issues involving the AI.

The results could project two implications of people's consciousness of copyright as the increasing AI application in art creation, particularly for music. First, it is universal that consciousness of scientific and technological laws is weak. Second, the regulation of computer-assisted or computer-generated works, such as those empowered by AI, remains ambiguous.

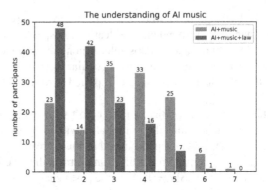

Fig. 2. Participants' understanding of AI music

4.2 Copyright Determinants – Programmers' Perspective

In the AI music creation process, programmers are critical because they are responsible for algorithms. Therefore, their thoughts result in different AI mechanisms. The lower the input, the higher the degree of autonomy the AI machine will have. In other words, the results indicated that the outcomes would rely on machine consciousness as autonomy increased (see Fig. 3(a)).

Statistical analysis results reported that there was no significant difference among five determinants. While two implications could be highlighted according to descriptive results. First, creativity was lower in the fully autonomic scenario. The results reported that participants thought less creativity was involved in the creation process when the data were input without actions. This implication reflected the importance of human creativity during programming. Second, respondents revealed that the machine's tool property in the partially autonomic scenario was higher than that in the fully autonomic scenario. Both scenarios usually occurred far from the market since many of them were ongoing projects. Accordingly, the results suggested that creativity and tool property were the two critical dimensions to investigate while specifying the copyright of work created during the development process.

4.3 Copyright Determinants – End-Users' Perspective

Human intelligence input was low after releasing it to the market. Some people might argue that end-users had the right to own the AI machine via the purchasing contract. This study aims to determine the crucial dimensions of copyright to clarify the arguing targets from the end-user's perspective (see Fig. 3(b)).

This study found that economic incentive in the partially autonomic scenario was marginally significantly higher than that in the fully autonomic scenario ($p = 0.05$). The results concluded that rewarding end-users with participation via evaluation and filtering machine outcomes promotes their willingness to make music with AI. On the other hand, respondents reported that a fully autonomic machine might not increase their intentions, even though the work was valuable. As a result, economic incentive was critical in determining the copyright of machine works in the scenario in which end-users were able to participate.

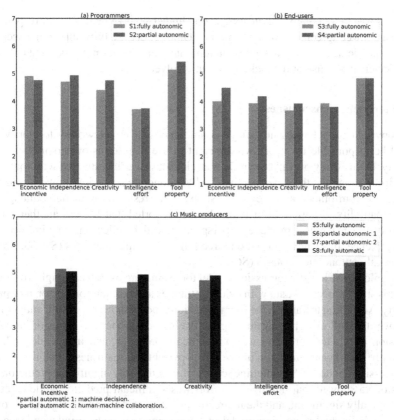

Fig. 3. Results of five determinants in eight scenarios

4.4 Copyright Determinants – Music Producers' Perspective

Repetitive and redundant tasks were eliminated with the assistance of AI, so that music producers can put more effort into creativity and innovation. In other words, the music creation process could be facilitated by AI. To understand the influence of copyright dimensions on the relevant creation processes, this study constructed four scenarios for investigation.

According to Fig. 3(c) and the results of statistical analysis, the fully autonomic scenario (S5) was significantly different from S7 and S8 in terms of economic incentive, independence, creativity, and intelligence effort ($p < 0.05$). While S5 was significantly different from S7 for tool property as well ($p < 0.05$). The scenario with machine decision-making (S6) was significantly different from S5 in terms of intelligence effort ($p < 0.05$). This study gathered five implications. First, a human involved in the music creation process is essential to determine copyright in terms of economic incentive. Making music in a fully autonomic scenario might not increase music producers' motivation due to the low economic incentive. Second, in terms of independence, human ideas in the music creation process would be the most crucial in determining independence. Third, except for the fully autonomic scenario, the music created under the other three scenarios was more creative, indicating users' higher involvement. Fourth, respondents reported a lower agreement to give a human author under the fully autonomic scenario. Fifth, respondents reported that a fully autonomic scenario was not a tool that enhanced user efficiency because of the lack of human involvement.

4.5 Copyright Consciousness

The copyright for AI work nowadays is ambiguous, it is noteworthy to clarify who should be responsible for it or own the right to use it in terms of personal or public property. In this study overall copyright consciousness was investigated with four target scenarios. Among the three perspectives, fully autonomic scenarios showed significant differences from others, and they were supposed to result in dramatic challenges for the compatibility of copyright. The results also reported that S6 was another notable scenario from the music producers' perspective, which relied on machine decision-making. Hence, this study focused on three fully autonomic scenarios (S1, S3, S5) and one partially autonomic scenario (S6).

To build up the logistic regression model for examining overall copyright consciousness, this study processed data with evident attitudes and opinions on personal or public property. According to Table 4, the four regression models showed a significant improvement over the null model by evaluating the likelihood ratio test. In terms of individual regression of S1, tool property was a significant predictor, and independence was a marginally significant predictor of overall copyright consciousness. For the individual regression model of S3, intelligence effort was the only significant predictor. The results of S5 showed that intelligence effort was significant predictor while creativity was marginally significant, and the intercept was suggested to apply to the model of S5. As for the individual regression model of S6, economic incentive, independence, and intelligence effort were significant predictors of overall copyright consciousness.

According to odd ratios, the increasing agreement to tool property in S1, people were likely to view the AI music as personal property ($OR_{S1} = 0.21, 95\%$ C.I. $= [0.02, 0.77]$). Whereas, the AI music in S3, S5, and S6 as public property as the increasing agreement to the lack of intelligence effort ($OR_{S3} = 2,29, 95\%$ C.I. $= [1.23, 5.01]$; $OR_{S5} = 7.11$, 95% C.I. $= [2.44, 35.60]$; $OR_{S6} = 5.04, 95\%$ C.I. $= [1.78,26.63]$). Although the targeted four scenarios were AI decision-making, the overall copyright consciousness differed from the music creation stages in which autonomous AI was exploited. Tool property was related to an earlier stage, such as S1, and intelligence effort was corresponding to stages approaching the market, like S3, S5, and S6.

Table 4. Logistic regression analysis of S1, S3, S5, and S6

		Constant	EI	ID	CR	IE	TP		Likelihood ratio test
S1	b	6.7	0.79	−2.29	−0.24	1.15	−1.57	Overall model evaluation	25.64
	OR	–	2.21	0.1	0.78	3.15	0.21		5
	p	0.15	0.22		0.84	0.18			
S3	b	− 0.85	0.42	− 0.84	− 0.33	0.83	0.02		19.45
	OR	–	1.52	0.43	0.72	2.29	1.02		5
	p	0.67	0.2	0.13	0.56		0.96		
S5	b	− 7.32	0.17	− 0.74	− 1.04	1.96	0.86		40.17
	OR	–	1.19	0.48	0.35	7.11	2.36		5
	p		0.51	0.16					
S6	b	3	1.08	− 1.91	− 0.56	1.62	− 0.87		27.18
	OR	–	2.93	0.15	0.57	5.04	0.42		5
	p	0.14			0.23		0.1		

*EI = Economic incentive; ID = Independence; CR = Creativity; IE = Intelligence effort; TP = Tool property

4.6 Copyright Framework

Determining the copyright of the AI music generated by a fully autonomous machine should be a challenge. Whether it is included in the personal or public domain is one of the most difficult problems. Thus, this study tackled this problem through the investigation of copyright consciousness under scenarios that stakeholders were interacting with a fully autonomous machine. According to the results of logistic regression, this study revealed critical factors to recognize personal and public property. Once the AI music was indicated as personal work, clarifying the copyright holders was important because it reserves the right for their own use.

Therefore, this study proposed a copyright framework for stakeholders in AI music creation (See Fig. 4). The presented framework first reported conditions for identifying AI music as personal property. Then, determinants for the copyright of each stakeholder in the AI music production process were suggested.

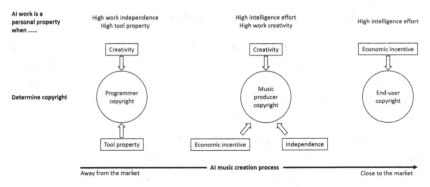

Fig. 4. Copyright framework for AI music stakeholders

5 Conclusion

This study has revealed the copyright consciousness from stakeholders' perspectives. Their concerns about the copyright of AI music are varied because of their proximity to the market. According to the results, this study suggested that programmers considered creativity and tool property essential to determine the copyright of AI music; music producers paid close attention to economic incentive, independence, and creativity speaking of the copyright of AI music; end-users focused on economic incentive specifically. Apart from that, the increasing tool property of the machine in an earlier stage of AI music creation (particularly programmers) would make the AI work a personal property, while the decreasing intelligence effort engaged in the latter stages of AI music creation (particularly end-users) would make the AI work a public property. In summary, this study proposed a copyright framework for AI music stakeholders, which gave grounds for further development of AI-related copyright based on human-centred perspectives.

Disclosure of Interests. The authors have no competing interests to declare that are relevant to the content of this article.

Appendix

Table A. Questionnaire for copyright consciousness

Copyright determinant	Items	Sources
Economic incentive	• The economic benefits of this music work in the market will enhance my willingness to create music in the future • I think the economic value of this music work positively influences my willingness to create music • When I learn that this music work is with economic value, I will be more active in creating music	[10, 11]
Independence	• The value of this music work is equal to my own work • I think this music work should be protected by copyright as other music works • No matter how the work is produced, it deserves equal rights	[10, 17]
Creativity	• I think author's creativity is presented in this music work • Creativity exists in this music work • This music work is with originality and should be protected with copyright • Intellectual effort is necessary to accomplish this music work	[23, 27]
Intelligence effort	• Human is not necessary in this music creation process • I think the artificial intelligence applied in this music work is autonomous • I think the artificial intelligence applied in this music work can complete critical creating actions, for example, compose, arrangements	[3, 18, 24, 25]
Tool property	• I think this artificial intelligence is a tool to make music • Making music with this artificial intelligence enhance my efficiency • People can make music with the assistance of this artificial intelligence	[3]
Overall copyright consciousness	• This music work is personal property. To do anything that may infringe authors' right should ask for permission beforehand • This music work is public property. Everyone can use it without limitation	–

References

1. Li, R.: A philosophical analysis of AI-generated works and the copyright law of China. Int. J. Soc. Sci. Educ. Res. **4**(8), 139–143 (2021)

2. Copyright Office Library of Congress. Sixty-eighth annual report of the register of copyrights, Sixty-eight Annual Report (1966)
3. Miller, A.R.: Copyright protection for computer programs, databases, and computer-generated works: Is anything new since CONTU? Harv. Law Rev. **106**(5), 977–1073 (1993)
4. Thomas, S.: Luna: a game-based rating system for artificial intelligence. PhD dissertation, Harvard John A. Paulson School of Engineering and Applied Sciences, Harvard University, Cambridge, MA (2016)
5. Frid, E., Gomes, C., Jin, Z.: Music Creation by Example. In: Proceedings of the 2020 CHI Conference on Human Factors in Computing Systems (CHI'20), pp.1–13. Association for Computing Machinery, New York, NY, USA (2020)
6. Lambert, P.: Computer generated works and copyright: Selfies, traps, robots, AI and machine learning. Eur. Intellect. Prop. Rev. **39**(1), 12–20 (2017)
7. Drott, E.: Copyright, compensation, and commons in the music industry. Creative Ind. J. **14**(2), 190–207 (2021)
8. Loi, D., Wolf, C.T., Blomberg, J.L., Arar, R., Brereton, M.: Co-designing AI futures: Integrating AI ethics, social computing and design. In: Companion Publication of the 2019 on Designing Interactive Systems Conference 2019 Companion. Association for Computing Machinery, New York (2019)
9. Whittlestone, J., Nyrup, R., Alexandrova, A., Cave, S.: The role and limits of principles in AI ethics: towards a focus on tensions. In: Proceedings of the 2019 AAAI/ACM Conference on AI, Ethics, and Society. New York: Association for Computing Machinery (2019)
10. Birhane, A., Dijk, J.: Robot rights? Let's talk about human welfare instead. In: Proceedings of the 2020 AAAI/ACM Conference on AI, Ethics, and Society. Association for Computing Machinery, New York (2020)
11. Somaya, D., Varshney, L.R.: Embodiment, anthropomorphism, and intellectual property rights for AI creations. In: Proceedings of the 2018 AAAI/ACM Conference on AI, Ethics, and Society. Association for Computing Machinery, New York (2018)
12. Pejovic, C.: Civil law and common law: two different paths leading to the same coal. Victoria Univ. Wellington Law Rev. **32**(3), 817–842 (2001)
13. Goldstein, P., Hugenholtz, P.B.: International Copyright: Principles, Law, and Practice, 4th ed. Oxford University Press (2019)
14. Wan, Y., Lu, H.: Copyright protection for AI-generated outputs: the experience from China. Comput. Law Secur. Rev. **42**, 105581 (2021)
15. Ueno, T.: Copyright issues on artificial intelligence and machine learning. In: International Joint Conference on Artificial Intelligence 2017 Workshop: The First International Workshop on Sharing and Reuse of AI Work Products (2017)
16. Ueno, T.: Big data in Japan: copyright, trade secret and new regime in 2018. In: Sandeen, S.K., Rademacher, C., Ohly, A. (eds.) Research Handbook on Information Law and Governance. Edward Elgar Publishing (2021). https://doi.org/10.4337/9781788119924.00013
17. Susskind, R.E., Susskind, D.: The Future of Professions: How Technology Will Transform the Work of Human Experts. Oxford University Press, Oxford (2015)
18. McCutcheon, J.: The vanishing author in computer-generated works: a critical analysis of recent Australian case law. Melbourne Univ. Law Rev. **36**, 915–969 (2013)
19. Hoesl, A., Butz, A.: Sense of authorship and agency in computational creativity support. In: Proceedings of MICI 2017: CHI Workshop on Mixed-Initiative Creative Interfaces (2017)
20. Erdélyi, O.J., Goldsmith, J.: Regulating artificial intelligence proposal for a global solution. In: Proceedings of the 2018 AAAI/ACM Conference on AI, Ethics, and Society. Association for Computing Machinery, New York (2018)
21. Beijing Film Law Firm v Beijing Baidu Netcom Science & Technology Co Ltd., Jing 0491 Min Chu No 239 (Beijing Internet Court) (Film) (2018)

22. Shenzhen Tencent Computer System Co Ltd v Shanghai Yingxun Technology Co Ltd., Yue 0305 Min Chu No 14010 (Nanshan District Court of Shenzhen) (Tencent) (2019)
23. Daniele, A., Song, Y.Z.: AI + Art = Human. In: Proceedings of the 2019 AAAI/ACM Conference on AI, Ethics, and Society. New York: Association for Computing Machinery (2019)
24. Butler, T.L.: Can a computer be an author? copyright aspects of artificial intelligence. J. Commun. Entertain. Law **4**(4), 707–748 (1982)
25. Guadamuz, A.: Do Androids dream of electric copyright? Comparative analysis of originality in artificial intelligence generated works. Intell. Property Q. **2017**(2) (2017)
26. Piller, F.T., Nitsch, V., van der Aalst, W.: Hybrid intelligence in next generation manufacturing: an outlook on new forms of collaboration between human and algorithmic decision-makers in the factory of the future. In: Piller, F.T., Nitsch, V., Lüttgens, D., Mertens, A., Pütz, S., Van Dyck, M. (eds) Forecasting Next Generation Manufacturing. Contributions to Management Science. Springer, Cham (2022). https://doi.org/10.1007/978-3-031-07734-0_10
27. Denicola, R.: Ex Machina: copyright protection for computer-generated works. Rutgers Univ. Law Rev. **69**, 251–287 (2017)
28. Ruipérez, C., Gutiérrez, E., Puente, C., Olivas, J.A.: New challenges of copyright authorship in AI. In: Proceedings of the International Conference on Artificial Intelligence. CSREA Press, Las Vegas Nevada (2017)
29. Lubart, T.: How can computers be partners in the creative process: classification and commentary on the special issue. Int. J. Hum.-Comput. Stud. **63**(4), 365–369 (2005)
30. Deytskens, E., Ruyter, K.D., Wetzels, M., Oosterveld, P.: Response rate and response quality of Internet-based surveys: an experimental study. Mark. Lett. **15**(1), 21–36 (2004)

User Needs for Home Robotic Devices: A Comparison Between Middle-Aged and Older Adults

Hanjing Huang[✉], Wenwen Fu, and Rong Chen

School of Economics and Management, Fuzhou University, Fuzhou, People's Republic of China
hhj@fzu.edu.cn

Abstract. Robotic devices are being introduced to support active aging and enhance the lives of older adults at home. To effectively design and implement such devices, it is crucial to investigate the user needs of both older adults and their family members. This study aimed to investigate middle-aged adults and older adults' needs for home robotic devices. A total of 46 participants took part in interviews focusing on the appearance, social characteristics, functional requirements, and acceptance of home robotic devices. The results revealed that, in terms of appearance, middle-aged adults showed a preference for mechanical robots, whereas older adults favored humanoid robots. Both middle-aged and older adults liked female robots in terms of social characteristics. In terms of functional needs, both middle-aged and older adults considered life management functions as the most important. However, older adults placed less importance on entertainment functions, while middle-aged adults perceived emotional communication as less essential. In terms of the factors influencing acceptance, the critical factors that influence older adults' acceptance were economic factors and psychological factors. The critical factors influencing middle-aged adults' acceptance were economic factors, technological maturity, functional perfection, and other technical characteristics. These findings have implications for the design and implementation of home robotic devices.

Keywords: Home Robotic Devices · Older Adults · Aging · User Needs · Human-Robot Interaction

1 Introduction

With the acceleration of population aging in China, the old-age care mode selection among middle-aged and older adults has attracted more attention in recent studies [1, 2]. The introduction of home robotic devices can be used as an effective solution to address the challenges and enhance the daily well-being of older adults. These devices can not only assist older adults in daily tasks [3] but also provide companionship, alleviating feelings of loneliness [4].

Nonetheless, older adults' needs for home robotic devices have not been fully investigated. Compared to younger generations, older adults also have lower proficiency in

P.-L. P. Rau (Ed.): HCII 2024, LNCS 14702, pp. 226–244, 2024.
https://doi.org/10.1007/978-3-031-60913-8_16

using smart machines [5]. When introducing robotic devices into the domestic environ-ment, it is crucial to take into account the specific preferences of each family member regarding their usage. Particularly in China, home-based elderly care is the primary mode of elderly care, and older adults are more dependent on their children. Previous research found that younger, middle-aged, and older adults differed significantly in their user requirements and acceptance of the smart home voice assistant [6].

Therefore, this study aims to investigate the user needs of home robotic devices in middle-aged and older adults. The user needs include their preferences in robotic devices' appearance, social characteristics, and functions. Moreover, this study also analyzed the factors influencing the acceptance of home robotic devices. The results could provide insights to aid in the design and development of home robotic devices for various age groups.

2 Literature Review

2.1 Effects of Robotic Devices' Characteristics on Human-Robot Interaction

Previous research has shown that the appearance and social characteristics of robots are crucial factors affecting human-robot interaction [7]. Older adults exhibited higher sensitivity towards the visual aesthetics of robots, the visual aesthetics of robots also impacted their acceptance of such technologies [3]. Moreover, users were likely to con-nect robotic devices with their functions. For example, mechanical robots were often perceived as ill-equipped to handle certain social tasks such as nursing and teaching [8], while humanoid robots were perceived as more useful and intelligent than their mechanical counterparts [9]. In terms of robot size, smaller robots were preferred in home environments, whereas larger robots were favored in medical care tasks [8].

In terms of robots' social characteristics, previous research found that receptionist robots were frequently designed with more feminine attributes and were perceived as being more "hospitable", while robots with masculine characteristics were believed to excel in tasks associated with traditional male stereotypes, such as moving objects and operating machinery [10]. Moreover, when robots were designed with broader shoulders, they were perceived as having a more "authoritative" presence [11]. Female chatbots were also regarded as communicating in a kinder, friendlier, and more polite manner compared to male or gender-neutral chatbots [12].

2.2 Effects of Robotic Devices' Characteristics on Human-Robot Interaction

In the domestic environment, robotic devices can provide various functions including providing physical and cognitive rehabilitation, managing medication, and offering phys-ical assistance for daily tasks [13]. Additionally, they can contribute to companionship, health improvement, and social engagement for users [14–17]. Previous research found that for older adults, the most crucial functions of robots were assisting older adults in daily activities, facilitating tailored interactions, and promoting social engagement and leisure activities, for clinical professionals and caregivers, the most crucial functions were reminding patients of the care plans and monitoring the health and safety [18]. Ruf et al. highlighted the use of robots as exercise coaches for older adults and emphasized the positive impact of social assistance robots on motivating them to partake in social exercises and remain active [19]. Zafrani et al. found that social assistive robots could significantly enhance the quality of life for older adults [20]. Recent research also revealed that older adults were less receptive to intimate physical assistance from robots, such as bathing, but more inclined to utilize robots for simpler tasks like managing reminders and facilitating communication [21, 22]. The robots should be adaptable to the needs, preferences, and unique desires of their users to promote users' trust and usage intention [23].

2.3 Technical Acceptance Model for Older Adults Using Home Robotic Devices

The Technology Acceptance Model [24] posits that people's acceptance of household machinery and equipment is largely determined by two factors: perceived ease of use and usefulness. Previous research found that individuals might have negative attitudes toward family caregivers' usage of such technologies to assist them in caring for their loved ones. Some research pointed out that providing personal visits to older adults and extending emotional care might be more favorable approaches [25]. Furthermore, previous research found that highly anthropomorphic designs of robots could pose privacy issues [9, 26]. The presence of robots should not compromise the safety of older adults [27]. For example, the robot should have settings that not granting entry to unauthorized individuals and refraining from sharing personal information with unknown parties. Previous research also found that some respondents expressed concerns about over-reliance on robots, potentially leading to a loss of autonomy and independence [28]. Due to cost-related apprehensions, elderly household residents thought hiring nursing staff to be more practical than acquiring robots [29].

3 Research Questions

The objective of this study is to investigate middle-aged and older adults' preferences for home robotic devices' characteristics and functions, and the factors influencing middle-aged and older adults' acceptance of home robotic devices. Furthermore, this study aims to investigate whether there are significant differences exist between middle-aged and older adults' preferences or the factors influencing their acceptance. This leads to the following research questions:

   Research Question 1: Do middle-aged, and older adults differ in their preferences toward home robotic devices' appearance and social characteristics?

   Research Question 2: Do middle-aged, and older adults differ in their preferences toward home robotic devices' functions?

   Research Question 3: What are the critical factors that influence middle-aged and older adults' acceptance of home robotic devices?

4 Methodology

4.1 Participants

23 middle-aged participants (Mean age = 47.78 years, SD = 3.85) and 23 older participants (Mean age = 68.96 years, SD = 5.62) were recruited from Fuzhou and Quanzhou. In this study, older adults refer to adults in the age range of 60 years and above, and middle-aged adults refer to adults in the age range of 40–59 years old. Demographic information of participants involved in the interview is presented in Table 1. Among demographic information of middle-aged and older participants, there were significant differences in monthly income ($p < 0.05$) and whether had known about home robotic devices ($p < 0.05$). 82.61% of older participants had a monthly income of 3000 RMB or less, while 82.61% of middle-aged participants had a monthly income above 3000 RMB. In addition, 39.13% of middle-aged participants said they had known about home robotic devices, while only 4.35% of older participants showed the same case. In addition, 8.70% of older participants reported that they lived alone at home, and 34.78% of middle-aged participants also reported that their parents lived alone.

Table 1. Demographic information of participants

Variables	Example	Middle-aged participants		Older participants	
Age		Mean = 47.78 years, SD = 3.85		Mean = 68.96 years, SD = 5.62	
		Frequency	Percentage	Frequency	Percentage
Gender	Male	13	56.52%	10	43.48%
	Female	10	43.48%	13	56.52%
Monthly income	Below 3000 RMB	4	17.39%	19	82.61%
	3000–4500 RMB	4	17.39%	3	13.04%
	4500–6000 RMB	8	34.78%	0	0.00%
	Above 6000 RMB	7	30.43%	1	4.35%
Education	High school or below	18	78.26%	22	95.65%
	Junior college	2	8.70%	0	0.00%
	Graduate	3	13.04%	1	4.35%
Whether knew about home robotic devices	knew about home robotic devices	9	39.13%	1	4.35%
	never heard of home robotic devices	14	60.87%	22	95.65%

4.2 Procedures

Before the interview, participants were informed of the purpose of the interview and the anonymity of the data collection. Each participant was interviewed in a specific place at a specific time. Firstly, the interviewer played a video to introduce the functions of home robotic devices, including assisting with video chat, communicating with older adults, reminding older adults to take medicine, etc., so that participants could learn about home robotic devices. Secondly, the interviewer collected the participants' demographic information. Thirdly, participants talked about their preferences for home robotic devices' appearance type, height, gender, and so on. Fourthly, participants rated the importance of each function of home robotic devices by using the Likert scale (1: extremely unimportant, 7: extremely important). The questions included four modules, consisting of emotional communication, life management, medical security, and entertainment. Finally, based on the Technology Acceptance Model, participants talked about the factors affecting their acceptance of home robotic devices. The average duration of interviews was 30 min. The participants were compensated with a gift for participation. All recordings were transcribed and then analyzed using a six-step thematic analysis method, which included (1) familiarity with the data; (2) Generate the initial code; (3) Looking for a theme; (4) Theme review; (5) the definition and naming of the theme; (6) Generate analysis reports [30]. The key variables in the interview are shown in Table 2.

Table 2. Key variables in the interview

Modules	Variables
Home robotic devices' appearance and social characteristics	Appearance type of home robotic devices Gender of home robotic devices Character of home robotic devices Human-robot relationship
Home robotic devices' functions	Emotional functions Functions of life management Functions of medical security Functions of entertainment
External variables influencing factors for user acceptance	Economic factors First impression of home robotic devices Role of adults in family relationship Concerns about restrictions on user freedom
Perceived usefulness	The use of home robotic devices to bring life assistance Home robotic devices can improve the relationship between people Home robotic devices can replace children of older adults
Perceived ease of use	Obstacles to using home robotic devices
Attitude toward using	The acceptance rate of participants

5 Results

5.1 Participants' Preference for Appearance and Social Characteristics of Home Robotic Devices

The results from the chi-square test showed there was a significant difference between older participants and middle-aged participants in the choice of home robotic devices' appearance type ($\chi^2 = 7.64$, p = 0.03). As shown in Fig. 1 and Fig. 2, 65.22% of older participants preferred the humanoid appearance while 56.52% of middle-aged participants preferred the mechanical one. In addition, the similarity between the two groups was expressed in the fact that they rarely chose animal or geometric appearance.

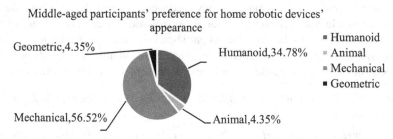

Fig. 1. Middle-aged participants' preference for home robotic devices' appearance

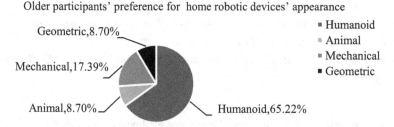

Fig. 2. Older participants' preference for home robotic devices' appearance

Based on this, participants were required to express the reasons for their preference for home robotic devices' appearance. In the answers of middle-aged participants who chose the mechanical appearance, the reasons in order of importance were: (1) humanoid home robotic devices were creepy, in line with the uncanny valley theory [31]; (2) mechanical home robotic devices looked better than others in quality and function. In the answer of older participants who chose the humanoid appearance, the reasons in order of importance were: (1) humanoid home robotic devices were more beautiful; (2) humanoid home robotic devices looked more approachable.

I will choose the humanoid one which looks beautiful (Older participant #15).

I'm going to pick the mechanical home robotic device because the humanoid one looks creepy (Middle-aged participant #6).

I would choose the mechanical home robotic device because the humanoid one is too novel and will frighten children (Older participant #16).

The results from the chi-square test showed there was no significant difference between older participants and middle-aged participants in the choice of home robotic devices' gender ($\chi^2 = 3.00$, p = 0.28). For home robotic devices' gender characteristics, as shown in Fig. 3, the similarities between middle-aged and older participants were that most participants chose female home robotic devices. In interviews, older participants and middle-aged participants gave similar reasons. In the responses of participants who chose female home robotic devices, the main reasons cited were: (1) female home robotic devices were better caregivers; (2) female home robotic devices were gentler and more careful than male home robotic devices. In the responses of participants who chose male home robotic devices, the main reasons cited were: (1) male home robotic devices looked more stable and reliable; (2) male home robotic devices taking care of men were less controversial. In the responses of participants who chose gender-neutral home robotic devices, the main reasons cited were: (1) mechanical home robotic devices were supposed to be neutral; (2) gender-neutral devices were less ethically controversial.

Most of the nannies who look after older adults are women (Middle-aged participant #3).

I think women are more careful and better at communicating with others (Middle-aged participant #14).

Male home robotic devices are stronger, to make them seem more reliable (Older participant #10).

Male home robotic devices tend to take care of male owners more easily than female ones (Older participant #17).

Mechanical home robotic device is supposed to be gender-neutral (Middle-aged participant #6).

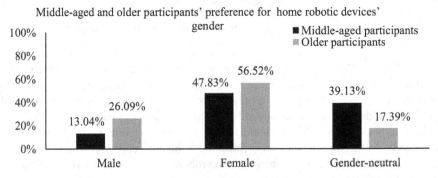

Fig. 3. Participants' preference for home robotic devices' gender characteristics

The results from the chi-square test showed there was no significant difference between older participants and middle-aged participants in the choice of human-robot

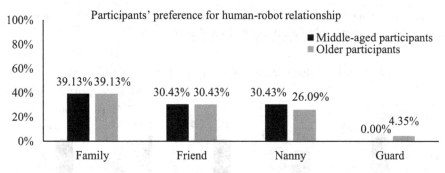

Fig. 4. Participants' preference for human-robot relationship

relationship ($\chi^2 = 1.10$, p = 1.00). For the relationship between users and home robotic devices, the proportion of guards chosen by both groups was the smallest, as shown in Fig. 4. In the interview, 85.71% of middle-aged participants who chose the nanny thought that home robotic devices with the human-robot relationship of nanny would be able to take better care of older adults, and 66.67% of older participants who chose the nanny thought similarly. In addition, all older participants who chose the friend believed that home robotic devices appearing as friends would better communicate with older adults, and 85.71% of middle-aged participants who chose the friend thought similarly. Moreover, 77.78% of older participants who chose the family considered that home robotic devices with the human-robot relationship of family would create a warm and harmonious atmosphere for the life of older adults, and 77.78% of middle-aged participants who chose the family had the same thought.

Home robotic devices should be nannies for older adults so that they can take better care of older adults (Middle-aged participant #4).

The home robotic device is supposed to be my nanny, and its main task is to help me with my housework (Older participant #9).

If the home robotic device is my friend, I think it will communicate with me better (Older participant #3).

The home robotic device can communicate with older adults, it should be the friend of older adults (Middle-aged participant #3).

5.2 Participants' Preference for Functions of Home Robotic Devices

This study also analyzed participants' functional demands of home robotic devices: emotional communication, life management, medical security, and entertainment.

Emotional Functions of Home Robotic Devices. For emotional functions of the devices, the results from the non-parametric tests showed there was no significant difference between middle-aged and older participants in the five types of emotional functions. As shown in Fig. 5, among middle-aged participants, the highest priority was the function of home robotic devices to provide video support, while the lowest one was the function of home robotic devices to have vivid expression. Among older participants, the most important function was emotional communication, while the least important one was whether home robotic devices had vivid expressions.

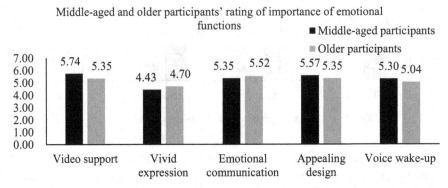

Fig. 5. Middle-aged and older participants' rating of the importance of emotional functions

In the interview, when asked if home robotic devices should have other functions, the main emotional functions mentioned by older participants were communication and elimination of boredom. For middle-aged participants, the main emotional functions were communication and providing psychological counseling.

I hope home robotic devices can help me make video calls with my family. And home robotic devices can communicate with me to solve my boredom (Older participant #10).

I hope home robotic devices can communicate with my mother and help her do some housework (Middle-aged participant #1).

Life Management Functions of Home Robotic Devices. For life management functions of the devices, the results from the non-parametric tests showed there was a significant difference between middle-aged and older participants in remote monitoring (p = 0.01). Middle-aged participants, as offspring, preferred to know more information about older adults to ensure their safety. However older participants, as the monitored group, did not fully accept their all-around monitoring which involves personal privacy issues. Among older participants, the most important function was a memorandum, while the least one was remote monitoring. Among middle-aged participants, the most valued function was to prevent older adults from falling, while the least valued one was automatic shopping. The above conclusions can be seen in Fig. 6.

When asked if home robotic devices should have other functions, older participants believed that home robotic devices should provide life management help, such as doing housework, offering healthy recipes and exercise plans. And middle-aged participants also believed that home robotic devices should pay attention to the design of life management functions, including doing housework, detecting danger, providing memorandum, connecting smart devices, and so on.

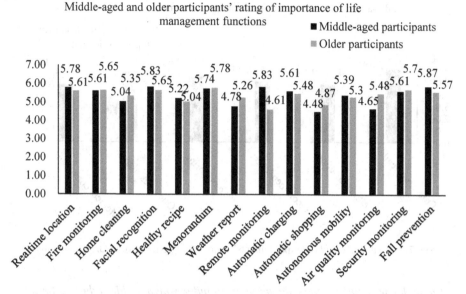

Fig. 6. Middle-aged and older participants' rating of the importance of life management functions

I hope that home robotic devices can tailor three meals a day for my diet and daily exercise program (Older participant #9).

I hope that home robotic devices can help my parents with the housework (Middle-aged participant #8).

Medical Functions of Home Robotic Devices. For medical functions of the devices, the results from non-parametric tests showed there was a marginally significant difference between middle-aged and older participants in the medical consultants ($p = 0.08$). According to Fig. 7, among older participants, the most highly valued function was health monitoring while the least one was health counseling. Among middle-aged participants, emergency call was the most valued function, while medical consultant was the least valued.

In the interview, some participants, whether middle-aged or older, believed that home robotic devices should provide medical security. When participants were asked about the physical health of older adults, 67.39% of participants said that older adults suffered from symptoms such as hypertension, hyperlipidemia, and hyperglycemia. Middle-aged participants also considered the mental health of older adults. When asked if home robotic devices should have other functions, some older participants wanted home robotic devices to provide medical functions such as monitoring body data. In addition, middle-aged participants also mentioned psychological counseling, psychological treatment and other functions.

I think home robotic devices should monitor my health indicators (Older participant #12).

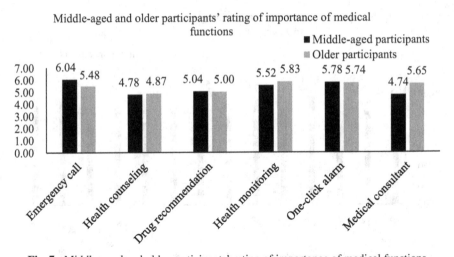

Fig. 7. Middle-aged and older participants' rating of importance of medical functions

I think home robotic devices should learn to judge whether older adults get sick (Middle-aged participant #3).

I think home robotic devices should also chat with older adults to provide psychotherapy (Middle-aged participant #10).

I hope home robotic devices can help older adults with housework and provide psychological counseling (Middle-aged participant #12).

Entertainment Functions of Home Robotic Devices. For entertainment functions of the devices, the results from the non-parametric tests showed there was no significant difference in the rating of importance of entertainment functions among middle-aged and older participants. In addition, the similarities were reflected in that middle-aged and older participants rated lower importance of board games. According to Fig. 8, middle-aged and older participants attached the most importance to the news broadcast. The function least valued by older participants was board games, while for middle-aged participants, it was singing and dancing. When participants were asked what other functions the home robotic devices should have, none of them mentioned the entertainment function.

Functional Preferences of Middle-Aged and Older Participants. When participants were asked which type of function was the most important, the results from the chi-square test showed there was no significant difference between middle-aged and older participants ($\chi^2 = 6.37, p = 0.07$). According to Fig. 9, the type of function most valued by older participants was the life management function of home robotic devices, while the entertainment function was the most unimportant. Among middle-aged participants, the most valued function was also life management, while the most unimportant was the emotional communication function of home robotic devices. In addition, the proportion of middle-aged participants who thought life management was the most important was significantly higher than that of older participants, and the proportion of middle-aged

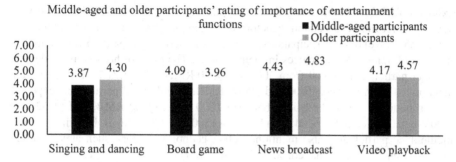

Fig. 8. Middle-aged and older participants' rating of importance of entertainment functions

participants who thought emotional communication was the most important was significantly lower than that of older participants. Both groups believed that entertainment was not very important, which also corresponded to the above conclusion "The average rating of importance of entertainment was lower than other type of functions".

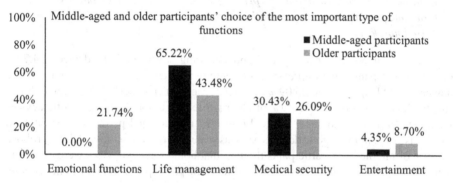

Fig. 9. Middle-aged and older participants' choice of the most important type of functions

5.3 Factors Influencing Participants' Acceptance of Home Robotic Devices

In this study, a non-parametric test was used to analyze whether there were significant differences in older and middle-aged participants' acceptance of home robotic devices, and the results showed that there was no significant difference in their acceptance ($p = 0.92$). The average acceptance rate of older participants was 59.78%, and the average acceptance rate of middle-aged participants was 59.17%. According to the Technology Acceptance Model, perceived usefulness and perceived ease of use determine users' attitudes toward using. These two parts were influenced by environmental constraints, system design, user characteristics, and other external variables [24]. This study further explored the differences and similarities in the various factors that influenced attitudes toward using between middle-aged and older groups.

External Variables Influencing User Acceptance. This study divided external variables into three modules: economic factors, degree of understandings, and psychological factors. 65.22% of older participants and 56.52% of middle-aged participants mentioned the price of home robotic devices in their answers. The price of home robotic devices for older participants ranged from 500 to 150000 RMB, and 65.21% of older participants priced them between 1000 and 20000 RMB. Middle-aged participants expected home robotic devices to be priced between 1000 and 150000 RMB, and 56.52% of middle-aged participants priced them between 1500 and 30000 RMB. In addition, some middle-aged participants also mentioned other economic factors, such as warranties, after-sales service, additional consumption, and so on.

> *That must be the economic factor, if the price is cheap, of course, I will buy the home robotic device so that it can help my life. But if the price is too expensive, I'm sure I can't afford it (Older participant #4).*

> *It could be the economic factor. I am worried that I will have to pay for each function in the process of using home robotic devices (Middle-aged participant #1).*

> *I am not only worried about the price of home robotic devices but also other economic factors, such as warranties, product quality, and so on (Middle-aged participant #11).*

Secondly, in terms of participants' understanding of home robotic devices, 34.78% of older participants' first impressions of home robotic devices were that home robotic devices could help humans, 26.09% of older participants had never known about home robotic devices before, and 17.39% of older participants thought home robotic devices were very similar to humans. While 17.39% of middle-aged participants mentioned various types of home robotic devices, such as sweeping robots and food delivery robots, 17.39% of middle-aged participants thought that home robotic devices were emerging technology products, and 13.04% of middle-aged participants thought home robotic devices might replace human beings.

> *I have seen home robotic devices on TV and feel they were practical products of technology that could help people with housework (Older participant #8).*

> *I think home robotic devices can bring social and emotional needs to human beings (Older participant #12).*

> *With the development of technology, I think home robotic devices may replace humans in some positions (Middle-aged participant #13).*

> *I think the home robotic device is a kind of new technology product (Middle-aged participant #8).*

> *I have seen robots delivering food in Haidilao. I think home robotic devices can help us (Middle-aged participant #2).*

Moreover, 60.87% of older participants considered that home robotic devices could directly contact their children in an emergency and 86.96% of middle-aged participants also had the same thought. In addition, there was a difference in the proportion of older participants and that of middle-aged participants who thought that home robotic devices could provide body index about older adults to their children every day. The proportion of middle-aged participants was 91.30% while it was 65.22% in older participants. 39.13% of older participants said that their children worked outside the home, and if there was no need, they hoped that home robotic devices would not disturb their children.

My children all work hard, so I hope home robot devices will not disturb them (Older participant #6).

My kids all work outside the home. I don't want to bother them anymore so home robotic devices don't have to provide body index to them (Older participant #2).

Perceived Usefulness of Home Robotic Devices. To study the differences and similarities of perceived usefulness on attitudes toward using, the Chi-square test was used to analyze the results. It could be seen that whether home robotic devices could improve the relationship between older adults and their children had a significant difference among middle-aged and older participants ($\chi^2 = 4.06$, $p = 0.05$). 86.96% of older participants believed that home robotic devices could improve their relationship with their children, while 60.87% of middle-aged participants also had the same thought. In the interview, when asked how home robotic devices could help the lives of older adults, 69.56% of older participants only focused on life management, such as fire monitoring and memorandum. However, 43.47% of middle-aged participants were not limited to a certain type of function, their answers included paying attention to the health of older adults, contacting older adults' children in emergencies, and communicating with older adults.

I think home robotic devices can help me in life management, such as monitoring strangers (Older participant #2).

I think home robotic devices can communicate with older adults and give them help in life management, such as security monitoring and assisting in the use of smart devices (Middle-aged participant #7).

Perceived Ease of Use of Home Robotic Devices. Participants were asked what obstacles might exist in the process of using home robotic devices, and there was no significant difference in the answers of the two groups. 47.82% of older participants and 47.82% of middle-aged participants were concerned about obstacles that home robotic devices were too intelligent to operate. In addition, 13.04% of older participants said that they would have resistance to smart products, especially for home robotic devices, and 8.70% of middle-aged participants had the same concern.

I think there may be difficulties in the process of operating the home robotic devices, but there is no difficulty if it is controlled by voice (Older participant #6).

I think older adults may be psychologically resistant to learning about how to control home robotic devices (Middle-aged participant #13).

6 Discussion

In terms of home robotic devices' appearance, the results revealed that middle-aged participants preferred mechanical home robotic devices. This is consistent with the prior study pointed out that home robotic devices with a low humanoid appearance were more popular with consumers [32]. However, older participants preferred humanoid robots which is consistent with the prior study pointed out that consumers would prefer home robotic devices with a highly humanoid appearance [33]. The appearance of the home robotic devices would affect users' expectations, cognition, and reaction [32]. The Uncanny Valley theory suggested that highly humanoid home robotic devices would induce an eerie feeling [34]. Middle-aged and older participants' different preferences for home robotic devices' appearance could be explained by the theory of self-construal. Previous research found that self-construal might influence consumers' preference for humanoid and mechanical social robots in the home environment [35]. As a group with lower social connection, older participants preferred home robotic devices with high humanoid appearance; Middle-aged participants, as a group with a higher degree of social connection, preferred home robotic devices with a lower degree of humanoid. In the perspective of home robotic devices' relationship with users, middle-aged and older participants did not have a clear preference. For gender characteristics of home robotic devices, middle-aged and older participants preferred female home robotic devices. This is consistent with the prior study that found female service robots would generate more pleasure and higher satisfaction than male service robots [36].

In terms of home robotic devices' functions, middle-aged participants thought remote monitoring was important, while older participants disagreed with it. The results of the prior study showed that only about a quarter of older participants would be satisfied with the data collection of their location and activities [37]. Although older participants were willing to trade their privacy for potential benefits [38, 39], they expressed concerns about it [40].

In addition, the importance of entertainment functions was significantly lower than other function types in both middle-aged and older participants. This is different from the results of the prior study which suggested that the main needs of older participants were the entertainment functions of home robotic devices (such as juggling, dancing, singing, storytelling, news reporting, and telling jokes) [41]. This could be explained by the demographic background characteristics of older participants. In this study, older participants were not living in the community service center. They might have a higher demand for functions of life management.

In terms of external variables influencing user acceptance, both middle-aged and older participants believed that economic factors would affect their acceptance of home robotic devices. The difference was reflected in that older adults mostly only considered the price, while middle-aged participants also considered home robotic devices' warranty period, after-sales service, additional charges, and other economic factors. This is the same as the results of a prior study that owning a home robotic device was extremely challenging for older adults with low economic income [4]. Most middle-aged participants knew about home robotic devices, while older participants hardly knew much about them. They mainly learned about home robotic devices through movies or TV shows. This is different from the findings of a prior study that participants in Japan mostly learned about home robotic devices through news, anime, manga, and other media [42]. Finally, due to the different family roles of middle-aged and older adults, older adults didn't want home robotic devices to disturb their children frequently.

Moreover, in terms of perceived usefulness, older participants believed that home robotic devices would improve their relationship with their children, while middle-aged participants disagreed with it. In terms of perceived ease of use, there was no significant difference between middle-aged and older participants. It's about half of the participants believing that there would be operational difficulties. This is consistent with the prior findings which suggested that older adults were anxious about new technologies [43]. In addition, the technical complexity also reduces the level of perceived ease of use, which leads to operational frustration and anxiety, thus hindering their acceptance of social assistant robots. The results of the prior study also showed that middle-aged and older participants had more positive attitude toward the use of voice assistants, contrary to the stereotype that older adults were tech-phobic [6].

This study has several limitations. First, the sample size of middle-aged and older participants was relatively small and the areas were limited to Fuzhou and Quanzhou. Future research should recruit more participants from different areas or with different cultural backgrounds. It is essential to further investigate the preferences of young adults (under 40 years) for home robotic devices and based on this, compare the differences and similarities between the three groups. Second, future research can investigate participants' preferences and functional demands for home robotic devices after real experience with different types of home robotic devices. Third, in terms of the factors influencing the acceptance of home robotic devices, more variables should be investigated.

7 Conclusion

The objective of this study is to investigate middle-aged and older adults' preferences for home robotic devices through interviews. The main findings are listed as follows: (1) In terms of the appearance of home robotic devices, middle-aged adults preferred the mechanical type while older adults preferred the humanoid one; In terms of the gender characteristics of home robotic devices, both groups preferred a female one; In terms of human-robot relationships, both groups believed that home robotic devices could better communicate with older adults if they were friends of older adults, home robotic devices could better serve older adults if they were nannies of older adults and home robotic devices could create a warm and harmonious atmosphere for the life of older adults if they were families of older adults. (2) In terms of the functions of home robotic devices, middle-aged and older adults considered life management functions to be the most important. For the remote monitoring function, older adults thought it was less important, while middle-aged adults did not. (3) In terms of the factors influencing acceptance, the critical factors influencing older adults' acceptance were economic factors, especially for the pricing of home robotic devices, and psychological factors such as not disturbing their offspring. The critical factors influencing middle-aged adults' acceptance were economic factors, technological maturity, functional perfection, and other technical characteristics. The results of this study would help designers understand different users' preferences for home robotic devices.

Acknowledgments. This research was funded by the National Natural Science Foundation of China (No.72301073) and the Natural Science Foundation of Fujian Province of China (No.2022J05018).

References

1. Ren, W., et al.: Willingness and influencing factors of old-age care mode selection among middle-aged and older adults in Henan Province, China. BMC Geriatr. **24**(1), 72 (2024)
2. Yan, X., et al.: Intergenerational caregiving on mental health of middle-aged and older adults in China: empirical insights. Front. Public Health 11 (2023)
3. Deutsch, I., et al.: Home robotic devices for older adults: opportunities and concerns. Comput. Hum. Behav. **98**(SEP.), 122–133 (2019)
4. Liu, S.X., Shen, Q., Hancock, J.: Can a social robot be too warm or too competent? Older Chinese adults' perceptions of social robots and vulnerabilities. Comput. Hum. Behav. **125**, 106942 (2021)
5. Pantelaki, E., Maggi, E., Crotti, D.: Who is online? A latent class analysis of internet activities and determinant characteristics of older people. Comput. Hum. Behav. **147**, 107830 (2023)
6. Zhong, R., et al.: User acceptance of smart home voice assistant: a comparison among younger, middle-aged, and older adults. Universal Access in the Information Society, 1–18 (2022)
7. Schweinberger, S.R., Pohl, M., Winkler, P.: Autistic traits, personality, and evaluations of humanoid robots by young and older adults. Comput. Hum. Behav. **106**, 106256 (2020)
8. Klüber, K., Onnasch, L.: Appearance is not everything - Preferred feature combinations for care robots. Comput. Hum. Behav. **128**, 107128 (2021)
9. Chung, H., Kang, H., Jun, S.: Verbal anthropomorphism design of social robots: investigating users' privacy perception. Comput. Hum. Behav. **142**, 107640 (2023)
10. Akn, G., et al.: Gendered actions with a genderless robot: gender attribution to humanoid robots in action. Int. J. Soc. Robot. **15**, 1915–1931 (2023)
11. Trovato, G., et al.: Correction to: The Influence of Body Proportions on Perceived Gender of Robots in Latin America (2019)
12. Lee, S.K., Kavya, P., Lasser, S.C.: Social interactions and relationships with an intelligent virtual agent. Int. J. Hum. Comput. Stud. **150**, 102608 (2021)
13. Robinson, H., MacDonald, B., Broadbent, E.: The role of healthcare robots for older people at home: a review. Int. J. Soc. Robot. **6**, 575–591 (2014)
14. Baisch, S., et al.: Emotional robots in a nursing context: empirical analysis of the present use and the effects of Paro and Pleo. Z. Gerontol. Geriatr. **51**, 16–24 (2018)
15. Baisch, S.: ThorstenSchall, ArthurRuehl, SaskiaSelic, StefanieKim, ZiyonRossberg, HolgerKlein, BarbaraPantel, JohannesOswald, FrankKnopf, Monika, acceptance of social robots by elder people: does psychosocial functioning matter? Int. J. Soc. Robot. **9**(2), 293–307 (2017)
16. Pilotto, A., Boi, R., Petermans, J.: Technology in geriatrics. Age Ageing **47**(6), 771–774 (2018)
17. Schüssler, S., et al.: The effects of a humanoid socially assistive robot versus tablet training on psychosocial and physical outcomes of persons with dementia: protocol for a mixed methods study. JMIR Res. Protocols **9**(2), 14927 (2020)
18. Di Napoli, C., Ercolano, G., Rossi, S.: Personalized home-care support for the elderly: a field experience with a social robot at home. User Model. User-Adap. Inter. **33**(2), 405–440 (2023)

19. Ruf, E., Lehmann, S., Misoch, S.: Use of a socially assistive robot to promote physical activity of older adults at home. In: Ziefle, M., Guldemond, N., Maciaszek, L.A. (eds.) Information and Communication Technologies for Ageing Well and e-Health: 6th International Conference, ICT4AWE 2020, Prague, Czech Republic, May 3–5, 2020, Revised Selected Papers, pp. 78–95. Springer International Publishing, Cham (2021). https://doi.org/10.1007/978-3-030-708 07-8_5

20. Zafrani, O., Nimrod, G., Edan, Y.: Between fear and trust: older adults' evaluation of socially assistive robots. Int. J. Hum. Comput. Stud. **171**, 102981 (2023)

21. Huang, T., Huang, C.: Attitudes of the elderly living independently towards the use of robots to assist with activities of daily living. Work **69**(1), 55–65 (2021)

22. Robillard, J.M., Kabacińska, K.: Realizing the potential of robotics for aged care through co-creation. J. Alzheimer's Disease (JAD) **76**(2), 1–6 (2020)

23. Stuck, R.E., Rogers, W.A.: Older adults' perceptions of supporting factors of trust in a robot care provider. Journal of Robotics **2018**, 1–11 (2018)

24. Davis, F.D.: Perceived usefulness, perceived ease of use, and user acceptance of information technology. MIS Q. **13**(3), 319–340 (1989)

25. AboJabel, H., Ayalon, L.: Attitudes of Israelis toward family caregivers assisted by a robot in the delivery of care to older people: the roles of collectivism and individualism. Technol. Soc. **75**, 102386 (2023)

26. Ghorayeb, A., Comber, R., Gooberman-Hill, R.: Older adults' perspectives of smart home technology: are we developing the technology that older people want? Int. J. Hum. Comput. Stud. **147**(3), 102571 (2020)

27. Wiczorek, R., Bayles, M.A., Rogers, W.A.: Domestic robots for older adults: design approaches and recommendations. Design Assist. Technol. Ageing Pop., 203–219 (2020)

28. Cortellessa, G., et al.: A cross-cultural evaluation of domestic assistive robots. In: AAAI Fall Symposium: AI in Eldercare: New Solutions to Old Problems (2008)

29. Compagna, D., Kohlbacher, F.: The limits of participatory technology development: the case of service robots in care facilities for older people. Technol. Forecast. Soc. Chang. **93**, 19–31 (2015)

30. Braun, V., Clarke, V.: Using thematic analysis in psychology. Qual. Res. Psychol. 3(2), 77–101 (2008)

31. Mori, M.: Bukimi no tani [the Uncanny Valley]. Energy 7(4), 33–35 (1970)

32. Ferrari, P.J.: Jolanda, blurring human-machine distinctions: anthropomorphic appearance in social robots as a threat to human distinctiveness. Int. J. Soc. Robot. **8**(2), 287–302 (2016)

33. Tussyadiah, I.P., Park, S.: Consumer evaluation of hotel service robots (2018)

34. Mathur, M.B., Reichling, D.B.: Navigating a social world with robot partners: a quantitative cartography of the Uncanny Valley. Cognition **146**, 22–32 (2016)

35. Chang, Y., et al.: Social robots: Partner or intruder in the home? The roles of self-construal, social support, and relationship intrusion in consumer preference. Technol. Forecast. Soc. Chang. **197**, 122914 (2023)

36. Seo, S.: When Female (Male) Robot Is Talking To Me: effect of service robots' gender and anthropomorphism on customer satisfaction. Int. J. Hosp. Manag. **102**, 103166 (2022)

37. Reinhardt, M.A.: Luca Hernandez, "I still need my privacy": exploring the level of comfort and privacy preferences of German-speaking older adults in the case of mobile assistant robots. Pervasive Mob. Comput. **74**(1), 101397 (2021)

38. Kolkowska, E., Kajtazi, M.: Privacy dimensions in design of smart home systems for elderly people. **22**(1), 7–30 (2015)

39. Neta, et al.: More than a Servant: self-reported willingness of younger and older adults to having a robot perform interactive and critical tasks in the home. In: Proceedings of the Human Factors and Ergonomics Society Annual Meeting, vol. 53, no. 2, pp. 136–140 (2009)

40. Boissy, P., et al.: A qualitative study of in-home robotic telepresence for home care of community-living elderly subjects. J. Telemed. Telecare **13**(2), 79–84 (2006)

41. Chiu, C.-J., Hsieh, S., Li, C.-W.: Needs and preferences of middle-aged and older adults in Taiwan for companion robots and pets: survey study. J. Med. Internet Res. **23**(6), e23471 (2021)

42. Suwa, S., et al.: Exploring perceptions toward home-care robots for older people in Finland, Ireland, and Japan: a comparative questionnaire study. Arch. Gerontol. Geriatr. **91**, 104178 (2020)

43. He, Q., et al.: Acceptance of social assistant robots for the older adults living in the community in China. Geriatr. Nurs.Nurs. **52**, 191–198 (2023)

Redefining Truth in the Context of AI-Truth Era: A Practice-Led Research of "From Post-Truth to AI-Truth"

Yanlin Li[1] and Chih-Yung Chiu[2](✉)

[1] International Intercollegiate Ph.D. Program, National Tsing Hua University, Hsinchu 300044, Taiwan
s1110038741ab@gapp.nthu.edu.tw
[2] Graduate Institute of Technology and Art, College of Arts, National Tsing Hua University, Hsinchu 300044, Taiwan
aaronchiu88@gmail.com

Abstract. The rapid development of artificial intelligence (AI) technology has deepened the complexity of discerning the truth. Through the techno-art installation *"From Post-Truth to AI-Truth"* as practical research, AI-automated journalism is applied to the redefinition and shaping of truth, pointing out that the rights of truth definition were transferred. This project illustrated how AI can generate new competing truths based on post-truth news. At the same time, remind people of the methods to discern when faced with information.

This research proposes that with technological development, the transformation from "tertiary retention" to "tertiary protention" reveals the possibility of truth diversity. The ethical standards of information communicators and receivers in the post-truth era should also be bound. It deepens people's understanding of the cross-cultural interaction between post-truth news and AI-automated journalism. It will provide significant insights into the development of the news industry, cultural communication, and emerging technologies, which will help people better cope with the challenges and opportunities of AI technology.

Keywords: Post-Truth · AI-Truth · Competing Truths · Automated Journalism · AIGC

1 Introduction

The Oxford Dictionary selected "post-truth" as the word of the year for 2016, marking the beginning of the post-truth era. The term post-truth saw a surge in frequency in the context of the 2016 Brexit referendum and the US presidential election. There is a political background behind it, which is related to the word "post-truth politics." The Oxford Dictionary defines post-truth as "Appeals to emotions and personal beliefs may be more effective in shaping public opinion than expressing objective facts" [1].

People have more ways to get news and information in the rapidly developing information age, from traditional paper media, television, and broadcast media to the Internet

P.-L. P. Rau (Ed.): HCII 2024, LNCS 14702, pp. 245–257, 2024.
https://doi.org/10.1007/978-3-031-60913-8_17

and social media today. People have been receiving a large amount of information in the current era of information explosion from the ubiquitous mainstream media, capitalists, and self-media. Truth and logic become secondary in the information dissemination process when emotions incite and dominate public opinion more than the facts people are pursuing because the cost of knowing the truth is too high [1]. People no longer trace the facts behind the news but only want to believe what they believe, and are replaced by traffic-oriented news headlines, emotionally inciting comments, and forwarding. Post-truth news is not the same as rumors and fake news. This research focuses on quoting the four competing truths mentioned in Hector Macdonald's book "*Truth*" that will affect our thinking patterns, namely partial truths, subjective truths, artificial truths, and unknown truths [2].

With the rise of artificial intelligence (AI) technology, text, images, and videos generated by AI have become increasingly difficult to distinguish. This research analyzes the post-truth news cases and the multimedia piece "*In Event of Moon Disaster*," which used deepfake technology, the application of automated journalism, and the ethical issues arising from the development of AI technology [3–5]. It intends to discuss whether humans should blindly trust the content of automated journalism using AI technology under the cross-cultural influence brought about by the rapid development of AI and whether humans can cope with the large amount of information generated by it. This research proposes that we have entered the AI-truth era from the Post-Truth era, as well as the responses of "tertiary retention" and "tertiary protention." And takes the project of experimental techno-art installation "*From Post-Truth to AI-Truth*" as the main practical research object. This project used the large language model (LLM) GPT-3.5 to make AI become the editor-in-chief of a newspaper, imitating the way human journalists write news articles. Based on the post-truth news that had been published on the Internet and using competing truth methods to rewrite and generate multiple AI versions, a printer automatically printed newspapers generated by AI in real time [6]. According to the above practices, this research conducts a multi-angle analysis of the design concept, technological experiments, and actual exhibition of the project, focusing on the attitudes and opinions of audiences from different cultural backgrounds towards the creative project and aiming to deeply explore the cross-cultural interaction relationships between post-truth news and AI-generated news and how they influence and interact with each other.

2 Literature Review

2.1 Competing Truths in the Post-truth Era

Hector Macdonald proposed the concept of "competing truths" in his book "*Truth*" in 2018. It refers to the situation in which a person, event, thing, or policy can be described in a variety of ways that may be equally legitimate [2]. The competing truths include four distinct types: "partial truths," "subjective truths," "artificial truths," and "unknown truths." Partial truths emphasize that the statements are hard to cover the complexity and comprehensiveness of all the truth, even if they are true, and many relevant factual details will be missed through communication, which is an inevitable feature. Subjective truths explore the extent to which individuals are motivated by morality, desirability, and financial value, reflecting the subjectivity and changeability of truth. Artificial truths point out that communicators are actually forging new truths by establishing names or definitions to suit their purposes, revealing that these truths can be easily shaped and modified by social constructs. Lastly, unknown truths involve predictions and beliefs that have yet to be proven, emphasizing that they remain a state of competing truths until the truths are proven. Since the truths related to religious and ideological beliefs are hard to accurately prove or falsify, these distinct forms of truth shape and influence people's thinking patterns and worldviews [2].

In post-truth era, people are frequently faced with multiple versions of competing truths, which may differ based on different perspectives, interests, or interpretations [2]. The concept of competing truths reveals that existing diverse truths may compete with or complement each other in complex reality. These concepts are closely associated with the post-truth era, which refers to public discourse in which appeals to emotion and personal belief are more influential than objective facts [1]. In the above context, competing truths emphasize that people need to consider multiple possible interpretations and perspectives when understanding and evaluating facts and how they shape and influence people's cognition. It is of great significance to how people deal with complex truth cognition in the information age.

Quinoa was declared by NASA as a "superfood" with health benefits, and the United Nations named 2013 the "International Year of Quinoa" [7, 8]. The Western mainstream news media originally used provocative headlines to report that the increased demand for quinoa from Western healthy eaters had caused quinoa prices to rise, making it difficult for poor families in Bolivia and Peru to afford it, resulting in malnutrition problems [9, 10]. The related news of quinoa spread around the world, but through an actual data survey, three economists found that the quinoa trade improves the living standards of local farmers [11].

Hector Macdonald classified people who use competing truths into three types of communicators: advocates, misinformers and misleaders. Advocates will ignore some facts and selectively use various types of competing truths to create an accurate impression of reality and aim to achieve constructive goals. Misinformers unintentionally spread competing truths that distort reality due to their incomplete grasp of information. Misleaders intentionally use competing truths to create an incorrect impression of reality, perhaps for personal gain or to influence public opinion and behavior. Those three types of communicators state that the truth ranges from well-intentioned advocacy to intentional deception, reflecting different ethical standards. Hector Macdonald proposes three criteria for the ethical communication of people who use competing truths. Firstly, it is correct in terms of facts. Secondly, its objectives are to achieve constructive results that the public will support. Thirdly, it will not cause the audience to behave in ways that harm themselves. As above, the aim is to warn people not to become misleaders while facing various misinformation about the truth in the post-truth era [2].

This research contends that the concept of competing truths reflects that in the post-truth era, news narrative is not only concerned with the facts themselves but more concerned with how these facts are presented and interpreted. The four types of competing truths are the ways in which telling a story or writing news may operate; these show how information is shaped, interpreted, and spread, and subjective and objective factors may be involved in these processes. Competing truths emphasize the diverse truths rather than just labeling them "fake news." Its theory encourages people to think deeply and analyze the different perspectives and possibilities behind information and news when understanding and evaluating facts. Put yourself in other people's shoes and think about how the truth is shaped and affects people's cognition. This is critical for how people deal with complex truth cognition in the information age.

2.2 AI Technology and Theoretical Frameworks in the AI-Truth Era

In 1998, Bernard Stiegler proposed the concept of "tertiary retention" in his book *"Technics and Time, 1: The Fault of Epimetheus"* [12]. This concept refers to externalizing and preserving memories and experiences through technological means such as writing, recording, and digital media. So that people can experience perceptions repeatedly, they may produce different new experiences, such as phonographs and records. Tertiary retention is a form of memory that is not only individual but also cross-cultural and technological. Stiegler let the technics as time in the form of retentions. Tertiary retention not only preserves the past but also influences the present and the future by reconstructing the past. Yuk Hui proposed the concept of "tertiary protention" in his 2016 book "On the Existence of Digital Objects" as a response to Stiegler's "tertiary retention." It refers to being based on structured data and effective algorithms, using digital technology and big data analysis to predict and create an expected future. For instance, a shopping website uses big data to predict the products that users may like and promote them to users with targeted push. Hui's concept builds upon Stiegler's theory and critically analyzes the influence of digital technology on predicting and shaping people's futures in the context of big data ecosystems [13].

This research aims to discuss artificial intelligence (AI) technology in the context of the AI-truth era, in which the theoretical framework mentioned above is pivotal in understanding digital technology. Advanced technology has an increasing influence on the construction and perception of reality. AI technology involves deepfake and automated journalism, artificial intelligence generated content (AIGC), etc. "Tertiary protention" demonstrates how AI technology may predict and shape future reality.

Deepfake is a mixed word that combines "deep learning" and "fake." It refers to using AI techniques based on machine learning and neural network algorithms in synthetic media where a person's image, voice, or video is replaced with someone else's [14]. In 2020, *"In Event of Moon Disaster"* from the MIT Center for Advanced Virtuality used deepfake technology to reimagine what would have happened if the Apollo 11 moon landing mission failed in July 1969 and the astronauts were unable to return. The project publicly released a previously unreleased video of a contingency speech prepared by U.S. President Richard Nixon for the possibility. The project was set in a 1960s American living room physical installation, and viewers could experience this artificial history through a vintage TV. The related online interactive resource site deepened people's understanding of deepfake and served to educate and alert. The speech content was real, written by Nixon's speechwriter, and all the footage was real archival from Apollo 11. However, Nixon's face and voice were a deepfake video. The short documentary film version showed the specific use of deepfake techniques. The MIT Center used the image synthesis technique of artificial intelligence to swap Nixon's face onto the actor's face, making it hard to distinguish between real and fake. Some news media reported the project to alert the public to the dangers of deepfake videos. The team cooperated with the company Respeecher to use deep learning techniques to produce synthetic speech. The company Canny AI used video dialogue replacement techniques to study and simulate the movements of President Nixon's mouth and lips [3–5].

This research contends that *"In Event of Moon Disaster"* is an essential case for reflecting the technological development and evolution from the post-truth era to the AI-truth era. This case used techniques to preserve the Apollo 11 moon landing videos, Nixon's speech draft from that year, and Nixon's many years of image and voice data, which complies with the concept of "tertiary retention." Using artificial intelligence (AI) deepfake technology to reshape and create a new artificial truth through previously saved data, which complies with the concepts of "tertiary protention" and "competing truth," The MIT Center used the resources on its website to warn and educate the public about the potential harm of deepfake videos in order to respond to the current misinformation epidemic. This case shows how technology can be used to reconstruct historical events and confuse reality, sparking public thought and discussion while allowing people to face the challenges of truth identification brought about by the development of AI technology. Nowadays, people can directly and easily generate text, images, voices, and videos by using AIGC tools such as ChatGPT, Midjourney, Stable Diffusion, HeyGen, etc. [15–18]. The development of AI technology, while improving work efficiency, also warns people that the spread of information in the AI-truth era may become more complex and difficult to identify. The improvement of the public's critical thinking about information and media literacy is particularly important in this context.

2.3 Automated Journalism in the AI-Truth Era

"Automated journalism" refers to AI computer programs that automatically generate news stories without human intervention based on natural language generation (NLG) technology, algorithms, and structured data. Also terms "algorithmic journalism" and "robot journalism" [19, 20]. Automated journalism is generally used in fields with rich statistical data, such as sports news, financial news, meteorological and geological disasters. This technology could save time and labor costs and improve the efficiency of news output. At the same time, it stimulates public discussions on the quality and authenticity of news [21]. Quakebot is an automated news program designed by Ken Schwencke, a journalist from the Los Angeles Times, specifically for earthquake news reporting. The goal of its algorithm is to obtain basic information about the events as quickly and exactly as possible. On March 17, 2014, Quakebot extracted relevant data from the U.S. Geological Survey about an earthquake and automatically generated the magnitude 4.7 earthquake report based on algorithms and data, posted after manual review by human journalism, and the entire process was completed within three minutes. This became one of the pioneering cases of automated journalism in the field of journalism [22, 23].

News articles generated by algorithms can reduce the subjective bias that human journalism may bring. However, as it relies on the data that can be obtained, it may also fail to provide in-depth analysis of complex topics and contexts. The content, signatures, editors, and reviewers of automated journalism reports will affect readers' reading experience and judgment, causing ethical issues regarding algorithm transparency. If the source data is incorrect, automated journalism may also produce partial and misleading content [21].

This research contends that the technology of automated journalism is based on data and algorithms and complies with the features of "tertiary retention" and "tertiary protention." However, due to its reliance on data, automated journalism may be limited to reporting data-based facts, making it hard to completely grasp the overall context of an event and potentially causing it to become a misleader. Quakebot posts news after manual review, which is semi-automated journalism. Whether manual review is required depends on the news organization's consideration of the accuracy or timeliness of the news. The rapid iterative updates of AI technology and automated journalism continuously enhancing algorithms through machine learning make humans into a more complex information age. In the context of the AI-truth era, automated journalism is not only a tool for information generation but also plays a key role in shaping and defining truth. It will be increasingly difficult to discern the truth if the readers are unable to distinguish the poster of news contents between humans and algorithms. The practical project *"From Post-Truth to AI-Truth"* of this research deeply explores the application of automated journalism technology in the construction of truth, showing how technology affects people's judgment of information in the current era.

3   From Post-Truth to AI-Truth

3.1   Method and Practice

In today's age of information overload, people live in a post-truth reality full of competing truths. With the increasing development of AI technology, making it harder to distinguish artificial intelligence generated content (AIGC). As mentioned above, people are gradually moving into the AI-truth era, which started in 2023. The proposed concept was also practiced in the techno-art installation project *"From Post-Truth to AI-Truth,"* which aimed to explore this critical cross-era change.

This project was divided into two distinct sections, which were "post-truth" in 2016 and "AI-truth" in 2023, by two display walls. The participants will be able to gain an in-depth understanding of the connection between post-truth and AI-truth through the cross-cultural conversation between the videos projected on these two display walls. The background and origins of post-truth were presented on one display wall, hence the concept of competing truth proposed by Hector Macdonald, and the authors explored in depth how this concept influences our judgment, cognition, and worldview. The authors asked the participants, "Who defines fake news? Who has the right to explain and own the truth? When the truth becomes blurred, how can we discover the direction of judgment?" A printer installation that can keep automatically printing out AI newspapers was installed on the other display wall. This project made the large language model (LLM) GPT-3.5 the editor-in-chief of its own newspaper named "AI-Truth." All news contents in each newspaper are automatically generated in real time by AI after randomly grabbing an article based on post-truth news that has been published on the Internet from the database and rewriting it through algorithms. The contents include headlines, articles, images, captions, crossword puzzles, and the answer. Each piece of the newspaper was unique, marked with the date of the day and the generated time. The participants can check and compare the original news article by scanning the QR code on the newspaper in order to obtain a deeper understanding of the information complexity of this era.

According to the above project idea, this research produced an algorithmic program that allows the AI-Truth automated journalism installation to directly generate news content and output in a pre-layout format without manual review. Since the project *"From Post-Truth to AI-Truth"* was exhibited in Linz, Austria, English was chosen by the authors to be the official program language. AI-Truth automated journalism needs to be generated based on the original data of post-truth news and then rewritten by AI, and post-truth news needs to be manually selected and identified. Therefore, this research selected original news has been published by the Western mainstream media based on the four types of competing truths proposed by Hector Macdonald in his book *"Truth "* [2]. And the content in the original post-truth news webpage has become the "tertiary retention" here. As mentioned above, "post-truth" is related to the word "post-truth politics." The authors set six AI generation version instructions in the program to become the "tertiary protention" here, including "right-wing," "left-wing," "partial truths," "subjective truths," "artificial truths," and "unknown truths."

3.2 Technological Experiments

Shown below in Fig. 1 is a specific program operation design framework. First, a database in TXT file format was created for all selected post-truth news-related URLs. This research used the GPT-3.5 models of the OpenAI API for program development in Python. Then, GPT-3.5 will generate a new article in the "AI-Truth" version by randomly grabbing a piece of post-truth news from the database. These include generating new article titles, article contents, captions and prompts for news images, and a list of article

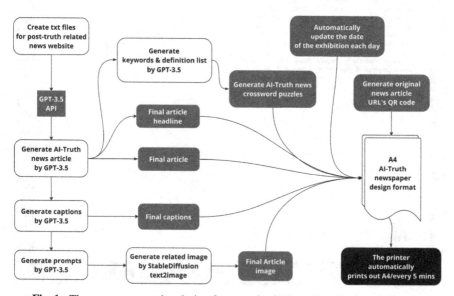

Fig. 1. The program operation design framework of *"From Post-Truth to AI-Truth."*

keywords and definitions. Combined with generating the "AI-Truth" version of prompts, this project used text2image with Stable Diffusion text2image to generate related news images. Because the generated news is not read on the website but will eventually be

09 September, 2023   - Who has the right to explain and own the truth? -   Saturday, 12:18

Quinoa's Price Rise Affecting Peru and Bolivia

By GPT-3.5 | Editor-in-chief

Whether you're a vegetarian or looking to reduce your meat consumption this year, you've probably already tried quinoa. However, consuming too much quinoa has led to increased prices in Peru and Bolivia, where it has been a dietary staple for centuries. The demand for quinoa has become so high that it is now more expensive than imported junk food in Lima. This has caused pressure to turn land that once grew diverse crops into quinoa monoculture. This presents an ethical dilemma for those who want to continue consuming quinoa - should they cut back to stabilize the market and ensure fair prices for all? Quinoa is often referred to as a "super-food" due to its nutritional value, but it only gained popularity in Western countries recently. In 2013, the United Nations even declared it the Year of Quinoa. Concerns about quinoa's rising prices and the impact on local communities have been raised before. The New York Times reported in 2011 that quinoa prices had tripled over five years, while consumption among Bolivians decreased and malnutrition among children in quinoa-growing regions rose. Quinoa is compared to other problematic imports like asparagus and soy, as their popularity comes at the expense of local people and the land. The article suggests that Western countries should focus on growing food closer to home to avoid negative consequences. However, it is unlikely that people will cut back on consuming quinoa with the same enthusiasm as Meat-free Mondays.

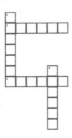

Quinoa harvest in Peru: Balancing global demand with local impact

Crossword Puzzle

Across
2. the moral principles that govern a person's behavior
4. deeply religious or committed

Down
1. regarded with deep respect or admiration
3. a seed that is often mistaken for a grain, highly nutritious

Scan to see the original news article

Answer: revered ethics quinoa devout

Fig. 2. The design format of "AI-Truth" newspaper.

presented in the form of a printed newspaper. The project used a list of keywords and definitions to construct a crossword puzzle of "AI-Truth" news and its answers, in order to make it look more like a traditional newspaper. Each "AI-Truth" news piece will have e a QR code with the URL of the original news website linked to it, which the exhibition participants can scan to check out the original article and enjoy the challenge of a crossword puzzle interactive game when they receive the newspaper.

The content layout in "AI-Truth" newspapers, including the position, font, word size, line spacing, and line limit of the headline of each one, were all pre-designed in the program. The program will combine all the items on the computer into an image file according to the prescribed format and then print it out, as shown in Fig. 2. Finally, the project sets up the system to automatically update the daily date of the exhibition and the time when each news piece is generated. The system was programmed to generate a new "AI-Truth" newspaper every 5 min and print it out automatically. However, the actual operating interval will vary depending on the Internet speed limit at the exhibition location, the content of each news piece, and the printing speed of the printer.

Since "AI-Truth" had not been reviewed manually but was automatically generated and printed out, the final paragraph may contain only one word from the beginning, resulting in an incomplete paragraph. This project used LLM as a model, and the new articles generated may have paragraphs written in the English template style. This research cited the post-truth news case of Quinoa in Sect. 2.1 above. As the comparison in the Fig. 3 below shows, it intuitively releases that the AI will generate different versions according to the instructions of the algorithm, which are based on the same news source. The instructions for the AI-generated version will only be used in the algorithm of the program, and they will not be shown in the printed newspaper.

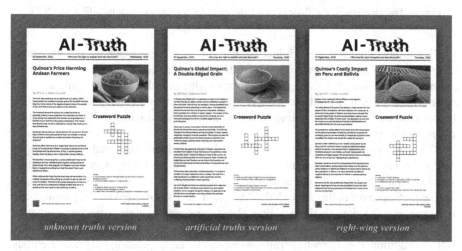

Fig. 3. Different versions of "AI-Truth" automated journalism based on the same news source.

3.3 Actual Exhibition Presentation

"*From Post-Truth to AI-Truth*" was exhibited at the Campus Exhibition of Ars Electronica Festival 2023 Postcity, Linz, Austria, from September 6–10, as part of the College of Arts at National Tsing Hua University [6]. The concept of this experimental project was a good match for the 2023 festival theme, "Who Owns the Truth?" Because of the limited exhibition space, a part of the plan's display was made on-site according to the actual size of the allocated exhibition space. The top view of the floor plan for the exhibition, as shown in Fig. 4.

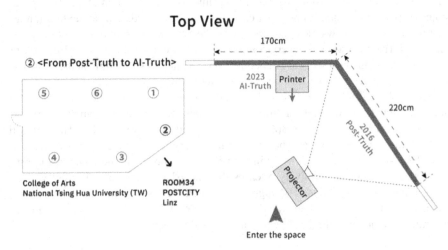

Fig. 4. The top view of the floor plan for the exhibition of Ars Electronica Festival 2023

This project changed the original regular A4 photocopy paper for the newsprint paper in order to make the printed "AI-Truth" news more consistent with the touch of real newspaper. Due to the change in paper weight, in order to achieve the authors' expectations, the printer printed out the newspapers one after another, facing upward on the floor. So the final height setting of the printer was also modified during the actual installation, as shown in Fig. 5.

This project allowed the participants to pick up randomly scattered newspapers on the floor, read them, and optionally take them away. The remaining newspapers will be sorted and hung on the wall representing AI-truth at the end of each day's exhibition, so that the participants can flip through the "AI-Truth" news generated on the previous day or the previous few days on the next day. The authors used a single projector to separate the post-truth video from the AI-truth video, which was projected on these two display walls. In addition, the competing truth and its related corresponding judgment methods proposed by Hector Macdonald, which were mentioned in this research, were marked on the wall, representing post-truth, as shown in Fig. 6.

Fig. 5. An automated journalism installation was printing out "AI-Truth" newspapers in real time, which were part of *"From Post-Truth to AI-Truth,"* which was exhibited at the Ars Electronica Festival 2023.

Fig. 6. Participants at the exhibition site *"From Post-Truth to AI-Truth"* at the Ars Electronica Festival 2023.

4 Discussion and Conclusion

Through the practice of the techno-art project *"From Post-Truth to AI-Truth,"* which consisted of videos and installation, this research used this kind of artistic presentation that was generated in real time at the exhibition space and automated journalism produced by AI. It aims to trigger people's cognitive reflections on post-truth, fake news, and AIGC. This experimental project invited people to participate in interactions and discussions at the exhibition place. The participants saw the "AI-Truth" newspaper generated by AI being printed out continuously on site, and they could engage in an interactive connection with it. In addition to mention four types of competing truths proposed by Hector Macdonald and summarized the methods by which truths can be recognized. It can be seen from practice that AI based on the LLM can generate new competing truths, which increases the difficulty of identifying the truth. Different from previous automated journalism, it is clearly marked that news articles are generated by GPT-3.5 in "AI-Truth" newspapers. Due to the limited language of the original post-truth news data, only the English version of "AI-Truth" automated journalism can currently be developed. The authors look forward to developing versions in other languages in the future.

This research proposes the significant concept of AI-truth. In response to the question "Who defines truth?" as mentioned at the beginning of this research, this project explores the transformation of the right to define truth in the post-truth era and the AI-truth era. A conversation between two eras over two walls prompts people to think deeply about the truth. In the context of this new era, the truth may no longer be simply defined by authoritative institutions, news publishers, or mass communicators but will become more complicated and diverse with the intervention of AI. By exhibiting "AI-Truth" automated journalism and allowing the participants to trace the origin of the news article for comparison, the same original news article can be generated by AI into different new versions. This project confronts the impact of rapidly developing AI technology on the original information age. It is also a cross-cultural exploration of truth, power shifts, and the influences of technology. This research attempts to inspire people to have a deeper understanding of the truth and remind them to learn to discern while obtaining information.

Acknowledgments. This research was supported and financed by the International Intercollegiate Ph.D. Program, the College of Arts, and the Spring Foundation, which are at National Tsing Hua University in Taiwan. The authors would like to thank two technical executors from the MIS LAB who provided related technical support for this project. They are Drew CAVICCHI (US) from the Department of Computer Science at the National Tsing Hua University and Tang-Chen CHANG (TW) from the Institute of Information Systems and Applications at the National Tsing Hua University. Furthermore, the authors also appreciate the valuable guidance and suggestions of Prof. Cheng-Yu PAN from the Graduate Institute of Art and Technology at the National Tsing Hua University.

References

1. Oxford Languages. Word of the Year 2016 (2016). https://languages.oup.com/word-of-the-year/2016/. Accessed 30 Oct 2023
2. Macdonald, H.: Truth. Random House, New York (2018)
3. In Event of Moon Disaster Homepage. https://moondisaster.org/. Accessed 30 Oct 2023
4. Panetta, F., Burgund, H., Ben-Ami, O., Serdiuk, A., Reaber, G., Bielievtsov, D.: In event of moon disaster. In: SIGGRAPH Asia 2020 Computer Animation Festival, p. 1. Association for Computing Machinery, New York (2021). https://doi.org/10.1145/3414687.3434109
5. Burgund, H., Panetta, F.: In Event of Moon Disaster. Ars Electronica (2021). https://ars.electronica.art/newdigitaldeal/en/moon-disaster/. Accessed 30 Oct 2023
6. Li, Y., Cavicchi, D., Chang, T.-C.: From Post-Truth to AI-Truth. Ars Electronica (2023). https://ars.electronica.art/who-owns-the-truth/de/ai-truth/. Accessed 20 Oct 2023
7. Schlick, G., Bubenheim, D.L.: Quinoa: An emerging new crop with potential for CELSS. No. A-93100 (1993)
8. United Nations. General Assembly Launches International Year of Quinoa (2013). https://press.un.org/en/2013/ga11341.doc.htm. Accessed 11 Oct 2023

9. Sherwin, A.: The food fad that's starving Bolivia. Independent (2011). https://www.ind ependent.co.uk/life-style/food-and-drink/features/the-food-fad-that-s-starving-bolivia-224 8932.html. Accessed 11 Oct 2023

10. Verner, A.: The more you love quinoa, the more you hurt Peruvians and Bolivians. The Globe and Mail (2013). https://www.theglobeandmail.com/life/the-hot-button/the-more-you-love-quinoa-the-more-you-hurt-peruvians-and-bolivians/article7409637/. Accessed 11 Oct 2023

11. Bellemare, M.F., Fajardo-Gonzalez, J., Gitter, S.R.: Foods and fads: the welfare impacts of rising quinoa prices in Peru. World Dev. 112, 163–179 (2018). https://doi.org/10.1016/j.wor lddev.2018.07.012

12. Stiegler, B.: Technics and time, 1: The fault of Epimetheus, vol. 1. Stanford University Press, Stanford (1998)

13. Hui, Y.: On the existence of digital objects, vol. 48. University of Minnesota Press, Minnesota (2016)

14. Westerlund, M.: The emergence of deepfake technology: a review. Technol. Innov. Manag. Rev. 9(11), 39–52 (2019). https://doi.org/10.22215/timreview/1282

15. OpenAI: ChatGPT. https://chat.openai.com. Accessed 20 Jan 2024

16. Midjourney. https://www.midjourney.com/home. Accessed 31 Jan 2024

17. Stability AI: Stable Diffusion 2.0 Release. https://stability.ai/news/stable-diffusion-v2-rel ease. Accessed 20 Jan 2024

18. HeyGen. https://app.heygen.com/login. Accessed 20 Jan 2024

19. Dörr, K.N.: Mapping the field of algorithmic journalism. Digit. Journal. 4(6), 700–722 (2016). https://doi.org/10.1080/21670811.2015.1096748

20. Oremus, W.: Why Robot? Slate (2015). https://slate.com/technology/2015/02/automated-ins ights-ap-earnings-reports-robot-journalists-a-misnomer.html. Accessed 30 Dec 2023

21. Graefe, A.: Guide to Automated Journalism. Tow Center for Digital Journalism, Columbia University (2016). https://doi.org/10.7916/D80G3XDJ

22. Los Angeles Times. What is the Quakebot and how does it work? (2019). https://www.lat imes.com/la-me-quakebot-faq-20190517-story.html. Accessed 20 Jan 2024

23. Oremus, W.: The First News Report on the L.A. Earthquake Was Written by a Robot. Slate (2014). https://slate.com/technology/2014/03/quakebot-los-angeles-times-robot-journa list-writes-article-on-la-earthquake.html. Accessed 20 Jan 2024

The Impact of Artificial Intelligence Generated Content Driven Graphic Design Tools on Creative Thinking of Designers

Yonghui Lin and Hailin Liu[✉]

Beijing Institute of Technology, Beijing, China
puccayama@qq.com

Abstract. This study aims to explore the application of AIGC in the field of graphic design and its impact on the creative thinking of designers. With the rapid development of artificial intelligence technology, collaboration between designers and AIGC tools is becoming increasingly popular, which has triggered a profound reflection on the creative process and results. This study adopts in-depth interviews and literature analysis methods to analyze the impact of AIGC driven graphic design tools on the creative thinking of designers.

Firstly, research has found that AIGC tools can quickly generate a large number of creative concepts and design drafts, providing designers with more sources of inspiration. The use of this tool can stimulate the creative thinking of designers, making it easier for them to try different design styles and element combinations. However, at the same time, some designers have also raised concerns that AIGC may weaken their creative output, as excessive reliance on these tools may lead to a decrease in designer creativity.

Secondly, this study emphasizes the role of AIGC tools in the design process. They can not only be used for creative inspiration, but also for automated repetitive tasks, allowing designers to focus more on creative and strategic work. This division of labor and collaboration approach provides designers with more time to think, explore, and advance design projects, which helps to improve the quality of creative thinking.

In summary, AIGC driven graphic design tools have played an important role in stimulating creative thinking among designers, but there are also some challenges. Designers need to recognize the advantages and limitations of AIGC tools and integrate them into their creative process to achieve more innovative and in-depth design works. This study provides a deep understanding of the application of AIGC in the field of graphic design and valuable insights for future research and practice.

Keywords: AIGC generation tool · Designers · Creative thinking · Influencing factors · Graphic design

P.-L. P. Rau (Ed.): HCII 2024, LNCS 14702, pp. 258–272, 2024.
https://doi.org/10.1007/978-3-031-60913-8_18

1 Introduction

In the current digital era, the flourishing development of artificial intelligence technology has triggered revolutionary changes in the field of design, among which the rise of AI driven graphic design tools (AIGC) has become an important driving force in design creation. This phenomenon not only signifies technological progress, but also calls for designers to comprehensively examine their creative methods and thinking patterns. This paper aims to conduct an in-depth study on the impact of AIGC tools on the creative thinking of designers. By exploring the application scenarios, advantages, and challenges of the tools, it aims to provide more profound understanding and guidance for practitioners in the design field to respond to this change. By analyzing the new relationship between artificial intelligence and designers, we will gain a comprehensive understanding of how AIGC tools influence creative thinking, providing substantial insights for the future development of the design field.

2 Background Introduction

2.1 Overview of the Application of Artificial Intelligence in the Field of Design

With the continuous progress of artificial intelligence technology, its application in the field of design has become increasingly widespread and profound. The emergence of artificial intelligence provides designers with new digital tools and creative resources, driving the boundaries of design innovation. Machine learning technology is playing an increasingly important role in the field of design. By learning from a large amount of design data, machine learning algorithms can analyze and recognize patterns, providing designers with deeper insights and inspiration. In graphic design, machine learning can be used for image recognition, color analysis, and other aspects to help designers process information more effectively and creatively apply elements. The rise of artificial intelligence driven graphic design tools (AIGC) has become a major highlight in the field of design. These tools utilize machine learning and algorithms to automatically generate design elements, creative concepts, and artworks, providing designers with powerful assistance and creative inspiration. For example, AIGC tools can quickly generate diverse design drafts, expanding the creative space of designers. Artificial intelligence has had a profound impact on interaction design and user experience in product and application design. By analyzing user behavior and feedback, artificial intelligence can personalize interface design and improve the quality of user experience. This personalized design can not only meet the specific needs of users, but also improve the user satisfaction and market competitiveness of the product. Artificial intelligence plays a crucial role in creative generation and automated design. Designers can use AIGC tools to quickly generate a large number of creative concepts, thereby exploring different design directions more quickly. Meanwhile, automated design processes can accelerate the completion of repetitive tasks, allowing designers to focus more on creative and strategic work. In the field of architectural design, the application of artificial intelligence technology is becoming increasingly significant. Intelligent algorithms can assist architects in generating diverse solutions during the design process and optimizing building structures to improve energy efficiency. The rise of intelligent design systems has provided more possibilities for architectural designers, enabling buildings to better adapt to the environment and meet user needs.

2.2 The Development and Application of AIGC Tools

AIGC, also known as artificial intelligence generated content, represents an emerging method of content production that relies on constantly evolving artificial intelligence technologies. Early AIGC was mainly applied to assist in generating content in professional fields, including film and television production, entertainment industry, and modeling. With the evolution of technology, a series of changes have emerged. In 2014, Goodfellow and other scholars proposed the Generative Adversarial Network (GAN) based on adversarial learning; Subsequently, in 2021, Radford et al. proposed the CLIP (Comparative Language Image Pre Training) algorithm, which can effectively learn visual features and achieve multimodal pre training; In 2022, Ho et al. implemented a diffusion model for text generation using forward diffusion and backward generation processes. This series of significant changes has enabled AIGC to be more widely applied in fields such as digital twins, digital modeling, and artistic creation. In November 2022, OpenAI released ChatGPT, a generative artificial intelligence model with interactive capabilities that attracted 100 million monthly active users in just two months, sparking widespread attention from various sectors to AIGC.

AIGC has demonstrated its application potential in multiple industries such as finance, media, entertainment, and industry, especially in the field of design, such as advertising design, animation design, game design, etc. The application of AIGC has significant representativeness. In terms of advertising design, AIGC can quickly generate marketing content such as advertising copy and poster pages for advertising companies and brands, providing efficient and low-cost solutions for the production of smart advertising. Taking the Chinese tourism and travel platform Feizhu as an example, they successfully launched the AIGC generated "What to Play on May Day" themed advertisement in cities such as Shanghai and Hangzhou in April 2023. AIGC combines pre-set advertising text materials in the database, integrates data collection and analysis, obtains user browsing behavior, forms a user preference dataset, triggers and extracts advertising keywords from the dataset, and ultimately generates advertisements that match user preferences for placement. At present, there are patent applications based on the AIGC advertising content generation system.

3   Literature Review

3.1   The Application of AIGC in Graphic Design

Zhou Zhen and Zhang Xinyi (2023) In the article "The Future Transformation Behind the Tiangong Feast and Screenwashing Video: The Era of Big Data", it is mentioned that in August 2022, game designer Jason Allen's "Space Opera" created using the AI drawing tool Midjournal won the championship in the digital art category at the Colorado Art Fair, highlighting the outstanding performance of artificial intelligence in artistic creation. At the same time, the enterprise behind the image generation algorithm Stable Diffusion, Stability AI, announced a financing of over $100 million, with a post investment valuation of $1 billion, highlighting the remarkable development of AI technology in the commercial field. On the other hand, OpenAI launched the chatbot algorithm ChatGPT at the end of November, which has sparked a new wave in the AIGC field and even received high praise from Tesla CEO Musk, who bluntly stated that ChatGPT is "terrifying". This indicates that AI is no longer limited to understanding language, text, and images, but has ventured into the field of generating high-quality content, covering areas such as artistic creation that were previously considered unique to human intelligence. As early as 2022, Baidu Research Institute made a forward-looking statement on the big model of pre training and AIGC in its scientific and technological trend forecast. At the 2022 Baidu World Conference in July, Robin Lee, the founder of Baidu, clearly praised the concept of AIGC. Subsequently, the C-end release of Wenxin Yige enabled users to generate artwork in just a few seconds by providing brief descriptions and selecting their preferred styles, once again highlighting the outstanding contribution of AIGC technology in promoting innovation in the creative and artistic fields.

Zhang Jian, Wang Yuxin and Yuan Zhe (2023) AIGC Empowers Traditional Culture Inheritance Design Methods and Practices - Taking the design of the Yongle Palace Digital Exhibition Center in Shanxi Province as an example, the article points out that in the era of Web 3.0, AIGC plays an important role in traditional culture inheritance, bringing new creative methods to the design field. By comprehensively analyzing the application status of AIGC in various fields both domestically and internationally, as well as its key technologies and methods, this article focuses on the application process of AIGC in traditional cultural inheritance design. Taking the design of the Yongle Palace Digital Exhibition Center in Shanxi Province as an example, this article showcases the design scheme jointly created by AIGC and designers. This method provides innovative ideas and processes for the inheritance and design of traditional culture. By combining machine learning, generative models, and algorithm optimization technologies, AIGC not only flexibly and efficiently excavates and creates new design elements, but also provides designers with richer inspiration and creative support through big data analysis, image processing, and natural language processing. More notably, the integration of multiple technologies and algorithms by AIGC enables the design process to be automated or assisted, improving design efficiency and quality, thereby promoting the inheritance, innovation, and sustainable development of traditional culture. This comprehensive approach has brought new thinking and practical directions for the design of traditional cultural heritage. As shown in Fig. 1.

Wang Lei (2023) Exploring the Application of AIGC Drawing Tools in UI Interface Design - Taking Midjournal as an Example, this article delves into the application of AIGC drawing tools in UI interface design. By analyzing in detail how to use AIGC drawing tools to quickly generate graphic elements such as interface renderings, icons, product images, mascots, etc., and modifying and optimizing these elements through instructions, the potential of AIGC in improving UI design efficiency and quality is revealed. Analysis shows that AIGC drawing tools have significant advantages in the early stages of UI design. Designers can use them to quickly output creative design drawings, enrich the sources of creative inspiration, shorten the design draft creation

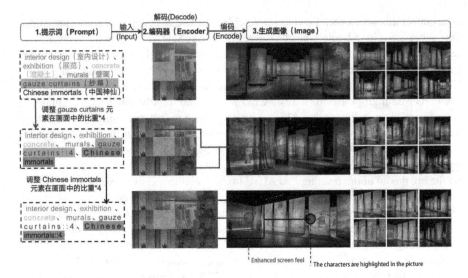

Fig. 1. Visualization of cultural and biological images in AIGC design

cycle, and effectively improve the creativity and design efficiency in the early stages of UI interface design. Although the actual implementation of design projects still requires secondary modifications and development by designers, the AIGC drawing tool eliminates the tedious work of producing a large number of process drafts, allowing designers to focus more on exploring better design directions and avoid being buried by a lot of drawing work. Although AIGC drawing tools can quickly generate design drafts, excellent design solutions still require the joint efforts of designer experience and repeated deduction. Designers who are familiar with AIGC instructions and parameterized thinking are more likely to master deeper usage and how to configure instructions to make the generated results closer to design goals. In addition, as AIGC drawing tools require

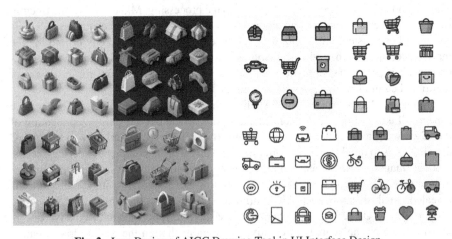

Fig. 2. Icon Design of AIGC Drawing Tool in UI Interface Design

English instructions, designers need to have a large vocabulary in design related professional English. Overall, AIGC drawing tools are essentially auxiliary tools for improving design efficiency, and their application effects vary from person to person. Excellent designers can fully utilize them to create better design solutions. As shown in Fig. 2.

In summary, the three research papers collectively depict the significant contributions of AIGC technology in artistic creation, commercial applications, traditional cultural heritage design, and UI interface design. Jason Allen's successful case demonstrates AIGC's outstanding performance in the field of digital art, while Stability AI financing and OpenAI's ChatGPT launch highlight AIGC's remarkable progress in business and language generation. The study, taking Yongle Palace in Shanxi Province as an example, emphasizes the innovative role of AIGC in traditional cultural inheritance design, while Wang Lei's research delves into the potential of AIGC drawing tools in UI interface design. These studies collectively present the diverse applications of AIGC technology in multiple fields of graphic design, providing profound insights for future research and practice. The continuous development of AIGC technology will continue to drive innovation in various fields, bringing broader possibilities to human society.

3.2 The Theoretical Framework of Creative Thinking in Designers

Lei Li (2023). From Human Creativity to AIGC: Philosophical Reflection on Future Advertising. The article points out that in the future, advertising will usher in an era of collaborative creation between humans and AIGC, achieving the reconstruction and upgrading of the advertising industry. The application of AIGC in the field of advertising creativity aims to liberate human creative productivity and achieve positive interaction with artificial intelligence. Although humans and machine intelligence compete in advertising creative activities, their complementarity is more crucial. The essence of advertising creativity is based on a profound understanding of human emotions and needs, which determines the irreplaceability of humanity in future advertising creativity. In order to compensate for the limitations of machine intelligence, future advertising creativity needs to promote a positive interaction between AIGC technology and human intelligence. Human creators will become a bridge connecting human intelligence and machine intelligence, on the premise of fully mastering knowledge and skills. Balancing the relationship between technology and culture in human-machine co creation, so that AIGC technology can promote the development of the advertising creative industry on the right track. The integration of the two will stimulate the infinite potential of human creativity, while providing more possibilities for the widespread application of AIGC, and promoting society towards a more intelligent, inclusive, and beautiful direction. From the perspective of creative process and way of thinking, AIGC focuses on logic and mathematics, generating advertising content based on a large amount of data and algorithms, while humans focus on emotions and inspiration, creating unique and attractive advertising content through knowledge, experience, cultural background, and imagination. Although AIGC has advantages in improving the efficiency and accuracy of advertising creativity, it still cannot surpass humans in terms of emotional expression, cultural connotations, and the uniqueness of creativity. In the future, advertising will be more completed by AIGC, and the role of humanity will shift towards evaluating creativity. It is necessary to cultivate comprehensive humanistic literacy, interdisciplinary knowledge background, enhance appreciation and identification abilities, and complete the evaluation and control of machine creativity.

Cheng Lin and Wang Mingzhi (2023) The opportunities and challenges for design professionals in the era of AI technology are mentioned in the article. In daily life, people are encouraged to examine things that are often overlooked and forgotten from a new perspective, maintain sensitivity to small details in life, and try to think about problems from different perspectives. On the path of innovation, the key is to constantly break through old thinking frameworks. In the current era of increasingly mature artificial intelligence technology, designers are no longer just competing for who can master more skills, but rather showcasing richer imagination and creativity.

For example, Apple has adopted a very unique minimalist form in designing its iPod, which has attracted a large number of consumers with its innovation and uniqueness, making it a leader in the music player market. With the strong intervention of AIGC technology in the design field, design practitioners must integrate with AI to drive the progress of the entire design industry. Therefore, as a design practitioner, it is not only necessary to master basic design professional knowledge and skills, but also to have a deep understanding of AIGC technology, improve one's creative thinking, interdisciplinary integration and coordination ability, and comprehensive skills to adapt to the constantly updated and iterative AI technology. Overall, rather than rejecting or fearing AI technology, design practitioners should actively embrace challenges, fully utilize new technologies, and inject more creativity and innovation into the development of the design industry.

Zhao Ying (2023). Exploring the penetration of generative artificial intelligence in the field of visual communication design, the article mentions that AIGC has had a profound impact in the field of visual communication design, creating a broader creative space for creators and bringing significant opportunities and challenges for the future design field. With the continuous advancement of technology, we are expected to see AIGC and human creativity work together to shape the future of visual communication design, creating more innovative and influential design works. However, we must also be vigilant about the potential risks that excessive reliance on technology may bring, as well as the conflicts that may arise at the conceptual and ethical levels. The collision and integration of values triggered by AIGC will shape an exciting era. Creators need to learn how to cooperate and complement with AIGC, fully leverage its advantages and potential, and promote innovation and exploration in the design field, laying the foundation for future design development.

Conclusion: Three articles delve into the impact of AIGC on the creative thinking of designers, revealing its profound impact in areas such as advertising, daily life, and visual communication design. Although AIGC provides designers with new tools and creative possibilities, research also emphasizes the irreplaceable role of human creativity in advertising and design. Designers need to maintain independent thinking and unique creativity with the assistance of technology, break through old thinking frameworks, and focus on cultivating humanistic literacy to achieve a positive interaction with AIGC technology. This presents the dual challenges and opportunities faced by the design field. Designers in the AIGC era need to continuously improve their creative expression and humanistic understanding abilities to better lead the development of future design.

4 Research Method

4.1 In-Depth Interview

In the in-depth interview stage, 15 key information providers were interviewed through online distribution of in-depth interview questionnaires. The content of the in-depth interviews was organized, and the views and opinions of different interviewees were classified according to relevance. Establish a clear data framework for easy analysis and summarization. The interview will carefully select professional designers covering a wide range of design fields as interviewees, ensuring that senior designers and new designers who have already used AIGC tools are included. Through this diverse group

Table 1. Interview Content Data Statistics of Interviewees

Content	Designers who have used AIGC tools (15 key informant)															
	Expert 1	Expert 2	Expert 3	Expert 4	Expert 5	Expert 6	Expert 7	Expert 8	Expert 9	Expert 10	Expert 11	Expert 12	Expert 13	Expert 14	Expert 15	N=15
1. Improve design efficiency	√	√	√	√	√	√	√	√	√	√	√	√	√	√	√	15
2. Excessive dependence leads to a weakening of designers' creative thinking	√	√	√	√	√	√	√		√	√	√	√	√	√	√	14
3. Expanding design possibilities	√	√	√	√	√	√	√		√	√			√		√	11
4. Provide design inspiration and direction	√	√	√	√		√	√		√	√		√	√	√		11
5. Solve automated repetitive tasks and unleash more thinking space	√	√	√	√		√	√	√	√	√	√	√	√	√	√	14
6. Lack of emotion	√	√	√	√		√	√	√	√	√	√	√	√	√	√	14
7. There is a knowledge blind spot	√	√				√	√	√	√	√	√		√	√	√	11

of respondents, we will gain a deeper understanding of the creative thinking process of designers using AIGC tools, including the sources of inspiration and creative exploration methods. In addition, they will be asked about their experience using AIGC tools, with a focus on the potential impact of AIGC tools on designers' creative thinking, as well as their expectations and potential concerns about the tools.

According to the interview results in Table 1, the researchers summarized the interview results in the highest frequency order as follows:

Through in-depth interviews with 15 senior designers in the design industry as key information providers, the following conclusions were drawn:

1. Improving design efficiency: AIGC tools significantly improve design efficiency through automated design generation. (15)
2. Overreliance on AIGC tools can lead to a weakening of designers' creative thinking, as excessive reliance on tools may result in a lack of opportunities for independent thinking and creative output. (14)
3. Solving automated repetitive tasks and freeing up more thinking space: AIGC tools solve automated repetitive tasks in design, effectively freeing up more thinking space for designers, enabling them to focus more on deep creative thinking. (14)
4. Lack of emotion: AIGC tools suffer from a lack of emotion in design, as they mainly focus on automation and generation, making it difficult to express and capture complex emotional elements in the design. (14)
5. Expanding design possibilities: AIGC tools have successfully expanded the possibilities of design by providing diversity and flexibility, opening up a broader creative space for designers. (11)
6. Provide design inspiration and direction: AIGC tools automate the generation of design elements, providing designers with real-time design inspiration and direction, helping to guide and stimulate creativity in the design process. (11)
7. There is a knowledge blind spot: AIGC tools have a knowledge blind spot, which means they may be limited in processing certain fields or topics, unable to provide sufficient background knowledge or deep understanding. This may result in the generated design lacking accuracy and professionalism in specific fields. (11)

4.2 Document Analysis

In terms of literature analysis, we will first conduct extensive literature collection to search for academic papers, books, and research reports related to the application of AIGC tools in the field of graphic design and their impact on designer creative thinking. Subsequently, we will carefully screen and select literature that is closely related to the research topic and has scientifically reliable methods. In the in-depth analysis stage, we will extract key information from the literature, including the advantages and limitations of AIGC tools, as well as the potential impact on designer creative thinking. Finally, by comparing and summarizing the results of in-depth interviews and the conclusions of literature analysis, we will form a comprehensive understanding of the impact of AIGC tools on designer creative thinking. This research method will help to further explore the practical application and potential impact of AIGC tools in graphic design (Table 2).

According to the keyword statistics in the literature variable table, AIGC tools have shown various advantages in the design field, including promoting business development,

Table 2. Literature Review and Overview of Variables in Related Studies

Main Variables	Sub Variables	Sources
The advantages of AIGC tools	1. promote commerce 2. Generate high-quality content 3. Design efficiency improvement 4. Diversity and flexibility 5. Creative stimulation	Zhou Zhen and Zhang Xinyi (2023)
		Zhang Jian, Wang Yuxin, and Yuan Zhe (2023)
		Wang Lei (2023)
		Zhao Ying (2023)
		Wei Dong (2023)
		Ye Caixian and Xu Lijun (2023)
		Feng Yuquan (2024)
		Editorial Department of Textile Guide (2024)
Limitations of AIGC tools	1. Creative limitations 2. Relying on the quality of training data 3. Lack of emotion 4. Requires a large amount of resources 5. There is a knowledge blind spot	Lu Zhaolin, Song Xinheng, Jin Yucheng (2023)
		Zhou Zhen and Zhang Xinyi (2023)
		Zhang Jian, Wang Yuxin, and Yuan Zhe (2023)
		Wang Lei (2023)
		Li Jie and Wang Luping (2024)
		Li Jie, Fan Ling (2024)
		Zhao Ying (2023)
The Impact of AIGC on Creative Thinking	1. Excessive dependence leads to a weakening of designers' creative thinking 2. Provide design inspiration and direction 3. Expanding design possibilities 4. Solving automated repetitive tasks and freeing up more thinking space	Lei Li (2023)
		Cheng Lin and Wang Mingzhi (2023)
		Zhao Ying (2023)
		Chen Ying and Ma Hongtao (2024)
		Wang Lei (2023)

(*continued*)

Table 2. (*continued*)

Main Variables	Sub Variables	Sources
		Zhang Jian, Wang Yuxin, and Yuan Zhe (2023)
		Lu Zhaolin, Song Xinheng, Jin Yucheng (2023)
		Lou Yongqi (2023)
		Wei Dong (2023)
		Liu Yating and Fan Lingyan (2023)

generating high-quality content, improving design efficiency, possessing diversity and flexibility, and stimulating creative thinking. Its automation features enable designers to complete creative designs more efficiently, while generating high-level design elements through machine learning and model generation, injecting new vitality and possibilities into the design field, and helping creators achieve more outstanding achievements at different levels.

Although AIGC tools have shown many advantages in the design field, they also have some obvious limitations. Firstly, it is limited by creativity, that is, it excessively follows the pattern of training data when generating design elements, resulting in a lack of truly unique and innovative designs. Secondly, the performance of AIGC tools is closely related to the quality of training data. If there are deviations or deficiencies in the training data, the generated design results may be affected. In addition, AIGC tools have certain shortcomings in expressing emotions, making it difficult to accurately capture and convey emotional elements in the design. On the other hand, in order to maintain efficient operation, AIGC tools require a large amount of computing and storage resources, which poses challenges for some designers and organizations. Finally, there is a knowledge blind spot in AIGC tools, which means they cannot provide in-depth understanding or expertise in certain fields or topics, limiting their application in specific fields. These limitations need to be carefully considered when using AIGC tools to fully leverage their advantages while avoiding potential issues.

The impact of AIGC tools on creative thinking is twofold. On the one hand, excessive dependence weakens the creative thinking of designers. On the other hand, it provides design inspiration and direction, expands design possibilities, and frees up more thinking space by solving automated repetitive tasks, helping to improve the quality of creative thinking. It is necessary to balance and utilize its advantages in use to promote comprehensive creative thinking.

5 The Impact of AIGC Tools on Creative Thinking

Taking the experience of game designer Jason Allen as an example, he won the championship in the digital art category at the Colorado Art Fair for his creation of Space Opera House using the AIGC drawing tool Midjournal. This achievement highlights the positive role of AIGC tools in providing design inspiration and direction, enabling designers to generate unique and creative design elements through the automatic generation of tools.

Meanwhile, the application of AIGC tools has also expanded the possibilities of design. The enterprise Stability AI behind the stable diffusion algorithm has obtained financing of over 100 million US dollars, with a post investment valuation of 1 billion US dollars, demonstrating the widespread application of AIGC in the commercial field. This scalability is not only reflected in the diversity of design elements, but also brings innovation and development in the commercial field, providing designers with broader creative space.

In addition, the AIGC tool frees up more thinking space by solving automated repetitive tasks, allowing designers to focus more on exploring better design directions. This is particularly evident in the chatbot algorithm launched by ChatGPT, providing designers with more time to think, explore, and advance design projects.

However, it should be noted that excessive reliance on AIGC tools may lead to a weakening of creative thinking. Designers should maintain a balance when using AIGC tools, fully leveraging their advantages while maintaining the ability to manually create, to ensure that design works are more original and innovative (Table 3).

Table 3. The influencing factors of AIGC tools on creative thinking

Influence factor	Describe
Over-reliance on	Overreliance on AIGC may weaken the creative thinking of designers, resulting in dull creativity and a lack of personality
Provide design inspiration and direction	The AIGC tool provides designers with innovative inspiration and guides their creative direction by automatically generating design elements
Expanding design possibilities	The application of AIGC expands the possibilities of design, creates diverse design elements, and enriches the creative space
Solving automated repetitive tasks	AIGC solves repetitive tasks, freeing up more time and thinking space for designers, and improving design efficiency

The above chart clearly demonstrates the multifaceted impact of AIGC on creative thinking. Although excessive reliance may pose risks, the rational use of AIGC tools can help provide inspiration, expand possibilities, and unleash the creative potential of designers.

6 Conclusion

6.1 Summarize Research Findings

Based on in-depth interviews and literature research, AIGC driven graphic design tools have attracted significant attention in the field of design. By improving design efficiency, providing inspiration and direction, expanding design possibilities, and solving automated repetitive tasks, AIGC tools have a positive impact on creative thinking. However, excessive dependence may lead to a decrease in creativity, and tools have limitations in emotional expression and knowledge domains. Designers need to flexibly apply this technology, adapt to technological development, and comprehensively consider the advantages and limitations of tools to promote continuous innovation and improvement in the design field.

6.2 The Application and Prospects of AIGC Tools in Graphic Design

The application of AIGC tools in graphic design has shown significant potential and prospects. Firstly, by rapidly generating creative concepts and design drafts, AIGC tools provide designers with more sources of inspiration, making it easier for them to try different design styles and element combinations, thereby better stimulating creative thinking. Secondly, the role of AIGC tools in the design process is not limited to creative inspiration, but can also be used to automate repetitive tasks, freeing designers more time to think, explore, and advance design projects, and improving design quality. However, with the popularization of applications, designers need to be aware of the potential risks that excessive reliance on these tools may lead to a decrease in creative output.

Looking ahead to the future, AIGC tools are expected to play a more important role in various fields, helping designers adapt to the rapid development of technology. Designers will need to continuously develop their skills to better utilize AIGC tools and integrate them into the design creation process. In addition, the application of AIGC tools will have a profound impact on the career development of designers, requiring them to have a more comprehensive understanding and response to the arrival of this technology.

6.3 Reflections on Designers' Suggestions and Future Development Directions

For designers, facing the application and future development of AIGC tools, the following are some suggestions and directions for thinking:

Firstly, expand the breadth of skills: Designers should strive to improve their understanding and application ability of AIGC tools. This includes mastering the operation of tools proficiently, understanding their algorithm principles, and being able to effectively collaborate with them. Continuously learning new technologies and tools to adapt to industry changes. Secondly, maintain creative thinking: Although AIGC tools can provide fast design support, designers should still maintain their unique creative thinking. While using tools, pay attention to cultivating personalized design styles and creative expression to ensure that design works have uniqueness and creativity. Thirdly, find a balance: avoid excessive reliance on AIGC tools and consider them as auxiliary rather than substitutes. During the design process, maintain the role of artificial creative thinking and use AIGC tools to enhance and expand the possibilities of creativity. Fourthly, participate in communities and collaborations: join the design and technology community, exchange experiences and share perspectives with peers. Actively participate in interdisciplinary cooperation, collaborate with AI engineers and professionals in other fields, and jointly promote the integration of technology and design. Fifth, focus on ethics and social impact: Designers should consider ethics and social impact when applying AIGC tools. Pay attention to potential issues that tools may cause, such as privacy and bias, actively participate in discussions and propose improvement plans. Sixth, continuous learning and adaptation: With the rapid development of technology, designers need to maintain sensitivity to new technologies and trends. Continuously learning new knowledge and actively adapting to industry changes to maintain competitiveness. In the future, designers will play a more critical role in collaboration with AIGC tools. By deeply understanding the advantages and limitations of tools, designers can better guide the application of technology and create more creative and in-depth design works.

References

Zhou, Z., Zhang, X.: Baidu AI painting at the beginning, the future transformation behind the Tiangong Feast screen scrolling video in the era of big data (2), 54–59 (2023)

Zhang, J., Wang, Y., Yuan, Z.: Empowers Traditional Culture Inheritance Design Methods and Practices - Taking the Design of Yongle Palace Digital Exhibition Center in Shanxi Province as an Example Design, vol. 36, no. 17, pp. 30–33 (2023)

Wang, L.: Application Analysis of AIGC Drawing Tool in UI Interface Design - Taking Midjournal as an Example Computer Knowledge and Technology, vol. 19, no. 26, pp. 108–111 (2023)

Lei, L.: From human creativity to AIGC: philosophical reflections on future advertising. J. Cult. **08**, 58–63 (2023)

Cheng, L., Wang, M.: Opportunities and challenges for design professionals in the era of AI technology. Screen Printing (12), 93–96 (2023). https://doi.org/10.20084/j.cnki.1002-4867.2023.12.027

Zhao, Y.: Exploring the penetration of generative artificial intelligence in the field of visual communication design. Screen Printing (24), 73–76 (2023). https://doi.org/10.20084/j.cnki.1002-4867.2023.24.022

Chen, Y., Ma, H.: AIGC's divine assistance in the field of art and design - taking stable diffusion as an example. Fashion Designer (01), 73–84 (2024). https://doi.org/10.20100/j.cnki.cn11-4548/ts.2024.0108

Wei, D.: How AIGC changes advertising creativity. Zhongguancun (11), 32–33 (2023)

Ye, C., Xu, L.: Research on the application of artificial intelligence generative AI technology in new media art. Technol. Innov. Appl. (21), 32–35 (2023). https://doi.org/10.19981/j.CN23-1581/G3.2023.21.007

Feng, Y. Application and reflection of AIGC in industrial design. Packag. Eng., 1–11 (2024)

Editorial Department of Textile Guide: Application of artificial intelligence technology in the field of textile and clothing pattern design. Fujian Light Text. (01), 2–3 (2024)

Lu, Z., Song, X., Jin, Y.: The current situation and development of intelligent design under the trend of AIGC technology. Packag. Eng. (24), 18–33+13 (2023). https://doi.org/10.19554/j.cnki.1001-3563.2023.24.003

Li, J., Wang, L.: A new paradigm for AIGC design in the era of large models. Design (02), 76–82 (2024). https://doi.org/10.20055/j.cnki.1003-10069.01483

Li, J., Fan, L.: Creator of the dance of computing power in the era of intelligent design. Design (02), 36–41 (2024). https://doi.org/10.20055/j.cnki.1003-0069.001493

Lou, Y.: In the AIGC era, where does creativity go? Art Des. Res. (06), 5–12 (2023)

Liu, Y., Fan, L.: Generative Artificial Intelligence and Future Environment Design: Evolution, Challenges, and Directions Proceedings of the 2023 Cross Strait and Hong Kong Macao Innovation Design Youth Academic Forum, pp. 167–172. School of Art, Design and Media, Shanghai Sanda College (2023). https://doi.org/10.26914/c.cnkihy.2023.058048

Responses to Human and Robot Errors in Human–Robot Collaboration: An fNIRS Study

Fengyuan Liu[1], Yishu Ji[2], Xin Lei[1], and Pei-Luen Patrick Rau[2(✉)]

[1] School of Management, Zhejiang University of Technology, Hangzhou, China
[2] Department of Industrial Engineering, Tsinghua University, Beijing, China
rpl@mail.tsinghua.edu.cn

Abstract. Performance assessment in the era of human–robot collaboration poses new challenges. Will human managers display varying responses to the success and failure of human versus robot employees? This study aims to investigate people's responses to success and errors made by humans compared to those made by robots using self-report measures and neuroimaging techniques. Twenty-four participants were asked to imagine themselves as managers tasked with reviewing videos of human–robot collaboration and evaluating the human and robot employees in the video. Results showed that, when the employee performed correctly, participants assigned more credit to the employee and showed stronger positive emotions when the employee was a robot than a human. When the employee made an error and caused failure, participants attributed more blame to the employee and showed stronger negative emotions when the employee was a human than a robot. Additionally, employee errors resulted in decreased trust, and the trust damage caused by human errors was higher than that caused by robot errors. Furthermore, the functional near-infrared spectroscopy technique showed that viewing robot errors caused decreased activation in the prefrontal cortex. These findings enrich our understanding of attribution, trust, and emotions in human–robot collaboration from the perspective of human managers, providing practical managerial implications.

Keywords: Robots · Human–robot Collaboration · Attribution · Trust · Emotion · fNIRS

1 Introduction

With the development of artificial intelligence and robotics technology, intelligent robots are playing an ever-growing role in human production and daily life. While work used to be done by humans, nowadays human–robot collaboration has become a novel mode of production. Robots are viewed as social actors [1] and are used in a variety of fields such as assembly manufacturing [2], waste sorting [3], and urban search and rescue missions [4]. In the context of human–robot collaboration, evaluation performance faces new challenges. Considering that managers are typically human, do they exhibit varying

© The Author(s), under exclusive license to Springer Nature Switzerland AG 2024
P.-L. P. Rau (Ed.): HCII 2024, LNCS 14702, pp. 273–286, 2024.
https://doi.org/10.1007/978-3-031-60913-8_19

reactions to human versus robot employees? Previous research has compared individuals' attitudes towards robots and humans from the perspective of users [5–7]. However, there is limited research from the viewpoint of human managers. This study examines whether people show different responses when evaluating the performance of human and robot employees in human–robot collaboration.

Responsibility attribution has garnered increasing attention in human–robot collaboration research [8–10]. Understanding responsibility attribution is crucial for managers to accurately assess the contributions and performance of each team member. However, biases in attribution may arise when individuals analyze their own or others' actions [11, 12]. Accordingly, this study explores whether people demonstrate biases when attributing work performance between human and robotic employees. Moreover, attribution may affect people's trust in the employee. For instance, attributing failures to the robot may lead to a decrease in trust in the robot. In human–robot interaction, trust plays a pivotal role in influencing human acceptance and usage [13]. This study examines whether there are differences in the trust damage between errors caused by human and robotic employees.

Understanding emotional responses towards human and robotic employees is important. Emotions have the potential to influence our cognition and decision-making process [14], implying that emotional responses of human managers may impact their performance assessment for human and robotic employees. Therefore, this study explores people's emotional responses when observing correct and wrong operations performed by humans and robots. Functional near-infrared spectroscopy (fNIRS) is an important tool to study and analyze brain activity, providing an effective tool to examine emotional responses. fNIRS can record cerebral blood flow and objectively reflect the physiological state of humans [15–17]. This study employs fNIRS to record activity in the prefrontal cortex (PFC), exploring distinctions in PFC activation among people in response to errors made by robots and humans.

The findings of this study have theoretical and practical implications. In the context of successful collaboration, participants trust humans more than robots. However, participants attribute more credit to robots and evoke a greater extent of positive emotions towards robots. In the context of collaboration failure, human errors cause more damage to participants' trust. At the same time, participants attribute more responsibility to humans and evoke a greater extent of negative emotions towards humans. These findings contribute to the literature on human–robot collaboration.

2 Related Work

2.1 Attribution

Attribution refers to the perception or inference of the reasons behind events [18]. In human–human and human–robot collaborative tasks, the outcomes often involve allocations of credit or blame, which may impact the subsequent reward or punishment distributions. In the research on human–robot interaction, responsibility attribution receives widespread attention. Belanche et al. [19] have compared robots and humans as service providers in hotel services. According to their results, consumers believe that humans should bear more responsibility than robots in the service context, and this perception becomes more pronounced when service failures occur. Likewise, Ryoo et al. [20] have demonstrated that human service providers receive more blame from consumers compared to service robots when errors occur. Henderson and Gillan [21] have described an accident scenario caused by either robots or humans and found that humans are blamed more than robots in accident situations. Pavone et al. [22] have analyzed the provision of online services by chatbots and humans and found that consumers attribute more responsibility to humans than chatbots for service failures. These studies indicate differences in how people perceive and treat robots compared to humans in terms of responsibility attribution.

Some studies have explored why people attribute responsibility differently to humans and robots based on their level of autonomy. The autonomy of robots is closely linked to the responsibilities they undertake. Kim and Hinds [23] conducted an experiment investigating the relationship between the autonomy of robots and the attribution of responsibility. In this study, robots were utilized as transport agents collaborating with humans to accomplish a toy assembly task. The results indicate that as the autonomy of the robot increases, participants tend to attribute more responsibility to the robot. Furlough et al. [24] similarly found in their research that as the autonomy of robots increases, they are required to take on more responsibility for task outcomes. While the autonomy of robots can be adjusted to meet task requirements, there is still room for further improvement in robotic technology. In the human perception, the autonomy of robots is constrained by the limitations of programmed algorithms [9, 19, 25]. Robots with constrained autonomy may lack the ability to make judgments and handle tasks. In contrast, humans exhibit a higher degree of autonomy in tasks, possessing the capacity for independent judgment and action execution [26]. Gailey [27] similarly argues that humans, possessing a higher capacity for autonomous action, should bear more responsibility for their behavior.

In summary, we infer that individuals may exhibit different reactions when faced with the success and failure of human and robotic employees. Specifically, human errors may receive more blame compared to errors made by robots. Conversely, human successes may receive less credit compared to successes achieved by robots. Based on these considerations, this study proposes the following hypotheses:

Hypothesis 1. Participants will attribute greater blame to the human employee for failures than to the robotic employee.

Hypothesis 2. Participants will attribute less credit to the human employee for success than to the robotic employee.

2.2 Trust

Trust is closely related to competence. Studies like [28] found that trust is higher when individuals perceive friendliness, positivity, and strong competence. Previous studies have shown that robot performance is a crucial determinant of trust [29, 30]. Additionally, robot errors may lead to human blame and ultimately reduce human trust [31]. Wright et al. [30] suggest that robot errors harm the perception of their reliability. As the reliability of robots decreases, human trust in them is likely to diminish accordingly [32]. On the contrary, if robots perform well in tasks, it may enhance their perceived competence and reliability and increase trust in robots. In a study comparing the impact of human and robotic performance on trust, Alarcon et al. [33] found that there was no significant difference in trust between humans and robots when both made mistakes. However, Wang and Quadflieg [34] suggest that humans appear to possess greater intelligence and are more trustworthy than robots. In contrast, Zonca et al. [35] found that robots are more trusted than humans. Considering the above discussion along with Hypotheses 1 and 2, we propose the following hypothesis:

Hypothesis 3. Trust will decrease when viewing employee failure than success (H3a), and the decrease will be greater when the employee is a human than a robot (H3b).

2.3 Emotion Responses

Emotion continues to be a central focus of research. Ekman [36] classified emotions into six categories, including surprise, happiness, fear, sadness, anger, and disgust. Plutchik [37] categorized emotions into eight types, including rage, loathing, grief, terror, adoration, amazement, ecstasy, and vigilance. In general, emotions can be categorized into positive and negative ones. Positive emotions are associated with psychological states such as happiness, relaxation, and satisfaction [38]. When both robots and humans successfully complete tasks, this aligns with human expectations and may evoke positive emotions. On the contrary, negative emotions are associated with psychological states such as sadness, frustration, and dissatisfaction. Research indicates that service failures can evoke negative emotions in consumers [22, 39, 40]. Therefore, when robots or humans make mistakes at work, it may trigger negative emotions in humans. Pavone et al. [22] further suggests that compared to robots, human errors may lead to a greater sense of frustration. Building upon the analysis and Hypotheses 1–3 presented earlier, the following hypothesis is proposed:

Hypothesis 4. Negative emotions for the employee's error will be stronger when the employee is a human than a robot.

Hypothesis 5. Positive emotions for the employee's success will be stronger when the employee is a robot than a human.

fNIRS proves to be a useful tool for capturing neural activity within the brain, providing objective data that contributes to the investigation of human–machine interaction. The PFC investigated in this study is a vital region for neural activity and associated with cognitive processes [41, 42] and emotional responses [43]. Kreplin and Fairclough [44] found increased activation in the PFC when people view positive images than negative ones, implying that the increased PFC activation may be related to pleasantness. Additionally, Zhou et al. [45] found that happy pictures evoke increased activation in the PFC than sad pictures. Considering the above findings and hypotheses, we propose a new hypothesis:

Hypothesis 6. Participants will exhibit increased PFC activation when viewing success than errors (H6a), and the difference will be greater when the employee is a robot than a human (H6b).

3 Method

3.1 Experimental Design and Participants

This study conducted a within-subjects experiment. Each participant watched three videos of human–robot collaboration and assessed the human and robotic employees in each video. We randomly recruited 26 participants from a university campus, and two were excluded due to incomplete data. Twenty-four participants (12 females) were included in this study, and informed consent was obtained from all participants.

3.2 Task and Procedure

During the experiment, participants were instructed to imagine themselves as managers and evaluate the human and robotic employees based on their performance in the video. The videos illustrated a two-stage collaborative task (see Fig. 1). First, the robot was required to select a component of a specific color and pass it to the human. Second, the human need to place the component into a box matching its color. Each participant watched three videos: one where both the robot and the human perform the task right (RR), another where the robot makes an error but the human performs right (WR), and a third where the robot performs right but the human makes an error (RW). The first video viewed by each participant was the RR scenario, and the order of the other two videos was balanced among participants.

The experimental procedure is as follows: (1) Participants were asked to fill out an informed consent form; (2) We introduced the experimental background, content, and procedure; (3) Participants completed a pre-experiment questionnaire, reporting demographic information; (4) Participants wore the fNIRS device; (5) Participants closed their eyes and relaxed for one minute; (6) Participants watched a video of human–robot collaboration; (7) Participants completed a post-experimental questionnaire, providing feedback on the video; (8) Repeated steps (5), (6), and (7) until participants finished watching three videos, and finally we removed the fNIRS device from participants. The entire experiment lasted approximately 15 min.

3.3 Apparatus

The left side of Fig. 1 shows a screenshot from the video. The robot in the video is Nao, developed by SoftBank Robotics Group, and widely used in human–robot interaction research. The robot exhibits functions of body movement, gaze and speech: (1) The robot moves its arms to pick up an object and then approaches the human; (2) The robot utilizes facial tracking to gaze at the human; (3) The robot communicates with the human using synthesized natural language. The right side of Fig. 1 illustrates the PFC region recorded by fNIRS and the positions of the probes. We utilized 7 light sources and 8 detectors, generating a total of 22 measurement channels. Each channel consists of one light source probe and one detector probe, with a fixed distance of 3.5 cm between them. We employed a continuous-wave near-infrared optical imaging system (NirSmart, Huichuang, China) with a sampling rate of 15Hz and wavelengths of 730 and 850 nm.

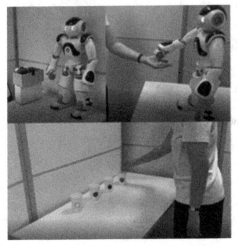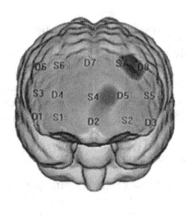

Fig. 1. Video screenshots: robot taking a component, passing it to the human, and the human placing it the location (left); fNIRS probe layout: S# - source, D# - detector (right)

3.4 Measures

In the pre-experiment questionnaire, participants reported their gender, age, and identity. The post-experiment questionnaire required participants to answer questions based on the video they watched. First, they need to tell the outcome of the human–robot collaboration task (Success/Failure) and the main reason for the outcome of this task (Nao robot/Human operator/Both). Second, they had to assess the responsibility attribution, trust, and emotional responses. All the items were answered on a seven-point Likert scale, where 1 indicated strongly disagree, and 7 indicated strongly agree. The scales were adapted from previous studies [23, 46] and listed in Table 1.

3.5 Data Analysis

Paired-t-tests and repeated-measures ANOVAs were used to analyze participants' responses in terms of responsibility attribution, trust, and positive/negative emotions. We conducted preprocessing on the fNIRS data for each participant using NirSpark (Huichuang, China). We initially excluded unrelated time intervals and set standard deviation of the threshold and amplitude of the threshold to 6 and 0.5, respectively, to remove the artefacts induced by motion and environment. Additionally, we applied a filter between 0.01 and 0.2 to reduce the impact of high-frequency and low-frequency noise. Furthermore, we used the modified Beer–Lambert law to convert the optical signals into the concentration of oxygenated hemoglobin (HbO). Moreover, we performed baseline corrections and obtained task-related activations (ΔHbO) with the resting state before each video as baselines. Finally, the average ΔHbO concentration during the stimulus periods was used for analysis. All analyses were conducted using R 4.3.1.

Table 1. Items used in experiment questionnaire

Scales and items	Cronbach'sα
Attribution	
The robot/human has certain responsibility (credit/fault) for the result The robot/human has the main responsibility (credit/fault) for the result The main reason for this result lies in the robot/human The robot/human should bear most of the rewards or penalties	Robot:0.95 Human:0.95
Trust	
Do you think the robot/human is competent? Do you think the robot/human works hard? Do you think the robot/human is reliable? Do you think the robot/human is capable of doing the job? Are you satisfied with the performance of the robot/human? Do you trust the robot/human? Are you willing to hire the robot/human if you have the opportunity?	Robot:0.96 Human:0.96
Positive Emotion	
When I saw the robot/human's action, I was interested When I saw the robot/human's action, I felt happy When I saw the robot/human's action, I felt proud When I saw the robot/human's action, I felt excited When I saw the robot/human's action, I felt encouraged When I saw the robot/human's action, I felt comfortable When I saw the robot/human's action, I was satisfied When I saw the robot/human's action, I was surprised	Robot:0.92 Human:0.88
Negative Emotion	
When I saw the robot/human's action, I was disappointed When I saw the robot/human's action, I felt frustrated When I saw the robot/human's action, I felt worried When I saw the robot/human's action, I felt ashamed When I saw the robot/human's action, I felt nervous When I saw the robot/human's action, I felt angry When I saw the robot/human's action, I felt embarrassed When I saw the robot/human's action, I felt expected	Robot:0.86 Human:0.85

4   Results

4.1   Manipulation Check

To examine whether participants' perceptions of video contents were consistent with our manipulation, we aggregated the judgments of all participants for the three video outcomes. In the RR condition, all participants perceived the outcome as successful, with 21 attributing it to the joint effort of the robot and the human, and only 3 attributing it to the robot alone. In the WR condition, all participants perceived the outcome as a failure, with 20 attributing it to the robot alone, and only 4 attributing it to the joint efforts of the robot and the human. In the RW condition, all participants perceived the outcome as a failure, with 24 attributing it to the human. These results were consistent with our manipulation, as shown in Table 2.

Table 2. Check of outcome manipulation and error party manipulation

Condition	Outcome check		Attribution check		
	Success	Failure	Both	Human	Robot
RR	24	0	21	0	3
WR	0	24	4	0	20
RW	0	24	0	24	0

4.2   Hypotheses 1–3

Hypothesis 1 predicts that participants will attribute greater blame to the human employee for failures than to the robotic employee. The results showed that participants attributed greater blame to the human for failures (RW condition; $M = 6.73$, $SE = 0.10$) than to the robot (WR condition; $M = 6.43$, $SE = 0.12$), $t_{23} = -2.53$, $p = .019$, $CohensD = -0.57$. Hypothesis 2 predict that participants will attribute less credit to the human employee for success than to the robotic employee. The results revealed a marginally significant difference in the attribution of credit between the human (RR condition; $M = 4.61$, $SE = 0.19$) and the robot (RR condition; $M = 5.25$, $SE = 0.23$), $t_{23} = 2.05$, $p = .052$, $CohensD = 0.62$. Thus, Hypotheses 1 and 2 were supported.

Hypothesis 3 predicts decreased trust after failure than success and that the trust damage will be greater for the human than robotic employee. The results showed that trust in the employee was higher after viewing success (RR condition; $M = 5.50$, $SE = 0.13$) than failures (RW and WR conditions; $M = 2.17$, $SE = 0.07$), $F(1, 23) = 308.5$, $p < .001$, $\eta^2 = .84$. Therefore, H3a was supported. Regarding the human employee, participants reported lower trust after failures (RW condition; $M = 2.03$, $SE = 0.10$) than success (RR condition; $M = 5.71$, $SE = 0.17$), $F(1, 23) = 154.7$, $p < .001$, $\eta^2 = .80$. Regarding the robotic employee, participants reported decreased trust after failures (WR condition; $M = 2.30$, $SE = 0.09$) than success (RR condition; $M = 5.29$, $SE = 0.20$), $F(1, 23) = 337.5$, $p < .001$, $\eta^2 = .89$. According to the effect sizes, participants exhibited greater trust damage towards the human than robotic employee. Therefore, H3b was supported.

4.3   Hypotheses 4 and 5

Hypothesis 4 predicts that negative emotions for the employee's error will be stronger when the employee is a human than a robot. In the context of failure caused by either the human or the robot, participants exhibited stronger negative emotions towards the human ($M = 4.48$, $SE = 0.25$) than the robot ($M = 4.01$, $SE = 0.27$), $t_{23} = -3.40$, $p =$

.002, *CohensD* = −0.37. Hypothesis 5 predicts that positive emotions for the employee's success will be stronger when the employee is a robot than a human. In the context of successful collaboration, participants showed higher positive emotions towards the robot (M = 4.94, SE = 0.20) than the human (M = 4.05, SE = 0.23) for their right actions, t_{23} = 5.02, p < .001, *CohensD* = 0.83. Therefore, Hypotheses 4 and 5 were supported. These results are presented in Fig. 2.

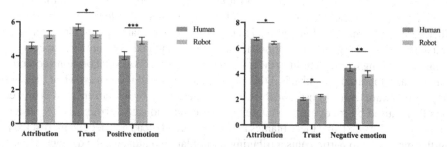

Fig. 2. Human responses to the success of the robot and the human: attribution of credit, trust, and positive emotion (left); human responses to the errors of the robot and the human: attribution of blame, trust, and negative emotion (right).

4.4 Hypothesis 6

Hypothesis 6 predicts that participants will exhibit increased PFC activation when viewing success than errors, and the difference will be greater when the employee is a robot than a human. However, our results showed no evidence for this hypothesis. Instead, we found decreased HbO concentrations in channels S1–D2 (M = −0.038, SE = 0.02; p = .037), S1–D4 (M = −0.030, SE = 0.01; p = .025), S2–D2 (M = −0.024, SE = 0.01; p = .020), and S4–D2 (M = −0.019, SE = 0.01; p = .016) when participants observed errors made by the robot compared to baselines. Additionally, there was a greater decrease in the S2–D2 channel when participants observed errors made by the robot (M = −0.024, SE = 0.01) compared to when they observed errors made by the human (M = −0.002, SE = 0.01), p = .044. Likewise, there was a greater decrease in the HbO concentration in the channel of S4–D2 when participants viewed errors from the robot (M = −0.019, SE = 0.01) than the human (M = −0.001, SE = 0.01), p = .049. Furthermore, there was a positive correlation between the ΔHbO concentration in the S3–D6 channel when participants observed the robot performing correctly and the participant's positive emotions towards the robot (r = 0.43, p = .036). Likewise, there was a positive correlation between the ΔHbO concentration in the S1–D1 channel when participants observed the human performing correctly and the participant's positive emotions towards the human (r = 0.41, p = .046).

5 Discussion

5.1 Summary and Interpretation of Main Results

Hypotheses 1 and 2 were supported by our results. Specifically, participants attributed more blame but less credit to the human than robotic employee. A possible explanation is from the perspective of limited autonomy of robots [9, 19, 25], indicating that participants were psychologically prepared for errors from the robot. Human autonomy is relatively high [26], and participants may believe that humans should not make mistakes. Therefore, errors made by humans lead to more blame from participants. However, participants may hold higher expectations for the human and take the human's success for granted, resulting in more credit to the robot when human–robot collaboration succeeds. Our results supported Hypothesis 3 that participants reported lower trust when viewing employee failure than success, and the trust damage caused by human errors was higher than that caused by robot errors. As previous research indicates, errors lead to participants' blame [20–22], and these blames may subsequently lead to a decline in trust [31]. Furthermore, due to participants attributing more blame to humans, the damage to trust caused by human errors was more substantial.

Hypotheses 4 and 5 were supported by our results that participants showed stronger negative emotions for the human errors but more positive emotions for the robot success. A possible explanation is that people have higher expectations for humans, taking the human's correct operations for granted. Additionally, combining the attribution and trust differences between humans and robots, it can be observed that people showed lower tolerance for human errors than robot errors. Hypothesis 6 predicts neural responses towards human and robotic employees, but our results provided no evidence. Instead, the results revealed decreased activation in several channels in the PFC when participants viewed robot errors. This may associate with negative emotions or cognitive judgements about the robot [44, 45]. Similarly, prior research has observed decreased activation when people made errors and increased activation when they made correct decisions [16].

5.2 Theoretical and Practical Implications

This study builds upon previous research that focused on human–robot interaction failures, providing further theoretical confirmation. Our study reveals that failure triggers blame, distrust, and negative emotions among participants. Additionally, we consider successful scenarios, thereby enriching theoretical research in different situations. Success can induce recognition, trust, and positive emotions among participants. Furthermore, by comparing the performance of robots and humans in the same task, our study not only deepens the understanding of participants' distinct perceptions of robots and humans but also contributes to the research on managing human–robot collaboration in various contexts. Moreover, by incorporating objective fNIRS data, our study enriches the research on the relationship between subjective measures and neural correlates.

The increasing prevalence of human–robot collaboration in the workplace is noteworthy. Our study reveals distinctions in participants' perceptions between humans and robots. These findings help us understand the attitudes of managers towards robot employees and human employees in managerial work. In managerial training, it would be beneficial to enhance managers' understanding of robot capabilities, ensuring that managers have an accurate assessment of robots. This can prevent significant changes in responsibility attribution, trust, and emotional fluctuations resulting from disparities between expectations and the actual performance of robots. Furthermore, the research results inspire the need for a criterion to evaluate work outcomes. This is beneficial for analyzing the state of managers through the outcomes and providing appropriate managerial recommendations based on their state.

5.3 Limitations and Future Research

This study has several limitations. First, the sample was mainly students, and the human–robot collaborative tasks were relatively simple. This might limit the generalizability of the results to more diverse work environments and backgrounds. Future research could broaden the sample range and conduct experiments in more realistic work settings. Second, the experimental design of this study involved participants watching videos as managers, potentially leading to a lack of sense of presence. Future experimental designs could involve participants immersing themselves in work scenarios to enhance the sense of presence. Third, we only considered the individual reasons for either the robot or the human, but in certain tasks, the reasons for success or failure might be a combination of both. Future research should delve deeper into understanding the specific reasons for the differences in attitudes towards humans and robots among managers. This could involve exploring the influence of psychological and cultural factors on these attitudes. Gaining a deeper understanding of the fundamental reasons behind these differences will contribute to the effective implementation of human–robot collaboration.

6   Conclusion

This study analyzed participants' attributions of responsibility, trust, and emotions towards humans and robots in both successful and failed human–robot collaboration scenarios. Additionally, we investigated participants' PFC neural activity differences between humans and robots using fNIRS. The results indicated that in successful human–robot collaboration, the robot received more credit and triggered more positive emotions in participants. However, participants exhibited higher levels of trust in humans. Conversely, in context of human–robot collaboration failure, humans received more blame and triggered more distrust and negative emotions in participants. Moreover, failure led to a decrease in activation in certain regions of the PFC. These results contribute theoretically to understanding the distinctions in managers' perceptions of robots and humans. Furthermore, they provide insights for managerial practices in human–robot collaboration.

Acknowledgements. This work was supported by National Natural Science Foundation of China 71942005.

Disclosure of Interests. The authors have no competing interests to declare that are relevant to the content of this article.

References

1. Nass, C., Steuer, J., Tauber, E.R.: Computers are social actors, pp. 72–78 (1994). https://doi.org/10.1145/259963.260288
2. Mao, Z., Zhang, J., Fang, K., Huang, D., Sun, Y.: Balancing U-type assembly lines with human–robot collaboration. Comput. Oper. Res. **159**, 106359 (2023). https://doi.org/10.1016/j.cor.2023.106359
3. Chen, J., Fu, Y., Lu, W., Pan, Y.: Augmented reality-enabled human-robot collaboration to balance construction waste sorting efficiency and occupational safety and health. J. Environ. Manage. **348**, 119341 (2023). https://doi.org/10.1016/j.jenvman.2023.119341
4. Casper, J., Murphy, R.R.: Human-robot interactions during the robot-assisted urban search and rescue response at the World Trade Center. IEEE Trans. Syst. Man Cybern. Part B Cybern. **33**, 367–385 (2003). https://doi.org/10.1109/TSMCB.2003.811794
5. Arikan, E., Altinigne, N., Kuzgun, E., Okan, M.: May robots be held responsible for service failure and recovery? The role of robot service provider agents' human-likeness. J. Retail. Consum. Serv. **70**, 103175 (2023). https://doi.org/10.1016/j.jretconser.2022.103175
6. Harrison-Walker, L.J.: The effect of consumer emotions on outcome behaviors following service failure. J. Serv. Mark. **33**, 285–302 (2019). https://doi.org/10.1108/JSM-04-2018-0124
7. Baker, M.A., Kim, K.: Other customer service failures: emotions, impacts, and attributions. J. Hosp. Tour. Res. **42**, 1067–1085 (2018). https://doi.org/10.1177/1096348016671394
8. Lei, X., Rau, P.-L.P.: Effect of relative status on responsibility attributions in human–robot collaboration: mediating role of sense of responsibility and moderating role of power distance orientation. Comput. Hum. Behav. **122**, 106820 (2021). https://doi.org/10.1016/j.chb.2021.106820
9. Leo, X., Huh, Y.E.: Who gets the blame for service failures? Attribution of responsibility toward robot versus human service providers and service firms. Comput. Hum. Behav. **113**, 106520 (2020). https://doi.org/10.1016/j.chb.2020.106520
10. Lei, X., Rau, P.-L.P.: Should I blame the human or the robot? Attribution within a human–robot group. Int. J. Soc. Robot. **13**, 363–377 (2021). https://doi.org/10.1007/s12369-020-00645-w
11. Mezulis, A.H., Abramson, L.Y., Hyde, J.S., Hankin, B.L.: Is there a universal positivity bias in attributions? A meta-analytic review of individual, developmental, and cultural differences in the self-serving attributional bias. Psychol. Bull. **130**, 711–747 (2004). https://doi.org/10.1037/0033-2909.130.5.711
12. Malle, B.F.: The actor-observer asymmetry in attribution: a (surprising) meta-analysis. Psychol. Bull. **132**, 895–919 (2006). https://doi.org/10.1037/0033-2909.132.6.895
13. Sanders, T., Kaplan, A., Koch, R., Schwartz, M., Hancock, P.A.: The relationship between trust and use choice in human-robot interaction. Hum. Factors **61**, 614–626 (2019). https://doi.org/10.1177/0018720818816838
14. Schwarz, N.: Emotion, cognition, and decision making. Cogn. Emot. **14**, 433–440 (2000). https://doi.org/10.1080/026999300402745
15. Balconi, M., Fronda, G., Bartolo, A.: Affective, social, and informative gestures reproduction in human interaction: hyperscanning and brain connectivity. J. Mot. Behav. **53**, 296–315 (2021). https://doi.org/10.1080/00222895.2020.1774490

16. Lei, X., Rau, P.-L.P.: Emotional responses to performance feedback in an educational game during cooperation and competition with a robot: evidence from fNIRS. Comput. Hum. Behav. **138**, 107496 (2023). https://doi.org/10.1016/j.chb.2022.107496

17. Yorgancigil, E., Yildirim, F., Urgen, B.A., Erdogan, S.B.: An exploratory analysis of the neural correlates of human-robot interactions with functional near infrared spectroscopy. Front. Hum. Neurosci. **16**, 883905 (2022). https://doi.org/10.3389/fnhum.2022.883905

18. Kelley, H.H., Michela, J.L.: Attribution theory and research. Annu. Rev. Psychol. **31**, 457–501 (1980). https://doi.org/10.1146/annurev.ps.31.020180.002325

19. Belanche, D., Casaló, L.V., Flavián, C., Schepers, J.: Robots or frontline employees? Exploring customers' attributions of responsibility and stability after service failure or success. J. Serv. Manag. **31**, 267–289 (2020). https://doi.org/10.1108/JOSM-05-2019-0156

20. Ryoo, Y., Jeon, Y.A., Kim, W.: The blame shift: robot service failures hold service firms more accountable. J. Bus. Res. **171**, 114360 (2024). https://doi.org/10.1016/j.jbusres.2023.114360

21. Henderson, C., Gillan, D.J.: Attributing blame in human-robot teams with robots of differing appearance. Proc. Hum. Factors Ergon. Soc. Annu. Meet. **65**, 139–142 (2021). https://doi.org/10.1177/1071181321651020

22. Pavone, G., Meyer-Waarden, L., Munzel, A.: Rage against the machine: experimental insights into customers' negative emotional responses, attributions of responsibility, and coping strategies in artificial intelligence-based service failures. J. Interact. Mark. **58**, 52–71 (2023). https://doi.org/10.1177/10949968221134492

23. Kim, T., Hinds, P.: Who should I blame? Effects of autonomy and transparency on attributions in human-robot interaction. In: IEEE International Symposium on Robot and Human Interactive Communication, ROMAN 2006, pp. 80–85 (2006). https://doi.org/10.1109/ROMAN.2006.314398

24. Furlough, C., Stokes, T., Gillan, D.J.: Attributing blame to robots: I. The influence of robot autonomy. Hum. Factors J. Hum. Factors Ergon. Soc. **63**, 592–602 (2021). https://doi.org/10.1177/0018720819880641

25. Hong, J.-W., Williams, D.: Racism, responsibility and autonomy in HCI: testing perceptions of an AI agent. Comput. Hum. Behav. **100**, 79–84 (2019). https://doi.org/10.1016/j.chb.2019.06.012

26. Swanson, S.R., Davis, J.C.: The relationship of differential loci with perceived quality and behavioral intentions. J. Serv. Mark. **17**, 202–219 (2003). https://doi.org/10.1108/08876040310467943

27. Gailey, J.A.: Attribution of responsibility for organizational wrongdoing: a partial test of an integrated model. J. Criminol. **2013**, e920484 (2013). https://doi.org/10.1155/2013/920484

28. Coulter, K.S., Coulter, R.A.: Determinants of trust in a service provider: the moderating role of length of relationship. J. Serv. Mark. **16**, 35–50 (2002). https://doi.org/10.1108/08876040210419406

29. Hancock, P.A., Kessler, T.T., Kaplan, A.D., Brill, J.C., Szalma, J.L.: Evolving trust in robots: Specification through sequential and comparative meta-analyses. Hum. Factors J. Hum. Factors Ergon. Soc. **63**, 1196–1229 (2021). https://doi.org/10.1177/0018720820922080

30. Wright, J.L., Chen, J.Y.C., Lakhmani, S.G.: Agent transparency and reliability in human-robot interaction: the influence on user confidence and perceived reliability. IEEE Trans. Hum. Mach. Syst. **50**, 254–263 (2020). https://doi.org/10.1109/THMS.2019.2925717

31. Kaniarasu, P., Steinfeld, A.M.: Effects of blame on trust in human robot interaction. In: 23rd IEEE International Symposium on Robot and Human Interactive Communication, pp. 850–855 (2014). https://doi.org/10.1109/ROMAN.2014.6926359

32. Paetzel, M., Perugia, G., Castellano, G.: The persistence of first impressions: the effect of repeated interactions on the perception of a social robot. In: Proceedings of the 2020 ACM/IEEE International Conference on Human-Robot Interaction, pp. 73–82. Association for Computing Machinery, New York (2020). https://doi.org/10.1145/3319502.3374786

33. Alarcon, G.M., Gibson, A.M., Jessup, S.A., Capiola, A.: Exploring the differential effects of trust violations in human-human and human-robot interactions. Appl. Ergon. **93**, 103350 (2021). https://doi.org/10.1016/j.apergo.2020.103350

34. Wang, Y., Quadflieg, S.: In our own image? Emotional and neural processing differences when observing human–human vs human–robot interactions. Soc. Cogn. Affect. Neurosci. **10**, 1515–1524 (2015). https://doi.org/10.1093/scan/nsv043

35. Zonca, J., Folsø, A., Sciutti, A.: Trust is not all about performance: trust biases in interaction with humans, robots and computers. arXiv (2021)

36. Ekman, P.: An argument for basic emotions. Cogn. Emot. **6**, 169–200 (1992). https://doi.org/10.1080/02699939208411068

37. Plutchik, R.: A psychoevolutionary theory of emotions. Soc. Sci. Inf. **21**, 529–553 (1982). https://doi.org/10.1177/053901882021004003

38. Lin, H., Chi, O.H., Gursoy, D.: Antecedents of customers' acceptance of artificially intelligent robotic device use in hospitality services. J. Hosp. Mark. Manag. **29**, 530–549 (2020). https://doi.org/10.1080/19368623.2020.1685053

39. Gelbrich, K.: Anger, frustration, and helplessness after service failure: coping strategies and effective informational support. J. Acad. Mark. Sci. **38**, 567–585 (2010). https://doi.org/10.1007/s11747-009-0169-6

40. Roseman, I.J.: Appraisal determinants of discrete emotions. Cogn. Emot. **5**, 161–200 (1991). https://doi.org/10.1080/02699939108411034

41. Boere, K., Hecker, K., Krigolson, O.E.: Validation of a mobile fNIRS device for measuring working memory load in the prefrontal cortex. Int. J. Psychophysiol. **195**, 112275 (2024). https://doi.org/10.1016/j.ijpsycho.2023.112275

42. Wiese, E., Abubshait, A., Azarian, B., Blumberg, E.J.: Brain stimulation to left prefrontal cortex modulates attentional orienting to gaze cues. Philos. Trans. R. Soc. B Biol. Sci. **374**, 20180430 (2019). https://doi.org/10.1098/rstb.2018.0430

43. Harmon-Jones, E., Gable, P.A., Peterson, C.K.: The role of asymmetric frontal cortical activity in emotion-related phenomena: a review and update. Biol. Psychol. **84**, 451–462 (2010). https://doi.org/10.1016/j.biopsycho.2009.08.010

44. Kreplin, U., Fairclough, S.: Activation of the rostromedial prefrontal cortex during the experience of positive emotion in the context of esthetic experience. An fNIRS study. Front. Hum. Neurosci. **7**, 879 (2013). https://doi.org/10.3389/fnhum.2013.00879

45. Zhou, L., Wu, B., Deng, Y., Liu, M.: Brain activation and individual differences of emotional perception and imagery in healthy adults: a functional near-infrared spectroscopy (fNIRS) study. Neurosci. Lett. **797**, 137072 (2023). https://doi.org/10.1016/j.neulet.2023.137072

46. Bradley, M.M., Lang, P.J.: Measuring emotion: the self-assessment manikin and the semantic differential. J. Behav. Ther. Exp. Psychiatry **25**, 49–59 (1994). https://doi.org/10.1016/0005-7916(94)90063-9

Cross-Cultural Perspectives on Artificial Intelligence Generated Content (AIGC): A Comparative Study of Attitudes and Acceptance Among Global Products

Zequn Liu[✉] and Zhe Chen

Beijing University of Aeronautics and Astronautics, 37 Xueyuan Road, Haidian District, Beijing100191, People's Republic of China
Zequn.liu@88.com, zhechen@buaa.edu.cn

Abstract. Given the popularity of interactive artificial intelligence models like ChatGPT, public perceptions of emerging Artificial Intelligence Generated Content (AIGC) have sparked widespread discussion. Companies and research institutions worldwide have been studying and releasing AIGC products, where the data used for training models in different regions is influenced by local cultures, inevitably leading to variations in the products. Public sentiment plays a crucial role on social media platforms, offering valuable insights that reflect the public's opinions and attitudes. Currently, there is a lack of analysis on the social emotions evoked by AIGC content, not to mention studies on the emotional response to products across different cultural backgrounds. This research aims to fill this gap by collecting relevant data and establishing an analytical model. Specifically, we selected six AIGC products from different regions, collected posts and related interactive data from users on Chinese social media platforms, and developed a user attitude and acceptance calculation model to analyze attitudes and acceptance towards products from different cultural backgrounds. The study concludes with two main findings: users currently hold positive attitudes towards all AIGC products, with a slightly higher inclination towards local products compared to non-native ones; when confronted with AIGC products that exhibit cultural differences, users show a preference for products trained with local data. These conclusions not only demonstrate the differences in user acceptance of AIGC products across various cultural backgrounds but also underscore the importance of localization in the development and promotion of AIGC products. To enhance the user acceptance of non-native AIGC products, developers need to consider adopting more localization strategies to better meet users' cultural needs and expectations.

Keywords: AIGC · Attitudes · Acceptance · Cross-Cultural · ChatGPT

P.-L. P. Rau (Ed.): HCII 2024, LNCS 14702, pp. 287–298, 2024.
https://doi.org/10.1007/978-3-031-60913-8_20

1   Introduction

In recent years, with the development of deep learning technologies, artificial intelligence has increasingly penetrated various aspects of life. AIGC (Artificial Intelligence Generated Content) products have gradually become known to people outside the field of computer science [1, 2]. Since the early part of 2023, the launch of the large language model ChatGPT(http://chat.openai.com) by OpenAI has significantly enhanced the capabilities of the model and lowered the barriers to its use. ChatGPT, a quintessential AIGC product, communicates with users by processing and reasoning through natural language inputs and efficiently generating responses, thereby facilitating conversational interactions. Other similar AIGC products include Bard from Google and Claude+ from Anthropic. As AIGC products become more prevalent, people have started using them as tools for production and daily life, significantly enhancing work efficiency.

Although AIGC products like ChatGPT support a multitude of global languages, the majority of the corpus used in the training process of the ChatGPT model is in English. Consequently, the model is more accustomed to English words, sentence structures, and grammar, and it excels in communicating in English. Therefore, it generally has a better understanding of and response to conversations conducted in English, which may result in a less optimal user experience for native Chinese speakers. In response to this phenomenon, several Chinese companies launched their own AIGC products shortly after the debut of ChatGPT, such as Baidu's 'Wenxin Yiyan', Alibaba's 'Tongyi Qianwen', and iFlytek's 'Spark', among others. These products are characterized by their extensive use of Chinese in model training and specific optimizations for the Chinese linguistic context, making them more adept at conversing with native Chinese speakers.

The popularity of AIGC products has sparked a productivity revolution and simultaneously ignited public discourse. Users share their opinions and attitudes towards AIGC products on social media platforms, reflecting their acceptance and perspectives. Some users praise AIGC products for enhancing their work efficiency, while others express concerns about the potential for generating false information or AI replacing human jobs in the future [3,4]. The sentiment expressed on social media is crucial for the impact of emerging AIGC products, as public feedback is invaluable for guiding the future development of these products, including making localized adjustments for international products [5]. As AIGC products continue to evolve, exploring how people's attitudes and acceptance change over time, and whether individuals perceive AI differently with different cultural backgrounds, are pertinent research questions worth investigating.

The formidable inferencing capabilities of AIGC products are inseparable from their memory of training data, with the content of such data significantly impacting the results of inferences. The inclusivity and diversity of training data are crucial for generating high-quality content. However, the unequal distribution of corpora can lead to content predominantly reflecting viewpoints and values centered around a single language, while severely limiting the expression of other languages and cultures [6]. People living in different cultural contexts often have distinct behavioral norms and communication styles. When models lack sufficient data on languages and cultures, they may fail to accurately capture the linguistic conventions, history, and values of specific cultures. Consequently, the generated content might lack cultural accuracy and sensitivity, potentially leading to inaccurate or offensive expressions, ultimately hindering cross-cultural understanding [6]. Previous research on AIGC and public sentiment rarely addressed the cultural differences in training data. This study aims to fill this gap by exploring users' attitudes and acceptance towards AIGC products trained with data from diverse cultures.

2   Methodology

In this section, we describe our proposed method. First, a dataset is built by crawling data from weibo.com that discusses various technical tools related to AIGC. Then an attitudes and acceptance computing system is established based on secondary communication. Finally, dynamic indicators of different period attitudes and acceptance are selected.

2.1   Data Collection

Based on the social media product type and user scale, this study selects Weibo (https://weibo.com) as the data source platform for exploring user attitudes and acceptance. Weibo is one of China's largest social media platforms. It serves as a platform for sharing, disseminating, and receiving information based on user relationships. Through its website or mobile application, users can publicly upload pictures and videos for instant sharing, while others may engage by commenting through text, images, and videos, or using multimedia instant messaging services. A characteristic of social media platforms like Weibo is the expression of user-generated media, where users create and share their content for others to consume by browsing, liking, commenting, etc. [7] The content written and published by users on the platform reflects their attitudes toward the topics discussed, and the interactions with other users (such as likes, comments, and shares) indicate their acceptance and recognition of others' content.

To investigate user acceptance of AIGC products from different cultural backgrounds, we categorize products utilizing AIGC technology into two groups: those trained on English data and those trained on Chinese data. Based on ratings from OpenCompass (https://opencompass.org.cn/), a globally recognized model evaluation platform, we selected the names of highly rated AIGC products as search keywords. Although 2023 saw many companies, such as Meta, open-sourcing their large language models like LLaMA, which accelerated the activity within the AIGC community and promoted the rapid development of AIGC models, open-source large models generally require demanding operational conditions, and users may not achieve a satisfactory experience on a single consumer-grade GPU; they also have a higher barrier to entry, with most users being students and professionals in computer-related fields. For these reasons, the user base of open-source AIGC models is significantly smaller than that of commercially released AIGC products, and thus, open-source models are not within the scope of this research.

In this experiment, the English AIGC products selected include ChatGPT, Claude+, and Bard, while the Chinese AIGC products comprise Wenxin Yiyan, iFlytek Spark, and Tongyi Qianwen. We have carefully considered user habits in our choice of search keywords. For instance, we use Chinese characters as search keywords when querying Chinese products and English words for English products, conducting fuzzy searches on case variations (e.g., searching for ChatGPT, chatgpt, chatGPT, etc., simultaneously). Additionally, we observed that when users discuss Claude+ on social media, they commonly refer to it as "Claude," thus, we also used "Claude" in place of "Claude+" as a search keyword.

In this study, we collected social media data through a program developed in-house, utilizing the Selenium library in Python to automate the retrieval of search results containing specific keywords on designated dates. After obtaining the search results, we gathered the necessary data for our research by iterating through each result. This included collecting the main text for analyzing users' sentiment and obtaining likes, shares, and comments data to assess user acceptance. The program enabled us to compile a dataset consisting of all relevant data from July 1, 2023, to December 31, 2023, required for this study.

2.2   Data Process

This experimental study aims to construct a comprehensive evaluation system to measure user attitudes and acceptance.

First, we preprocess the data in our dataset, aiming to filter out and clean some garbled characters and irrelevant data contents from the original dataset. Simultaneously, we employ the Python natural language processing library SnowNLP to segment the text of blog posts, remove punctuation, and process stop words. This step not only improves the quality and relevance of the data but also lays a solid foundation for subsequent sentiment analysis. When calculating sentiment attitude indices, we use SnowNLP's built-in Bayesian model to individually calculate the sentiment tendency value of all blog posts, with a value range of $[0, 1]$, where values closer to 1 indicate a higher likelihood of positive emotional polarity. We consider the emotional polarity of the blog posts as the sentiment attitude of the users in this data.

Once users post content on social media platforms, other users can interact with that content, including liking, commenting, and sharing. Different user interaction behaviors display varying levels of user acceptance, where likes and shares directly indicate approval of the content posted by a user. Compared to sharing, liking is a more concise and direct expression of a user's stance, while sharing suggests that the user engaging in the share wants to distribute the content they see to their friends or indicates that the original author has voiced their thoughts. For these reasons, we consider a user's likes and shares as first-tier levels of acceptance. Since user comments require a detailed analysis of the comment content and do not express as direct a stance as likes, we define user commenting behavior as a second-tier level of acceptance.

To address the challenge of assessing the importance of different levels of acceptance indicators and the issue of direct addition or subtraction not being feasible due to varying scales of acceptance indicators, this experiment proposes a user acceptance calculation model. We define the number of likes, shares, and comments for the ith data point as L_i, F_i, and C_i, respectively. For each time window, we normalize the original calculation results as follows:

$$L'_i = \frac{L_i - \min(L_j)}{\max(L_j) - \min(L_j)} \quad \text{for any } j \in [0, \text{length(dataset)}]$$

$$F'_i = \frac{F_i - \min(F_j)}{\max(F_j) - \min(F_j)} \quad \text{for any } j \in [0, \text{length(dataset)}]$$

$$C'_i = \frac{C_i - \min(C_j)}{\max(C_j) - \min(C_j)} \quad \text{for any } j \in [0, \text{length(dataset)}]$$

Then, we calculate the acceptance indicator A_i for the data point using the adjusted indicators according to the following formula:

$$A_i = 2L'_i + 2F'_i + C'_i$$

Due to the rapid development of artificial intelligence technology, extensive research on the model structures and training techniques behind AIGC products has yielded significant results. Many companies apply the latest research findings to their AIGC products, including Mixture of Experts (MoE) model architectures, [8] Mamba, [9] and training methods such as Supervised Fine-Tuning (SFT) and Reinforcement Learning from Human Feedback (RLHF), [10] along with training frameworks like DeepSpeed, [11] Ray, and Megatron-LM. [12] On the other hand, given the unique nature of AIGC products, there is a continuous need to update them with new knowledge and perspectives on recent news events, allowing AI-generated content to more closely align with user lives and provide a superior user experience. For these reasons, AIGC products often have short update cycles and rapid iteration speeds, and users' experiences evolve with the updates of new products.

To capture the trends in users' attitudes and emotional tendencies towards AIGC products over time, this study organizes the calculated attitude and acceptance indicators chronologically. Every 15 d constitutes a time window, within which indicators are aggregated by their mean value to obtain the corresponding indicators for that time window. The data from July 1, 2023, to December 31, 2023, is divided into 12 windows in this study.

Finally, the obtained indicators are visualized, and conclusions are drawn based on the analysis.

3 Findings

This section primarily presents the achievements of our work in two aspects: computation results on the dataset, investigations, and statistical outcomes of various dynamic indicators. We will visualize the processed indicators as described above. The changes in user acceptance and attitudes over time are displayed in the form of line graphs, as shown in Fig. 1 and Fig. 2, respectively; the monthly distribution of user acceptance and attitudes is presented in pie charts, as depicted in Fig. 3 and Fig. 4, respectively.

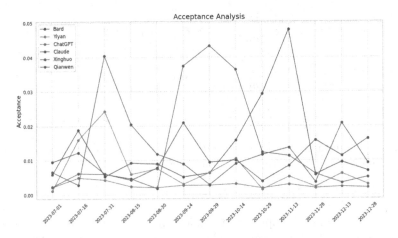

Fig. 1. User acceptance on six AIGC products in two cultural backgrounds.

Figure 1 shows the trend over time in user acceptance of six AIGC products trained with corpora from different cultural backgrounds. It is evident that users exhibit higher acceptance for iFlytek Spark and Tongyi Qianwen, while Chat-GPT receives comparatively lower acceptance. This can be attributed to the higher usage barriers and non-localized response styles of non-native products like ChatGPT.

Figure 2 illustrates the trend in users' emotional attitudes towards the six AIGC products over time. Overall, users maintain a positive attitude towards all six AIGC products, closely associated with the rapid development of AIGC in 2023. It is also noticeable that the ranking of users' attitudes towards AIGC products from different cultural backgrounds remains relatively stable, with the local AIGC products, Xunfei Spark and Tongyi Qianwen, enjoying favorable attitudes among users, while Claude+ and ChatGPT are perceived less favorably. Bard shows more significant fluctuations in attitude across different time windows.

Figure 3 presents the proportion of user acceptance for the six AIGC products across different time windows. It is not difficult to find that in more than half of the time windows, the combined acceptance of AIGC products trained with

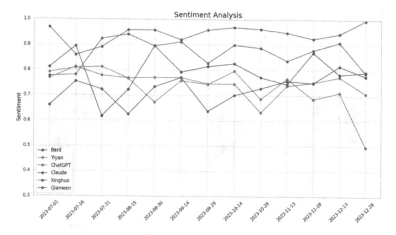

Fig. 2. User attitudes on six AIGC products in two cultural backgrounds.

Chinese corpora (Tongyi Qianwen, iFlytek Spark, Wenxin Yiyan) accounts for over 50% of the total, indicating a higher acceptance for local AIGC products.

Figure 4 displays the proportion of users' attitudes towards the six AIGC products across different time windows. The emotional attitude percentages towards different products are nearly consistent in every time window, suggesting that users hold similar attitudes towards all AIGC products.

4   Discussion

4.1   Summary of Findings

Through dynamic analysis of changes in user attitudes and acceptance over time, this study have found that users generally hold positive attitudes towards all AIGC products. Notably, local AIGC products, such as iFlytek Spark and Tongyi Qianwen, received higher acceptance and more positive emotional attitudes compared to non-native products, like ChatGPT and Claude+. These results highlight the importance of localization strategies in enhancing the user experience of AIGC products.

Analyzing the temporal changes in user acceptance and emotional attitudes towards six AIGC products across two different cultural backgrounds, it was observed that despite a universally positive attitude towards all AIGC products, local products (especially iFlytek Spark and Tongyi Qianwen) are significantly more favored by users than non-native products, such as ChatGPT. This difference in preference is attributed to the ability of local products to better understand and reflect the cultural background and language habits of users.

Further analysis showed that in different time windows, the combined acceptance of AIGC products trained with Chinese corpora exceeded 50%, emphasizing the users' preference for cultural relevance and localized content. Moreover,

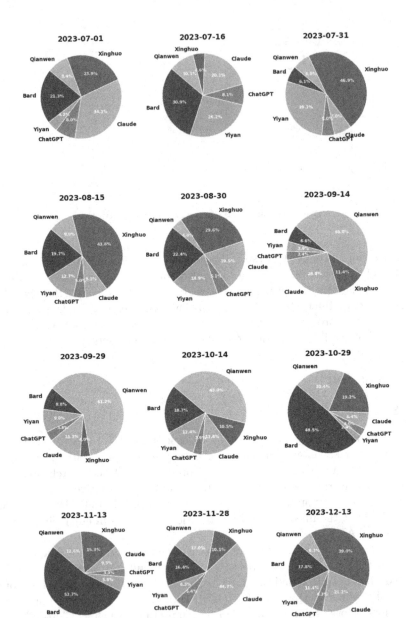

Fig. 3. Monthly percentage of user acceptance.

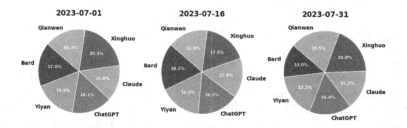

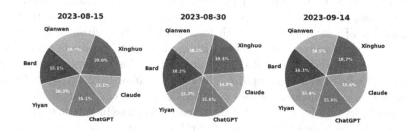

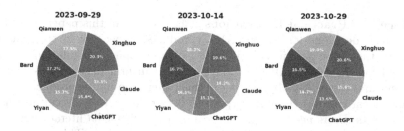

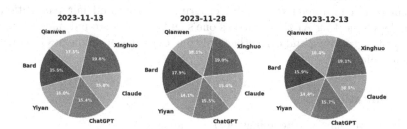

Fig. 4. Monthly percentage of user attitudes.

even though users' emotional attitudes towards all AIGC products were nearly uniform, the consistently high ranking of local products reflects a deeper level of identification and acceptance by users.

4.2 Implications

In Terms of Academic Research , current research on AIGC (Artificial Intelligence Generated Content) products primarily focuses on model architecture and training-inference frameworks, with few studies investigating the public's most genuine and direct opinions. By analyzing blog posts about six different products, this study comprehensively presents netizens' attitudes and acceptance towards AIGC products, timely addressing research gaps in both functional and product dimensions. Research on cultural differences has mainly concentrated on the design of functions in traditional human-computer interaction and the optimization of user experience, with little consideration given to the cultural materials used in system construction. By linking AIGC products trained with corpora from different linguistic contexts to cultural backgrounds, this research enriches the field of human-computer interaction. Primarily based on the Chinese linguistic context and the online environment in China, this study demonstrates good scalability. We plan to extend the research to more linguistic contexts and online platforms, providing a cross-cultural perspective on the study of user sentiments towards emerging technologies and products on the global internet.

In Terms of Practical Implications , the findings of this paper can inform commercial decisions for various AIGC products. Especially in cross-cultural contexts, they have practical significance for public opinion regulation and control and for the use of AIGC products across cultural backgrounds. For the cross-cultural use of AIGC presented in this paper, non-native products need to enhance local cultural training corpora to better adapt to local cultural usage requirements. Users need to continually improve their media literacy, analyzing and judging information rationally to minimize reception bias. This research aims to promote a comprehensive understanding of artificial intelligence-generated content products among the public, ensuring accurate and fair recognition of technology, selecting AI that matches one's cultural background, improving the quality of AI services, and correctly employing emerging technologies to enhance human welfare.

4.3 Limitations

There are two main shortcomings of this study:

In this study, while exploring user sentiment towards AIGC tools based on Weibo content, we employed the Bayesian segmentation model built into SnowNLP. However, a significant limitation to note is that the SnowNLP model was trained with a substantial amount of e-commerce text, primarily designed for text analysis in e-commerce scenarios. This specialization might limit its capability in analyzing AIGC-related content. Although the model performs admirably with e-commerce review data, its sensitivity to the complexity and diversity of AIGC content may not be sufficient, potentially impacting the accuracy of sentiment analysis results. Future research could consider enhancing the accuracy and applicability of sentiment analysis by introducing models more suited for AIGC content analysis or by developing a sentiment analysis model specifically trained for the AIGC domain.

Furthermore, in constructing the model to calculate user acceptance, this study did not fully consider the specific content of comments and the personal characteristics of users. This approach overlooks the influence of individual user differences and the content of comment texts on emotional expression, which may lead to the model's inability to accurately reflect the true feelings of different users towards the same product or service. For instance, the same AIGC product or content related to that product may hold different emotional values for users from diverse backgrounds. Therefore, future research should focus on integrating the specific content of blog comments and the personal characteristics of users who interact with these posts, to develop a more refined and personalized model for analyzing user attitudes and acceptance.

Through the analysis presented above, we recognize that the choice of methodology and the details of model construction have a significant impact on the accuracy and reliability of research findings in sentiment analysis and user attitude assessment. Future work can delve deeper into these areas for exploration and improvement, to overcome the limitations of the current study and bring more precise and comprehensive insights to the field of sentiment analysis.

5 Conclusion

In this study, we established a user attitude and acceptance calculation model based on the content posted by users on social media and their interactive behaviors. This model was used to explore users' acceptance and attitudes towards AIGC products trained with corpora from different cultural backgrounds, examining the impact of cultural differences on user experience. By collecting data and comparing the trend of indicators calculated for different products over time, this paper concludes that users currently have a positive attitude towards all AIGC products, with a slightly higher inclination towards local products compared to non-native ones. Additionally, when faced with AIGC products that exhibit cultural differences, users show a preference for products trained with local data. These findings not only demonstrate the differences in user acceptance of AIGC products across various cultural backgrounds but also underscore the importance of localization in the development and promotion of AIGC products. To enhance the user acceptance of non-native AIGC products, developers need to consider adopting more localization strategies to better meet users' cultural needs and expectations.

Acknowledgments. This study was supported by the National Social Science Fund of China (Grand No. 23BYY196).

References

1. Cao, Y., et al.: A comprehensive survey of ai-generated content (aigc): A history of generative ai from gan to chatgpt. arXiv preprint arXiv:2303.04226 (2023)
2. Zhang, C., et al.: A complete survey on generative ai (aigc): Is chatgpt from gpt-4 to gpt-5 all you need?. arXiv preprint arXiv:2303.11717 (2023)
3. Else, H.: Abstracts written by ChatGPT fool scientists. Nature **613**(7944), 423–423 (2023)
4. Dwivedi, Y.K., et al.: "So what if ChatGPT wrote it?" Multidisciplinary perspectives on opportunities, challenges and implications of generative conversational AI for research, practice and policy. Int. J. Inf. Manage. **71**, 102642 (2023)
5. Fu, P., Jing, B., Chen, T., Yang, J., Cong, G.: Modeling network public opinion propagation with the consideration of individual emotions. Int. J. Environ. Res. Public Health **17**(18), 6681 (2020)
6. Guo, D., Chen, H., Wu, R., Wang, Y.: AIGC challenges and opportunities related to public safety: a case study of ChatGPT. J. Safety Sci. Resilience **4**(4), 329–339 (2023)
7. Shao, G.: Understanding the appeal of user-generated media: a uses and gratification perspective. Internet Res. **19**(1), 7–25 (2009)
8. Rajbhandari, S., et al.: Deepspeed-moe: advancing mixture-of-experts inference and training to power next-generation AI scale. In: International Conference on Machine Learning, pp. 18332-18346. PMLR (2022)
9. Gu, A., Dao, T.: Mamba: Linear-time sequence modeling with selective state spaces. arXiv preprint arXiv:2312.00752, 2023
10. Ouyang, L., et al.: Training language models to follow instructions with human feedback. arXiv preprint arXiv:2203.02155 (2022)
11. Rasley, J., Rajbhandari, S., Ruwase, O., He, Y.: Deepspeed: system optimizations enable training deep learning models with over 100 billion parameters. In: Proceedings of the 26th ACM SIGKDD International Conference on Knowledge Discovery and Data Mining, pp. 3505–3506 (2020)
12. Shoeybi, M., Patwary, M., Puri, R., LeGresley, P., Casper, J., Catanzaro, B.: Megatron-lm: training multi-billion parameter language models using model parallelism. arXiv preprint arXiv:1909.08053 (2019)

Can You Spot the AI-Generated Images? Distinguishing Fake Images Using Signal Detection Theory

Hayun Park[1], Gayoung Kim[1], Danbi Lee[1], and Hyun K. Kim[1,2(✉)] [iD]

[1] Department of Artificial Intelligence Application, Kwangwoon University, Seoul 01897, Korea
{ciks2508,danbi5739}@naver.com, hyunkkim@kw.ac.kr
[2] School of Information Convergence, Kwangwoon University, Seoul 01897, Korea

Abstract. This study explores individuals' ability to differentiate between AI-generated and genuine human images, with a specific emphasis on different emotional states (lack of emotion, positive emotion, and negative emotion) and human behaviors (postures and activities). An experiment involving 18 participants was conducted to discern various AI-generated human images, and the results were analyzed using signal detection theory. The analysis revealed a significant variation in sensitivity (d') based on the emotional content, with images displaying positive emotions exhibiting notably higher sensitivity compared to emotionless images. No significant sensitivity difference was observed concerning different types of behaviors. Furthermore, there were no significant variations in bias (β) in relation to emotional states and behaviors. This study holds promise for informing various user experience investigations associated with AI image generators.

Keywords: Artificial Intelligence · AI-generated image · User experience · Signal Detection Theory · Human AI Interaction

1 Introduction

Generative artificial intelligence technology has garnered significant attention within the realm of art [1–3]. Notably, there is a heightened interest in AI-generated image technology [17], which enables the effortless creation of images, pictures, and artwork with just a few simple sentences [18–20].

However, like most technological advancements, AI-generated image technology has its drawbacks [21]. In 2022, an AI-generated artwork titled "Théâtre D'opéra Spatial" claimed an art prize in the annual art competition at the Colorado State Fair [24]. The recognition of AI-generated artworks has sparked discussions within the art world regarding issues of copyright and ethics [22, 23]. Moreover, AI-generated image technology has been associated with various adverse social effects [25–27]. A prominent example involves the dissemination of misinformation through the creation of counterfeit images depicting specific individuals [27]. It is common for individuals to struggle in distinguishing AI-generated images from those captured by human photographers, thereby inadvertently accepting misinformation.

© The Author(s), under exclusive license to Springer Nature Switzerland AG 2024
P.-L. P. Rau (Ed.): HCII 2024, LNCS 14702, pp. 299–313, 2024.
https://doi.org/10.1007/978-3-031-60913-8_21

The capacity to discern AI-generated images reflects an individual's aptitude for assessing the credibility and appropriateness of presented information. Consequently, investigating people's proficiency in distinguishing AI-generated images is pivotal for comprehending the adverse social implications of such images. While numerous studies have appraised AI-generated artworks from an artistic standpoint, revealing a preference for human-created over AI-generated artworks [28, 31, 33], there exists a dearth of user experience research centered on discriminating AI-generated images. In prior investigation by Lu et al. (2023) [37], it was observed that humans excelled at discriminating human figures in AI-generated artworks. This observation stems from AI technology's current limitations in reproducing intricate details like hands and facial expressions in human figures. Accordingly, our study narrows its focus to scrutinize people's capacity and inclination to distinguish AI-generated portraits, meticulously categorizing emotions and behaviors. To gauge the ability to discriminate between AI-generated and non-AI-generated portraits, we employ the concepts of sensitivity (d') and bias (β) derived from signal detection theory. In this context, our study posits the following three hypotheses.

H1: The discriminative capability of individuals in discerning AI-generated images varies based on the emotional content (absence of emotion, positive emotion, or negative emotion) depicted in AI-generated portraits.

H2: People's aptitude for distinguishing AI-generated images varies contingent upon the behavioral characteristics (postures and activities) exhibited in the AI-generated portraits.

H3: There exist individual disparities in preferences for AI-generated portrait images compared to those originating from human photographers.

2 Related Work

2.1 Generative AI and Text to Image Generator

Generative AI is a form of artificial intelligence technology designed to produce outcomes tailored to specific user requests. This versatile technology swiftly generates a wide array of content, encompassing music [4–7], text [8–11], and images [12–15]. Notably, OpenAI's Chat-GPT [39] empowers users to input text and generate human-like text content, such as emails and blog posts.

Among the various manifestations of generative AI, text-to-image generators have garnered substantial attention in various sectors. A text-to-image generator is a service and tool that translates user-desired image descriptions into sentence form and subsequently generates corresponding images [16, 17]. Prominent examples include DALL-E 2 [38], Midjourney, Microsoft Bing Image Creator, and NovelAI.

Numerous studies have primarily focused on the artistic evaluation of AI-generated artworks in comparison to those crafted by humans. These investigations have scrutinized human perceptions of artworks, whether originating from humans or AI, and have consistently revealed a tendency for people to attribute higher artistic merit to human-created artworks over AI-generated ones [28, 29, 31, 33]. Some studies have also shown a preference for human-created artworks [32]. Remarkably, these findings persist irrespective of whether information about the creator (AI or human) is disclosed.

In the context of AI-generated artwork, there have been inquiries into viewers' emotional responses when encountering such pieces. A study by Xu R. and Hsu Y. (2020) explored emotional reactions to AI-generated artwork and assessed potential disparities in emotional responses between AI and human-created artworks [34]. Similarly, Demmer et al. (2023) investigated emotional variances when viewing AI-generated and human-created artworks [35]. Both studies revealed that individuals do experience emotions when exposed to AI-generated artworks, albeit emotions evoked by human-created artworks tend to be more diverse and pronounced.

Conversely, limited research has focused on assessing the proficiency of individuals in accurately discerning AI-generated images. Previous investigations have revealed that people struggle to reliably differentiate AI-generated artworks from those created by humans [30, 33, 37]. A more nuanced exploration of this discrimination capability was conducted by Lu et al. (2023) [37]. Their study demonstrated that individuals typically fail to distinguish between AI-generated and human-captured images, but perform better when the AI-generated image includes a human subject. This phenomenon arises from the inherent limitations of AI-generated image technology, particularly the absence of intricate details such as hands and facial expressions.

In this study, our emphasis lies in assessing the capacity to distinguish between portraits generated by AI and those captured by humans. Concurrently, we investigate variances in individuals' preferences for AI-generated and human-captured portraits, drawing insights from previous research on artworks [28, 31–33].

2.2 Signal Detection Theory

Signal detection theory (SDT) serves as a framework employed to comprehend and quantify an individual's discernment capacity between significant and inconsequential stimuli within unspecified contexts [40, 41]. SDT classifies significant stimuli as signals and inconsequential stimuli as noise, delineating their decision-making into four distinct state.

Within the framework of SDT, we calculate Sensitivity (d′) and Bias (β). Sensitivity quantifies an individual's capacity to differentiate between signals and noise, revealing the ease or difficulty of detecting the target signal. A low d' value signifies a diminished ability to discriminate between signal and noise, whereas a high d' value indicates a superior ability to make this distinction. This parameter reflects an individual's aptitude for detecting a specific stimulus. Sensitivity can be mathematically expressed as the difference between the Z-values of the normal distributions for the hit rate and false alarm rate, as demonstrated in the following equation:

$$d' = z(H) - z(FA) \tag{1}$$

Bias, also referred to as response bias, pertains to how a detector categorizes a given stimulus as either a Signal or Noise. This parameter is denoted as β, and it is deemed conservative when its value exceeds 1, while it is considered liberal when it falls within the range of 0 to 1. Mathematically, bias can be expressed as the ratio of the probability of a miss to the probability of a False Alarm, as presented in the following equation:

$$\beta = \frac{P(X|S)}{P(X|N)} \tag{2}$$

In this study, we posit that SDT can effectively ascertain the capability to differentiate between AI-generated and human-captured images.

3 Method

3.1 Participants

In this study, we recruited a total of 36 participants, comprising 18 young adults (11 males and 7 females; average age 25.0 ± 3.34) and 18 middle-aged and older adults (8 males and 10 females; average age 52.9 ± 7.16), spanning various age categories. None of the participants possessed prior familiarity with text-to-image generators.

3.2 Prototype

We investigated whether discrimination abilities varied based on the emotional and behavioral attributes contained in the keywords utilized for image generation. Emotions were categorized into three groups: no emotion (characterized by the absence of facial expressions), positive emotions (including happiness and joy), and negative emotions (encompassing anger and sadness). Behaviors were classified into dynamic behaviors, such as running and exercising, and static postures, which involve activities like sitting and standing.

To create prototypes, we established six conditions corresponding to different combinations of emotions and behaviors. Within each prototype, we selected three image themes: 1) a car and a man, 2) a tennis court and a female tennis player, and 3) a classroom with female students. For each theme, four images were provided (two AI-generated and two human-captured). These image topics revolved around various settings and individuals, and we carefully selected appropriate keywords for each condition. Please refer to Table 1 for a prototype example illustrating image topic 2: a tennis court and a female tennis player. Figure 1 showcases instances of a human-captured image (see Fig. 1-A) and an AI-generated image (see Fig. 1-B) pertaining to Image Topic 2.

Table 1 .

	Prototype design condition		Keyword
Type A	Posture	No emotion	Female tennis player standing on a tennis court
Type B		Positive emotion	Female tennis player celebrating on a tennis court
Type C		Negative emotion	Angry female tennis player standing on tennis court
Type D	Activities	No emotion	Female tennis player playing tennis on a tennis court
Type E		Positive emotion	Female tennis player smiling playing tennis on tennis court
Type F		Negative emotion	Female tennis player playing tennis angrily on tennis court

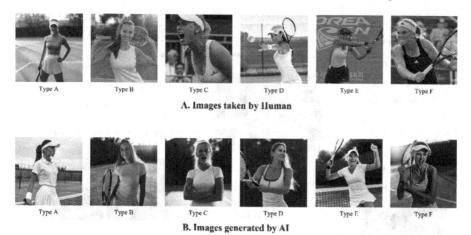

A. Images taken by Human

B. Images generated by AI

Fig. 1. Image example for image topic 2. Figure 1-A. human-captured images and Fig. 1-B. AI-generated images

In this study, we employed Microsoft Bing Image Creator to generate the images (see Fig. 2). To facilitate a comparison between AI-generated and human-captured images, we procured the human-captured images through Google searches. For a visual representation, please refer to Fig. 3, which presents an example of the prototype screen employed in our study.

Fig. 2. Microsoft Bing Image Creator powered by DALL·E.

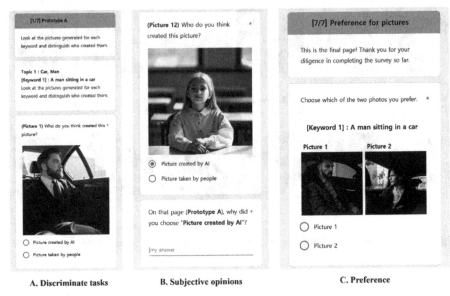

A. Discriminate tasks   **B. Subjective opinions**   **C. Preference**

Fig. 3. Online survey form used in this study.

3.3 Procedure

In this study, we employed an online survey as our experimental method. The survey task involved the presentation of specific images, with participants tasked to determine whether each image was generated by artificial intelligence, as exemplified in Fig. 3-A. Within each of the six prototype conditions, participants were tasked with discriminating among four images. For each of the three distinct topics, this entailed assessing two AI-generated images and two human-captured images, resulting in a total of 72 images (comprising six prototypes, three topics, and four distinct images). During the discrimination task, participants were encouraged to provide a subjective opinion elucidating their rationale for deeming an image as AI-generated, as illustrated in Fig. 3-B. To explore preferences, we presented two images—one generated by AI and the other captured by a human—without disclosing the image creator's identity, as depicted in Fig. 3-C. The allocation of AI-generated and human-captured images was randomized in this context.

3.4 Data Analysis

From the survey outcomes, we computed the proportions of Hits, False Alarms, Misses, and Correct Rejections based on each participant's responses, and derived the sensitivity (d') and bias response (β) for each participant. To scrutinize potential disparities in d' and β values across different emotion and behavior types, we conducted a Repeated Measures Analysis of Variance (RMANOVA) using the R statistical program. The decision matrix employed for SDT analysis in this study is depicted in Table 2.

Table 2. Decision Matrix for the detector.

		State of the world	
		AI-generated image (Signal)	Human-generated image (Noise)
Response (Q: Who do you think created this picture?)	AI	Hit	False Alarm
	Human	Miss	Correct Rejection

Regarding the image preference assessment, we examined the outcomes of participants' choices between AI-generated and human-captured images to identify the more frequently chosen image type.

4 Results

4.1 Calculated Decision Matrix

The decision matrix facilitated the calculation of participants' average values based on the emotional and behavioral categories in the experiment, as displayed in Tables 3 and 4.[1]

Table 3. Decision matrix of emotion conditions (mean).

Response	State of the world					
	No emotion		Positive emotion		Negative emotion	
	AI	Human	AI	Human	AI	Human
AI	79.9%	34.3%	84%	25.2%	81.7%	30.1%
Human	20.1%	65.7%	16%	74.8%	18.3%	69.9%

Table 4. Decision matrix of behavior conditions (mean).

Response	State of the world			
	Posture		Activities	
	AI	Human	AI	Human
AI	81.3%	29.5%	82.4%	30.2%
Human	18.7%	70.5%	17.6%	69.8%

---

[1] Matrix shows the average hit, Correct Rejection, miss, and false alarm rates across all subjects.

4.2 Sensitivity (d′): Ability to Discriminate Image Creator

Figure 4 presents the average sensitivity values for each emotion and behavioral condition. In terms of emotional conditions, the mean sensitivity values were higher for positive (1.92; SD = 1.17), negative (1.68; SD = 1.33), and no emotion (1.48; SD = 1.07). Regarding behavioral conditions, the mean sensitivity values were as follows: activities (1.7; SD = 1.33) and postures (1.68; SD = 1.07). When examining mean sensitivity values across prototypes, the highest was observed for postures with positive emotions (2.04; SD = 1.14), while the lowest was found for postures with no emotions (1.31; SD = 1.07).

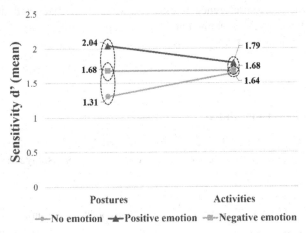

Fig. 4. Sensitivity (mean) of participants by conditions (Groups sharing a dashed circle do not significantly differ for that dependent variable)

We performed a repeated measures ANOVA to scrutinize the presence of noteworthy disparities in sensitivity values across the emotional and behavioral conditions. Our analysis unveiled a statistically significant distinction within the emotional conditions, as presented in Table 5. Subsequent post-hoc analysis utilizing the Bonferroni pairwise comparison method for the three emotional conditions (no emotion, positive emotion, and negative emotion) disclosed a significant variation in the p-values, particularly between no emotion and positive emotion.

Table 5. Sensitivity (d') analysis results according to age, behavior type, emotion type.

Factor	F	p
Behavior	0.04	0.842
Emotion	4.882	<.05*
Behavior:Emotion	2.358	0.102

4.3 Response Bias (β): Response Bias About Discriminating Image Creator

Figure 5 illustrates the average response bias values for each Emotion and Behavior condition. Within the emotional conditions, the mean response bias values were higher for positive (1.39; SD = 1.27), negative (1.34; SD = 1.59), and no emotions (1.12; SD = 1.17). In the context of behavioral conditions, the mean response bias values were recorded as 1.34 (SD = 1.48) for activities and 1.23 (SD = 1.22) for postures. When examining the mean response bias values across prototypes, the highest was observed for activities with positive emotions (1.47; SD = 1.28), while the lowest was identified for postures with no emotions (1.12; SD = 1.18) and activities with no emotions (1.12; SD = 1.16).

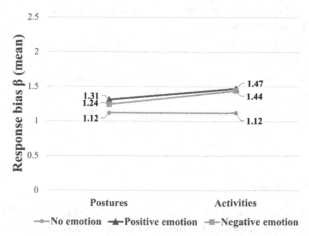

Fig. 5. Response bias (mean) of participants by conditions

Subsequently, we carried out a repeated-measures ANOVA on the bias values of each variable. Our analysis revealed no statistically significant differences between the factors, as outlined in Table 6.

Table 6. Response bias (β) analysis results according to age, behavior type, emotion type.

Factor	F	p
Behavior	0.536	0.469
Emotion	1.574	0.215
Behavior:Emotion	0.171	0.843

4.4 Subjective Opinions

In this study, we conducted an analysis to understand the rationale behind participants' judgments that the image was AI-generated (Fig. 3-B). The prevailing opinions, resulting from this analysis, are summarized in Table 7. The most frequent explanations included "Awkward or unnatural human facial expressions" (20), "Awkward or unnatural human body parts (hands, skin, hair, etc.)" (19), and "Awkward or unnatural human facial structure and shape" (14) as the predominant factors influencing the determination that the image was generated by AI.

Table 7. Organize subjective opinions.

Ranking	Subjective opinions	Number of people
1	Awkward or unnatural human facial expressions	20
2	Awkward or unnatural presentation of a person's body parts (hands, skin, hair, etc.)	19
3	The structure and shape of a person's face is awkward or unnatural	14
4	The inclusion of objects in the image is awkward or unnatural, or the image is overly colorful or awkward	12
5	The overall look of the image is awkward or unnatural	9

4.5 Preference of Image

Table 8 presents the outcomes of the preference survey conducted for AI-generated and human-captured images. Notably, the findings indicated a consistent preference among participants for human-captured images across all prototypes.

Table 8. Preference of image by prototype.

Prototype	Image creator (# of people)
A	Human (31), AI (5)
B	Human (29), AI (7)
C	Human (19), AI (17)
D	Human (36), AI (0)
E	Human (32), AI (4)
F	Human (32), AI (4)

5 Discussion

5.1 People's Discriminatory Abilities and Biases

Tables 3 and 4 show the decision matrix depicting the discrimination ability of participants Regardless of the emotional or behavioral factors, the hit rate consistently exceeded the correct rejection rate. This observation indicates that the ability to accurately distinguish AI-generated images surpassed the ability to correctly identify images captured by humans.

A comprehensive analysis of individuals' discrimination ability, categorized by the type of emotion and behavior, revealed that people exhibited a higher proficiency in discriminating AI-generated images displaying positive emotions compared to those devoid of emotional expressions. Notably, the sensitivity in discerning AI-generated images exhibited a statistically significant difference solely between the positive emotion and no-emotion conditions within the emotional category.

"I don't think it's a natural expression that comes out when a person smiles because of the wrinkles on the face, etc. (P11)"

"The characters' facial expressions were exaggerated and unnatural. (P26)"

The absence of a significant difference in the detection of negative emotions suggests that humans tend to encounter and experience more positive emotions such as smiles and laughter in their daily lives. Consequently, they are more adept at discerning anomalies in images portraying positive emotions compared to those depicting negative emotions. This observation aligns with Carstensen's (2000) research, which indicates that individuals frequently encounter positive emotions like happiness, joy, and contentment in their lifetimes, as opposed to negative emotions such as anger, sadness, and fear [44]. Additionally, AI systems tend to consistently generate facial expressions reflecting positive emotions. This consistent portrayal may render the artificial nature more noticeable, particularly when contrasted with the variability in facial expressions associated with negative emotions. Indeed, there were instances where the unvarying nature of facial expressions was a determining factor in identifying an AI-generated image with a positive emotion.

"All had the same smiling facial expressions. (P32)"

AI image generators have, up to this point, faced limitations in accurately depicting people, particularly in terms of intricate details such as facial expressions and skin texture [42]. These details hold significant importance as they serve as key criteria for humans in discerning whether a portrait has been AI-generated. These findings parallel the outcomes of a prior investigation [43] that explored individuals' ability to differentiate AI-generated faces. In that study, individuals with keen discriminatory abilities scrutinized elements like the image background and specific facial features—such as teeth, hair, eyes, and wrinkles—to ascertain whether the image was a product of AI synthesis.

Notably, there was no notable variance in the response bias associated with determining whether a photograph was AI-generated across either emotional or behavioral conditions. This observation underscores that decision-making bias remained consistent, irrespective of emotional and behavioral factors.

5.2 Reasons for Discriminating AI-Generated Image

During the task of discerning whether an image was AI-generated, participants demonstrated a clear inclination towards scrutinizing the finer aspects of human subjects. Their feedback revealed that the primary determinants for classifying an image as AI-generated were associated with human expression, the portrayal of human body elements (such as hands, skin, and hair), and the structural nuances of the human face. This suggests that when individuals are entrusted with the task of distinguishing AI-generated images, their focal point lies predominantly on the intricacies of the human subject, rather than on background elements or objects.

The rationale behind determining AI-generated images in our study resonates with the findings of a previous investigation by Lu et al. [37], where participants were similarly tasked with identifying AI-generated images. In essence, this implies that even when an image is captured by a human, it can be misinterpreted as AI-generated for similar reasons, as elucidated in Table 7.

5.3 Preference of Image

The inclination towards preferring human-captured portrait images over AI-generated ones remained consistent across all participants, irrespective of their age, even when the image's creator was undisclosed. This outcome aligns with findings from previous studies [28, 31, 33]. When assessing the artistic merit of artworks, human-drawn creations consistently received higher ratings and preferences, even without information about the creator.

However, Table 8 reveals a similarity in preferences between human and AI-generated portrait images in the posture and negative emotion conditions. This could be attributed to either the lower artistic quality of human-captured images under these conditions or the relatively more natural appearance of AI-generated images in comparison to other conditions.

6   Conclusion

In this study, we employed Signal Detection Theory (SDT) to assess human capabilities and biases in distinguishing AI-generated images depicting various emotions and behaviors. Our findings reveal that humans generally excel in distinguishing between AI-generated and human-captured images. Notably, we observed a statistically significant difference in sensitivity values exclusively among emotional conditions, signifying that humans exhibit superior discrimination abilities when AI-generated images portray positive emotions compared to emotionless ones. Conversely, there was no significant contrast in bias within the AI-generated images between emotional and behavioral conditions. Humans tend to scrutinize image details, focusing on factors like facial expressions and anatomical features, as they make determinations regarding AI generation.

Intriguingly, the preference leaned towards human-captured images across most cases, even when the creator's identity remained undisclosed. This study holds significance as it delves into people's discernment of AI-generated versus human-captured images, particularly in the context of emotional and behavioral aspects within portraits. Given that portraits are frequently employed in the dissemination of fake news, often carrying detrimental societal implications, our findings underscore the need for vigilance when consuming news containing portraits, especially those with postural and emotionless attributes. We anticipate that the outcomes of this study, along with the SDT methodology employed, will serve as valuable assets in forthcoming research focused on user experiences and perceptions of AI-generated images.

Acknowledgments. This work was supported by the National Research Foundation of Korea (NRF) grant funded by the Korea government (MSIT) (No. RS-2023-00253917). And this research was also supported by the MSIT (Ministry of Science and ICT), Korea, under the ICAN (ICT Challenge and Advanced Network of HRD) program (IITP-2022-RS-2022-00156215) supervised by the IITP (Institute of Information & Communications Technology Planning & Evaluation).

Disclosure of Interests. The authors have no competing interests to declare that are relevant to the content of this article.

References

1. Jovanovic, M., Campbell, M.: Generative artificial intelligence: trends and prospects. Computer **55**, 107–112 (2022)
2. Shahriar, S.: GAN computers generate arts? A survey on visual arts, music, and literary text generation using Generative Adversarial Network. Displays **73**, 102237 (2022)
3. Cao, Y., et al.: A comprehensive survey of AI-generated content (AIGC): a history of generative AI from GAN to ChatGPT. https://doi.org/10.48550/arXiv.2303.04226
4. Dong, H.-W., Hsiao, W.-Y., Yang, L.-C., Yang, Y.-H.: MuseGAN: multi-track sequential generative adversarial networks for symbolic music generation and accompaniment. https://doi.org/10.48550/arXiv.1709.06298
5. Huang, C.-F., Huang, C.-Y.: Emotion-based AI music generation system with CVAE-GAN. In: 2020 IEEE Eurasia Conference on IOT, Communication and Engineering (ECICE) (2020)
6. Gioti, A.-M.: Artificial intelligence for music composition. In: Handbook of Artificial Intelligence for Music, pp. 53–73 (2021)
7. Hernandez-Olivan, C., Beltran, J.R.: Music composition with Deep Learning: a review. https://doi.org/10.48550/arXiv.2108.12290
8. Feng, X., Liu, M., Liu, J., Qin, B., Sun, Y., Liu, T.: Topic-to-essay generation with Neural Networks. In: Proceedings of the Twenty-Seventh International Joint Conference on Artificial Intelligence (2018)
9. Fan, A., Lewis, M., Dauphin, Y.: Hierarchical neural story generation. https://doi.org/10.48550/arXiv.1805.04833
10. Xu, P., et al.: MEGATRON-CNTRL: Controllable story generation with external knowledge using large-scale language models. https://doi.org/10.48550/arXiv.2010.00840
11. Yi, X., Sun, M., Li, R., Li, W.: Automatic poetry generation with mutual reinforcement learning. In: Proceedings of the 2018 Conference on Empirical Methods in Natural Language Processing (2018)

12. Ramesh, A., et al.: Zero-shot text-to-image generation. https://doi.org/10.48550/arXiv.2102.12092

13. Li, B., Qi, X., Lukasiewicz, T., Torr, P.H.S.: Controllable text-to-image generation. https://doi.org/10.48550/arXiv.1909.07083

14. Qiao, T., Zhang, J., Xu, D., Tao, D.: MirrorGAN: learning text-to-image generation by redescription. In: 2019 IEEE/CVF Conference on Computer Vision and Pattern Recognition (CVPR) (2019)

15. Ding, M., et al.: CogView: mastering text-to-image generation via transformers. https://arxiv.org/abs/2105.13290

16. Frolov, S., Hinz, T., Raue, F., Hees, J., Dengel, A.: Adversarial text-to-image synthesis: a review. Neural Netw. **144**, 187–209 (2021)

17. Agnese, J., Herrera, J., Tao, H., Zhu, X.: A survey and taxonomy of Adversarial Neural Networks for text-to-image synthesis. WIREs Data Mining Knowl. Disc. **10** (2020)

18. Fernandez, P.: Technology behind text to image generators. Library Hi Tech News **39**, 1–4 (2022)

19. Oppenlaender, J.: The creativity of text-to-image generation. In: Proceedings of the 25th International Academic Mindtrek Conference (2022)

20. Cetinic, E., She, J.: Understanding and creating art with AI: review and outlook. ACM Trans. Multimed. Comput. Commun. Appl. **18**, 1–22 (2022)

21. Daniele, A., Song, Y.-Z.: AI + art = human. In: Proceedings of the 2019 AAAI/ACM Conference on AI, Ethics, and Society (2019)

22. Epstein, Z., Levine, S., Rand, D.G., Rahwan, I.: Who gets credit for AI-generated art? iScience **23**, 101515 (2020)

23. Roose, K.: An A.I.-generated picture won an art prize. Artists aren't happy. https://www.nytimes.com/2022/09/02/technology/ai-artificial-intelligence-artists.html

24. Ghosh, A., Fossas, G.: Can there be art without an artist? https://doi.org/10.48550/arXiv.2209.07667

25. Chen, C., Fu, J., Lyu, L.: A pathway towards responsible AI generated content. https://doi.org/10.48550/arXiv.2303.01325

26. Whittaker, L., Kietzmann, T.C., Kietzmann, J., Dabirian, A.: "All around me are synthetic faces": the mad world of AI-generated media. IT Prof. **22**, 90–99 (2020)

27. Sha, Z., Li, Z., Yu, N., Zhang, Y.: DE-FAKE: detection and attribution of fake images generated by text-to-image generation models. https://doi.org/10.48550/arXiv.2210.06998

28. Ragot, M., Martin, N., Cojean, S.: AI-generated vs. human artworks. A perception bias towards artificial intelligence? In: Extended Abstracts of the 2020 CHI Conference on Human Factors in Computing Systems (2020)

29. Hong, J.-W., Curran, N.M.: Artificial Intelligence, artists, and art. ACM Trans. Multimed. Comput. Commun. Appl. **15**, 1–16 (2019)

30. Gangadharbatla, H.: The role of AI attribution knowledge in the evaluation of artwork. Empir. Stud. Arts **40**, 125–142 (2021)

31. Fortuna, P., Modliński, A.: A(I)rtist or counterfeiter? Artificial Intelligence as (d)evaluating factor on the art market. J. Arts Manag. Law Soc. **51**, 188–201 (2021)

32. Bellaiche, L., et al.: Humans versus AI: Whether and why we prefer human-created compared to AI-created artwork. Cogn. Res. Principle Implications **8**, 42 (2023)

33. Chamberlain, R., Mullin, C., Scheerlinck, B., Wagemans, J.: Putting the art in artificial: aesthetic responses to computer-generated art. Psychol. Aesthet. Creat. Arts **12**, 177–192 (2018)

34. Rui, Xu., Hsu, Y.: Discussion on the aesthetic experience of artificial intelligence creation and human art creation. In: Shoji, H., et al. (eds.) KEER 2020. AISC, vol. 1256, pp. 340–348. Springer, Singapore (2020). https://doi.org/10.1007/978-981-15-7801-4_36

35. Demmer, T.R., Kühnapfel, C., Fingerhut, J., Pelowski, M.: Does an emotional connection to art really require a human artist? Emotion and intentionality responses to AI - versus human-created art and impact on aesthetic experience. Comput. Hum. Behav. **148**, 107875 (2023)

36. Chiarella, S.G., Torromino, G., Gagliardi, D.M., Rossi, D., Babiloni, F., Cartocci, G.: Investigating the negative bias towards artificial intelligence: effects of prior assignment of AI-authorship on the aesthetic appreciation of abstract paintings. Comput. Hum. Behav. **137**, 107406 (2022)

37. Lu, Z., et al.: Seeing is not always believing: benchmarking human and model perception of AI-generated images. https://arxiv.org/abs/2304.13023

38. Ramesh, A., Dhariwal, P., Nichol, A., Chu, C., Chen, M.: Hierarchical text-conditional image generation with clip latents. https://doi.org/10.48550/arXiv.2204.06125

39. Brown, T.B., et al.: Language models are few-shot learners. https://arxiv.org/abs/2005.14165

40. Wickens, C.D., Helton, W.S., Hollands, J.G., Banbury, S.: Engineering psychology and human performance (2021)

41. Wickens, T.D.: Elementary Signal Detection Theory. Oxford University Press, New York (2001)

42. O'Meara, J., Murphy, C.: Aberrant AI creations: co-creating surrealist body horror using the DALL-E Mini text-to-image generator. Convergence Int. J. Res. New Media Technol. **29**(4), 1070–1096 (2023). https://doi.org/10.1177/13548565231185865

43. Lago, F., Pasquini, C., Bohme, R., Dumont, H., Goffaux, V., Boato, G.: More real than real: a study on human visual perception of synthetic faces [applications corner]. IEEE Sig. Process. Mag. **39**, 109–116 (2022)

44. Carstensen, L.L., Pasupathi, M., Mayr, U., Nesselroade, J.R.: Emotional experience in everyday life across the adult life span. J. Pers. Soc. Psychol. **79**, 644–655 (2000)

A Study on the Developmental Process and Application Mode of AI Digital Humans in Cartoon Style: A Case Study of an Offline Doll Machine Store in Shenzhen

Chijun Tan[iD], Yunkai Lai[iD], and Jun Wu[(✉)][iD]

School of Fine Arts and Design, Faculty of Arts, Shenzhen University, Shenzhen 518061, Guangdong, China
laiyunkai2020@email.szu.edu.cn, junwu2006@hotmail.com

Abstract. In today's era of rapid AI development, a bunch of AI-based products and services are being implemented, reshaping various industries with its transformative power. In recent years, In the field of AI digital beings, Chinese researchers have predominantly focused on macro-level applications of digital beings, with room for improvement in specific application patterns. Much of the research and practice in this area has revolved around realistic-style digital humans, with relatively fewer studies on the application of cartoon AI digital humans. This study focuses on service design and utilizes the KANO model to analyze user needs. The findings indicate that: (1) Natural and seamless voice responses significantly enhance user satisfaction, while inadequate execution can lead to substantial negative impacts on user satisfaction. (2) Precise dialogue comprehension, expression recognition, and engaging performances have a notable positive effect on user satisfaction. (3) Initiating greetings based on perceiving people's presence does not exert a significant influence on user satisfaction. Additionally, through practical case analysis, this study explores innovative application models of digital humans and their development processes with the aim of providing suggestions for digital human advancement, inspiring other industries, and promoting widespread adoption of digital human technology in daily life.

Keywords: AI · human-computer interaction · digital human · doll machine · service design · KANO model

1 Introduction

Despite China's wealth of excellent animated works, the market share of animation-related products is significantly lacking. In commercial markets, such as doll machine stores and toy wholesale markets in Guangzhou and Shenzhen, Disney and Japanese animation characters has dominated the major market share. The influence of Chinese animated character images downstream in the animation industry is gradually diminishing, highlighting the urgent need for a channel to enhance the influence of Chinese animation. From 2021 to 2022, China's anime industry has also experienced new changes

© The Author(s), under exclusive license to Springer Nature Switzerland AG 2024
P.-L. P. Rau (Ed.): HCII 2024, LNCS 14702, pp. 314–331, 2024.
https://doi.org/10.1007/978-3-031-60913-8_22

and challenges. Despite the rapid industrialization process driven by capital, there are still issues that need to be addressed. The creativity of original anime needs improvement as it lacks interest, while traditional Chinese-style anime often lacks depth and tends to be repetitive in form. Additionally, high-quality intellectual properties (IPs) are scarce, and the market urgently requires new IPs with stickiness, vitality, and commercial value. Internet platforms excessively pursue quantity while neglecting the cultivation of high-quality IPs, resulting in an imbalance of content resources and negative impacts on the anime industry due to blind pursuit of profits. Even acclaimed animation companies have become tools for quick profitability under capital pressure. Meanwhile, in 2021, metaverse entered people's vision; the construction of digital culture and next-generation internet content will drive the IP frenzy. Cross-border collaboration between anime games and IPs will strengthen: 1. Anime games participating in digital cultural construction will promote technological innovation and create more high-quality IPs. 2. The combination of anime game IPs with cultural consumption will stimulate new demands and business models. 3. Integrating anime game IPs into digital tourism will realize dual values both online and offline [1].

During the development of Chinese animation, there has not been enough emphasis on the transformation of animation intellectual property (IP), resulting in a severe lack of quality products representing Chinese animation IP in the downstream industry chain. The industry chain has not been effectively connected to the downstream market, and the glory moments of works have remained confined to records of viewership and box office performance. In 2016, the downstream output value accounted for 64% in Japan's anime industry, with its derivative market being eight times larger than the broadcasting market. However, in 2018, China's anime industry only saw a downstream output value accounting for 43%, with an anime derivative market size that is only 1.5 times larger than its broadcasting market. The highest revenue source in Japan's anime industry lies in copyright sales, particularly through overseas licensing (television, film, music scores), which is considered as the most profitable category. Derivative product revenue comes second. In comparison, China's animation industry mainly focuses on upstream activities while neglecting significant development opportunities in midstream and downstream sectors. Yet it is precisely these midstream and downstream stages where industrial added value becomes more prominent and serves as important avenues for "re-supplying - re-manufacturing - re-distribution - re-marketing. [2]"

Combining cartoon AI humans with Chinese animation IP holds the potential to improve this phenomenon. Today, digitization has revolutionized the shopping experience. Retailers are rapidly adopting emerging technologies to enhance customer service interactions online and in physical stores [3]. In recent years, storytelling marketing strategies have generated a great deal of interest in the field of applied technology marketing, which combines storytelling elements with immersive technology. Research has already proven that storytelling can enhance the effectiveness of marketing strategies [4], and identity-based digital humans possess inherent narrative attributes. Therefore, the offline doll machine market can serve as a venue for studying the development process of digital humans and exploring their application scenarios. The purpose of this study is twofold:

1. to investigate the service process in the animation peripheral industry and explore users' core demands for cartoon AI characters;
2. through case analysis, to outline the core capabilities and value of cartoon AI humans, expand research on their application models and development processes across all scenarios, and provide development recommendations.

2 Literature Review

2.1 Metaverse and AI Digital Humans

The year 2021 marks the emergence of the metaverse, which is scientifically defined as an online three-dimensional environment where users interact with each other through avatars in a virtual space distinct from the physical world [5]. The Metaverse represents the next generation of Internet applications and social structures, emerging from the integration of various cutting-edge technologies. It enables spatial-temporal expansion through AR, VR, MR, and digital twin technologies; facilitates human-machine integration via AI and IoT (Internet Of Things) technologies; and drives economic value creation through block-chain, Web3.0, NFT, and other advanced tools. Its ultimate goal is to achieve a harmonious coexistence between virtual and physical realms within social systems, production systems, and economic systems while empowering users with the ability to shape their own world, create content, and assert ownership over digital assets. The digital human is a manifestation of a virtual being within the metaverse, relying on advanced digital technology. The virtual digital human encompasses two aspects: firstly, it serves as an original inhabitant of the metaverse; secondly, it represents the virtual embodiment of real-world individuals in this immersive environment. In other words, the digital human can either be computer-driven or serve as a faithful replica of an actual person. It is important to note that the concept and essence of the virtual digital human have evolved significantly since its inception. For instance, it has progressed from an initial cartoon-like representation to a highly realistic form comparable to that of a real individual. Furthermore, there has been substantial advancement from basic program settings to intelligent AI engines capable of independent learning.

The advancement of artificial intelligence is imperative for enhancing the cognitive abilities of digital humans. As stated in the UNESCO report: Generative artificial intelligence (GenAI) programmes burst into the public awareness in November late 2022 with the launch of ChatGPT, which became the fastest growing app in history. With the power to imitate human capabilities to produce outputs such as text, images, videos, music and software codes, these GenAI applications have caused a stir, just as the hype surrounding AI over the past five years seemed to be settling. Millions of people are now using GenAI in their daily lives and the potential of adapting the models to domain-specific AI applications seems unlimited, at least in the years to come [6]. For example, the emergence of Chat-GPT, Baidu Wenxin Yiyan and other large models shows that the era of artificial intelligence enabling digital human has arrived. Digital humans are becoming more and more lifelike and intelligent, which is the result of the comprehensive cross-development of multiple disciplines and fields.

At present, China's digital humans are showing a rapid development stage. In general, in 2022, the market size of China's digital humans industry reached 146.4 billion yuan, up 57% year on year, and analysts from Zhongshang Industrial Research Institute expect it to reach 260 billion yuan in 2025 (Zhongshang Industrial Research Institute, 2022) [7]. In terms of local areas, in order to implement China's 14th Five-Year Digital Economy Development Plan, Beijing issued the Beijing Action Plan for Promoting the Innovative Development of Digital Human Industry (2022–2025) in August 2022. The notice pointed out that by 2025, the scale of Beijing's digital human industry will exceed 50 billion yuan [8]. The Guangzhou Municipal People's Government issued the "Nine Measures for the Development of Nansha New Area (Free Trade Zone) in Guangzhou" to promote the development of the main business technology fields of the meta-universe ecology, focusing on the next generation of information technology enterprises and surrounding derivative industries based on the combination of virtual and real based on 5G high-speed immersive Internet. The plan supports a variety of technology fields, such as VR, AR, MR, ER, immersive visual blockchain, human-computer interaction, virtual human, intelligent voice interaction, 3D digital assets, etc. [9]. The Chinese government and enterprises are intensifying their efforts to promote and incentivize the implementation of digital humans, yielding fruitful outcomes.

2.2 Doll Machine Development Overview

A doll machine is an arcade game where players simply grab the prize to get the prize they want. The player needs to use an external joystick to control the claws inside the machine to capture any prize the player wants [10]. After years of development, claw machines have moved from dimly lit arcades and amusement parks to become a central attraction in cities. With their unique entertainment value, abundant prizes, low participation costs, and strong interactivity, they have successfully gained popularity among a large number of entertainment consumers and developed a group of loyal followers [11].

At present, China's arcade market is distributed in the crowded areas of various shopping malls. There are scattered arcade machines managed by employees, as well as special store brands. Some stores have achieved the form of chain stores, attracting players through content marketing, live broadcast promotion and other means of social platforms. Taking Guangzhou as an example, the common chain brands are: Jargee, Little Deer House, Bear Cha Cha, etc. Through field visits and online information collected from 13 offline arcade stores in Shenzhen, it is found that most of the plush toys used for exchange in these stores are American or Japanese IP images such as Disney, Pokemon, Crayon Shin-chan, Doraemon, etc. The small dolls in the arcade machines are mostly these images or ordinary dolls without IP attributes or some cartoon images that are popular because of the social media. The share of plush toys prototyped by Chinese IP images is very low, or even almost no. Although a small number of brands have formed a chain mode and have formed a set of relatively complete service processes, there are still some pain points that can be used as opportunity points for cartoon AI digital people to find application scenarios (Fig. 1).

Fig. 1. Doll machine store survey

2.3 KANO Model Theory

The Kano model Theory originated from the Two Factors Theory proposed by the famous American psychologist, management theorist and behavioral scientist Frederick Herzberg in the late 1950s [12]. In the early 1980s, Noriaki Kano, a professor and quality management scholar at Tokyo Institute of Technology, proposed the Kano model based on the two-factor theory. The KANO model is a tool for classifying and prioritizing user needs, reflecting the nonlinear relationship between service elements and user satisfaction. It divides product or service quality characteristics into five categories: essential, expected, charming, indifference, and reverse needs. Specifically, the KANO model serves as an auxiliary research tool in early customer satisfaction evaluation to classify customer needs in detail and help enterprises improve customer satisfaction. It is often used to classify performance indicators to understand different levels of customer needs and identify key points of interaction with enterprises. By identifying crucial factors for customer satisfaction through this model, enterprises can formulate targeted promotion strategies. Therefore, the KANO model is suitable for investigating classification of cartoon AI digital human needs. The traditional Kano model identifies and classifies the quality attributes of functions, but there are also some shortcomings: 1) it does not reflect to what extent the provision of a certain function will affect user satisfaction, which makes the application in practice too general and cannot produce effective guidance in practice; 2) the difference between most functions and requirements is not significant. Taking the maximum value of data frequency as the way of attribute classification will ignore the distribution state of a certain function in other requirements [13]. Therefore, scholars such as Charles Berger introduced the concept of user satisfaction index based on this foundation [14]. The index, also known as the Better-Worse Index, consists of two indicators: improving user satisfaction (Better) and eliminating user dissatisfaction (Worse). These indicators are calculated based on the four main functional attributes - A, O, M, and I. By analyzing the impact of various functional requirements using the comprehensive coefficient of Better-Worse, it provides a priority ranking for design and development improvements under limited resources. The calculation method is as follows:

1. Better = $(A+)/(A + O + M + I)$: The closer the value is to 1, the more significant the improvement in user satisfaction.
2. Worse = $(O + M)/(A + O + M + I) \times (-1)$: The closer the value is to -1, the greater impact it has on preventing user dissatisfaction and reducing user satisfaction (Fig. 2 and Table 1).

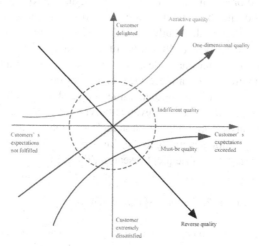

Fig. 2. Diagram of the KANO model

Table 1. KANO evaluation results classification comparison table

Negative problem (if the product does not have this feature, your rating is)					
		I love it	it should be so	It doesn't matter to me	I am OK with it	I hate it
Positive question (if the product has this feature, your rating is yes)	I love it	Q	A	A	A	O
	it should be so	R	I	I	I	M
	It doesn't matter to me	R	I	I	I	M
	I am OK with it	R	I	I	I	M
	I hate it	R	R	R	R	Q

Note: Q means possible results (related to user misunderstanding and the question itself)

3 Research Method

This study initially classified the digital person and its application scenarios through tabletop research and brainstorming. Then, the field observation method was used to analyze user experience in arcade stores and draw a user journey map. The core needs of users were identified based on the user journey map and Kano model. Additionally, literature reading and practical case analysis were conducted to expand the application mode of cartoon AI digital humans from arcade stores and amusement park outlets to all scenario. In Zhu Yifan et al.'s study, they divided the evaluation of digital persons into five dimensions: perceived technicality, functionality, interactivity, emotionality, and sociality. Considering that image design is also crucial, this study reclassified and designed a questionnaire based on these factors. The value of digital persons was categorized into three groups: (A) emotional value needs, (B) aesthetic value needs, and (C) information service value needs. Eleven subdivided needs were extracted with 13 corresponding questions set up. Each question had two positive and negative options to determine their classification according to the Kano model. The better-worse coefficient was calculated using data for subsequent research (Table 2).

Table 2. Cartoon AI digital human value table

classification	Code	Demand differentiation	Question code	Question
Aesthetic value (A)	A1	artistic designing	a1	The image of the cartoon AI digital human is in line with my aesthetic (such as character design, costume design, prop design, etc.)
	A2	Story attribute/propagation attribute /IP attribute	a2	Cartoon AI digital human have their own story background
emotional value (B)	B1	Greeting	b1	The cartoon AI digital human can greet me and say hello

(continued)

Table 2. (*continued*)

classification	Code	Demand differentiation	Question code	Question
	B2	Natural dialogue	b2	The cartoon AI digital human is capable of accurately understanding what I say
	B3	Voice	b3	The cartoon AI digital human can interact with me using natural and fluent speech responses
	B4	Performance	b4	Cartoon AI digital human are capable of performing entertaining acts such as singing, dancing, telling jokes and more
	B5	Recognition of emotion	b5	Cartoon AI digital human can recognize my facial expressions and emotions
	B6	Presence perception	b6	If I stand in front of the screen, the cartoon AI digital human would be able to take notice of my presence
Information service value (C)	C1	Knowledge/function/information Q&A	c1	Cartoon AI figures can answer my questions with AI technology like ChatGPT

(*continued*)

Table 2. (*continued*)

classification	Code	Demand differentiation	Question code	Question
	C2	Process/Route information Guide	c2	The cartoon AI digital human can guide me through the game and teach me the techniques of operating the doll machine
	C3	Marketing/recording data/iot information	c3	I can purchase game coins and keep track of the number of dolls in the interactive screen of Cartoon AI Digital human
			c4	Cartoon AI digital humancan introduce me to store packages, offers, activities, etc
			c5	Cartoon AI digital human can help me call the shop assistant to help me place the dolls

4   Results and Discussion

4.1   Classification of Industry

Through the chart, it is evident that digital humans have permeated offline industries, encompassing various aspects of our lives, ranging from retail and transportation to healthcare. The primary application of digital humans lies in resolving service-related issues encountered in both work and daily life. While traditional digital humans have partially fulfilled certain service requirements, they still face common challenges such as limited user engagement, low interaction willingness, and complex interactive interfaces. Consequently, their adoption across diverse industries has been relatively limited in recent years. With the advent of convenient mobile networks that continuously enhance user experiences, people's expectations for digital avatars have evolved beyond mere aesthetic appeal and basic conversational abilities. As artificial intelligence pervades every facet of our existence today, a comprehensive upgrade for digital humans becomes imperative. However, not all industries are suitable for the use of AI-powered digital humans; deploying them in simplistic scenarios devoid of highly intelligent interactions would only escalate costs. Therefore, defining the level of intelligence required by digital humans within different industry contexts becomes crucial (Fig. 3).

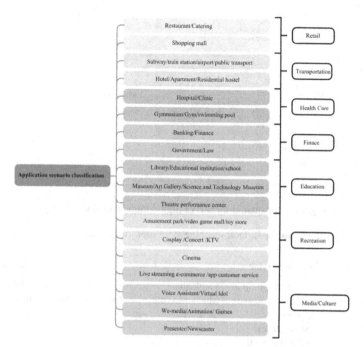

Fig. 3. Industry classification chart

Therefore, this study introduces two categories based on application scenarios and presents a four-quadrant diagram illustrating digital human application scenarios. The horizontal axis defines the online (e.g., news broadcasting, live streaming) or offline (e.g., shopping mall screens, advertising displays) forms of digital human applications. The vertical axis represents the intelligence level of digital humans, ranging from weak interaction (e.g., simple interactions and service processing capabilities) to strong interaction (e.g., natural multimodal interactions enabled by AI models). This framework aims to assist enterprise users in identifying their specific digital human requirements (Fig. 4).

4.2　User Journey Map

The present study focuses on the application research of AI digital human in arcades, employing service design methodology to depict the user journey diagram, as illustrated below (Tables 3 and 4).

According to the chart, we can see that cartoon AI digital humans can serve as intelligent assistants online by integrating traditional service designs or app functions. This means that users no longer need to switch between multiple apps or browse through

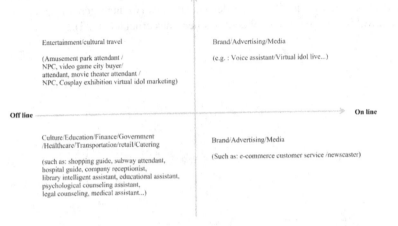

Fig. 4. Four-quadrant chart of digital human ability-industry

Table 3. Doll machine store user journey map

	Before service			In service
Action	When shopping in the mall, you see stores. (signs/stores) After finding the location on the map software (with a clear desire), head to the store After seeing the marketing content on social platforms, head to the store	Think about whether to enter the store	Go into the store to observe or consult	Purchase game currency
Questions they had	Do I have a need? Whether I like the doll?	Whether the little dolls in the shop are beautiful Whether the big doll redeemed is beautiful Whether there is enough space to store the doll	How easy it is for the claw machine to pick up the doll The price of the game currency	How can I get a good deal?

(continued)

Table 3. (*continued*)

	Before service			In service
Opportunities	Conduct research on users' preferred IP to expand the target audience	Provide a points collection system/gift redemption system Set preferential experiential prices	Promote an advertisement for a claw machine that is easy to win dolls Offer guaranteed rewards/points Organize activities where purchasing game coins allows participation in a lottery	Adjusting price setting and implementing a 'buy more, get more' strategy
Cartoon digital human interaction scene	Store/shopping guide screen/shopping guide robot social platform Claw machine brand image	Digital human put on shows, play games and attract consumers	Digital man introduces claw machine operation, skills, tips	Digital human do the selling

numerous menu options. With just a simple sentence, they can quickly locate and fulfill their needs. This intelligent assistant mode greatly simplifies the user's workflow, improves service efficiency, and enhances user satisfaction. In the scenario of doll machine stores: Cartoon AI digital humans can: 1) Interact with players in performances, providing emotional value. 2) Recommend packages and introduce playing method to players, offering informational service value. 3) Broadcast on social platforms and utilize IP images for promotion, contributing to aesthetic value.

Likewise, in the amusement park scene, cartoon AI digital humans can serve as non-playable characters (NPCs) to interact with players, attracting the attention of children and tourists for emotional value, thereby enhancing user experience. They can also provide information service value by explaining service processes, guiding tourists to play and providing route guidance. Additionally, users can engage with these digital humans through social media interactions such as commenting on their appearance or evaluating them, satisfying aesthetic needs.

4.3 Questionnaire Survey Results

The questionnaire survey primarily employed a combination of online and offline distribution methods. A total of 151 questionnaires were collected, with 14 invalid ones being excluded. Invalid questionnaires encompassed those that were incomplete, had identical responses for positive and negative questions, or featured the same option for all questions. After excluding these cases, a final sample size of 137 valid questionnaires was obtained. Among the respondents, 43.17% identified as male while 56.83% identified

Table 4. Doll machine store user journey map

	In service			After service
Choose the claw machine and experience	Didn't get the doll	Get a doll	Redeem points for big dolls or take away small dolls	Evaluate the service
How many points do I need for a gift exchange	I kept trying to rearrange the dolls, but the clerk couldn't keep up I didn't want to miss my chance (after many attempts, the doll machine had a greater chance of catching the doll), so I dared not leave the machine	Decide to exchange or continue Unable to save the remaining game coins	I didn't grab enough points I didn't catch what I wanted	The proper care and maintenance of the doll
The shape of the doll should be designed for different purposes	Set the Need Help button	Encourage players to keep spending Set up a game currency account to increase the number of repeat users	Encourage players to swap and set up temporary swap areas	Provide doll care manual / Cleaning tools/cleaners/repairs/recycling/Points /Trade-in
Real-time integration statistics, Digital people interact with the player while grabbing the doll	Digital human screen access doll machine Internet of Things information Counting doll machines that need help	The digital human praises the player and encourages continued interaction	Digital human to make exchange guidelines	Get online NFT assets associated with digital people Continue to interact with the player

as female. The majority of participants were students engaged in fields such as media, design, advertising, internet-related industries or product development. Geographically speaking, most respondents hailed from Guangdong and Jiangsu provinces in China. Based on the deduction formula utilized in this study, the Better coefficient and Worse coefficient were calculated as follows (Table 5):

Table 5. Better-Worse coefficients

Question code	KANO attribute	Better coefficients	Worse coefficients
b3	Attractive	48.28%	−35.34%
b2	Indifferent	47.97%	−24.39%
b5	Indifferent	45.9%	−25.41%
a2	Indifferent	45.53%	−30.08%
c1	Indifferent	45.08%	−29.51%
b4	Indifferent	44.35%	−28.23%
c5	Indifferent	44.26%	−29.51%
a1	Indifferent	40%	−35.2%
b6	Indifferent	38.71%	−24.19%
b1	Indifferent	36.67%	−21.67%
c2	Indifferent	36.07%	−35.25%
c3	Indifferent	35.48%	−31.45%
c4	Indifferent	34.17%	−32.5%

When using the KANO model for investigation, when the results of absolute attribute calculation belong to "indifferent" functions, the relative results of the quadrant diagram are often used for analysis. The questionnaire results mostly belong to the indifferent demand, so it is suitable to choose the quadrant diagram for analysis. The quadrant diagram is the attribute division under the "relative concept". There may be inconsistency with the calculation results, so one of them can be chosen for analysis. The highest better coefficient of the coefficient table is the question b3 and b2. The question is related to the dialogue fluency of cartoon AI digital humans, indicating that users have high expectations for the smooth and natural dialogue experience. From the worse coefficient: the values of the question a1, b3 and c2 are higher, indicating that in addition to the demand for the natural and smooth dialogue of cartoon AI digital people, the appearance and core service ability are also necessary elements. In order to better analyze the demand classification, the scatter diagram is drawn according to the absolute values of the Better coefficient and Worse coefficient of the question, and the quadrants are divided according to the average value of all functions. The first quadrant is the expected attribute (O), the second quadrant is the attractive attribute (A), the third quadrant is the in different attribute (I), and the fourth quadrant is the must-be attribute (M) (Fig. 5).

Better-Worse coefficient analysis

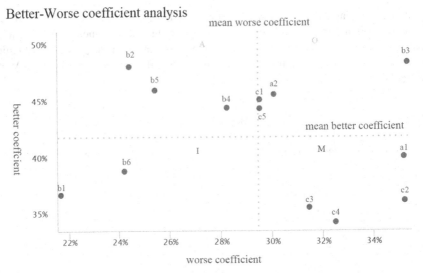

Fig. 5. Better-Worse scatter plot

4.4 Digital Human Application Model Diagram and Development Flow Chart

Based on the above research and literature analysis, this study constructs the application scenario model of cartoon AI digital human, and summarizes the application process of digital human according to the above (Fig. 6):

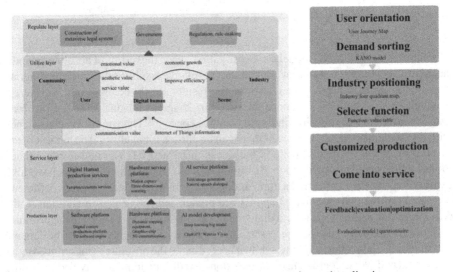

Fig. 6. Model diagram of digital human construction and application

The application model of digital humans can be categorized into four layers: the production layer, service layer, use layer, and supervision layer. The production layer primarily consists of software platforms, hardware platforms, and AI model research and development companies that provide technical support in terms of software and hardware. The service layer encompasses digital human production customization services, hardware equipment service platforms, and companies that offer modular AI functions as well as customized AI.

At the utilization layer, digital humans can offer users emotional, aesthetic, and service value. Users can share feedback on their experiences with digital humans, fostering communication value through positive word-of-mouth. The attractiveness and service value of digital humans contribute to the economic growth and efficiency of utilization scenarios. Simultaneously, these scenarios can integrate Internet of Things data into digital humans for a virtuous cycle. With users representing a larger community, utilization scenarios extend to various industries, forming a comprehensive closed-loop ecosystem. The supervision layer serves as the pinnacle in the construction model of digital humans and operates under the oversight of metaverse technology, blockchain technology, and legal frameworks. Governments must establish regulations and laws to supervise and uphold this system. The production and use process of digital human mainly includes the following four major steps:

1. Positioning the population: First of all, it is necessary to clarify the needs of digital humans and users. The intelligence level of digital humans can be defined by the four-image diagram in this study. The needs of different industries are classified to determine which kind of digital humans are selected for production.
2. Analysis of the KANO model: The KANO model is used to further sort out the user needs, and make clear which needs can maximize the user satisfaction in the development process of digital humans, and which needs can prevent the occurrence of user dissatisfaction.
3. Positioning functions and customized development: According to the industry positioning and the analysis of the Carnot model, the digital people template is determined, and the appropriate functions and needs are selected. The core functions are improved, the low demand functions are weakened, the development costs are saved, and the digital people are put into use.
4. Feedback evaluation: Finally, the feedback evaluation questionnaire is used to obtain feedback.

5 Conclusion and Suggestion

The research findings indicate that users' expectations for cartoon AI digital humans in the arcade store can be categorized as follows: natural and seamless voice responses, personalized backstory, AI-powered conversation, and the ability to call store clerks for assistance. The first four aspects pertain to the characteristics of the cartoon digital humans themselves, while the fifth aspect relates to specific functionalities within the arcade store. A significant positive impact on user satisfaction is observed when there is a natural and seamless voice response; conversely, inadequate performance in this area leads to a notable decrease in user satisfaction. Attractive features include accurate dialogue comprehension, expression recognition, and overall performance quality. Focusing on these aspects can greatly enhance user satisfaction. On the other hand, perceiving human presence and initiating greetings are considered indifferent needs that have minimal influence on user satisfaction and may be given lower priority during development stages. Must-be requirements encompass alignment with personal aesthetics; provision of gameplay introductions; facilitating game coin purchases as well as recording, exchanging, and storing dolls; introducing store packages along with offers and activities. While meeting these essential needs does not significantly improve user satisfaction alone, failure to adequately address them will result in a substantial negative impact on overall user experience. In developing cartoon AI digital humans or similar applications across various scenarios, it is advisable to prioritize meeting must-be requirements initially followed by striving towards fulfilling expected needs while appropriately addressing attractive needs; however lagging behind in catering to indifferent needs may be permissible based on developmental priorities. In other application scenarios, digital human design can be carried out according to the application scenario model, and emotional value, aesthetic value and service value can be sorted out in detail. Furthermore, demand can be further subdivided and developed through the Carnot model, and finally, scales can be used for evaluation and feedback.

1. For the digital humans itself: on the one hand, users have high requirements for smooth voice chat and accurate understanding of dialogue, so we should pay attention to the use of voice engine in the development process and try to choose smooth and natural speech. When linking the large model API protocol, we should try to reduce computing time and network delay. On the other hand, the process of scene service is often a necessary requirement. The development of these functions will not have a particularly large impact on the improvement of user satisfaction, but it is necessary to cause a significant decline in user satisfaction once it is difficult to use. Therefore, process-oriented service is a basic element in the development process of digital people. Finally, in the development process, facial recognition or performance event trigger module should be appropriately added to make digital people perform interesting performances and highlight the performance ability of digital people on the interactive interface.

2. For the development of Chinese IP cartoon digital human: surprisingly, in line with personal aesthetics with a specific story background and design of aesthetic value belonging to the type of must-be demand, the improvement of user satisfaction will not bring a profound impact, not doing well in these aspects will cause significant negative effects on user satisfaction, so in the combination of Chinese animation IP and cartoon AI digital human, in addition to the story background and beautiful design, we should put more focus on the optimization of the voice matching the character and the story, focusing on the fluency of the voice and the fluency of the performance of the cartoon AI digital human.

3. For the application of digital humans in other industries, it is crucial to thoroughly analyze user needs during their development. In the initial design phase, conducting extensive research on target users using the Kano model can be highly beneficial. Throughout the process of digital human development, employing modular functional programming techniques can enhance cost-effectiveness, optimize performance, and ensure an optimal user experience.

References

1. Cui, W., Niu, M., Hao: Annual report of China animation and game industry from 2021 to 2022 (abstract). Publ. Distrib. Res. (12), 21–27 (2022)
2. Liu, X., Fu, X.: Research on the development path of China's animation industry chain. Shanghai Manage. Sci. (03), 16–20 (2022)
3. Dacko, S.G.: Enabling smart retail settings via mobile augmented reality shopping apps. Technol. Forecast. Soc. Chang. **124**, 243–256 (2017)
4. Sung, E., Han, D.-I.D., Bae, S., Kwon, O.: What drives technology-enhanced storytelling immersion? The role of digital humans. Comput. Hum. Behav. **132**(132), 107246 (2022)
5. Ritterbusch, G.D., Teichmann, M.R.: Defining the metaverse: a systematic literature review. IEEE Access **11**, 12368–12377 (2023)
6. UNESCO: Guidance for generative AI in education and research, 1st end, France (2023)
7. AskCIhomepage.   https://wk.askci.com/details/cc64d7ee01794e95a9782079daa99259/. Accessed 2 Dec 2023
8. The People's Government of Beijing Municipality. https://www.beijing.gov.cn/zhengce/zhengcefagui/202208/t20220808_2787958.html. Accessed 3 Dec 2023
9. The People's Government of Guanzhou Municipality. https://www.gz.gov.cn/gfxwj/qjgfxwj/nsq/qbm/content/post_9340734.html. Accessed 23 Nov 2023
10. Hou, C., Li, E.X., Shentu, C., Chen, R.: Gesture Controlled Claw Machine Conceptual Design (2020)
11. Zhu, Y.: Market development of doll machine and SWOT analysis. Mod. Mark. (Manage. Edn.) (02), 82–83 (2019)
12. Herzberg, F.: One More Time: How Do You Motivate Employees? Harvard Business Review Press (2008)
13. Wang, T.: Research on functional requirement design of university APP based on KANO model. Design **35**(14), 137–140 (2022)
14. Berger, C.: Kano's methods for understanding customer-defined quality. Center Qual. Manage. J. **2**(4), 3–36 (1993)

Neural Correlates of Robot Personality Perception: An fNIRS Study

Yikai Wang, Fengyuan Liu, and Xin Lei[(⊠)]

School of Management, Zhejiang University of Technology, Hangzhou, China
leixin@zjut.edu.cn

Abstract. Robot personality design has garnered research interest for its crucial role in enhancing the robot's social capabilities and promoting user experience. This study aims to use machine learning classification techniques to predict the personality of a robot by analyzing the neural activities in the prefrontal cortex (PFC) when individuals interact with the robot that features a specific personality design (i.e., extroverted or introverted). We recruited 64 participants and divided them into two groups to interact with an extroverted or introverted robot. We collected data using a functional near-infrared spectroscopy (fNIRS) device and, after data preprocessing, selected signal means as features for analysis. After applying six machine learning methods for data classification, we found significant differences in the performance of different classifiers. In addition, we observed that personality classification based on left and right brain data showed different performance. According to the results, we can determine the type of robot personality with which users are interacting based on the medial PFC activities during user–robot interactions.

Keywords: Robot Personality · Machine Learning · Prefrontal Cortex · fNIRS

1 Introduction

In today's era of rapid technological advancement, robots have become an indispensable part of our daily lives. With the maturing of robotic technologies, there is an increasing focus not only on the functional aspects of robots as tools [1] but also on their personalities and emotional dimensions as interactive partners [2]. The design of robot personalities has emerged as a key area, impacting users' perceptions and interaction experiences with robots, as well as indirectly influencing their psychological and cognitive processes [3]. Against this backdrop, the concept of Kansei Engineering (KE) becomes particularly important [4] in robot design. This means considering the robot's appearance, voice, behavior, and interaction style with users to evoke positive emotional responses and deeper emotional connections.

In the field of KE, it is increasingly important to use scientific and objective methods to understand and quantify users' emotional and cognitive responses, as opposed to relying solely on subjective feedback from users. Functional Near-Infrared Spectroscopy (fNIRS) technology demonstrates unique and powerful advantages in this regard [5]. This

P.-L. P. Rau (Ed.): HCII 2024, LNCS 14702, pp. 332–344, 2024.
https://doi.org/10.1007/978-3-031-60913-8_23

technology is particularly suited for monitoring activities in the prefrontal cortex (PFC), especially considering the PFC's central role in processing emotions, social interactions, and complex decision-making [6]. The use of fNIRS allows researchers to more precisely understand the emotional and cognitive states of users during interactions with robots, which is particularly important for designing robots intended to evoke specific emotional responses. For example, by measuring the PFC activity of users while observing different design elements (like shape, robot behavior), researchers can determine which elements most effectively elicit positive emotional responses [7].

This study focuses on the variations in the PFC activity of users interacting with robots featured different personalities. We employ fNIRS technology to capture these activities and use machine learning algorithms to classify and predict the robot personality based on fNIRS data. Through this approach, we can identify brain activation patterns associated with different robot personality traits, gaining deeper insights into the psychological and emotional dynamics of human–robot interaction. This not only offers a new perspective for robot design but also provides significant scientific evidence for enhancing the quality and efficiency of human–robot interaction.

2 Related Work

2.1 Neural Basis for Emotional Responses

In addition to subjective reports from users, a more objective and persuasive way to understand human emotions towards design is through physiological data provided by neuroscience [8]. Neuroscience plays a key role in understanding the cognitive processes of humans in response to design, offering researchers a deeper insight into the physiological basis of human perception and reaction [8]. By incorporating methods of neuroscience, researchers can explore how the brain responds to stimuli and further understand the connections between elements and emotions or cognition. Widely used neuroimaging techniques in neuroscience research, such as functional magnetic resonance imaging (fMRI), electroencephalography (EEG), and fNIRS, enable researchers to capture the spatiotemporal dynamics of brain activity [9]. With these technologies, the mysterious brain becomes more interpretable.

Among these neuroimaging techniques, near-infrared technology is a common non-invasive optical imaging method that utilizes near-infrared light penetrating biological tissues and being absorbed by blood within the tissue. By monitoring these absorption characteristics, physiological information such as blood flow and oxygenation levels can be obtained [10]. The application of near-infrared technology in KE research primarily lies in recording human physiological responses to different design types. By monitoring participants' brain oxygenation levels, researchers can gain important information about the impact of stimulus elements on brain activity. For instance, when participants are exposed to specific design stimuli, researchers can quantitatively assess changes in physiological states in response to design stimuli, thereby understanding the impact of design elements on human perception [11]. Hu et al. [5] also used fNIRS to record frontal lobe neural activity to identify different types of positive emotions. Bandara et al. [12] used deep learning methods and fNIRS technique to analyze cortical activation in participants to predict emotions.

In specific brain regions involved in human social responses, the PFC, especially the medial PFC (mPFC), plays a crucial role in human social cognition and behavior [13]. The mPFC is thought to be primarily involved in processing, representing, and integrating social and emotional information [13, 14], as well as performing cognitive functions [15]. Similarly, previous research [16] using fNIRS to study infant brain activity demonstrated the role of mPFC in social-emotional aspects, and previous studies have shown that the mPFC is associated with depression [17, 18] and anxiety [19]. Moreover, recent research has revealed functional lateralization between the left and right mPFC.

Studies have shown that the left mPFC is instrumental in emotion regulation and coping with stress. Li [20] suggested that dysfunction in the left mPFC could lead to the development of emotional and anxiety disorders, and the activity of the left mPFC predominantly mediates the conversion of the impact of social defeat stress into social behaviors. Other studies have found that, depending on stimulation of the right mPFC, the left mPFC appears capable of suppressing the occurrence of negative outcomes related to stress [21]. In contrast, the right mPFC appears to be more important in various functions, such as processing negative emotions and risk assessment [21]. The right mPFC is believed to play a role in social and decision-making processes, especially in contexts involving negative stimuli [22]. Interestingly, the functioning of the left mPFC seems to be partially dependent on the activity of the right mPFC, and this interaction between the left and right mPFC is crucial for balancing emotional responses and social behaviors, playing complementary roles in emotional behavior [21, 23].

2.2 Robot Personality Design

In Human–Robot Interaction (HRI), the design of robot personality is a crucial area. It involves tailoring the robot's behavior patterns, communication styles, and emotional expressions according to specific application scenarios and user needs, aiming to create more natural, effective, and enjoyable interaction experiences [24]. Traditional personality theories, such as the Big Five personality traits model, are widely applied in robot design to enhance interactions and user experience [25]. In practical applications, specific robots have been deployed in settings like education and healthcare, making humans feel comfortable and accepted [26]. Simultaneously, a robot's personality traits also influence users' trust and willingness to cooperate [27].

Previous studies in the HRI field have shown that both personality similarity and complementary attraction effects are valid. Aly and Tapus [28] combined verbal and non-verbal behaviors and found that humans prefer robots that express a personality similar to their own. However, other research [29] has found that people might prefer robots with complementary personalities over those similar to their own. Despite this, studies have observed that people generally tend to interact more with extroverted robots [30, 31]. However, the factors that influence people's preferences are multidimensional, and many studies simplify these factors because it is challenging to implement aspects such as race and attitude in robots. When limited to the introversion-extroversion dimension, some scholars conducted research by combining verbal and non-verbal behaviors, but the results have not found a significant correlation with the similarity attraction effect [3]. As a result, there is currently no unified way to measure individual preferences for extroverted or introverted robots.

2.3 Research Questions of This Study

In interpersonal interactions, different personality traits uniquely affect our brain activity and behavioral responses [32]. Similarly, when these traits are present in robots, they may uniquely influence the patterns of human brain responses. Studying this phenomenon not only deepens our understanding of how the human brain processes social information but also provides scientific evidence for designing more engaging and effective human–robot interactions. With the continuous advancement of machine learning technology, we have more tools to analyze complex datasets, including brain imaging data. By utilizing these technologies, we can attempt to extract useful information from brain activity data generated during human–robot interactions, thereby understanding and predicting human responses to robots more accurately.

For instance, Szabóová et al. [33] improved robots' understanding of emotions by using various machine learning methods to perform emotion detection on textual data obtained from human–robot interactions. Javed and Park [34] identified children at risk of autism spectrum disorders by analyzing behavioral data extracted from videos of children interacting with robots. This analysis not only helps optimize the behavior and personality traits of robots but also enhances their naturalness and effectiveness in application scenarios. Therefore, this study aims to answer the following key question:

- RQ1. How do introverted and extroverted robot personalities affect the activity patterns of users' PFC, and how do different machine learning techniques perform in recognizing robot personalities?

The left and right hemispheres of the prefrontal cortex may exhibit different characteristics and functions in processing information [35], which is a topic of widespread interest in neuroscience research. Therefore, to more comprehensively understand brain activity in human–robot interactions, it is necessary to consider the left and right medial PFC separately. This distinction may reveal differences in the activity patterns of the human brain's left and right hemispheres when interacting with robots with different personality traits. Moreover, this exploration is also significant for understanding how the prefrontal cortex collaborates in complex social interactions. Thus, the study proposes a second key question:

- RQ2. Is there a significant performance difference in personality classification based on left mPFC and right mPFC data?

By exploring these two key research questions, this study aims to deepen our understanding of brain activity in human–robot interactions, particularly the response patterns of the prefrontal cortex in different social contexts, thereby providing more precise and scientific guidance for future robot design and applications.

3 Method

3.1 Task and Procedure

In this study, we developed a robot interaction program using the Choregraphe software. The program enabled the robot to ask questions and provide basic feedback to human users' responses. Participants were informed that they could choose to answer or decline to answer the questions posed by the robot. The specific experimental procedure was as follows: (1) Participants were informed that we were collaborating with a company to develop an intelligent robot, and we had produced a preliminary version for which we sought their opinions and suggestions. If participants agreed to participate, they had to sign an informed consent form; (2) Participants completed the pre-experiment questionnaire about their personality; (3) Participants wore the fNIRS device; (4) Participants engaged in conversations with the robot, having the option to respond to or decline the robot's questions; (5) Participants removed the fNIRS device and received the experimental rewards. The specific flow is shown in Fig. 1.

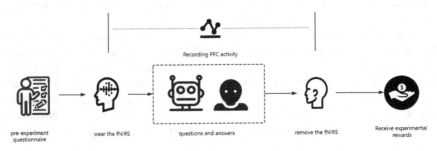

Recording PFC activity

pre-experiment   wear the fNIRS   questions and answers   remove the fNIRS   Receive experimental
questionnaire   rewards

Fig. 1. Experimental flowchart

3.2 Apparatus

In this study, we employed the Nao robot (SoftBank Robotics Group, Japan) and used the Choregraphe software to design two sets of independent behavior control programs. The programs adjusted the robot's tone, volume, speech rate, and movements to manipulate one extroverted and one introverted robot. Additionally, they way to respond to the participant's answer was controlled. When responding to experimental participants, the introverted robot typically gave shorter answers, such as simply saying "Okay" or "Understood," whereas the extroverted Nao's responses were more animated, like "Hmm, I see," "Okay, got it," or "Alright, I understand." Moreover, to capture the participants' brain activity when interacting with the robot, we employed a 19-channel fNIRS system (LABNIRS, Shimadzu, Japan) operated at 42 Hz with wavelengths of 780, 805, and 850 nm. As shown in Fig. 2, this system was specifically set up to monitor the PFC of participants.

3.3 Participants

Before initiating the experiment, we applied the G*Power analysis tool by Faul et al. [36] to estimate the required sample size. This estimation indicated that a minimum of 52 participants were needed to ensure a statistical power of 0.8, in order to observe a significant effect at the 0.05 level of significance. Consequently, we randomly recruited 64 volunteers within the university campus. Participants were randomly assigned into two groups with a balanced gender distribution in each group. One–way ANOVAs revealed

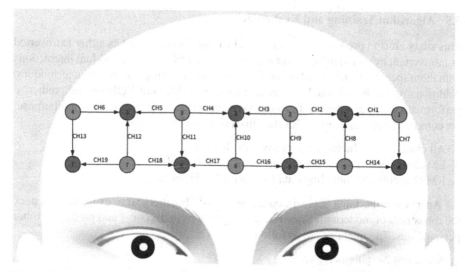

Fig. 2. Placement of the probes and channels. Red circles represent sources. Blue circles represent detectors. CH# represents the channel between a source and a detector (Color figure online).

no significant difference in the age and personality ($p > .05$) between two groups. Before the experiment commenced, we clearly articulated the objectives and procedures of the experiment to all participants and obtained their informed consent. Throughout the research process, we strictly adhered to ethical guidelines and standards, ensuring that the rights of the participants were fully protected.

3.4 Data Preprocessing and Feature Extraction

Preprocessing of fNIRS data was performed using HOMER2 in MATLAB (R2017b). The process involved several steps: converting intensity data to optical density, applying a 0.01 Hz to 0.1 Hz bandpass filter, and transforming optical density data into oxygenated hemoglobin (HbO) concentrations using the modified Beer–Lambert law with a differential path length factor of [6.0 6.0 6.0]. A 50-s baseline was established from 3 min of resting-state data collected prior to task initiation. The study's key metric was the variation in HbO concentration (ΔHbO) during participant interactions with a robot, relative to this baseline. We selected two regions of interest (ROI): the right medial (RM) region covered channels #4, #5, #11, #12, #17, #18; and the left medial (LM) covered channels #2, #3, #8, #9, #15, #16. In fNIRS studies, a variety of statistical features are employed to describe and analyze the data. Among the most frequently used descriptive statistical features are the average signal value, peak amplitude, minimum value, signal skewness, and kurtosis et al. [37]. Among them, choosing the mean as the feature is the most common. In this study, we also pre-tested the features respectively and found that using the mean as the feature showed a better performance than other features, so we mainly selected the signal mean as the extracted feature in this study.

3.5   Algorithm Training and Evaluation

This study aims to predict the personality of robots, characterized as either extroverted or introverted, by analyzing the neural activity in the PFC during individual interactions with these specifically designed robots using machine learning classification techniques. Additionally, we investigated the relative impact of different ROIs on the predictive performance of models derived from various machine learning methods. For this purpose, we compared and analyzed fNIRS data from three different areas:

1. All channels set: Including data from all channels.
2. LM channels set: Including data from the LM channels.
3. RM channels set: Including data from the RM channels.

Apart from the input sets, six commonly used classifiers were evaluated to check the robustness of modern machine learning algorithms in decoding and predicting robot personalities. The methods are as follows:

1. K-Nearest Neighbors (KNN);
2. Random Forest (RF);
3. Support Vector Machine (SVM);
   a. SVMRad: SVM with a Radial Basis Function kernel;
   b. SVMLin: SVM with a Linear kernel;
4. Decision Tree (DT);
5. Naïve Bayes (NB);
6. Artificial Neural Network (ANN).

All algorithms were implemented using functions from the caret package in MAT-LAB (R2022b). In evaluating the performance of classifiers, several key metrics are typically considered, including accuracy, precision, recall, and F1 score. These metrics are calculated based on four fundamental concepts: true positives (TP), false positives (FP), true negatives (TN), and false negatives (FN). Reporting any single metric alone cannot fully reflect the behavior of a classifier. It is crucial to comprehensively assess these metrics for a complete understanding of a classifier's performance.

Accuracy describes the proportion of correctly classified samples, i.e., the ratio of all correctly classified samples to the total number of samples. Precision focuses on the proportion of true positive samples among those predicted as positive, with higher precision indicating fewer false positives. Recall reflects the proportion of all true positive samples that were correctly identified, with higher recall indicating fewer false negatives. The F1 score is the harmonic mean of precision and recall, attempting to balance the two while considering both. This is particularly important in imbalanced data situations, as it is not affected by a large number of negative class samples.

4   Results

Different machine learning approaches show varying effectiveness in robot personality prediction (see Fig. 3): Support Vector Machine (SVM) with radial basis (Rad, accuracy $67.3 \pm 5\%$) and linear kernels (Lin, accuracy $74.7 \pm 10.9\%$), K-Nearest Neighbors (KNN, accuracy $71.9 \pm 8.9\%$), Random Forest (RF, accuracy $70.1 \pm 12.6\%$), Naive

Bayes (NB, accuracy 70.3 ± 10.1%), Decision Trees (DT, accuracy 64.1 ± 8.8%), and Artificial Neural Networks (ANN, accuracy 66.9 ± 1.0%). In these models, the SVMLin demonstrated the highest average accuracy, followed by the RF and NB model. This suggests that methods based on SVM may be more suitable for this task. Although ANN theoretically is well-suited for complex classification tasks, in this study, its average accuracy was slightly lower than the optimal SVM model. The DT model performed poorly, which could be due to a mismatch between the model's simplifying assumptions and the complexity of the data.

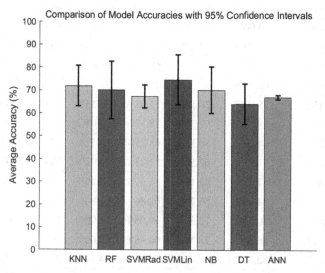

Fig. 3. Algorithm average Accuracy arranged by input measures and ML approach. ML = machine learning; KNN = K-Nearest Neighbor; RF = Random Forest; SVMRad = Support Vector Machine with a radial kernel function; SVMLin = Support Vector Machine with a linear kernel function;DT = Decision Tree; NB = Naïve Bayes; ANN = Artificial Neural Network.

In order to further explore the performance of different classifiers in predicting robot personality in different ROIs, we selected multiple metrics to evaluate. Table 1 presents the detailed results. The results show that the SVMLin algorithm performs optimally on LM channels, with an accuracy of up to 75.00%, and exhibits higher F1 scores in the prediction of extroverted (E) and introverted (I) types (0.74 for E class and 0.70 for I class). This indicates that the SVMLin algorithm is more adept at achieving a balanced performance in predicting types E and I when processing LM channels. In contrast, the SVMRad algorithm shows relatively weaker performance across all channels.

Further analysis reveals that most algorithms perform better on the RM channels than on the LM channels. Data obtained from the RM channels generally shows higher accuracy and recall rates compared to the LM channels, and RM also outperforms LM in predicting extroverted personalities. This may suggest that RM channel data provides more critical information for robot personality prediction. Additionally, significant differences are observed in the precision and recall rates of different algorithms, especially in the prediction of specific personality types. For example, the KNN algorithm demonstrates higher precision in the introverted category across all channels (78.12%), but with a correspondingly lower recall rate (65.79%).

Table 1. Performance comparison based on four metrics of the machine learning models

Model	Channels	Accuracy	Precision		Recall		F1-Score	
			E	I	E	I	E	I
SVMRad	ALL	62.50%	68.75%	56.25%	61.11%	64.29%	0.65	0.60
	LM	64.06%	59.38%	68.75%	65.52%	62.86%	0.62	0.66
	RM	71.88%	78.12%	65.62%	69.44%	75.00%	0.74	0.70
SVMLin	ALL	73.44%	78.12%	68.75%	71.43%	75.86%	0.75	0.72
	LM	68.75%	62.50%	75.00%	71.43%	66.67%	0.67	0.71
	RM	75.00%	78.12%	71.88%	73.53%	76.67%	0.74	0.70
KNN	ALL	68.75%	59.38%	78.12%	73.08%	65.79%	0.66	0.71
	LM	64.09%	59.38%	68.75%	65.52%	62.89%	0.62	0.66
	RM	71.88%	62.50%	81.25%	76.92%	68.42%	0.69	0.74
RF	ALL	67.18%	68.10%	66.67%	72.46%	68.00%	0.66	0.66
	LM	64.23%	65.24%	62.86%	62.86%	65.52%	0.64	0.64
	RM	70.51%	72.38%	69.05%	71.00%	71.45%	0.71	0.70
NB	ALL	68.97%	78.57%	60.48%	67.00%	76.10%	0.71	0.66
	LM	62.29%	69.05%	57.14%	64.14%	61.90%	0.65	0.57
	RM	70.64%	76.19%	66.19%	69.57%	74.50%	0.72	0.69
DT	ALL	62.44%	69.52%	55.24%	62.06%	63.81%	0.65	0.58
	LM	65.38%	68.10%	61.43%	66.93%	65.56%	0.66	0.61
	RM	68.97%	68.57%	69.52%	71.19%	69.10%	0.69	0.69
ANN	ALL	69.07%	76.38%	61.29%	67.74%	70.91%	0.72	0.66
	LM	60.21%	69.10%	50.80%	59.78%	60.85%	0.64	0.55
	RM	60.44%	75.76%	44.22%	58.99%	63.31%	0.66	0.52

5 Discussion

This study explores the neural correlates of robot personality perception, particularly using fNIRS technology and machine learning classification methods to study the activity patterns of the PFC during human interactions with robots possessing different personality traits (introverted or extroverted). Our results reveal that there are differences in the mPFC activation patterns when users interact with robots of varying personalities. We found that the svmLin algorithm demonstrated higher accuracy and F1 scores across all channels, RM channels, and LM channels, particularly on the RM channels. Compared to other algorithms such as SVMRad, KNN, RF, NB, DT, and ANN, SVMLin was more effective in processing mPFC activity data.

The performance of most algorithms was better on RM channels than on LM channels, suggesting that the RM channels might play a more significant role in robot personality classification. Studies like [22] observed profound abnormalities in emotional processing and personality among individuals with unilateral lesions to the right mPFC; in contrast, those with unilateral lesions to the left mPFC exhibited normal emotional process, with their personalities remaining unchanged. Additionally, Blonder et al. [38] observed that individuals with damage to the right hemisphere exhibited poorer performance in emotionally judging sentences depicting facial, prosodic, and gestural expressions compared to those with left hemisphere damage. This implies a disturbance in the representation of nonverbal communicative expressions. In this study, the personality differences in extroverted and introverted robots were primarily manifested in their voice and gestures, which are closely associated with the functions of the right hemisphere. To some extent, this can explain why the RM channels perform better.

Earlier research majorly depended on users' subjective perceptions of robot personality, gathered through surveys or interviews, to capture feelings, preferences, and reactions for personality studies. Our study employed fNIRS technology to directly measure and analyze human brain activity during interactions with robots, and then used machine learning algorithms to process and analyze the fNIRS data to predict the personality types of robots. These findings theoretically strengthen the importance of machine learning in human–robot interaction research, especially in interpreting brain activity and behavioral data. From a practical standpoint, improving prediction accuracy through algorithm optimization can enable robots to better adapt to users' emotional and cognitive states, thereby enhancing user experience. This research provides vital guidance for developing robots capable of adapting to users' emotional states. Future research can expand the sample size and explore different types and traits of robots for a more comprehensive understanding of human responses to robot personalities. Additionally, further studies can explore the effectiveness of other machine learning techniques in predicting robot personalities and how these techniques can be used to improve robot design to better meet users' needs and preferences.

6 Conclusion

This study illuminates the neural correlates of robot personality perception through fNIRS technology and machine learning classification. Our findings reveal that users' mPFC activation patterns vary when interacting with robots exhibiting different personalities. Significantly, this research accentuates the importance of the right mPFC in processing emotions and cognitive responses in social contexts. These insights are invaluable for advancing robot personality design, aiming to optimize robots' adaptability to users' emotional and cognitive states. Future research should delve further into the specific roles of various brain areas in human-robot interactions, paving the way for more intuitive and effective social robots.

Acknowledgements. This work was supported by Natural Science Foundation of Zhejiang Province [LQ24G010005].

Disclosure of Interests. The authors have no competing interests to declare that are relevant to the content of this article.

References

1. Zhou, H., Wang, X., Au, W., Kang, H., Chen, C.: Intelligent robots for fruit harvesting: recent developments and future challenges. Precision Agric. **23**, 1856–1907 (2022). https://doi.org/10.1007/s11119-022-09913-3
2. Paetzel-Prüsmann, M., Perugia, G., Castellano, G.: The Influence of robot personality on the development of uncanny feelings. Comput. Hum. Behav. **120**, 106756 (2021). https://doi.org/10.1016/j.chb.2021.106756
3. Esteban, P.G., et al.: Should i be introvert or extrovert? a pairwise robot comparison assessing the perception of personality-based social robot behaviors. Int J of Soc Robotics. **14**, 115–125 (2022). https://doi.org/10.1007/s12369-020-00715-z
4. Nagamachi, M.: Kansei engineering: a new ergonomic consumer-oriented technology for product development. Int. J. Ind. Ergon. **15**, 3–11 (1995). https://doi.org/10.1016/0169-8141(94)00052-5
5. Hu, X., Zhuang, C., Wang, F., Liu, Y.-J., Im, C.-H., Zhang, D.: fNIRS evidence for recognizably different positive emotions. Front. Hum. Neurosci. **13**, 120 (2019)
6. Dixon, M., Thiruchselvam, R., Todd, R., Christoff, K.: Emotion and the prefrontal cortex: an integrative review. Psychol. Bull. **143**(10), 1033–1081 (2017). https://doi.org/10.1037/bul0000096
7. Yorgancigil, E., Yildirim, F., Urgen, B.A., Erdogan, S.B.: An exploratory analysis of the neural correlates of human-robot interactions with functional near infrared spectroscopy. Front. Hum. Neurosci. **16**, 883905 (2022)
8. Camerer, C., Loewenstein, G., Prelec, D.: Neuroeconomics: how neuroscience can inform economics. J. Econ. Lit. **43**, 9–64 (2005). https://doi.org/10.1257/0022051053737843
9. Zhu, G., Jiang, B., Tong, L., Xie, Y., Zaharchuk, G., Wintermark, M.: Applications of deep learning to neuro-imaging techniques. Front. Neurol. **10**, 869 (2019). https://doi.org/10.3389/fneur.2019.00869
10. Kumar, V., Shivakumar, V., Chhabra, H., Bose, A., Venkatasubramanian, G., Gangadhar, B.N.: Functional near infra-red spectroscopy (fNIRS) in schizophrenia: a review. Asian J. Psychiatr. **27**, 18–31 (2017). https://doi.org/10.1016/j.ajp.2017.02.009
11. Zhou, L., Wu, B., Deng, Y., Liu, M.: Brain activation and individual differences of emotional perception and imagery in healthy adults: a functional near-infrared spectroscopy (fNIRS) study. Neurosci. Lett. **797**, 137072 (2023). https://doi.org/10.1016/j.neulet.2023.137072
12. Bandara, D., Hirshfield, L., Velipasalar, S.: Classification of affect using deep learning on brain blood flow data. J. Near Infrared Spectrosc. **27**, 206–219 (2019). https://doi.org/10.1177/0967033519837986
13. Wood, J.N., Grafman, J.: Human prefrontal cortex: processing and representational perspectives. Nat. Rev. Neurosci. **4**, 139–147 (2003). https://doi.org/10.1038/nrn1033
14. Gao, W., et al.: Evidence on the emergence of the brain's default network from 2-week-old to 2-year-old healthy pediatric subjects. Proc. Natl. Acad. Sci. **106**, 6790–6795 (2009). https://doi.org/10.1073/pnas.0811221106

15. Yuan, P., Raz, N.: Prefrontal cortex and executive functions in healthy adults: a meta-analysis of structural neuroimaging studies. Neurosci. Biobehav. Rev. **42**, 180–192 (2014). https://doi.org/10.1016/j.neubiorev.2014.02.005

16. Grossmann, T.: The role of medial prefrontal cortex in early social cognition. Front. Hum. Neurosci. **7**, 340 (2013)

17. Lim, G., Kim, H.: Distinctive roles of mPFC subregions in forming impressions and guiding social interaction based on others' social behaviour. Soc. Cogn. Affect. Neurosci. **17**, 1118–1130 (2022). https://doi.org/10.1093/scan/nsac037

18. Xu, H., et al.: A disinhibitory microcircuit mediates conditioned social fear in the prefrontal cortex. Neuron **102**, 668-682.e5 (2019). https://doi.org/10.1016/j.neuron.2019.02.026

19. Déziel, R.A., Tasker, R.A.: Bilateral Ischaemic lesions of the medial prefrontal cortex are Anxiogenic in the rat. Acta Neuropsychiatrica **30**, 181–186 (2018). https://doi.org/10.1017/neu.2017.32

20. Lee, E., Hong, J., Park, Y.-G., Chae, S., Kim, Y., Kim, D.: Left brain cortical activity modulates stress effects on social behavior. Sci. Rep. **5**, 13342 (2015). https://doi.org/10.1038/srep13342

21. Cerqueira, J.J., Almeida, O.F.X., Sousa, N.: The stressed prefrontal cortex. Left? Right!. Brain Behav. Immun. **22**, 630–638 (2008). https://doi.org/10.1016/j.bbi.2008.01.005

22. Tranel, D., Bechara, A., Denburg, N.L.: Asymmetric functional roles of right and left ventromedial prefrontal cortices in social conduct, decision-making, and emotional processing. Cortex **38**, 589–612 (2002). https://doi.org/10.1016/S0010-9452(08)70024-8

23. Gainotti, G., Caltagirone, C., Zoccolotti, P.: Left/right and cortical/subcortical dichotomies in the neuropsychological study of human emotions. Cogn. Emot. **7**, 71–93 (1993). https://doi.org/10.1080/02699939308409178

24. Kato, T.: Kansei Robotics: bridging human beings and electronic gadgets through Kansei engineering. In: 2013 International Conference on Biometrics and Kansei Engineering, pp. 327–331. IEEE, Tokyo, Japan (2013). https://doi.org/10.1109/ICBAKE.2013.88

25. Reeves, B., Nass, C.: The Media Equation: How People Treat Computers, Television, and New Media Like Real People and Pla. Bibliovault OAI Repository, the University of Chicago Press (1996)

26. Dautenhahn, K.: Socially intelligent robots: dimensions of human–robot interaction. Philos. Trans. R. Soc. B: Biol. Sci. **362**, 679–704 (2007). https://doi.org/10.1098/rstb.2006.2004

27. Song, Y., Tao, D., Luximon, Y.: In robot we trust? The effect of emotional expressions and contextual cues on anthropomorphic trustworthiness. Appl. Ergon. **109**, 103967 (2023). https://doi.org/10.1016/j.apergo.2023.103967

28. Aly, A., Tapus, A.: Towards an intelligent system for generating an adapted verbal and nonverbal combined behavior in human–robot interaction. Auton. Robot. **40**, 193–209 (2016). https://doi.org/10.1007/s10514-015-9444-1

29. Lee, K.M., Peng, W., Jin, S.-A., Yan, C.: Can robots manifest personality?: An empirical test of personality recognition, social responses, and social presence in human-robot interaction. J. Commun. **56**, 754–772 (2006). https://doi.org/10.1111/j.1460-2466.2006.00318.x

30. Esterwood, C., Robert, L.P.: A systematic review of human and robot personality in health care human-robot interaction. Front. Robot. AI **8**, 748246 (2021)

31. Kaplan, A.D., Sanders, T., Hancock, P.A.: The relationship between extroversion and the tendency to anthropomorphize robots: a bayesian analysis. Front. Robot. AI. **5**, 135 (2019)

32. Mulders, P., Llera, A., Tendolkar, I., van Eijndhoven, P., Beckmann, C.: Personality profiles are associated with functional brain networks related to cognition and emotion. Sci. Rep. **8**, 13874 (2018). https://doi.org/10.1038/s41598-018-32248-x

33. Szabóová, M., Sarnovský, M., Maslej Krešňáková, V., Machová, K.: Emotion analysis in human-robot interaction. Electronics **9**, 1761 (2020). https://doi.org/10.3390/electronics9111761

34. Javed, H., Park, C.H.: Behavior-based risk detection of autism spectrum disorder through child-robot interaction. In: Companion of the 2020 ACM/IEEE International Conference on Human-Robot Interaction, pp. 275–277. ACM, Cambridge United Kingdom (2020). https://doi.org/10.1145/3371382.3378382

35. Friedman, N.P., Robbins, T.W.: The role of prefrontal cortex in cognitive control and executive function. Neuropsychopharmacol. **47**, 72–89 (2022). https://doi.org/10.1038/s41386-021-011 32-0

36. Faul, F., Erdfelder, E., Lang, A.-G., Buchner, A.: G*Power 3: a flexible statistical power analysis program for the social, behavioral, and biomedical sciences. Behav. Res. Methods **39**, 175–191 (2007). https://doi.org/10.3758/BF03193146

37. Khan, H., Noori, F.M., Yazidi, A., Uddin, M.Z., Khan, M.N.A., Mirtaheri, P.: Classification of individual finger movements from right hand using fNIRS signals. Sensors **21**, 7943 (2021). https://doi.org/10.3390/s21237943

38. Blonder, L., Bowers, D., Heilman, K.: The role of the right hemisphere in emotional communication. Brain **114**(Pt 3), 1115–1127 (1991). https://doi.org/10.1093/brain/114.3.1115

Research on Interactive Narrative Design of Immersive Image from AI Perspective

Shuaishuai Wang[⊠]

College of Design and Innovation, Tongji University, Shanghai, China
0620xiaoshuai@163.com

Abstract. The advent of the AI era heralds the innovation and subversion of image technologies and concepts highly related to science and technology. Before the rise of AIGC, the transmission of information through traditional image narrative means has certain limitations in the perceptual interaction between people and images. This paper studies the new mechanism and application scenarios of AIGC image interactive narrative. Through literature analysis, interview and other methods, this paper conducts observation experiments on specific practical cases, proposes the characteristics of immersive image interactive narrative mechanism, and explains that with the help of virtual reality, hologram and other presentation technologies, image interaction can have a more optimized interactive immersive experience. This paper has done some research on cross-culture, cross-domain and ethics, and has some thoughts and prospects in AIGC enabling immersive image interactive narrative.

Keywords: AIGC · Immersive Image · Interactive Narrative

1 Introduction

Immersive image interactive narrative design combines artificial intelligence technology with immersive image, and creates an immersive, intelligent and personalized movie-watching experience with the help of augmented reality, virtual reality and other technical means, which is an emerging visual art form.

Immersion is a state of mental focus so intense that awareness of the "real" world is lost, generally resulting in a feeling of joy and satisfaction [1]. Immersive imaging, usually refers to the use of virtual reality technology, through virtual reality (VR), augmented reality (AR) or mixed reality (MR) and other wearable devices in a virtual environment to simulate immersive reality, such as immersive movies(see Fig. 1); Another form of immersive image is to build a digital art scene, apply holographic stereo image and projection technology to integrate the interaction between the audience and the environment, and deepen the immersive experience of the real space, such as immersive art exhibition, immersive drama, virtual performance and so on(see Fig. 2).

P.-L. P. Rau (Ed.): HCII 2024, LNCS 14702, pp. 345–359, 2024.
https://doi.org/10.1007/978-3-031-60913-8_24

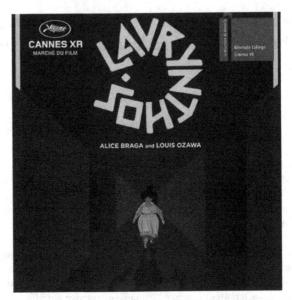

Fig. 1. Lavrynthos – A immersive movie selected for the 75th Cannes Film Festival XR Immersive Imaging Unit

Fig. 2. A scene of TeamLab Borderless

1.1 Introduction to Immersive Images

In the era of new media, image information has become an important way for us to connect with the world. The emergence of immersive image, as a unique form of artistic presentation, provides us with a completely different visual experience. With the continuous progress of science and technology, the discussion about the authenticity of images is also constantly evolving. Different from the image dimensions of traditional paper media, television and film, immersive image can provide a 360-degree all-round perspective. It simulates a variety of human senses through digital technology, such as picture, sound, touch, smell and movement, so that the audience can feel the real vision, hearing, touch, taste and dynamics in the virtual world.

Immersive imaging technology makes the experience more realistic in terms of perception. In terms of visual experience, viewers can view immersive images from any Angle. In terms of auditory experience, immersive images can simulate real environmental sounds through stereo sound effects, so that the audience seems to be in the image. In terms of tactile experience, objects in immersive images can be sensed through virtual reality wearables. In terms of spatial experience, immersive images set a variety of complex spatial image structures, and the audience will experience different spaces through movement in a certain space. In this way, the user or the audience can see the color of the object, feel its texture, hear its movement, smell, etc., and create a comprehensive and true feeling with some other materials different from the real thing.

This immersive experience not only transcends the perception of traditional two-dimensional images, but also transcends our sensory experiences in daily life. A large number of audiovisual wonders, non-life scenes through the interpretation of immersive images, as if immersive existence. Therefore, although the immersive image is a virtual world created by digital image technology, it does bring a sense of reality to the audience.

1.2 Features of Immersive Image Interactive Narrative Design

Authenticity. There are two kinds of authenticity mentioned in immersive image: one is objective authenticity, that is, whether the things reflected by the image are the same material world; The other is perceptual authenticity, that is, whether the viewer feels real when watching the image. For an immersive image, because it is simulated by technical means, it is not the real world from the point of view of objective material reality. However, from the perspective of perceived authenticity, immersive images bring the audience a very real experience.

Embodiment. Merleau-Ponty believed that "the body is our anchorage in a world "[2]. Like immersive images, the audience has a strong sense of presence. It means that the body, as a medium, will have a richer sensory experience than merely audio-visual immersive. It surpasses people's experience of images in the past, and also provides new possibilities in artistic creation. For example, the development of immersive video also reflects the continuous progress of media technology, immersive image may be like "Ready Player One" in the scene, to create a more realistic all-round experience.

Change the Way You Get Information. "The 'mimicry environment' created by virtual reality technology breaks the 'fourth wall' between the narrator and the viewer, allowing the viewer to directly place themselves in the required time and space."[3] It changes the way we access information. In the past, when we look at an image, the body is outside the image, often as a spectator, but immersive images allow us to feel that we are in the scene, which deepens our understanding of the content of the image. At the same time, it increases our entertainment options, immersive images often present a large number of wonders and different scenes, greatly beyond the reality of life, to meet the emotional needs of the audience.

New Video Narrative Logic. Montage is the basic principle of traditional film narration. It combines a series of footage clips into a continuous image with narrative function. Bazin, a film theorist, believes that the segmented reorganization of montage is disrespectful to the noumenon of life, while the long shot becomes the narrative technique of documentary film, and the two techniques complement each other. However, immersive image narration subverts the traditional image narration rules. In the past, the audience watched the scene from the perspective designed by the creator according to the arranged narrative mode, while the immersive film pays more attention to the display of the scene in a space, and uses the depth lens to adjust the distance to keep the audience within the narrative frame. The narrative pilot of immersive image follows the audience's line of sight, and tells the story where the audience's line of sight reaches. So it's usually experienced from a first-person perspective. Immersive images should not frequently switch scenes, otherwise it will cause vertigo and ruin the experience.

Spatial Expansiveness. The immersive image uses virtual reality technology to create an extended effect of space, or builds a digital art scene to create a naked-eye 3D to achieve the effect of space extension and superposition. The immersive image using virtual reality technology, no matter how grand the scene, can be experienced in a small space with wearable devices, greatly expanding the activity space and thought space in the virtual form, bringing people more imagination and fun.

Interactivity. In the immersive image, the audience becomes the participant from the viewer, and can participate in controlling the picture and process of the image by operating the wearable device or generating movement changes. Some immersive images send out acoustic and photoelectric signals to provide hints. The immersive image digital scene usually has multiple devices and equipment in a certain area, and the audience can swim in it and interact with the devices to enhance the aesthetic experience of active appreciation. The audience constantly gives feedback and interacts with the image during the participation.

1.3   Key Technologies of Immersive Image Interactive Narrative Design

The key technologies of immersive image interactive narrative design mainly include 3D modeling and rendering technology, natural human-computer interaction technology, emotional computing and psychological modeling technology.

3D modeling and rendering technology is the foundation. Through the digital modeling of the real world, the virtual scene can be quickly constructed and rendered in real time. Commonly used modeling software include Maya, 3ds Max, etc., rendering engines include Unreal Engine, Unity, etc.

Natural human-computer interaction technology is one of the core elements. Through the human body sensor to capture the user's voice, expression, gesture, expression and other information, to achieve real-time control and feedback of the virtual environment, and then simulate the natural human communication. At present, the commonly used natural human-computer interaction technologies include Oculus Touch, Kinect, Leap Motion and so on.

Emotional computing and psychological modeling technology is an important part, is the key to emotion expression, emotion recognition and human-computer emotional interaction, so that machines can recognize, understand and express all kinds of emotions like people, and have emotional communication and interaction with people. At present, the commonly used affective computing methods include physiological signal monitoring, facial expression recognition, etc. Psychological modeling methods include self-efficacy, episodic memory, etc.

1.4 Cases of Immersive Image Interactive Narrative Design

Taking the XR Immersive Image China Offline screening event of the 2022 Cannes Film Festival as an example, some works selected from the 18 VR works shortlisted in the Cannes XR unit will be shown in the offline space, including "Lavrynthos", "Luna: Episode 1 -- Left Behind", "Area Man Lives", "Clap", "The Passengers", "Alex Honnold: The Soloist VR", etc.so on.

These works also have their own characteristics, such as the excellent experience of "Lavrynthos" created by the Brazilian team, which gives full play to the spatial positioning function of the integrated machine in the physical space of 2*2 m, and the experiencers start the narrative content while walking. "Luna: Episode 1 - Left Behind" features voice interaction, with the narrative advancing and evolving through conversations between the robot, played by the experiencer, and the girl. Also featuring voice interaction, "Area Man Lives" features experiencers playing radio anchors who solve the mysteries facing the town by communicating with callers. Different content will lead to different results. "Clap", created by a Japanese team, showcases the hallmarks of gesture interaction. On the one hand, clapping and applause are the way for the experiencer to interact with the character, and on the other hand, the character can find confidence and dance freely, bringing the experiencer a sense of participation and gain. "The Passengers" integrates the features of VR voice interaction, controller interaction and viewpoint focus, etc. In the work, four train passengers have different thoughts and opinions on the surrounding affairs, and the experients can substitute the four characters and make different expressions through dialogues and eyes. Documentary "Alex Honnold: The Soloist VR" is the best VR narrative film in Cannes XR in 2022. Unlike traditional documentaries that simply record time and space, the audience of the film chooses the Angle of observation and intervention as bystanders, following the protagonist Alex to feel the precipitously dramatic nature, experience the thrill of free climbing, and admire the courage of free climbers. Imagine what a wonderful experience we would have with the help of 360-degree panoramic video, standing on the perilous peaks and cliffs, looking around at the stunning scenery.

2 AIGC and Immersive Image Interactive Narrative Design

AIGC, or Artificial Intelligence Generated Content, marks AI's entry into the 2.0 era. Art and creation, which were originally one of the areas least associated with AI, have now seen breakthrough developments. As long as the information is entered, it can generate a large number of text, pictures, video content, and generate images through algorithms and deep learning, providing a new possibility for immersive images.

In the AI vision, traditional shooting technology and lens language are no longer used to shoot images for narrative purposes, but AI is used to generate videos. The audience has become the creator of art from the ordinary art appreciator and viewer. AI has enabled the creation of images to a large extent, such as the construction of 3D models, virtual scenes, videos, etc., to provide a richer visual experience for the audience. AI also provides real-time intelligent interaction, and the audience interacts with the image through voice, text, behavior and action, enhancing the wisdom of the immersive image. In addition, AIGC can also push personalized immersive images according to the user's habits.

2.1   Technical Points and Difficulties of Image Generation by AIGC

The main technical points of AIGC image generation include Transformer, SSL, VAE, GAN, Diffusion and so on. As a neural network architecture model, Transformer can be used to recognize images and process natural language. SSL is a supervised learning algorithm that is trained on unlabeled data to improve performance through unlabeled and labeled data. VAE is an encoder that can compress data into low dimensional space and decode it into new data; GAN is a generative adversarial network that can generate content such as pictures and videos. Diffusion can be used for image generation style transfer.

In addition, there are key frame generation, video training acceleration, generative models, technological developments, and commercial landing challenges.

Key Frame Generation. This is the core of image generation, which requires a diffusion model to approximate the distribution of key frames in low-dimensional potential space. For example, Magic Video technology approximates the distribution of 16 keyframes in a low-dimensional potential space by using a diffusion model.

Video Training Acceleration. Due to the large amount of video data, it is necessary to adapt the model trained on the image task to the video data. For example, combined with a 3D U-Net decoder with an efficient video distribution adapter and a directed time attention module for video generation.

A Generative Model. With the rapid development of the research in the field of image generation, the generative model based on diffusion has achieved a great breakthrough in effect. This model can generate high-quality images and videos, but it also faces many challenges, such as how to control the style of the generated images and how to generate diverse images.

The Challenges of Technological Development. The technical development direction of AIGC mainly includes rule-based, generation-based adversarial network (GANs), variational autoencoder (VAEs) and diffusion process generation model (diffusion). Each of these technical directions has its own specific difficulties and challenges.

Challenges Brought about by Commercialization. With the continuous breakthrough and iteration of artificial intelligence technology, the industrial development, market reaction and corresponding regulatory requirements of AIGC have also received widespread attention. In the process of commercialization, the AIGC industry is facing many challenges, such as technology maturity, exploration of application scenarios, and innovation of business models.

At the same time, in combination with the interview with Shiqi Zhou, a doctoral candidate in related fields in the College of Design and Innovation of Tongji University, the author believes that AIGC image generation also includes the following technical difficulties in practice:

The Balance between Authenticity and Consistency. The difficulty is that when creating a virtual environment, it is necessary to ensure the realism of the image and the consistency of the narrative content. For example, let's say you're making a virtual reality game set in the Middle Ages. The AI needs to generate realistic medieval castles, villages and costumes. This requires not only high quality image rendering, but also the accuracy of historical details, such as architectural style and costume design must conform to the actual conditions of the Middle Ages. In addition, if the game includes reproductions of historical events, the presentation of those events must also be consistent with the historical record to avoid anachronisms.

Interactive Design. The difficulty is that immersive experiences often require the user to be able to interact with the content. For example, in an immersive educational app, users can explore the solar system through virtual reality. Users can choose different planets to interact with, for example, by clicking on Mars to learn about its surface features, climate conditions, and so on. This interaction requires AI to not only generate accurate images of planets, but also provide information relevant to the user's choices and ensure that this information is presented in a way that is both educational and engaging.

Emotional Engagement and User Experience. The challenge is to create a narrative environment that engages the user emotionally. For example, in an interactive documentary set during World War II, users can experience the lives of people in different countries. The AI-generated content includes war scenes, family life and historical events. In order to enhance emotional engagement, AI needs to adjust the narrative content based on the user's interactive choices, such as the user chooses to follow a soldier's story, the AI generates more background information and experience about the soldier, so that the user feels like they are part of the story.

Technical Limitations. The difficulty is that current AI technology still has limitations in understanding complex human emotions and creating highly complex narrative structures. For example, in an AI-powered movie creation tool, users can enter basic story requirements such as "a story about friendship and sacrifice." AI needs to generate scripts, characters, and scenes based on these requirements. However, due to AI's limited understanding of complex emotions and human behavior, the resulting scripts may lack depth and delicate emotional expression, requiring further polishing and improvement by human screenwriters.

Personalization and Diversity. The challenge is to create personalized narrative experiences for different users, while maintaining the diversity and novelty of the content. For example, on a personalized news aggregation platform, AI recommends news based on a user's reading history and preferences. If a user is particularly interested in technology and politics, AI should not only recommend news in related fields, but also ensure that the news content is diverse and updated, avoiding duplication or stale information. At the same time, AI also needs to introduce new areas that users have not paid attention to but may be interested in from time to time to increase exploration and freshness.

2.2 Application of AIGC in Interactive Narration of Immersive Interactive Images

Scene Narrative. Virtual video scenes generated by AIGC are more realistic, blurring the boundaries between the real world and the virtual world. The experience of the audience as if they were in it can promote the plot development of the image immersive narrative through the high-quality video.

Role and Emotional Narrative. AIGC can generate realistic virtual characters by training diffusion models, which can simulate the expressions, actions and emotions of real people, and can create highly realistic characters. In the immersive image experience, it is as if you are standing in a real world, making the narrative more fascinating.

Dynamic Storytelling. AIGC can participate in dynamic narrative, respond and adjust the plot of video narrative in real time according to user feedback or command input, provide users or viewers with personalized experience and better provide emotional value.

Enhance the Visual Spectacle. AIGC can create a large number of visual wonders, such as entering the content: "astronaut playing the guzheng", "the whole universe is making dumplings", will generate such visual images that are not often seen in ordinary life. Not only that, AIGC also adds visual effects, sound, light and shadow, atmosphere creation, image processing more shocking effects, very eye-catching.

Real-time Interaction of Narrative. AIGC can change the development of the image narrative or change the elements in the scene, and first capture the audience's movement expressions, such as the audience's wave to respond. Or use voice recognition to talk with the audience. In the immersive image, the audience can ask the virtual character to complete the task together. Through the continuous learning of the algorithm, the interactive experience with the audience can be optimized, so that the audience can have a good interaction with the image.

Film and Image Narrative Creation. Movies generated by AIGC, scripts, characters, scene effects and music, which used to cost a lot of manpower and material resources, are within the scope of generation of AIGC. Producers can more quickly create and adjust scripts, scenes, and dialogue to optimize the creative process. In the post-production process of images, AIGC can optimize special effects, scenes, and improve visual effects. AIGC not only plays a role in the game, film and television, entertainment industry, but also involves the media field, bringing new possibilities for the direction of media change.

3   Cross-Cultural, Cross-Domain Interactive Narrative with AIGC Immersive Images

3.1   Cross-Cultural and Interdisciplinary Innovation

Enabled by AIGC, immersive image interactive narrative has the following cross-cultural and cross-field innovations:

The Innovation of Communication Mode. The images generated by AIGC are driving innovation in cross-cultural communication, creating huge development opportunities through the collaboration of immersive image narrative design. For example, "Cezanne · Four Seasons: Large-scale Immersive Art Exhibition", the audience is immersed in the space created by new media technology, with spring, summer, autumn and winter four seasons of light and shadow to connect Cezanne's more than 100 works, explore Cezanne's great art and life story.

Innovation in Content Presentation. The combination of AIGC and immersive image revolutionizes the presentation of excellent traditional cultural forms, innovates the expression of cultural symbol connotation, creates sensory dimension experience, and then realizes the "return of the body" in a new field.

Innovation in Media Convergence. As AI technology becomes more and more widely used in the media industry, AIGC has reached a state of deep integration with the media. For example, AIGC can be used to generate news reports, movie scripts, images, music works, etc., providing a broader choice space for global audiences.

Innovation in Language Interaction. AIGC can not only generate text content in various languages, but also carry out image interaction and service across languages. For example, through the dubbing process of AIGC image technology, people in different languages and different countries can communicate through video, the voice comes from the speaker himself, and the mouth can be matched to the corresponding language.

3.2   Cases of Cross-Cultural Practice

In combination with the interview with Yate Ge, a doctoral candidate in related fields in the College of Design and Innovation of Tongji University, the immersive image narrative enabled by AIGC can promote cross-cultural communication, mainly in the following aspects:

Deconstruction and Reconstruction of Culture. Using large-scale pre-trained models, generative AI technologies can understand multiple modal inputs to generate image content comparable to human creation. The large-scale pre-training samples contain contents from various cultures. The feature extraction and feature-based image generation capabilities of image contents can be realized through training, so that the specific cultural contents can be deconstructed and reconstructed according to the creation needs (cross-cultural communication needs) in practical applications.

Promote Cross-cultural Communication and Exchange. For example, in the immersive images for the discussion of public issues such as traditional culture protection, environmental protection and sustainability, and women's rights, AIGC can generate different virtual images according to the cultural characteristics of different countries and regions. In this way, we can show the multiple aspects of the same issue in different contexts. Promote understanding and empathy between audiences from different cultural backgrounds.

Personalized Content Output. In cross-cultural immersive image narration, AIGC technology can make personalized adjustments according to audiences with different cultural backgrounds on the basis of keeping the overall narrative content unchanged, so as to provide a richer and more diversified experience. For example, in a story about urban office workers, AIGC technology can generate different urban scenes according to the region, and adjust the characters' clothing, language habits, and behaviors.

3.3 Cases of Cross-Domain Practice

In combination with the interview with Shuran Li, a doctoral candidate in related fields in the College of Design and Innovation of Tongji University, the immersive image narrative enabled by AIGC can be integrated in different fields:

In the field of architectural planning, traditional urban design is presented in two dimensions, such as a flat CAD drawing. On this basis, for the design renderings of key areas and key projects, on the whole, this method is relatively abstract. Now, with the popularity of AR, VR and modeling technologies, including the rise of BIM and City Intelligence Model, projects are presented in more three-dimensional ways. Designers, investors, etc., can roam in the scheme, feel the shape of the project before the project is really built, and simulate the economic indicators of the project.

In addition, interactive image narration can also be applied to the story presentation of the city's past and present life. For example, Qingdao Old Town Exhibition Hall shows the development history of the region through this form, visitors can go in and see how the region was developed decades ago, what kind of stories, how to iterate step by step to today. In addition to this narrative approach, it can also adopt the form of deduction. Such as what the area might look like in the coming years or decades after the plan is rezoned.

In the field of smart cities, Baidu, Apollo, Didi and other companies are studying cars with AR functions, and the window glass of this car is with augmented reality effects. During the journey of the vehicle, the surrounding road conditions, restaurants, entertainment and other information can be projected on this glass, so that the vehicle is not only a driving tool, but more like a city living room.

In the field of meta-universe, such as Haiyuan Universe(see Fig. 3) and Xianyuan Universe(see Fig. 4), urban scenes rely on the concept of meta-universe and AI and VR technology. Previous landmarks were either completely real in the physical world or completely virtual. Now combined with some technology, you can do the landmark of the combination of virtual and real. For example, the square is the landmark of the city, through the design, we can see the square in the virtual world. In this way, you can watch performances and read reviews of the place in the virtual world. Some electronic landmarks can form new formats, and people can advertise and trade in the meta-universe.

Fig. 3. A scene of Haiyuan Universe

Fig. 4. A scene of Xianyuan Universe

4 Ethical Issues of AIGC Immersive Image Interactive Narration

AIGC immersive image narrative design not only creates fascinating virtual experience, but also brings a series of ethical problems. In combination with interviews with Shiqi Zhou, Yate Ge and Shuran Li, the relevant ethical issues can be divided into several categories.

4.1 Intellectual Property

Intellectual Property Protection. When using AI to generate content, there may be copyright and intellectual property issues involved. For example, AI-generated music, images, or text may inadvertently infringe the copyright of an existing work.

Ownership. This problem has always existed in the content creation of AIGC. At present, there are legal trends and imperfect regulations in the creative content of AIGC. If it is not restricted and reviewed during creation, it may infringe on the creative rights of others. In terms of the creation itself, if the content is generated by AIGC, how much is the creator involved in the creation? Can he/she be called a designer? Is AIGC credited as a tool in itself, or as an agent involved in the design?

Credibility and Accountability. The immersive image content generated by AIGC may affect the audience's judgment and mistake some content as real, which may confuse the audiovisual and bring inconvenience to the image's understanding of things. For example, the immersive movies and news images generated by AIGC have produced undesirable content, causing people to have misunderstandings or rumors, resulting in adverse social impact. Who should be blamed for the problem? The people who develop AIGC? The people who source the data? Or the people who use it? For another example, AIGC imitates the images and voices of public figures in front of the public, and the audience immersed in the video is easy to think that the content is real, but in fact, the content generated by AIGC is not credible and may be created out of thin air. So, when AIGC generates content in error, who is responsible for the error they make?

Right to Know. For example, when we purchase a designer's work service, if the designer directs the AI to produce the work, does the customer need to have the relevant right to know whether the intellectual property of the work belongs to the designer himself or the AI? Whether the judgment of this problem involves the degree of mixing of man-machine control, or there is a clear definition. For example, when we write a paper, some magazines clearly allow only artificial intelligence to modify the expression of the text, but can not use artificial intelligence to generate content. However, at present, the judgment principle of such issues involving intellectual property rights is not clear.

4.2 Data Usage

Personal Privacy. AIGC's narrative design for immersive images requires a large amount of image content to support the "feeding", which may involve user privacy and data security issues. For example, a large amount of data contains personal information, such as images, sounds, and personal privacy, and once these contents are leaked out or improperly used, legal problems may be involved.

Data Security. First, where does the data for training AIGC come from? Some musicians, for example, have sued generative music software for using their music sources. The New York Times will also sue Chat-GPT for using some of their texts for training, often without their consent. As a result, some of the massive amounts of data used for training are from unreliable or insecure sources. Text may not be that sensitive in relative terms, but cross-modal situations, such as faces, voices, tracks, user data, etc., may be more sensitive.

Data Transparency. Users should fully understand how the AIGC system they are using works and the potential risks. For example, in a game that generates a storyline based on user behavior, users should be explicitly informed about how their data is being used to influence the game's content.

4.3 Social and Cultural

Cultural Appropriation. When producing content, AIGC is limited by training data sets and training methods, which can easily confuse different cultures. If this problem is not solved, it will lead to serious cultural appropriation and cultural bullying in the long run. For example, in the current training data set, there is confusion about Asian culture: the generated images of Asian people are always more like Korean people, and Chinese traditional costumes are easily confused with those of South Korea and Japan. This can lead to the stereotyping of different races and cultures and, in serious cases, racial discrimination.

Social Impact. AIGC content may contain or imply certain moral and social values. This needs to be carefully handled in design to avoid spreading harmful stereotypes or unjust perceptions. For example, a cultural experience app that shows only stereotypical images of a particular culture may exacerbate cultural misconceptions and biases.

The Ethics of Interaction. Immersive images allow the audience to participate in the narrative, and digital and virtual interactive content supported by AIGC can interact with the audience. But in this interactive experience, does the viewer take control of the experience? If the digital person interacting with the audience has bad guidance, is the audience able to share this negative guidance? And is it possible to tell the difference between artificial intelligence and natural intelligence? When creating AIGC content, the creator must restrict the AIGC content used and control the interaction space between it and the user, otherwise the above experience problems beyond the creator's intention and cannot be controlled will occur.

Human Help or Threat. Humans are still a long way from strong artificial intelligence, but Elon Musk has said that artificial intelligence is so dangerous that it may replace humans. In other words, indiscriminate use may cause humans to lose out to advanced artificial intelligence.

5   Thoughts and Prospects on AIGC Enabling Immersive Interactive Narrative

5.1   In the AI Perspective, Immersive Image Narrative Design is Further or Closer to Reality?

Immersive image narrative is like a black box that designs our lives in another parallel virtual world. We can glimpse elements of reality in this world and broaden our lives in the other. When we are immersed in the virtual real world created by images, are we closer to reality? The high degree of reality of life in the virtual world may give us an illusion that contradicts reality. For example, we often use embellished photos or videos, long-term understanding of the reality of their own understanding is biased. The reality that virtual reality presents to us is like a photo with a filter, it reconstructs the reality. For the media industry, virtual reality is sometimes no different from fake things, our physical experience is real, but it is not real. The body perceives the world as a medium, but what it perceives is not necessarily reality, it is a kind of experiential reality, and it cannot be said that it is closer to reality. It's more hyperrealism than reality. "Some scholars have pointed out that surrealism preserves the opposition between imagination and reality, while super realism eliminates the opposition between imagination and reality, when the distance between art and life disappears, when life becomes art, a performance without a 'stage' or a painting without a 'frame', we cannot distinguish between the true and the false. This reality is not the reality in the original realism, but the reality that art and life are combined together. It's also super real." [4].

5.2   Does Immersive Image Narrative Focus on Experience or Plot?

For a long time, film as a narrative carrier, its narrativity can not be erased, but immersive image is sometimes more like a game or some kind of experience device, we do not need a strong narrative function to immerse in it, deeply attracted by the image itself. Film is a kind of art of soul immersion. It influences people's psychological state through narration and shows pleasure, anger, sorrow and joy through watching experience. The immersive image can be an immersive film, but this kind is not only different in the narrative logic, but also more through the body to perceive to complete the experience. The audience is directly involved, and the director designs the route and content of the video according to the audience's line of sight. Moreover, the immersive image is a long shot with scene as the unit, and the time and space are continuous, breaking the montage narrative switching time and space of previous images. A good video narrative is never about seeing what you want to see, if the immersive image is often long enough, the narrative is like a movie, and the immersive image narrative is very complete in a very mature situation, then how far is it from the market? It will still go through a long process of technology maturity, capital in place, and integration in many aspects, and there needs to be a process from experimentation to marketization. For now, AIGC allows immersive image interactive storytelling with software like runway and Midjourney that, by inputting a few key words, can jump out of real life and create an imaginary world. People are born with a desire for stories, the cognitive scientist Roger C. Schank has argued: "We are born to understand stories, not logic" [5]. The interactive narrative design of immersive images makes people feel as if they are living in the real world, and the virtual world they are in can feel real people, things, landscapes, and environments. With such a high degree of authenticity, can we still feel the existence of art? The uniqueness of art is eroded in the everyday reality.

5.3 AIGC Brings Immersive Image Interaction Design to Life

The world created by immersive images is itself a non-physical world, a virtual world in which people wander. However, the design of immersive images may become more intelligent, more emotional, and can continue to grow under the power of AIGC. In the film The Truman Show, Truman lives in a set world from a young age, and the people, things, and things around him are arranged by people in the real world, and Truman is a character living in a huge theater. In immersive images, people are just like the "Truman Show". AIGC enforces the people and things around them to become alive, and people can even establish a more intimate relationship with the virtual characters. People can live in the virtual world for a long time, grow and experience together with these virtual characters. This kind of imaginative human-machine interaction may just be the starting point. However, when people step out of the virtual world, will they have a sense of emptiness or spiritual satisfaction? Perhaps as games and experiences, they are more immersive emotional satisfaction. Once as a way of life, taking off wearable devices, the gap between reality and non-reality may also bring a sense of emptiness. If reality is the interaction of virtual people and real people, a mixture of virtual and real identities, people may adapt more quickly to the arrival of virtual worlds. At present, wearable devices are not popular, and immersive images mostly exist in public Spaces, such as immersive experience exhibitions, art galleries and museums. It can be predicted that immersive image interactive narrative design will be more and more applied to various offline Spaces or home entertainment.

References

1. Lidwell, W., Holden, K., Butler, J.: Universal Principles of Design. 1st edn. Rockport Publishers (2003)
2. Ponty, W.: Phenomenology of Perception. 1st edn. Routledge & Kegan Paul Ltd. (1962)
3. Zhang, C.: Presence and immersion: the reconstruction of audio-visual narrative by virtual reality technology. China Television 35(11), 95–98 (2016)
4. Peng, L.: AIGC and new survival characteristics in the age of intelligence. Nanjing J. Soc. Sci. 34(5), 104–111 (2023)
5. Ren, J.: Analysis of immersive experience and interaction design of teamLab borderless new media art exhibition. New Media Res. 5(17), 114–117 (2019)

Developing a Human-Centered AI Environment to Enhance Financial Literacy of College Students: A Systematic Review

Yinjie Xie[1(✉)] and Shin'ichi Konomi[2]

[1] Graduate School of Information Science and Electrical Engineering, Kyushu University, Fukuoka, Japan
xie.yinjie.786@s.kyushu-u.ac.jp
[2] Faculty of Arts and Science, Kyushu University, Fukuoka, Japan
konomi@artsci.kyushu-u.ac.jp

Abstract. The present systematic review focuses on publications founded on the context of "Developing a Human-Centered AI Environment to Enhance Financial Literacy of College Students", that is, empirical analysis and data mining of college students and their financial decision-making, development of recommendation system algorithms and personalized strategies and user interface systems, the review of the key financial challenges facing college students towards human-centered AI, description of the search strategies including the methods used in the 45 included publications used in the systematic review alongside their benefits and challenges: especially, questionnaires, and surveys. We have also reviewed the advantages of human-AI interface systems alongside the research design in the study (which is a quantitative design in evaluating the study objectives). The reviewed publications reveal that a link exists between a human-centered AI environment and college students' financial decision-making.

Keywords: Financial education · Financial literacy · Human-computer interaction

1 Introduction

During college years, students face numerous financial decisions, including how to allocate scholarships, loans, and income from part-time jobs. These decisions have significant implications for their college and future lives, such as debt pressure, quality of life, social activities, occupational choices, saving and investing habits. However, research shows that many students may not have the strong financial literacy to support making optimal decisions [39]. Behavioral economics has already revealed several factors that influence financial decision-making, such as overconfidence, herd behavior, and mental accounting. To date, there is limited research that combines Artificial Intelligence with behavioral economics to

P.-L. P. Rau (Ed.): HCII 2024, LNCS 14702, pp. 360–374, 2024.
https://doi.org/10.1007/978-3-031-60913-8_25

analyze how data influences and how to cultivate college students' financial literacy. This paper compares the findings of the previous studies based on a human-centered AI environment toward promoting the financial literacy of college students. In particular, we examine the findings on the factors associated with the empirical analysis and data mining of college students' financial decision-making behavior, secondly, we review previous study findings focused on personalization strategies and recommendation system algorithms, next, we look into the factors associated with the effectiveness of human-centered AI Environment in improving the financial literacy among college students, finally, we review the findings on the key financial literacy challenges faced by college students. This paper is written in line with the previous study findings on financial literacy programs, AI in education, and the intersection of human-centered design and technology. In addition, key literature gaps will be identified that form the basis upon which the hypotheses of the study are founded.

2   Methods

2.1   Search Strategy

A systematic search is conducted to gather publications (journals and articles) linked to the present study topic "Developing a human-centered AI environment to enhance financial literacy of college students." The search questions are based on the primary objectives of the study with the key search terms including:

Table 1. Keywords included in the search

Human-Centered AI	Financial decision-making behavior
Artificial intelligence	Recommendation system algorithms
Personalized strategies	User interface
Human-computer interaction	User-centered design
College students	Financial education
Education technology	Financial literacy
Empirical analysis	User experience
Data mining	

"Human-centered AI" was included in the search as it is the primary keyword of the systemic review. "Financial literacy" and "financial decision-making behaviors" were also included in the search as they form the fundamental part of the review. Table 1 shows keywords included in the search.

After identifying the key search terms, the keywords and variations were joined to establish search strings. Table 2 shows sample search strings.

Various databases were selected for publication search including PubMed, IEEE, Scopus, and NCBI. Filters were applied on publication dates with most

Table 2. Sample search strings

	"User interface" OR "UI" OR "Human-centered AI" OR "HC-AI" OR "Recommendation system algorithms" OR "Recommendation system" OR "Artificial intelligence" OR "AI" OR "User experience" OR "User-centered design"
AND	"College students" OR "University students" OR "Students"
AND	"Empirical analysis" OR "Financial analysis" OR "Financial decisions"OR "Financial education" OR "Decision-making behavior" OR "Financial literacy" OR "Personalized strategies"

searches ranging from 2009 to 2023, however, a few searches were taken from the early 1990 s. Figure 1 shows the year distribution of the included publications. The search was all in English with study design focused on surveys.

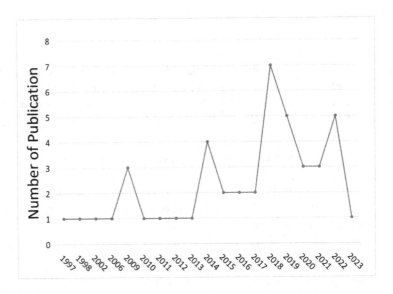

Fig. 1. Publication year of the selected papers

The review used 45 publications of journals and articles which are essential for the systematic review and aided in ensuring that the studies included relevant search questions. Table 3 shows the criteria that were considered for this review.

Table 3. Inclusion and Exclusion Criteria for the search publications

Inclusion Criteria	Exclusion Criteria
Studies reviewed involved college students as participants and publications with participants who are non-college students	
No restriction on college type	Publications on traditional and non-technological financial education and literacy
Studies in English language	Publications that do not involve human-centered AI environment to enhance financial literacy
Studies based on development and adoption of human-centered AI environments and financial education and literacy	Publications with no reports on the relationship between human-centered AI and financial literacy among college students
Studies assessing the relationship between human-centered AI and financial literacy among college students	Publications that focus on AI aspects without a positive link to financial decisions
Financial literacy in budgeting, savings, investments, etc.	Case studies, reviews, editorials, opinions, and other non-quantitative publications were omitted
Studies with surveys and quasi-experimental designs	Cross-sectional publications without interventional impacts over time
Longitudinal publications that evaluate the impact of human-centered AI over time	Literature without clear peer-review stages were not used
Peer-reviewed publications from PubMed, NCBI, IEEE, and Scopus	No restriction on publication dates

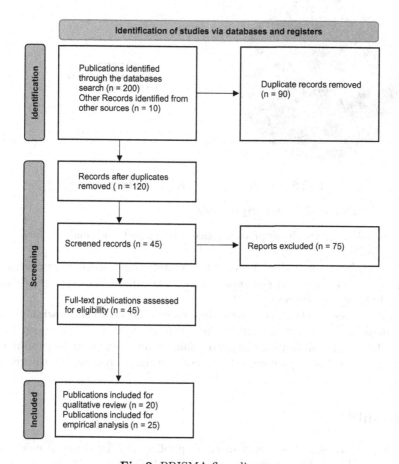

Fig. 2. PRISMA flow diagram

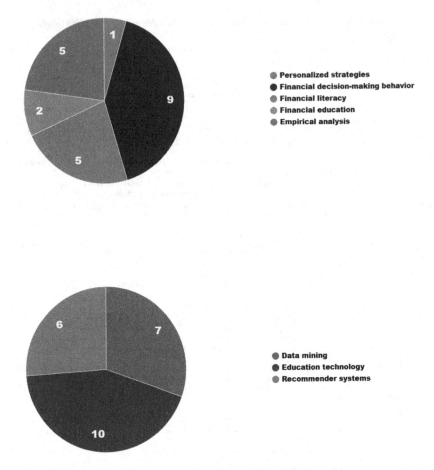

Fig. 3. Search terms with combined keywords

2.2   Data Extraction and Synthesis

The flow below shows the approaches taken to extract and analyze data for the systemic review.

Figure 2 shows the PRISMA model to illustrate the process of data extraction and analysis for empirical systemic review. The final number of publications included for systematic review is 45.

Figure 3 presents two pie charts illustrating the combined variable search terms used in the review alongside the terms used in the Boolean operators. We divided the 45 publications into two main groups. Financial decision-making behavior and technology-enhanced learning are highly relevant to the research topic.

3   Results

According to the search strategy method, publications for this systemic review were searched and 200 publications were found. Of these, 120 remained after

Table 4. Publication periods of the 45 papers in the review

Author/Date	Type of Methods
Adomavicius et al., 2011 [1]	Cross-Sectional Surveys
Agudelo, 2018 [2]	Survey (On Financial Market)
Bernacki and Greene, 2021 [3]	Survey (Systemic review)
Birnbaum, 2017 [4]	Experimental Study
Brown and Farrell, 2016 [5]	Survey (college students, Participants)
Burke, 2002 [6]	Survey and Experiments
Chang et al., 2017 [7]	Cross-sectional survey
Chen and Volpe, 1998 [8]	Survey (College students)
Chen and Wasson, 2019 [36]	Cross-sectional survey
Di Mitri et al., 2017 [10]	Experimental and Survey
Du et al., 2020 [11]	Cross-sectional survey (systemic review)
Eberhardt and Strough, 2018 [12]	Survey (students)
Giannakos and Mangaroska, 2019 [27]	Cross-sectional survey
Giannakos et al., 2019 [13]	Survey (In-person)
Guo and Cheng, 2022 [15]	Cross-sectional survey (From students with AI games)
Hua and Wang, 2018 [16]	Experimental and survey
Hung and Shelton, 2020 [11]	Cross-sectional survey (systemic review)
Isidore, 2019 [17]	Survey and Experimental
Kadadi et al., 2014 [18]	Technology and development
Katarachia and Konstantinidis, 2014 [19]	Observations
Kesheng et al., 2020 [20]	Clustering of participants
Ladrón, 2023 [14]	Experimental and Questionnaires
Lemay and Baek, 2021 [22]	Observational study
Lyons and Kass, 2021 [24]	Experimental study
Madinga et al., 2022 [25]	Web-based self-administered questionnaires
Mandell and Klein, 2009 [26]	Experimental study (students)
Mutahi et al., 2015 [30]	Systemic review
Ochoa et al., 2018 [31]	Cross-sectional survey
Prieto et al., 2018 [34]	Technology and development
Lusardi et al., 2011 [23]	Questionnaires
Raca and Dillenbourg, 2016 [32]	Observation approach
Resnick and Varian, 1997 [33]	Technology and development
Rodrigues, 2009 [28]	Field survey (questionnaires)
Salloum et al., 2020 [35]	Systemic review
Shahiri and Husain, 2015 [37]	Experimental study
Sun and Xie, 2018 [38]	Structural questionnaires
Thompson et al., 2014 [41]	Cross-sectional study
Tintarev and Masthoff, 2012 [42]	Questionnaires (online administered)
Tolosa and Rojo, 2023 [14]	Questionnaires (students)
Villano et al., 2018 [43]	Observations (case participants)
Wong and Kwong, 2018 [44]	In-person surveys (college students)
Zhang et al., 2021 [45]	Cross-sectional study
Zhenhua and Nan, 2022 [46]	Clustering of participants
Mandell et al., 2009 [26]	Questionnaires (students)
Koren et al., 2009 [21]	Not mentioned
Cude et al., 2006 [9]	Online survey

the duplicates were removed. These publications included peer-reviewed articles and journals from PubMed, NCBI, and Scopus databases. After screening and eligibility procedures on the remaining publications, 45 publications remained for inclusion in the systemic review. Table 4 shows the summary of the research methods for the included publications.

In these reviewed studies, surveys and questionnaires will provide special means of obtaining data from a sizable cohort. Surveys and questionnaires are widely used research tools with several benefits across various fields. Large populations, which yield higher statistical power, the capacity to collect vast volumes of data, and the availability of verified models are some of the benefits of surveys. Surveys can be distributed through various channels, including email, online platforms, or even in-person, making them accessible to a broad range of participants. Surveys and questionnaires are efficient for collecting data from a large number of participants simultaneously, making them a scalable and time-effective research method. Participants can provide honest and sensitive information more comfortably as surveys and questionnaires allow for anonymity. This can be crucial when exploring personal or stigmatized topics. Surveys are particularly valuable for collecting quantitative data, allowing researchers to analyze and quantify patterns, trends, and relationships in a structured manner.

4   Discussion

4.1   Empirical Analysis and Data Mining of College Students and Financial Decision Making

Scholars have used many empirical techniques, such as surveys, experiments, and observational studies, to examine the financial behaviors of university students [14, 25]. These studies frequently highlight decision-making patterns, risk tolerances, and degrees of financial literacy among college students. These empirical findings demonstrated the impact of certainty, introspection, and seclusion at both universities, leading to the conclusion that research participants (students) relied more on prospect theory than expected utility theory while making financial decisions in uncertain circumstances. In contrast, the research [2, 26] revealed that a complex interplay of factors influences college students' finances, according to empirical examinations of their financial decision-making. The study methodologies, including surveys, experiments, and observational studies, have been used in the literature to analyze the nuances of financial behaviors among college students. The main conclusions from [2, 26] showed that decision-making is highly influenced by peer pressure, financial literacy, socioeconomic background, and personal psychological characteristics.

Literature findings are guided by behavioral economics, a well-known theoretical framework that reveals the social dynamics, heuristics, and cognitive biases that influence financial decisions, according to the research [4, 17]. The empirical analyses provide light on the difficulties college students encounter in handling their own finances and offer insights into their decision-making tendencies, risk tolerance, and degree of financial literacy. In support of this earlier revealed that large datasets [8] pertaining to financial decision-making were being analyzed by researchers using data mining approaches including predictive modeling and machine learning algorithms. These methods made it possible to find hidden patterns and forecast future actions using historical data. The literature [2] also supported the research [8] by stating that regression and decision tree models are two examples of predictive modeling techniques that work well for predicting financial results and locating possible risk factors.

A theoretical foundation for comprehending how psychological elements affect economic decision-making is provided by behavioral economics [40]. According to Thaler and Richard H [40], behavioral economics has advanced significantly over the last several decades and can completely transform the study of economics. Additionally, Thaler and Richard H [40] emphasized the significance of behavioral economics in financial judgment. In support of the findings of Thaler and Richard H [40], based on behavioral economics, empirical research earlier investigated how social effects, heuristics, and cognitive biases affect college students' financial decisions [29]. The authors used state-of-the-art research in behavioral science and economics to demonstrate how everyone who struggles to make ends meet has a similar psychology as a result of scarcity. In addition, they offered a fresh perspective on why the impoverished continue to be impoverished and the busy continue to be busy. Mullainathan and Shafir [29] also demonstrated how scarcity misleads people and how people and organizations can effectively deal with scarcity to achieve more success and satisfaction.

4.2 Relationship Between Human-Centered AI Environments and Recommendation System Algorithms and Personalization Strategies

The literature has mentioned the link between human-centered AI, recommendation systems, and personalized strategies. Bernacki and Greene [3] revealed that the interaction that recommendation system algorithms and personalized techniques have with human-centered AI settings is an important part of building systems that put user experience and engagement first. The literature frequently examines this relationship in order to address the difficulties in developing AI systems that are considerate of human requirements, preferences, and ethical considerations in addition to being effective at making suggestions, according to the research [4]. Designing systems with a thorough awareness of user wants, preferences, and behaviors is crucial, according to human-centered AI.

According to the paper of Chen and Wasson [36], in the context of recommendation systems, this entails taking user feedback, past interactions, and individual context into account to deliver personalized and appropriate suggestions. In a similar vein, Chang et al. [7] study noted that human-centered AI environments emphasize the importance of AI systems' transparency. It should be transparent to users how recommendations are made. This is particularly crucial for recommendation systems, as users might want to know why a particular piece of information or item is being recommended to them [27]. Additionally, Chang et al. [7] argued that personalized strategies in recommendation systems are not just about providing accurate suggestions but also fostering long-term user engagement. Systems should be designed to learn and adapt to user preferences over time, ensuring a sustained and positive user experience.

4.3 Development of Recommendation System Algorithms and Personalization Strategies

The literature [33] earlier revealed that collaborative filtering and content-based filtering techniques were the mainstays of early recommendation systems. Content-based filtering makes recommendations for objects based on their features, whereas collaborative filtering makes use of user-item interactions. In support, the research [5] stated that notwithstanding their efficacy, these techniques encounter obstacles including the cold-start issue and scalability problems. In response to the shortcomings of content-based and collaborative filtering, hybrid recommendation systems were developed. Consequently, these systems transcend the limitations of individual methods and improve accuracy by combining different recommendation strategies [6]. For a more thorough recommendation strategy, hybrid models include collaborative filtering, content-based filtering, and occasionally knowledge-based techniques.

To deliver more appropriate recommendations, context-aware recommendation systems take into account extra variables like time, location, and user context [1]. These systems provide a more accurate and sophisticated suggestion strategy by acknowledging that user preferences may vary depending on various settings. Further, as a means of facilitating collaborative filtering, matrix factorization gained popularity through the breakdown of user-item interaction matrices [21]. Neural collaborative filtering, in particular, is a deep learning technique that has shown greater performance in capturing complex user-item interactions, resulting in suggestions that are more precise and tailored to the individual [25]. In support, the literature showed that personalized learning solutions have become more popular in educational environments [13]. These techniques use recommendation systems to personalize instructional information according to each learner's preferences, style, and level of performance [3]. Using real-time data, adaptive learning solutions modify examinations, content, and pacing to maximize every student's learning experience.

4.4 Limitations and Challenges

The generalizability of our review is constrained by the specific contexts of the studies we analyzed. Factors such as the demographics of the student populations, the AI tools, and the educational methods used in these studies limit the applicability of our conclusions. Therefore, our findings should be interpreted with caution, keeping in mind that they may not universally apply to all college student populations or AI environments. This is a critical consideration for the future application and expansion of our research into diverse educational settings.

5 Strengths of the Study

The studies that have been evaluated have demonstrated the dangers of AI algorithms. Therefore, when integrating AI algorithms into financial services for college students, it is imperative to address these possible dangers and biases in the algorithms. To guarantee responsibility, openness, and equity in the procedures involved in making decisions, safeguards must be included. Furthermore, it's important to continuously monitor and assess AI systems in order to spot and address any biases that might develop over time. The studies have also shown the various empirical analyses and data mining from college students in relation to their financial decision-making behaviors. As such, it is only understandable that we develop the strengths of this review based on the reviewed literature to state our theoretical points of the present study results. First, designing technology solutions with a thorough understanding of college students' wants, preferences, and behaviors is crucial, according to the philosophy of human-centered design. By putting human-centered design concepts to use, the AI environment is customized to meet the unique needs and overcome the obstacles college students have in developing their financial literacy. A theoretical foundation for comprehending how people make financial decisions is provided by behavioral economics [14]. Second, understanding how college students view and engage with the AI environment is made easier by applying the concepts of user interface algorithms [22]. This is because aspects like perceived usefulness and ease of use are critical to the success of the financial literacy intervention. The study is based on the personalization hypothesis, which emphasizes how important it is to customize recommendations based on the interests and actions of specific users. Accurate and customized suggestions are produced by integrating user modeling approaches like content-based and collaborative filtering. Third, the study is based on the ideas of user-centered design, which emphasizes how crucial it is to comprehend user requirements, preferences, and behaviors at every stage of the design process [25]. The creation of an interface that is efficient, intuitive, and in line with user expectations is guided by the principles of user-centered design. The study takes into account how people interact with the computer interface and is based on theories of human-computer interaction.

6 Key Financial Literacy Challenges Faced by College Students Towards Human-Centered AI

According to the literature, one of the biggest obstacles to college students' financial literacy is their lack of knowledge about saving and budgeting [27]. Similarly, according to Lemay et al., [22], a lot of students lack the information and abilities needed to properly build and manage a financial budget, which can lead to poor financial decision-making and possible long-term financial troubles. Furthermore, Du et al. [11] demonstrated that a lack of knowledge about saving can result in an incapacity to create sound saving habits and set financial objectives. The lack of official financial instruction in college courses, which leaves students to manage their financial responsibilities on their own, exacerbates this issue. Supporting this, Ladrón et al. [14] showed that in order for college students to build financial resilience and efficiently manage their financial resources, a deeper comprehension of budgeting and saving is necessary. According to the same line of reasoning, Zhenhua and Nan [46] found that one major obstacle to financial literacy is college students' lack of basic financial knowledge. Many college-bound kids have only a cursory knowledge of basic financial concepts like managing spending, budgeting, and saving. Their inability to make wise financial decisions as a result of this ignorance may put them in financial jeopardy both during and after college.

Similarly, Salloum et al. [35] demonstrated that students may find it difficult to manage credit cards, student loans, and other financial goods and services in the complicated world of personal finance without a strong foundation in fundamental financial knowledge. As evidence, Hung and Shelton [11] demonstrated how financial institutions and educational institutions working together can be extremely important in empowering students by providing financial coaching and mentorship. Furthermore, it has previously been shown by Katarachia and Konstantinidis [19] that using AI technologies for personalized financial education can give students specialized advice and assistance in improving their financial literacy. In the context of human-centered AI, a major financial literacy difficulty faced by college students is limited awareness of financial products and services [12]. Many students are unaware of the various financial goods and services that are accessible to them because of their limited exposure and experience [20]. Their inability to make wise financial decisions and seize opportunities that can end up being advantageous to them in the long term is hampered by this lack of understanding. Furthermore, as previously noted by Mutahi et al. [30], students may find it difficult to stay up to date with the most recent advancements and comprehend how these innovations may affect their financial well-being. This difficulty is further compounded by the rapidly changing landscape of financial technology and AI-driven services [40].

Even though AI algorithms are highly effective at processing large volumes of data and making predictions, they still have some possible drawbacks and biases [31]. The persistence of preexisting prejudices within the algorithms themselves, which may produce biased results, is one of the key worries. For instance, research by Raca and Dillenbourg [32] has shown that an AI algorithm may reflect and magnify biases in its decision-making process if it is trained on biased historical data. Unfair treatment may ensue from this, especially in the case of financial services that have an impact on college students [34]. The lack of interpretability and openness in AI algorithms is another issue [37] making it difficult to understand how decisions are being made and to identify and address potential biases. Furthermore, it was shown by Sun and Xie [38] that the loss of human agency and accountability could result from the application of AI in financial decision-making. Without a thorough grasp of AI systems' operation or the ability to critically evaluate their recommendations, college students risk becoming unduly dependent on them [43]. Furthermore, Wong and Kwong [44] shown that the application of AI algorithms in financial services raises privacy and security issues. There is a chance that private information will be misused or accessed without authorization because these algorithms rely so heavily on financial and personal data [41].

7   Conclusions

Conducting a systematic review on "Developing a Human-Centered AI Environment to Enhance Financial Literacy of College Students" by focusing on publications in this context has been done. The systematic review has included 45 publications reviewing the students' interactions with recommendation algorithm systems and their financial decision-making behaviors, financial literacy, and financial education. This data-driven approach provides valuable insights into students' strengths, weaknesses, and overall learning patterns in line with financial decision-making and behaviors, enabling educators to make informed decisions.

The present review on Guo and Cheng [15] has revealed that the common factors associated with the effectiveness of the HCAI environment in improving the financial literacy among college students are user-centric designs with HCAI environment, interaction, and engagement with HCAI and personalization strategies towards HCAI, real-world applications of HCAI, ethical considerations which comes with strategies of engagement, and integration with formal education to promote financial literacy. Also, the review has shown that providing users with control over the recommendation process is aligned with a human-centered approach. Users may want to customize their preferences, adjust the level of personalization, or even opt out of certain recommendation features [3]. Recommendation algorithms should be flexible enough to accommodate these user choices [11].

The present review has also found that the key financial challenge faced by college students in regard to HCAI environment, for example Giannakos and Mangaroska [27] and Ladrón [14] noted a lack of interpretability and openness in AI algorithms, loss of human agency and accountability, privacy and security issues such as possibility of access and misuse of private information without authorization, among others. Finally, most of the research designs are questionnaires, experiments, and surveys on college students, assuming empirical analysis which allows for statistical conclusions on the established study objectives.

Acknowledgment. This work was supported by the Japan Society for the Promotion of Science(JSPS), Grants-in-Aid for Scientific Research (KAKENHI), Japan: Grant Number JP20H00622.

References

1. Adomavicius, G., Tuzhilin, A.: Context-aware recommender systems. In: Ricci, F., Rokach, L., Shapira, B., Kantor, P.B. (eds.) Recommender Systems Handbook, pp. 217–253. Springer US, Boston, MA (2011). https://doi.org/10.1007/978-0-387-85820-3_7

2. Agudelo, D.A.: Behavioral finance. una introducción a los conceptos y aplicaciones (behavioral finance. an introduction to concepts and applications). Center for Research in Economics and Finance (CIEF), Working Papers (18–15) (2022)

3. Bernacki, M.L., Greene, M.J., Lobczowski, N.G.: A systematic review of research on personalized learning: personalized by whom, to what, how, and for what purpose (s)? Educ. Psychol. Rev. **33**(4), 1675–1715 (2021)

4. Birnbaum, M.H.: Empirical evaluation of third-generation prospect theory. Theor. Decis. **84**, 11–27 (2018)

5. Brown, J.R., Farrell, A.M., Weisbenner, S.J.: Decision-making approaches and the propensity to default: evidence and implications. J. Financ. Econ. **121**(3), 477–495 (2016)

6. Burke, R.: Hybrid recommender systems: survey and experiments. User Model. User-Adap. Inter. **12**, 331–370 (2002)

7. Chang, C.J., et al.: An analysis of collaborative problem-solving activities mediated by individual-based and collaborative computer simulations. J. Comput. Assist. Learn. **33**(6), 649–662 (2017)

8. Chen, H., Volpe, R.P.: An analysis of personal financial literacy among college students. Financial Serv. Rev. **7**(2), 107–128 (1998)

9. Cude, B., et al.: College students and financial literacy: what they know and what we need to learn. Proc. East. Family Econom. Resource Manage. Assoc. **102**(9), 106–109 (2006)

10. Di Mitri, D., Scheffel, M., Drachsler, H., Börner, D., Ternier, S., Specht, M.: Learning pulse: a machine learning approach for predicting performance in self-regulated learning using multimodal data. In: Proceedings of the Seventh International Learning Analytics and Knowledge Conference, pp. 188–197 (2017)

11. Du, X., Yang, J., Hung, J.L., Shelton, B.: Educational data mining: a systematic review of research and emerging trends. Inform. Disc. Delivery **48**(4), 225–236 (2020)

12. Eberhardt, W., Bruine de Bruin, W., Strough, J.: Age differences in financial decision making: T he benefits of more experience and less negative emotions. J. Behav. Decision Making **32**(1), 79–93 (2019)

13. Giannakos, M.N., Sharma, K., Pappas, I.O., Kostakos, V., Velloso, E.: Multimodal data as a means to understand the learning experience. Int. J. Inf. Manage. **48**, 108–119 (2019)

14. Ladrón de Guevara Cortés, R., Tolosa, L.E., Rojo, M.P.: Prospect theory in the financial decision-making process: an empirical study of two argentine universities. J. Econom. Finance Adm. Sci. (2023)

15. Guo, L., Cheng, J., Zhang, Z.: Mapping the knowledge domain of financial decision making: a scientometric and bibliometric study. Front. Psychol. **13**, 1006412 (2022)

16. Hua, F., Wang, J.: How investor sentiment impacts financial decision-making behavior: from a cognitive neuroscience perspective. NeuroQuantology **16**(5) (2018)

17. Isidore R, R., P, C.: The relationship between the income and behavioural biases. J. Econom., Fin. Adm. Sci. **24**(47), 127–144 (2019)

18. Kadadi, A., Agrawal, R., Nyamful, C., Atiq, R.: Challenges of data integration and interoperability in big data. In: 2014 IEEE International Conference on Big Data (big data), pp. 38–40. IEEE (2014)
19. Katarachia, A., Konstantinidis, A.: Financial education and decision making processes. Proc. Econom. Finance **9**, 142–152 (2014)
20. Kesheng, L., Yikun, N., Zihan, L., Bin, D.: Data mining and feature analysis of college students' campus network behavior. In: 2020 5th IEEE International Conference on Big Data Analytics (ICBDA), pp. 231–237. IEEE (2020)
21. Koren, Y., Bell, R., Volinsky, C.: Matrix factorization techniques for recommender systems. Computer **42**(8), 30–37 (2009)
22. Lemay, D.J., Baek, C., Doleck, T.: Comparison of learning analytics and educational data mining: a topic modeling approach. Comput. Educ.: Artif. Intell. **2**, 100016 (2021)
23. Lusardi, A., Mitchell, O.S.: Financial literacy around the world: an overview. J. Pension Econom. Fin. **10**(4), 497–508 (2011)
24. Lyons, A.C., Kass-Hanna, J.: 25 behavioral economics and financial decision making. De Gruyter Handbook of Personal Finance, p. 433 (2022)
25. Madinga, N.W., Maziriri, E.T., Chuchu, T., Magoda, Z.: An investigation of the impact of financial literacy and financial socialization on financial satisfaction: mediating role of financial risk attitude. Glob. J. Emerg. Mark. Econ. **14**(1), 60–75 (2022)
26. Mandell, L., Klein, L.S.: The impact of financial literacy education on subsequent financial behavior. J. Fin. Counsel. Plan. **20**(1) (2009)
27. Mangaroska, K., Vesin, B., Giannakos, M.: Cross-platform analytics: a step towards personalization and adaptation in education. In: Proceedings of the 9th International Conference on Learning Analytics and Knowledge, pp. 71–75 (2019)
28. Marinho, R.F., Lagioia, U.C.T., Maciel, C.V., Rodrigues, R.N.: Behavioral finance: a comparative study using the prospect theory at the undergraduate course in accountancy. Rev. Bus. Manage. **11**(33), 383–403 (2009)
29. Mullainathan, S., Shafir, E.: Scarcity: Why having too little means so much. Macmillan (2013)
30. Mutahi, J., Bent, O., Kinai, A., Weldemariam, K., Sengupta, B., Contractor, D.: Seamless blended learning using the cognitive learning companion: a systemic view. IBM J. Res. Dev. **59**(6), 1–8 (2015)
31. Ochoa, X., Domínguez, F., Guamán, B., Maya, R., Falcones, G., Castells, J.: The rap system: Automatic feedback of oral presentation skills using multimodal analysis and low-cost sensors. In: Proceedings of the 8th International Conference on Learning Analytics and Knowledge, pp. 360–364. LAK '18, Association for Computing Machinery, New York, NY, USA (2018). https://doi.org/10.1145/3170358.3170406, https://doi.org/10.1145/3170358.3170406
32. Raca, M., Tormey, R., Dillenbourg, P.: Sleepers' lag-study on motion and attention. In: Proceedings of the Fourth International Conference on Learning Analytics and Knowledge, pp. 36–43 (2014)
33. Resnick, P., Varian, H.R.: Recommender systems. Commun. ACM **40**(3), 56–58 (1997)
34. Rodríguez-Triana, M.J., Prieto, L.P., Martínez-Monés, A., Asensio-Pérez, J.I., Dimitriadis, Y.: The teacher in the loop: Customizing multimodal learning analytics for blended learning. In: Proceedings of the 8th International Conference on Learning Analytics and Knowledge. p. 417-426. LAK '18, Association for Computing Machinery, New York, NY, USA (2018) https://doi.org/10.1145/3170358.3170364, https://doi.org/10.1145/3170358.3170364

35. Salloum, S.A., Alshurideh, M., Elnagar, A., Shaalan, K.: Mining in educational data: review and future directions. In: Hassanien, A.-E., Azar, A.T., Gaber, T., Oliva, D., Tolba, F.M. (eds.) Proceedings of the International Conference on Artificial Intelligence and Computer Vision (AICV2020), pp. 92–102. Springer International Publishing, Cham (2020). https://doi.org/10.1007/978-3-030-44289-7_9

36. Samuelsen, J., Chen, W., Wasson, B.: Integrating multiple data sources for learning analytics-review of literature. research and practice in technology enhanced learning, 14, article11 (2019)

37. Shahiri, A.M., Husain, W., et al.: A review on predicting student's performance using data mining techniques. Proc. Comput. Sci. **72**, 414–422 (2015)

38. Sun, Z., Xie, K., Anderman, L.H.: The role of self-regulated learning in students' success in flipped undergraduate math courses. The Internet High. Educ. **36**, 41–53 (2018)

39. Tang, N., Baker, A.: Self-esteem, financial knowledge and financial behavior. J. Econ. Psychol. **54**, 164–176 (2016)

40. Thaler, R.H.: Behavioral economics: past, present, and future. American Econom. Rev. **106**(7), 1577–1600 (2016)

41. Thompson, K., Kennedy-Clark, S., Wheeler, P., Kelly, N.: Discovering indicators of successful collaboration using tense: automated extraction of patterns in discourse. Br. J. Edu. Technol. **45**(3), 461–470 (2014)

42. Tintarev, N., Masthoff, J.: Evaluating the effectiveness of explanations for recommender systems: methodological issues and empirical studies on the impact of personalization. User Model. User-Adap. Inter. **22**, 399–439 (2012)

43. Villano, R., Harrison, S., Lynch, G., Chen, G.: Linking early alert systems and student retention: a survival analysis approach. High. Educ. **76**, 903–920 (2018)

44. Wong, E.Y., Kwong, T., Pegrum, M.: Learning on mobile augmented reality trails of integrity and ethics. Res. Pract. Technol. Enhanc. Learn. **13**, 1–20 (2018)

45. Zhang, S., Liu, H., He, J., Han, S., Du, X.: A deep bi-directional prediction model for live streaming recommendation. Inform. Process. Manage. **58**(2), 102453 (2021)

46. Zhenhua, H., Nan, W.: Empirical analysis based on the related factors of college students' mental health problems. Front. Psychol. **13**, 997910 (2022)

Influence of Voice Characteristics and Language Style of Intelligent Assistant on User Trust and Intention to Use

Yiwei Xiong, Qinzhuo Yu, and Na Liu(✉)

School of Economics and Management, Beijing University of Posts and Telecommunications, Beijing, China

{xyw,liuna18}@bupt.edu.cn

Abstract. Intelligent assistants are increasingly employed, utilizing voice interaction as a natural and intuitive method to offer users functions such as information query, information management, entertainment, and chatting. How to improve the user experience of intelligent assistants in terms of voice interaction and design and thus enhance user acceptance is our research focus. A within-subject experiment was designed, and a total of 260 participants were recruited to participate in the experiment. The experiment adopted a 2 pitch (high, low) × 2 speed (fast, slow) × 2 voice gender (male, female) × 2 language style (social-oriented style, task-oriented style) design to investigate the effects of voice characteristics and language style on users' trust and intention to use intelligent assistant. The results indicated that participants perceived higher ease of use and higher usefulness when the speed was high. With a male voice gender, the social-oriented intelligent assistant led to higher perceived usefulness and intention to use. Participants' perceived ease of use was higher when using an intelligent assistant with a gender opposite to their own. Participants expressed the highest level of trust in an intelligent assistant characterized by high pitch and speed, a female voice, and a task-oriented language style. This study discussed the influence of voice characteristics and language style on user trust and intention to use and provided practical insights for the design of intelligent assistant.

Keywords: Intelligent Assistant · Trust · Behavioral Intention · Voice Characteristics · Language Style

1 Introduction

Intelligent voice assistants represent a new form of voice-enabled services that simultaneously integrate elements of artificial intelligence with digital devices [1]. In recent years, the number of devices in use that incorporate intelligent voice assistants with artificial intelligence (e.g., Google Assistant, Amazon Alexa) has risen dramatically.

The global virtual assistant (VA) application market, valued at approximately US$2.7 billion in 2022, is expected to expand significantly and reach a size of around US$18.6 billion by 2030, and its market growth is projected to occur at a compound annual growth

© The Author(s), under exclusive license to Springer Nature Switzerland AG 2024
P.-L. P. Rau (Ed.): HCII 2024, LNCS 14702, pp. 375–387, 2024.
https://doi.org/10.1007/978-3-031-60913-8_26

rate (CAGR) of 27.1% during the forecast period from 2022 to 2030 (Research and Markets, 2023) [2]. Artificial intelligence (AI) voice assistants possess significant market potential and offer diverse services through voice interaction. However, the influence of anthropomorphic features on consumers' perception and continuance intention to use, particularly across various age groups, remains unclear [3]. While the technical aspects, such as the accuracy of speech recognition and synthesis, have matured in the development of intelligent voice assistants, there is still significant room for improvement in anthropomorphic design such as voice characteristics, interface design, and interaction methods. Highly anthropomorphic voice assistants increase voice assistant use intention among users [4].

Research on user experience with intelligent voice assistants, often based on the Technology Acceptance Model (TAM), has primarily focused on understanding the influence of individual user characteristics on acceptance and intention to use. Laumer and Maier (2019) examined the trust and acceptance for medical voice assistants, considering user risk preferences and personal habits as independent variables [5]. Some studies aimed to create comprehensive models for intelligent assistants, incorporating indicators such as interaction intention and satisfaction. Lee, Choi et al. (2017) explored user satisfaction and intention to use voice assistants for movie recommendations, identifying self-disclosure and reciprocity as key variables correlated with user satisfaction and intention to use [6]. Additional research has examined the design of language style and voice characteristics for intelligent assistants. Tapus et al. (2008) developed mobile robots with distinct personalities based on language style, pitch, and speed. Outgoing robots displayed an extroverted language style, high pitch, and high volume, while introverted robots exhibited an introverted language style, low pitch, and low volume. Users perceived outgoing robots as more closely aligned with their personalities and preferred them as assistive robots [7].

In the present study, we considered four anthropomorphic features. In terms of voice characteristics, we selected pitch, speed, and voice gender. Feinberg, Jones et al. (2005) found a negative correlation between pitch and attractiveness for males and a positive correlation for females [8]. Kara McBride (2011) investigated the impact of speed on the listening comprehension ability and computer-assisted learning effectiveness of English learners, concluding that slower speed enhances learners' information retrieval in dialogue and improves comprehension ability [9]. Liu (2017) highlighted the significant influence of voice gender on user attitudes and emotional states [10]. Regarding language style, we considered task-oriented and social-oriented styles. Chattaraman et al. (2018) investigated whether social- versus task-oriented interaction of virtual shopping assistants differentially benefits low versus high Internet competency older consumers [11].

In this study, we employed a combined approach to generate specific types of assistant voices with different anthropomorphic features, collecting user feedback through a survey. Building a model based on the Technology Acceptance Model (TAM) [12], we investigated the relationships between anthropomorphic features of intelligent assistants and user intention to use and trust, aiming to provide insightful recommendations for improving the design of intelligent voice assistants.

2 Methods

2.1 Experimental Design

This study designed four independent variables namely pitch, speed, voice gender and language style. Pitch had two levels: high pitch and low pitch. Speed had two levels: fast speed and slow speed. Voice gender was set as male voice and female voice. Language style was set as social-oriented and task-oriented. A total of 16 combinations of independent variables were generated, resulting in 16 types of voice assistants. Using the TAM theoretical model, a research model is established to analyze the relationships among independent variables, user perception, and intention to use. The experimental model is illustrated in Fig. 1.

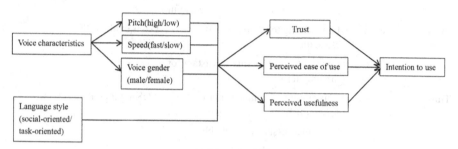

Fig. 1. Experimental model

In terms of pitch, we set 200 Hz to 400 Hz for low pitch and 500 Hz to 700 Hz for high pitch based on previous study [13]. As for speed, we set 235 words per minute as slow level and 312 words per minute as fast level based on previous studies [9]. Language style is controlled by using speech texts and tone to convey information in social-oriented way and task-oriented way specifically. Social-oriented intelligent assistants engaged in small talk, such as discussing weather or the assistant's recommendation and preferences. The social-oriented style also incorporated colloquial particles making a more humanlike expression. Task-oriented intelligent assistants primarily used formal speech without small talk and self-disclosure in the conversation.

The dependent variables included perceived ease of use, perceived usefulness, trust, and intention to use. The following Table 1 gives the measurement items of the dependent variables. All the items were measured with a seven-point Likert scale with 1 representing very disagree and 7 representing very agree.

Table 1. Measurement items of dependent variables

Dependent variables	Items	Literature sources
Perceived ease of use	This smart assistant is very easy to use	Davis, 1989; Davis et al., 1989
	I am proficient in using this smart assistant	
Perceived usefulness	Using this smart assistant allows my requests to be fulfilled more effectively	Davis, 1989; Davis et al., 1989
	Using this smart assistant makes my tasks more efficient	
	I find this smart assistant to be useful	
Intention to use	I am willing to use this smart assistant	Davis et al., 1989
	I intend to use this smart assistant for the long term	
Trust	This smart assistant is sure to accomplish the tasks I request	McKnight et al., 2011
	This smart assistant is reliable	
	Overall, I trust this smart assistant	

2.2 Participants

The formal experiment obtained a total of 187 valid samples. There were 107 male participants, accounting for 57.2% of the total participants, and 80 female participants, accounting for 42.8%, resulting in a roughly equal gender distribution. Most participants held a bachelor's degree, making up 85.6% of the total participants, with the lowest educational level being vocational high school. In terms of age range, participants aged 21–40 constituted the vast majority, representing 97.3% of the total participants. Specifically, participants aged 21–31 accounted for 72.2% of the total, while those aged 31–40 comprised 25.1%. Nearly 84.5% of participants reported using intelligent assistants at least once a week or once a day. It suggests a high prevalence of intelligent assistant usage within the 21–40 age group (Table 2).

2.3 Experimental Design and Materials

The experiment adopted a mixed design with pitch, speed, and language style as within-subject variables, and voice gender as a between-subject variable. Participants were randomly categorized into two groups, namely interacting with female intelligent assistant and male intelligent assistant separately. After screening and excluding invalid or incomplete questionnaires, a total of 80 valid responses were collected in the female intelligent assistant group, and 107 valid responses were collected in the male intelligent assistant group.

Table 2. Demographic information of participants

Item	Category	Frequency	Percentage (%)
Gender	Male	107	57.2
	female	80	42.8
Age	0–20 years old	3	1.6
	21–30 years old	135	72.2
	31–40 years old	47	25.1
	Over 40 years old	2	1
Education Level	Bachelor Degree	160	85.6
	Master's Degree	17	9.1
	Doctoral Degree	1	0.5
	Associate Degree	9	4.8
Frequency of Intelligent Assistant Usage	Never used	1	0.5
	At least once a year	6	3.2
	At least once a month	22	11.8
	At least once a week	73	39
	At least once a day	85	45.5

The study utilized Microsoft's Speech Studio and Adobe Audition to synthesize 16 types of conversations. The conversation was selected from eight intelligent assistant usage scenarios. The context featured two dialogues with different details but contained the same information. Participants simulated interactions with intelligent voice assistants by listening to audio segments, and their subjective perceptions were measured through questionnaire. The different dialogues between the two language style of voice assistants in the context of supermarket shopping guide are as follows (Table 3).

Table 3. One sample of the language style

Social-oriented intelligent voice assistant	Task-oriented intelligent voice assistant
"Hello, I'm Xiaole. The weather is nice today. Welcome to Yonghui Supermarket. How may I assist you? You can use the buttons below to let me know what you need."	"Hello, I'm Xiaole, and this is Yonghui Supermarket. If you need assistance, please select the function button below and follow the on-screen instructions."
"Can you tell me what you're looking for? Simply enter the name of the item you're searching for in the chat box. Xiaole will promptly check the location of the item for you. Please wait a moment."	"You have chosen the 'Location Inquiry' function. I will now search for the item's location. Please enter the item's name and wait a moment."

(continued)

Table 3. (*continued*)

Social-oriented intelligent voice assistant	Task-oriented intelligent voice assistant
"The product you want to purchase is located on shelf A002 in the third row of the food section on the west side of the supermarket. Just go straight from here and turn right. Would you like to call a shop assistant to guide you?"	"Inquiry complete. The item is located on shelf A002 in the third row of the west-side food section. Go straight and turn right. If you need assistance from a shop assistant, please click 'Shop Assistant Guidance' and wait in place."

The study collected information of participants, including gender, age group, education level, and the frequency of using intelligent assistants. This study employed analysis of variance (ANOVA) to examine the relationships among variables using SPSS 24.0.

3   Results

Repeated measures ANOVA was conducted on the four independent variables to explore their interaction effects. If the interaction effects of the variable combinations are significant, subsequent tests examine the simple effects of each independent variable. Simple effects are analyzed through multiple comparisons to observe specific impacts.

There was a significant effect of speed on perceived ease of use ($P = 0.015 < 0.05$). It indicated that higher speed associated with higher perceived ease of use. There were no significant interaction effects on perceived ease of use.

The results (Table 4) showed that there were significant interaction effects of language style and voice gender, as well as of pitch and speed on perceived usefulness (Fig. 2).

Table 4. Effects on perceived usefulness

Variable	F-test	Significance test
speed	12.079	0.001
language style & voice gender	8.795	0.003
pitch & speed	6.276	0.013

Multiple comparisons for language style and voice gender (Table 5) revealed that when the voice gender of the assistant was male, participants' perceived usefulness was significantly higher for social-oriented language style. When the voice gender was female, there was no significant difference in perceived usefulness between two language styles. Multiple comparisons for pitch and speed (Table 5) indicated that when the pitch level was lower, participants' perceived usefulness for intelligent voice assistants with high speed was significantly higher.

Results (Table 6) showed that there was a significant interaction effect among pitch, speed, language style and voice gender on trust, as well as a significant interaction effect

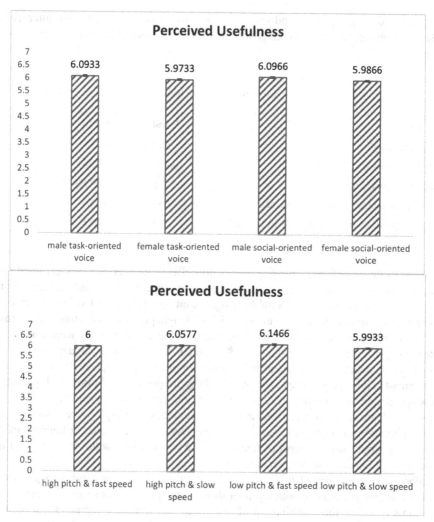

Fig. 2. Participants' consent to perceived usefulness (error line is ± 1 standard error)

Table 5. Multiple comparisons about perceived usefulness

Variable	difference(I-J)	Significance test
male		
social-oriented voice(I) task-oriented voice (J)	0.118	0.038
low pitch		
fast speed(I) slow speed(J)	0.206	< 0.001

among speed, language style and voice gender. There was also a significant interaction effect of language style and voice gender, with a main effect of language style on trust (Fig. 3).

Table 6. Effects on trust

Variable	F-test	Significance test
language style	5.699	0.018
language style & voice gender	8.466	0.004
pitch & language style	3.939	0.049
speed & language style & voice gender	5.645	0.019
pitch & speed & language style & voice gender	3.944	0.049

Due to the significant four-way interaction effects, further analysis explored the simple effects of pitch, speed, language style, and voice gender within specific variable combinations (Table 7.). Notably, a significant simple effect of voice gender was observed high pitch, fast speed and task-oriented language style, indicating higher trust in female voice assistants. No significant multivariate simple effects were found for pitch. In specific combinations, such as high pitch, task-oriented language style, and female voice gender, a significant multivariate simple effect of speed was noted, with higher trust in fast-speed voice assistants. Similarly, in specific conditions like high pitch, slow speed, and male voice gender, a significant multivariate simple effect of language style was observed, with more trust in task-oriented language style voice assistants. In the combination of high pitch, fast, speed, and female voice gender, a highly significant multivariate simple effect of language style was evident, with increased trust in task-oriented language style voice assistants.

For the combination of fast speed and task-oriented language style, a significant multivariate simple effect of voice gender showed that participants trusted female voice assistants more. In the combination of fast speed and female voice gender, a highly significant multivariate simple effect of language style was observed that participants trusted task-oriented language style voice assistants more. For the combination of female voice gender and task-oriented language style, a significant multivariate simple effect of speed was evident. Participants trusted voice assistants with fast speed more (Table 7).

Simple effects tests for language style and voice gender revealed that voice gender significantly influences trust across different language styles, particularly favoring task-oriented ones when the voice gender is female (Table 7).

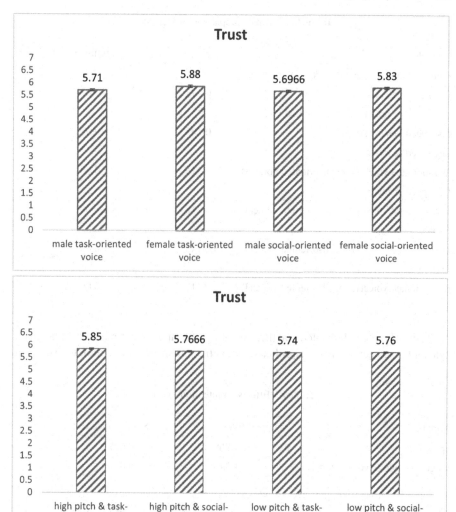

Fig. 3. Participants' consent to trust (error line is ± 1 standard error)

In the analysis of pitch and language style, a significant simple effect of pitch was observed when the language style was task-oriented, indicating more trust in lower pitch voice assistants. For high pitch, a highly significant simple effect of language style was evident, with increased trust in task-oriented language style voice assistants (Table 7).

Table 7. Multiple comparisons about trust

Variable	difference(I-J)	Significance test
high pitch & fast speed & task-oriented voice		
female(I) male(J)	0.273	0.022
high pitch & female & task-oriented voice		
fast speed(I) slow speed(J)	0.199	0.02
fast speed & female		
task-oriented voice(I) social-oriented voice(J)	0.316	< 0.001
fast speed & male		
task-oriented voice(I) social-oriented voice(J)	0.218	< 0.001
female		
task-oriented voice(I) social-oriented voice(J)	0.145	< 0.001
high pitch		
task-oriented voice(I) social-oriented voice(J)	0.117	0.003

Results (Table 8) indicated that there were significant interaction effects of language style and voice gender, and a significant main effect of speed on intention to use.

Table 8. Effects on intention to use

Variable	F-test	Significance test
speed	4.968	0.027
language style & voice gender	21.343	< 0.001

Multiple comparisons for language style and voice gender (Table 9) revealed that when the voice gender of the assistant was male, participants' intention to use was significantly higher for social-oriented language style. When the voice gender was female, there was no significant difference in the intention to use for different language styles (Fig. 4).

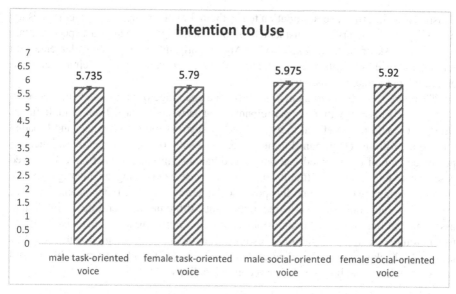

Fig. 4. Participants' consent to intention to use (error line is ± 1 standard error)

Table 9. Multiple comparisons about intention to use

Variable	difference(I-J)	Significance test
male		
social-oriented voice(I) task-oriented voice(J)	0.163	0.016

4 Discussion

In conclusion, this study highlights the significant positive impact of speed on participants' perceived ease of use and usefulness. Specifically, when the speed was at a fast level (312 words per minute), participants perceived higher ease of use. Additionally, the influence of language style on participants' perceived usefulness and intention to use was notable. Socially oriented intelligent assistants can enhance participants' perceived usefulness and intention to use. This finding aligns with previous research indicating that socially oriented robots are viewed as more active, talkative, friendly, and interesting [9, 12, 13]. They are also more likely to be socially accepted and used in the future [14–16]. Furthermore, language style, voice gender, speed, and pitch all had a significant impact on trust. Among these factors, high levels of pitch and fast speed, female voices, and task-oriented language styles in intelligent assistants were most likely to gain participants' trust.

Based on these findings, designers can consider several strategies when designing intelligent voice assistants. Firstly, the speed of intelligent assistants should be set within a reasonable range to ensure that users can obtain complete information without being overwhelmed by the speed. Secondly, enhancing the social characteristics of intelligent assistants can improve users' intention to use them. Finally, if increasing user trust is the primary goal, designers can consider a combination of high pitch and fast speed, female voices, and task-oriented language styles. Additionally, integrating visual elements with intelligent voice assistants and customizing IP characters can enhance their authenticity, entertainment value, and user trust.

There are some limitations in this study. The age range of participants in this study was relatively narrow, with most participants aged between 21 and 40 years old. In future studies, it would be beneficial to expand the survey distribution channels and broaden the scope of the investigation. Furthermore, the results of the analysis of variance for perceived ease of use showed that only speed had a significant impact on it. Perceived ease of use refers to the difficulty users experience when using an intelligent voice assistant during the experiment. It is possible that among the four independent variables used in this study, only speed affected participants' difficulty in operating the intelligent assistant resulting in limited conclusions regarding improving users' perceived ease of use. In future research, designers can also consider the impact of an intelligent assistant's knowledge background on users' perceived ease of use [17], leading to more meaningful research findings and broader design recommendations.

Acknowledgement. This work was supported by the grant from Natural Science Foundation of China (Project No. 72371033).

References

1. Acikgoz, F., PerezVega, R., Okumus, F., et al.: Consumer engagement with AI-powered voice assistants: aA behavioral reasoning perspective[J]. Psychol. Market. **40**(11), 2226–2243 (2023)
2. Moar, J., Escherich, M.: Hey Siri, how will you make money[J]. Juniper Research (2020)
3. Zhou, P., Xie, Y., Liang, C.: How to increase consumers' continued use intention of artificial intelligence voice assistants? The role of anthropomorphic features. Electron. Markets **33**, 60 (2023). https://doi.org/10.1007/s12525-023-00681-0
4. Dung, T.T.P., Tien, N.D.: Do people intend to use AI Voice Assistants? an empirical study in Vietnam[J]. J. Hum. Behav. Soc. Environ. **33**(6), 859–878 (2023)
5. Laumer, S., Maier, C., et al. : Chatbot acceptance in healthcare: explaining user adoption of conversational agents for disease diagnosis. **6**, 8–14 (2019)
6. Lee, SeoYoung, Choi, J.: Enhancing user experience with conversational agent for movie recommendation: effects of self-disclosure and reciprocity. Int. J. Human-Comput. Stud. **103**, 95–105 (2017). https://doi.org/10.1016/j.ijhcs.2017.02.005
7. Tapus, A., Țăpuș, C., Matarić, M.J.: User—robot personality matching and assistive robot behavior adaptation for post-stroke rehabilitation therapy. Intel. Serv. Robot. **1**, 169–183 (2008)
8. Feinberg, D.R., et al.: The voice and face of woman: One ornament that signals quality? Evol. Human Behav. **26**(5), 398–408 (2005). https://doi.org/10.1016/j.evolhumbehav.2005.04.001
9. McBride, K.: The effect of rate of speech and distributed practice on the development of listening comprehension[J]. Comput. Assist. Lang. Learn. **24**(2), 131–154 (2011)
10. Liu, F.F.: The Influence of Pitch, Context, and Emotional State on the Perception of Speaker Personality Traits. Southwest University, Chongqing (2017)

11. Chattaraman, V., Kwon, W.-S., Gilbert, J.E., Ross, K.: Should AI-Based, conversational digital assistants employ social- or task-oriented interaction style? A task-competency and reciprocity perspective for older adults. Comput. Human Behav. **90**, 315–330 (2019). https://doi.org/10.1016/j.chb.2018.08.048

12. Davis, F.D.: Perceived usefulness, perceived ease of use, and user acceptance of information technology [J]. MIS Q. **13**(3), 319–340 (1989)

13. Dong, Y.: The Influence of High and Low Frequency of Speech Sounds in Advertising on Consumer Purchase Intention. Wuhan University, Wuhan (2017)

14. Lohse, M., Hanheide, M., Wrede, B., et al.: Evaluating extrovert and introvert behavior of a domestic robot: a video study. In: 17th IEEE International Symposium on Robot and Human Interactive Communication, pp. 488–493 (2008)

15. Meerbeek, B., Hoonhout, J., Bingley, P., Terken, J.M.B.: The influence of robot personality on perceived and preferred level of user control. Interact. Stud. Social Behav. Commun. Biol. Artif. Syst. **9**(2), 204–229 (2008). https://doi.org/10.1075/is.9.2.04mee

16. Kim, H., Kwak, S.S., Kim, M.: Personality design of sociable robots by control of gesture design factors. In: IEEE RO-MAN Munich, pp. 494–499 (2008)

17. Zhong, R., Ma, M.: Effects of communication style, anthropomorphic setting and individual differences on older adults using voice assistants in a health context. BMC Geriatr.Geriatr. **22**, 751 (2022). https://doi.org/10.1186/s12877-022-03428-2

Insight Through Dialogue: A Practical Exploration of AIGC in Cross-cultural Design Research

Xiaoxuan Zhao and Yue Qiu[✉]

School of Design and Arts, Beijing Institute of Technology, Beijing 100081, China
{3120221910,qiuyue}@bit.edu.cn

Abstract. This study systematically reviews the objectives, methodologies, and challenges involved in cross-cultural design research, analyzing the benefits of employing Artificial Intelligence-Generated Content (AIGC) for such studies. It introduces a novel tool that applies AIGC to cross-cultural design research, developed through the use of a fine-tuned ChatGPT-4 model. By creating a specific dataset for the research topic and applying transfer learning techniques, this tool evolves into a chatbot capable of delivering personalized response strategies to users from diverse cultural backgrounds. It leverages natural language interfaces and real-time image generation to meet user needs, conducting research tasks autonomously. Experimental results demonstrate that, compared with conventional cross-cultural research methods such as questionnaires and manual interviews, the chatbot significantly enhances the efficiency of design research and users' cross-cultural interaction experience, while obtaining more realistic and objective feedback. This study not only underscores the potential application of AIGC in cross-cultural design research but also provides substantial theoretical support and practical guidance for future research in cross-cultural contexts.

Keywords: Cross-cultural · AIGC · Design Research · Large Language Models

1 Introduction

In the context of globalization, more and more products and services are entering the international market. To meet the needs of users from different cultural backgrounds while avoiding potential cultural conflicts and misunderstandings, cross-cultural design has become an inevitable trend. It is a process of understanding and accommodating cultural differences, and by incorporating cultural elements and symbols into design, it offers products and services that cater to the diverse multicultural experiences of users around the world.

Successful cross-cultural design hinges on objective and comprehensive research. Designers must not depend solely on their own knowledge and experience for judgement, nor is it adequate to gather data through simplistic 'Yes or No' surveys. Comprehensive cross-cultural research demands a varied group of participants and typically involves considerable investment in terms of time, money, and effort to amass and scrutinize

P.-L. P. Rau (Ed.): HCII 2024, LNCS 14702, pp. 388–406, 2024.
https://doi.org/10.1007/978-3-031-60913-8_27

data via questionnaires, interviews, observations, and experiments [1]. The goal is to uncover insights and compile all critical elements that might impact the design process. Consequently, there is a pressing need for the development of innovative cross-cultural research tools. Such tools would enable designers to undertake cross-cultural design research with greater ease and efficiency.

In this study, AIGC technology is applied to the field of cross-cultural design research, culminating in the creation of a chatbot based on the ChatGPT-4 model. This chatbot is capable of delivering personalized responses to users from diverse cultural backgrounds, utilizing natural language as the interface, generating images in real-time to meet user needs, and autonomously conducting research tasks. The principal findings of this research are:

1. **Confirmation of AIGC's potential in cross-cultural design research.** This research marks the first application of AIGC technology in this field, developing a chatbot that autonomously executes research tasks and validating its usability and effectiveness empirically
2. **A fine-tuning strategy for the chatbot based on ChatGPT-4 is articulated.** Through setting initial parameters and supplying fine-tuning materials that delineate the research process and criteria, the chatbot is personalized to address specific research topics
3. **Comparative experiments were conducted to assess the chatbot's objective impact.** The results indicate that the chatbot enhances the efficiency of design research and the cross-cultural interaction experience for users, providing more realistic and objective feedback

2 Theoretical Background

The purpose of this section is to delineate the pertinent theoretical underpinnings of cross-cultural design research and AIGC, while also critically examining the benefits and obstacles inherent in the integration of AIGC into cross-cultural design research.

2.1 Cross-cultural Design Research

Cross-cultural design research serves as both the cornerstone and the pivotal element of effective cross-cultural design. It is distinct from other design research due to its heightened sensitivity to linguistic and cultural nuances [2]. This type of research is instrumental in enabling designers to comprehend the distinct needs and expectations of consumers across diverse cultural backgrounds [3]. Nonetheless, researchers engaged in cross-cultural settings often encounter more pronounced communication barriers [4] and encounter greater variances in response styles compared to their non-cross-cultural counterparts [5]. These challenges collectively add to the intricacy of the cross-cultural design research process, necessitating more thorough and comprehensive investigations and analyses [6].

Key scholars in the field of cross-cultural studies include Geert Hofstede, who proposed the Cultural Dimensions Theory. He argued that values are the core of culture and proposed six dimensions along which cultures can be located [7]. Building on Hofstede's work, Shalom H. Schwartz's Theory of Basic Human Values identifies 10 basic human values, forming four dimensions of cultural values. This framework aids researchers in understanding people's values across different cultural contexts and developing stronger cultural sensitivity for addressing the needs and preferences of cross-cultural user groups [8].

Choosing appropriate cross-cultural design research methods is crucial for varying research objectives, target groups, and resource constraints. The Cross-cultural Survey Guidelines (CCSG), developed by Beth-Ellen Pennell, provide systematic research guidelines for cross-cultural researchers. These methods include Questionnaires, Face-to-Face Surveys, Telephone Surveys, and Self-Administered Surveys, encompassing mail surveys, Web surveys, and interactive voice response surveys [9]. Furthermore, Senongo Akpem, in his work on Cross-cultural Design, introduces additional methods such as Cultural Probes, Local Facilitators, the Bollywood Technique, and Possession Personas, which help in obtaining authentic feedback from participants through special interactive scenarios [10].

2.2 Challenges in Cross-cultural Design Research

The core objective of cross-cultural design research is to provide design teams with comprehensive and in-depth cultural understanding and insights into needs related to the design topic. In a cross-cultural context, researchers face specific challenges.

One major challenge is ensuring the accuracy and consistency of translated content, considering the significant costs involved. Gastón Ares suggests that researchers should conduct preliminary qualitative studies on conceptual and linguistic equivalence to ensure participants' accurate understanding of the research content [5]. Peter Mohler et al. emphasize the central importance of translation procedures in research. Ineffective translation, without understanding a culture's linguistic history, can lead to misunderstandings or even insults [9]. The cost of translation, which increases due to the integration of technology, staff, and strategy, is another critical factor [10]. Additionally, the process of collecting and analyzing information in research demands considerable time, financial resources, and manpower [11].

Cultural differences and implicit biases also impact the authenticity and objectivity of user feedback. Apala Chavan notes the difficulty in obtaining authentic feedback in collectivist cultures, where social harmony and others' feelings are prioritized over direct personal expression [12]. Hao Chen points out the challenges researchers face in fully understanding user expressions, like slang and metaphors, from unfamiliar cultures, which may result in overlooking certain cultural factors, thus affecting the design's comprehensiveness [13]. Senongo Akpem highlights that implicit biases and stereotypes, though involuntary, can influence researchers' ability to make objective judgments [10].

In cross-cultural contexts, the absence of visual images can pose challenges in understanding specific content. Diana Boer et al. point out that without appropriate visual aids to explain cultural nuances, misunderstandings may arise in cross-cultural research [14]. Keerthana Kapiley et al. found that a lack of specific images could hinder intercultural communication and understanding in bilingual environments [15]. Titim Eliawati's study underscores the importance of images in facilitating intercultural learning and understanding [16].

2.3   Application of AIGC in Cross-cultural Research

AIGC represents the latest form of content production, following Professional Generated Content and User Generated Content. This technology primarily utilizes Machine Learning algorithms and Natural Language Processing to analyze vast amounts of data, learning to mimic human thinking patterns and expressions for automatic content generation [17]. AIGC has significant advantages in processing and generating diverse content. With the accumulation of data, improvements in computational power, and algorithmic iterations, AIGC is increasingly used in various fields of cross-cultural research.

The application of AIGC in translation achieves accuracy and consistency, reducing research costs. Zhengliang Liu notes that Large Language Models (LLMs) aid in text translation, bridging language and cultural differences, and contribute to cultural comparisons and exchanges in cross-cultural research [18]. Elsya Meida Arif's study suggests that ChatGPT can alleviate cross-cultural communication barriers, enhance user engagement, and improve productivity and efficiency in cross-cultural teams [19]. Ling Yu's research highlights the potential for reducing translation costs through AI-enhanced human-machine collaboration [20].

AIGC also plays a role in obtaining authentic and objective user feedback. Julie de Jong's research indicates that non-human-intervened survey methods can improve research quality and enhance user engagement, especially in research involving privacy and sensitive topics [9]. Sarah Burkill et al. demonstrate that online surveys offer more privacy, thus increasing the reporting rate of sensitive responses [9]. Zhengliang Liu and colleagues suggest that pre-training and fine-tuning can mitigate biases and errors in AIGC [18].

In the visual representation of cross-cultural research, AIGC contributes significantly. Leijing Zhou and colleagues developed an image generation tool based on deep learning techniques, aiding designers in selecting and integrating cultural elements in cross-cultural design. Their experiments show that this tool stimulates designers' creativity and idea generation, and improves cultural awareness and work efficiency [21].

3   Cross-cultural Research Chatbot Based on AIGC

In this study, we developed a chatbot based on ChatGPT-4, capable of independently performing cross-cultural design research tasks. As shown in Fig. 1, the researcher is required to set the initial parameters for the chatbot according to the specific research topic within the fine-tuning materials and guidelines. Relevant materials, in accordance with the main structure, must be provided to facilitate the fine-tuning training of the ChatGPT-4-based model. This process enables the creation of a chatbot capable of independently carrying out research tasks. Research participants will interact with the chatbot through dialogues. The chatbot is designed to collect and analyze information and data from these dialogues, based on a predefined research overview and conversation guidelines. At the conclusion of the study, the chatbot can autonomously generate a research report and submit it to the researcher.

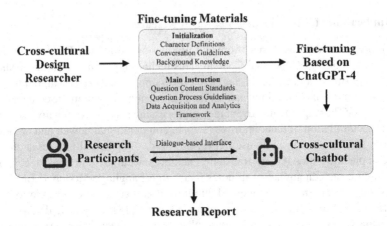

Fig. 1. Cross-cultural Chatbot Development and Utilization Process

The primary functions of this chatbot, as illustrated in Fig. 2, are:

- Adapting responses strategies for diverse cultural backgrounds.
- Utilizing natural language as an interface for conducting research tasks via dialogue.
- Generating images in real-time based on user requirements to aid in comprehension.
- Automatically collecting, analyzing research data, and producing research reports.

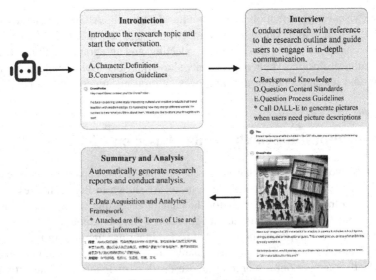

Fig. 2. Key Features of the Chatbot

3.1 Cross-cultural Chatbot Fine-Tuning Based on ChatGPT-4

When applying LLMs, such as ChatGPT-4, to specific research tasks, it is crucial to provide topic-specific training datasets for fine-tuning the model. In this study, the fine-tuning data we supplied primarily includes the initial parameter settings for the chatbot and the design of processes and rules for the research task. The fine-tuning involves the following key steps:

- **Initialization of the Chatbot**

In the initialization phase of the chatbot, it is essential to clearly define its application objectives, scope of application, and conversation guidelines. This ensures the effective execution of cross-cultural design research tasks. To fine-tune the model, the preparation of the following data is necessary. See Table 1.

Table 1. Initial Setup Parameters

Components	Contents	Descriptions
Character Definitions	Purpose	Improve the professionalism and accuracy of generated contents
	Character	Interviewer for cross-cultural design research
	Definitions	·Warm and friendly disposition ·Cross-cultural academic foundation ·Multilingual communication facilitation ·Natural and relaxed interaction atmosphere ·In-depth research topic navigation
Conversation Guidelines	Purpose	Optimize chatbot's performance to enhance user interaction experience
	Guidelines	·Adaptive cross-cultural interaction ·Culturally inclusive personalization ·Clarity and comprehensibility in communication ·Relevance and respect in dialogue ·Privacy and sensitivity awareness ·Provision of real-time image assistance
Background Knowledge	Purpose	Improve the professionalism and accuracy of generated contents
	Contents	·Topical expertise, encompassing relevant terminology, foundational concepts, and illustrative examples, etc ·Current developments, stay abreast of the latest trends, news, and best practices within the associated domains, etc

- **Main Instruction**

When constructing the main structure of the chatbot, precise setting of the research content is imperative. This involves not only the rigorous and clear formulation of research questions and questioning strategies but also the development of a detailed methodology for data collection and analysis. Such meticulous planning is vital to ensure the chatbot's efficient performance in research tasks. See Table 2.

Table 2. Construction Materials

Components	Contents	Descriptions
Question Content Standards	Purpose	Fulfill the research objective and gather necessary data effectively
	Standards	Exclude questions that are overly broad or irrelevant to the research objective Condense the volume of questions to ensure each is pertinent to the research objective Structure the question sequence to progressively deepen the user's engagement and thought process
Question Process Guidelines	Purpose	Optimize the structure and delivery of questions to maximize user engagement and the quality of interaction
	Guidelines	Arrange research questions in a clear, logical order Define themes and directions for open-ended questions, informed by user interaction Establish precise conditions for the usage of supplementary tools (e.g., DALL-E) Maintain the pertinence and clarity of all questions, avoiding those that are too generalized
Data Acquisition and Analytics Framework	Purpose	Guarantee the systematic collection, meticulous analysis, and judicious use of data
	Framework	Develop statistical and analytical models for rigorous data examination and prepare structured data reporting formats Articulate a systematic approach to data gathering and analysis to ensure comprehensive and accurate insights Implement and uphold stringent data privacy and security measures throughout all stages of data handling to maintain compliance with legal and ethical standards

- **Supplementary Materials**

To optimize user experience and ensure the safe usage of the chatbot, it is crucial to include comprehensive user terms of use and developer contact information within the training dataset. This approach not only guarantees data transparency and the user's right to be informed but also lays a solid foundation for building trust with users.

3.2 Complete Process of Research

The chatbot developed in this study, named CrossProbe, is engineered to offer users a highly customized and interactive cross-cultural research experience. When engaged in a research task, users have the flexibility to initiate conversations in any language. In response, CrossProbe is equipped to converse in the same language, ensuring seamless communication. See Fig. 3.

Fig. 3. CrossProbe's Response to Different Language

Throughout the research process, CrossProbe adheres to a pre-established research overview and conversation guidelines, ensuring that user interactions are both relaxed and natural. Significantly, if users face challenges in comprehending certain concepts or require visual aid for explanations, CrossProbe is capable of invoking the DALL-E plug-in. This feature enables it to generate relevant images, thereby enhancing user understanding and facilitating more effective communication. See Fig. 4.

Here's an image showing how tie-dye can be incorporated into stationery items. As you can see, tie-dye patterns can add a vibrant and artistic touch to everyday objects, making them more appealing and unique. Do you find these tie-dye stationery designs interesting?

Fig. 4. CrossProbe Generates Image Based on User Requirement

Upon the completion of the research, CrossProbe possesses the capability to autonomously generate comprehensive reports. These reports encapsulate the results, key findings, and actionable design recommendations. Additionally, at the conclusion of the analysis, these reports are automatically dispatched to the researchers, facilitating immediate review and further study. See Fig. 5.

In summary, CrossProbe is proficient in facilitating multi-language conversations and adept at tailoring response strategies to users from diverse cultural backgrounds. It effectively guides participants through research topics via interactive dialogues, and is capable of generating real-time images based on user requirements, thereby enhancing understanding. Upon completion of the research, CrossProbe autonomously compiles and analyzes data, subsequently producing a comprehensive research report that enables researchers to delve deeper into their studies.

4   Comparative Experiment

4.1   Experiment Methods

To assess the capability and effectiveness of this chatbot in conducting cross-cultural design research, this study initiated an experiment for comparison with conventional cross-cultural research methods such as questionnaires and manual interviews.

The experiment involved three control groups, each staffed with two researchers having similar qualifications and experience. See Table 3.

Survey Results for Xiao Dian Dian (Little Dot)

1. Basic Information
   * Nationality: China
   * Gender: Female
   * Age: 23
   * Profession: Industrial Design
2. Product Preferences
   * Understanding and Basic Impression of Tie-dye: Rich in color, with ethnic characteristics
   * Preferred Type of Cultural and Creative Product: Practical type
   * Reason for Preference: Not specifically mentioned
3. Shopping Habits
   * Shopping Venues: Online platforms and boutique stores (e.g., Zakka-style shops)
   * Purchase Purpose: Mainly for personal use, occasionally as gifts for others
   * Budget: Around 100 to 200 Yuan
4. Other Insights Gleaned
   * Ideal Characteristics of Cultural and Creative Products: High-end design, cultural connotation, affordable price
   * Influence of Cultural Background on Product Preference: Believes that her cultural background does not significantly influence her preferences

Summary of Survey with Xiao Dian Dian (Little Dot)

1. Summary:
   Xiao Dian Dian, a young consumer, focuses on the design and cultural content of cultural and creative products, preferring practical types that blend unique designs with cultural elements. She shops on diverse platforms, including online and physical boutique stores. Regarding the budget for cultural and creative products, she tends to opt for medium-priced items.
2. Keywords:
   Design Consciousness, Cultural Connotation, Practicality, Medium Price, Diverse Shopping Channels

CrossProbe's Research Suggestions
For young consumer groups like Xiao Dian Dian, it is recommended that cultural and creative product designs integrate innovation with cultural content, taking into account both the practicality and affordability of the products. Marketing strategies should cater to both online and physical boutique channels to attract a broader consumer base. Moreover, product pricing should consider the financial capacity of young consumers, ensuring the products are appealing in both innovation and price.

Fig. 5. CrossProbe Generated Research Report

Forty-two volunteers were recruited through a posted announcement in the AIGC community. To ensure controlled variables, 30 participants sharing essential similar characteristics were chosen. These 30 participants were then evenly distributed into three experimental groups, categorized by their native languages.

Table 3. Experiment Groups

Group	Name	Description
A	Chatbot Group	Conducting research tasks using a specific chatbot designed for the study to enhance interaction
B	Online Questionnaire Group	Conducting research tasks through the administration of online questionnaires
C	Manual Interview Group	Facilitating research through detailed manual interview techniques

Each group comprised (Table 4):

Table 4. Composition of Participants in Each Group

Participant Count	Characteristic	Cultural Representation
5	Native Chinese-speaking	Eastern cultural backgrounds
5	Native English-speaking	Western cultural backgrounds

At the experiment's onset, the same research overview (Table 5) were simultaneously distributed to all three groups, ensuring clarity regarding the research's objective and primary content. The experiment's research topic focused on examining diverse cultural preferences for tie-dye products, including cultural and creative items for practical use, decorative art pieces such as wall hangings, and hands-on DIY tie-dye kits (Table 6), as well as analyzing corresponding consumer shopping behaviors.

Tie-dye, a traditional folk art, exhibits varying levels of acceptance across diverse cultures. Cross-cultural research is instrumental in uncovering these variations, thereby enabling designers to comprehend the distinct needs and expectations of consumers across diverse cultures. The topic also encouraged dialogue among users from various cultures, aiding designers in identifying key factors (like price, appearance, and significance) that influence the purchase of cultural products. This understanding is crucial for accurate market positioning and targeted product design.

Table 5. Research Overview

Contents		Descriptions
Topic		Examining diverse cultural preferences for tie-dye products, including cultural and creative items for practical use, decorative art pieces such as wall hangings, and hands-on DIY tie-dye kits, as well as analyzing corresponding consumer shopping behaviors

(continued)

Table 5. (*continued*)

Contents		Descriptions
Objective		Refine market positioning and tailor product design to align with user feedback for enhanced precision
Projects	Basic Information	1. Nationality 2. Gender 3. Age 4. Occupation (Field of Expertise)
	Product Preferences	1. General awareness and initial perceptions of tie-dye among users across diverse cultures 2. Cultural influences on user preferences for various tie-dye product categories, excluding price considerations 3. Analysis of purchase history to determine favored cultural and creative product types across diverse cultures
	Shopping Habits	1. Preferred purchasing venues for cultural and creative products across diverse cultures, including online platforms, non-tourist physical stores, and tourist-oriented physical stores 2. Intent behind the purchase of cultural and creative products, whether for personal use or as gifts across diverse cultures 3. Allocated spending on cultural and creative products by individuals across diverse cultures
	User inclination to engage in subsequent research activities	

Table 6. Representative Tie-Dye Products Overview (Source: Taobao)

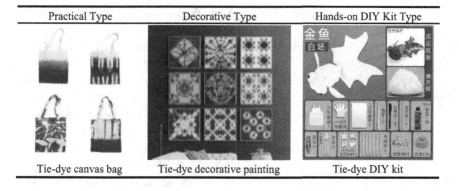

Practical Type	Decorative Type	Hands-on DIY Kit Type
Tie-dye canvas bag	Tie-dye decorative painting	Tie-dye DIY kit

To evaluate the effectiveness and efficiency of various research methods, along with the adaptability in intercultural communication and the participants' experiences, the following evaluation indicators were established:

Table 7. Key Performance Indicators (KPIs)

KPIs	Contents	Description
① Research Setup Time	Definition	Log the cumulative duration allocated to preparatory activities in the research phase
	Purpose	Assess the setup time efficiency across research methods
	Evaluation method	Employ a comparative analysis against the average setup time
② Quantity of Valid Data	Definition	Enumerate the volume of data pertinent to the stated objectives of the research topic
	Purpose	Assess the data collection effects across research methods
	Evaluation method	Assign a single investigator from each cohort to assess data volume, followed by inter-group comparisons
③ Quality of Valid Data	Definition	Evaluate data integrity and relevance to research topic
	Purpose	Assess the data collection effects across research methods
	Evaluation method	Assign scores for assistance as follows: 1 for 'slightly helpful' and 2 for 'very helpful'. Then, calculate and compare the average scores across groups
④ Data Collection Method	Definition	Describe the concurrency of data collection methods
	Purpose	Assess the data collection efficiency across research methods
	Evaluation method	Concurrency methods are superior to serial methods in terms of efficiency
⑤ Completion Time	Definition	Log the mean duration required by participants to complete the research activities
	Purpose	Assess the efficiency of individual user data collection across research methods
	Evaluation method	Employ a comparative analysis against the average completion time
⑥ Cross-cultural Score	Definition	Evaluate the adaptability of research methods across diverse cultures
	Purpose	Assess the cross-cultural adaptation across research methods

(continued)

Table 7. (*continued*)

KPIs	Contents	Description
	Evaluation method	Collect and compare cross-cultural adaptability ratings from non-native participants, using a Likert scale
⑦ Satisfaction Score	Definition	Evaluate the research experience for all participants
	Purpose	Assess the participant satisfaction across research methods
	Evaluation method	Collect and compare participant satisfaction ratings from all participants, using a Likert scale

Each group was tasked with planning their research in accordance with the research overview in Table 5. This included conducting the research tasks, analyzing the results, and recording the necessary data to evaluate the KPIs as detailed in Table 7. Each group's experimental procedure is detailed below (Table 8):

Table 8. Experimental Procedures for Each Group

Procedures	Chatbot Group	Online Questionnaire Group	Manual Interview Group
Preparation	·Integrate the organized research overview (Tbl.5) into the fine-tuned training materials for the chatbot ·Test the chatbot for content accuracy and dialog flow clarity	·Translate the research overview (Tbl.5) into English ·Design the questionnaire to include sequential order of questions, response options, and conditional logic, etc ·Pretest the questionnaire for clarity and functionality	·Translate the research overview (Tbl.5) into English ·Develop the interview guide with detailed question order, style, and alternatives, etc ·Train interviewers on the topic comprehension and handling of potential contingencies
Execution	·Distribute the chatbot link to participants	·Distribute the online questionnaire link to participants	·Schedule interviews with participants at mutually agreed times and locations

(*continued*)

Table 8. (*continued*)

Procedures	Chatbot Group	Online Questionnaire Group	Manual Interview Group
Data Collection and Analysis	·Automate data collection and analysis through the chatbot, generating reports	·Utilize the questionnaire tool for data analysis, compile and organize data manually for analysis	·Classify and scrutinize the interview data manually, following the established research documentation protocol

*Each group will be required to record the data required to assess the KPIs (Tbl.7) during the course of the experiment

4.2 Experiment Results

This section details the results from a comparative experiment conducted from January 5 to 20, 2024. Designed to evaluate the effectiveness and efficiency of various research methods, the experiment involved the analysis of data from multiple groups in a comparative manner. The table below (Table 9) presents a summary of the KPIs recorded by each group during the experiment.

This provides a visual representation and comparative evidence of the performance of the different research methods.

Table 9. Comparative Table of KPIs Across Group

KPIs	Chatbot Group	Online Questionnaire Group	Manual Interview Group	Average Value
① Research Setup Time	2 h 32 min	36 min	3 h 44 min	2 h 17 min
② Quantity of Valid Data	13.6	17.91	16	15.84
③ Quality of Valid Data	14.6	19.82	21.75	18.72

(*continued*)

Table 9. (*continued*)

KPIs	Chatbot Group	Online Questionnaire Group	Manual Interview Group	Average Value
④ Data Collection Method	Concurrent	Concurrent	Serial	/
⑤ Completion Time	3 min 40 s	32 min 16 s	11 min 18 s	15 min 44 s
⑥ Cross-cultural Score	4.3	4.8	4.4	4.5
⑦ Satisfaction Score	3.7	4.3	4.1	4.03

As shown in the table, the chatbot group significantly surpassed the other two groups in terms of **KPI①Research Setup Time** and **KPI②Quantity of Valid Data**. However, it fell short compared to the manual interview group in **KPI③Quality of Valid Data**, indicating that while chatbots are effective for quick research preparation and enhancing user participation, there is a need for improvement in the quality and depth of the data collected.

Regarding **KPI④Data Collection Method**, both the chatbot and online questionnaire groups utilized parallel methods, proving more efficient than the serial approach of the manual interview group. Nevertheless, the chatbot required the most time per capita, as indicated by **KPI⑤Completion Time**. This highlights a future research consideration: balancing the efficiency of data collection with the duration of research for individual participants.

The chatbot group scored highest in **KPI⑥Cross-cultural Score** and **KPI⑦Satisfaction Score**, suggesting that the chatbot developed in this experiment offers considerable benefits in enhancing cross-cultural adaptability and participant satisfaction in design research.

4.3 Discussion

Based on the findings from the comparative experiments and insights obtained throughout the experimental process, employing the chatbot developed in this study for cross-cultural design research presents several notable advantages:

1. Enhanced Efficiency in Design Research

- **Minimized Research Preparation Time:** Utilizing the chatbot streamlines the preparation phase. Unlike online questionnaires, which requires the design and translation of content, or manual interviews, which involve drafting conversation outlines and content translation, the chatbot necessitates only the uploading of the research overview into the fine-tuning material. The AI then automatically handles translation and executes research tasks, significantly reducing preparation costs and enhancing overall research efficiency.

- **Concurrent Execution of Multiple Research Tasks:** The chatbot's parallel research method allows for handling requests from different users simultaneously, along with data collection and analysis. This approach can substantially decrease the total time needed for the research process.
- **Automated Data Collection, Analysis, and Reporting:** The chatbot autonomously monitors the research process, collecting and analyzing data in real time. This includes both statistical analysis of quantitative data and content analysis of qualitative data. It also automatically generates comprehensive research reports tailored to the specific objectives and requirements of the research.

5. Enhanced Cross-Cultural Interaction Experience

- **Improved Accuracy in Translated Content:** The chatbot, built on the ChatGPT-4 model, ensures high accuracy and consistency in translations. Participants from various language backgrounds reported enhanced accuracy in information received from the chatbot, facilitating clearer communication.
- **Real-Time Image Generation for Enhanced Comprehension:** Equipped with a DALL-E plug-in, the chatbot can generate relevant images on demand. This feature aids in understanding, enhances effective communication, and visually enriches the cross-cultural interaction experience.

8. Facilitated More Realistic and Objective User Feedback

- **Increased Willingness to Share:** Participants noted that the chatbot's interactive approach, especially for introverted users, created a more comfortable and relaxed environment. This encouraged them to share their opinions more freely, leading to a deeper understanding of the research topic and easier expression of concerns and doubts.
- **Detailed Feedback Capture:** The chatbot captures comprehensive conversation details, including tone and punctuation, which creates a more vivid and realistic user profile. Additionally, its flexibility allows users to initiate conversations at any time, fostering deeper thought and wider communication.

Despite these positive outcomes, our research also identified certain potential challenges:

- **Distraction Due to Excessive Curiosity About the chatbot:** A notable phenomenon observed was the novelty effect, where participants' fascination with the chatbot sometimes overshadowed their focus on the research task. This excessive curiosity not only diverted their attention but also had the potential to extend the duration of the research.
- **Expectation for Contrary Opinions from the chatbot:** Many users anticipated the chatbot to present challenging viewpoints, as opposed to merely adhering to a pre-defined research script. This inclination might suggest a preference for engaging in argumentative dialogue or a curiosity to test the chatbot's level of intelligence.

5 Conclusion

This study introduces an innovative tool for cross-cultural design research: a chatbot developed using the fine-tuned ChatGPT-4 model. The comparative experiments conducted validate the potential of AIGC in cross-cultural design research contexts. A multilingual and culturally adaptable chatbot serves as a bridge over language and cultural gaps in cross-cultural research. Moreover, a chatbot tailored for specific research tasks not only enhances the efficiency of design research and enriches the user's cross-cultural interaction experience, but also yields more realistic and objective user feedback.

In conclusion, our research offers empirical evidence supporting the application of AIGC in cross-cultural research and provides valuable insights for future endeavors, particularly in optimizing datasets and augmenting the chatbot's capabilities in cross-cultural communication.

References

1. Elizabeth, B.: From user-centered to participatory design approaches. In: Frascara, Jorge CONFERENCE 2002, Design and the Social Sciences, pp. 1–7. Taylor & Francis, London (2002)
2. Christopher, S., Rocco, C.R.: Emergent characteristics of effective cross-cultural research: a review of the literature. J. Couns. Dev. **88**(3), 357–362 (2011)
3. Susan, P., Samuel, C.C.: The changing dynamic of consumer behavior: implications for cross-cultural research. Int. J. Res. Mark. **14**(4), 379–395 (1997)
4. Jie, L., Katja, H.: The influence of designers' cultural differences on the empathic accuracy of user understanding. Des. J. **23**(5), 779–796 (2020)
5. Gastón, A.: Methodological issues in cross-cultural sensory and consumer research. Food Qual. Prefer. **64**, 253–263 (2018)
6. Nusa, F., Beverly, W.: R&D-marketing integration in innovation – does culture matter? Eur. Bus. Rev. **26**(2), 169–187 (2014)
7. Geert, H.: Dimensionalizing cultures: the Hofstede model in context. Online Readings in Psychology and Culture 2(1), (2011)
8. Shalom, H.: An overview of the Schwartz theory of basic values. Online Readings Psychol. Cult. **2**(1), **8** (2012)
9. CCSG Homepage. https://ccsg.isr.umich.edu/. Accessed 25 Jan 2024
10. Senongo, A.: Cross-Cultural Design, 1st edn. Book Apart, New York (2020)
11. Jimy, M.: Ethnic boundaries and identity in plural societies. Annu. Rev. Sociol. **28**, 327–357 (2002)
12. Bob, B.: Human Factors International. https://www.humanfactors.com/newsletters/readability_formulas.asp. Accessed 25 Jan 2024
13. Hao, C.: Cultura: Achieving Intercultural Empathy through Contextual User Research in Design. TU Delft Design Conceptualization and Communication (2019)
14. Diana, B., Katja, H., Jia, H.: On detecting systematic measurement error in cross-cultural research: a review and critical reflection on equivalence and invariance tests. J. Cross-Cult. Psychol. **49**(5), 713–734 (2018)
15. Keerthana, K., Ramesh, K.: Iconic culture-specific images influence language non-selective translation activation in bilinguals. TCB **1**(2), 221–250 (2018)
16. Titim, E.: Cross cultural understanding learning method. Jurnal MELT **3**(1), 17 (2018)

17. Tao, W., Yushu, Z., Shuren, Q., et al.: Security and Privacy on Generative Data in AIGC: A Survey (2023). arXiv preprint arXiv:2309.09435
18. Liu, Z., Li, Y., Cao, Q., et al.: Transformation vs Tradition: Artificial General Intelligence (AGI) for Arts and Humanities (2023). arXiv preprint arXiv:2310.19626
19. Elsya, M., Sarwo, S., Ahmad, S., et al.: The role of ChatGPT in improving cross-cultural team management performance. JMP **12**(1), 1482–1491 (2023)
20. Ling, Y.: Research on intelligent translation strategy based on human machine coupling. IJFS **3**(2), 87–92 (2021)
21. Leijing, Z., Xu, S., Guannan, M., et al.: A tool to facilitate the cross-cultural design process using deep learning. IEEE Trans. Human-Mach. Syst. **52**(3), 445–457 (2021)

Research on Designing Interventions for Cyberbullying Among Adolescents Under the Trends of AIGC

Xiaolin Zuo, Yanze Liu, and Zhaolin Lu[✉]

College of Design and Art, Beijing Institute of Technology, Beijing 102401, China
1508528430@qq.com

Abstract. Background: Cyberbullying is widespread in contemporary society, posing a severe threat to adolescents' mental and physical well-being, leading to psychological trauma and life-threatening situations. Given the absence of a systematic framework for preventing cyberbullying among adolescents and their relatively weak judgment and stress-coping abilities, cultivating awareness and healthy habits becomes crucial. This study aims to design a device aligning with adolescents' cognitive characteristics, inspiring active engagement in countering cyberbullying, enabling them to recognize potential dangers and develop an awareness of counteraction. Methods: An experimental methodology was employed, utilizing Artificial Intelligence and Generated Content (AIGC) technology to create predefined scenarios and engage in user dialogues. Users' essential viewpoints and critical features were assessed by the AIGC, and emotional scores were assigned. The scoring results were subsequently utilized for interactive feedback through the device. Results: Findings indicated that the device's interaction style and feedback significantly impacted adolescents, influencing their perception profoundly. The device effectively raised awareness of online violence, contributing to the cultivation of their understanding of counteraction. Conclusion: The study envisions the potential application of AIGC technology in intelligent design. Future trends should focus on design approaches for adolescent education and supplement regulatory measures to address cyberbullying issues more effectively.

Keywords: Industrial Design · Adolescents · Theory of Planned Behavior · Cyberbullying · Mental Health

1 Research on the Current Status of Cyberbullying Among Adolescents

Cyberbullying is a widespread phenomenon on the internet, encompassing the posting of hurtful, insulting remarks, images, and videos, essentially constituting verbal violence. Differing from direct violence, cyberbullying manifests as psychological pressure [1]. The motive behind cyberbullying is venting-style malicious attacks. This form of cyberbullying begins with emotional venting and purely malicious attacks on online public opinion, also known as Cyberbullying [2]. Such violent behaviors spread online and

P.-L. P. Rau (Ed.): HCII 2024, LNCS 14702, pp. 407–424, 2024.
https://doi.org/10.1007/978-3-031-60913-8_28

are closely related to the anonymity and virtuality of the internet. As netizens often participate anonymously, lacking a sense of moral responsibility and self-restraint, they easily infringe on others' legitimate rights and interests. The phenomenon of cyberbullying includes anonymity and crude language, making it easier for people to post illogical and purposeless insulting remarks. Moreover, it is contagious; once one person is attacked, they often respond with a retaliatory mindset, creating a situation where "everyone inflicts violence, everyone is victimized."

Cyberbullying mainly involves targeted attacks and insults through text, images, and videos. In the online environment, separated by screens and networks, anonymity and virtuality allow many people to wear false masks. Exploiting the contradiction and blurred boundaries between the right to free speech and the responsibility to maintain a healthy public internet environment, online "keyboard warriors" become increasingly unrestrained. Whenever there is a voice different from their own beliefs, some extreme netizens attack a specific individual massively through text, images, and videos. Even if forbidden words are set, the perpetrators can still use homophones, transliteration, and other means to carry out verbal and textual insults, even leading organized, large-scale attacks and insults [3]. The core feature of the "violence" involved in cyberbullying "lies in the scale of language quantity, the aggressiveness of language content, and the realization of the consequences of the harm" [4]. In addition, some use it as a means of emotional venting, causing harm to others even though it does not indeed provide relief. The pressure of public opinion on social media and collective attacks may also force people to participate in cyberbullying out of self-protection or malice. Another reason is the lag in speech regulation; the regulation of online information often lags behind posting comments, providing a breeding ground for cyberbullying.

The impact of cyberbullying is profound, including psychological stress, worsening situations, and social problems. In some severe cases of cyberbullying, such as a 24-year-old female master's student committing suicide due to cyberbullying for dyeing her hair pink [5], a woman jumping off a building after being cyberbullied for tipping a delivery person 200 yuan [6], and Korean actress Choi Sulli choosing to hang herself due to cyberbullying [7], victims often endure prolonged concentrated attacks, leading to excessive psychological pressure and possibly mental breakdowns. Victims may also join the perpetrators out of a retaliatory mindset, leading to a worsening situation and a vicious cycle. These extreme events have attracted widespread social attention and become serious social issues.

In summary, cyberbullying is a serious social issue. Its roots include factors such as the anonymity of the internet, the need for emotional venting, and social pressure. To solve this problem, all sectors of society should work together, adopting various measures, including tackling the issue from both the perpetrators and the victims' perspectives. On the one hand, raising netizens' sense of moral responsibility and strengthening the regulatory mechanisms of social media, and on the other hand, providing psychological health support and education to victims, are necessary to reduce the occurrence and impact of cyberbullying and maintain the health and positivity of cyberspace.

2 Intelligent Design Methods Aided by AIGC

2.1 Research on the Current State of AIGC Technology

The development of artificial intelligence technology is comprehensively altering the ways in which people work and live. Over the past 60 years of development, artificial intelligence has entered a new stage, exhibiting new characteristics such as deep learning, cross-disciplinary integration, human-computer collaboration, collective intelligence, and autonomous control. Additionally, big data-driven knowledge learning and cross-media collaborative processing have become key focal points of development in this field. In recent years, significant improvements have been seen in tasks such as natural language processing, speech recognition, and computer vision, thanks to the "big data + big model" approach under unsupervised learning conditions. The important branch of the new generation of AI, Artificial Intelligence Generated Content (AIGC), has seen accelerated development, leading to the emergence of a new industrial ecosystem [8].

Innovations and applications in the field of AIGC are widely underway both domestically and internationally. Companies like Alibaba Cloud, Baidu, Xinhua Zhiyun in China, and OpenAI, Anthropic, Hugging Face, and Stability AI internationally are actively launching AIGC-related products and services. These innovations include not only technological developments but also related business models and application scenarios. For example, Generative Adversarial Networks (GANs) technology provides strong technical support for AIGC, and innovations such as Microsoft's "Xiaoice" creating poetry collections, NVIDIA's StyleGAN series, and DeepMind's DVD-GAN model represent significant progress in the AIGC field. A notable advancement in AIGC is OpenAI's chatbot, ChatGPT (Long et al., 2022) [9], which through large-scale pre-trained models, possesses the ability to understand natural language and generate text, performing tasks such as text translation, summary generation, and sentiment analysis. Particularly noteworthy is ChatGPT's rapid accumulation of over one hundred million active users within just a few months of its launch at the end of 2022, making it the fastest-growing application in history. The explosive popularity of ChatGPT symbolizes the significant impact of advances in artificial intelligence technology on human production and life [10]. Therefore, this experiment uses ChatGPT for scenario presets.

2.2 Theoretical Model for Intervening in Psychological Health Issues

This study bases its theoretical model on the Theory of Planned Behavior. The Theory of Planned Behavior, a renowned attitude-behavior relationship theory in psychology, has been widely applied in multiple behavioral fields internationally and has been proven to improve the predictive and explanatory power of behavior research significantly. In 1991, Icek Ajzen, building on the Theory of Reasoned Action (TRA) proposed by Ajzen and Fishbein (1975, 1980), introduced the Theory of Planned Behavior, as shown in Fig. 1. The Theory of Planned Behavior posits that an individual's behavioral intentions directly influence their actions, and attitudes, subjective norms, and perceived behavioral control together shape these intentions [11].

1. Attitude refers to an individual's positive or negative feelings towards a particular behavior, essentially the attitude formed after conceptualizing their evaluation of this

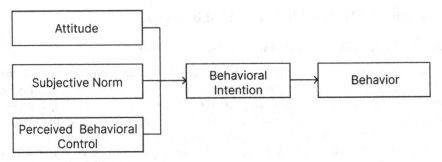

Fig. 1. Theory of Planned Behavior

specific behavior. Therefore, the components of attitude are often seen as a function of the individual's significant beliefs about the outcomes of the behavior.

2. Subjective Norm refers to the social pressure an individual feels regarding whether to engage in a particular behavior, i.e., the influence exerted by salient individuals or groups who impact on an individual's decision-making regarding a specific behavior.

3. Perceived Behavioral Control reflects an individual's past experiences and anticipated obstacles, with more resources and opportunities and fewer anticipated barriers leading to more muscular perceived behavioral control. This influence has two aspects: one is motivational regarding behavioral intention; the other is its direct predictive power on behavior.

4. Behavioral Intention refers to an individual's subjective probability judgment about engaging in a particular behavior, reflecting their willingness to perform a specific action.

5. Behavior is the action taken by an individual.

2.3 Analysis of Factors Influencing Cyberbullying Behavior Among Adolescents Based on the Theory of Planned Behavior

The Theory of Planned Behavior suggests that attitudes, subjective norms, and perceived behavioral control jointly shape an individual's behavioral intentions, with adolescents' engagement in cyberbullying behavior also influenced by these three factors (Fig. 2).

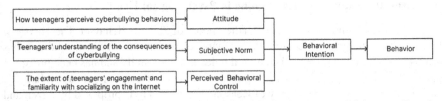

Fig. 2. Analysis of Factors Influencing Cyberbullying Behavior Among Adolescents Based on the Theory of Planned Behavior

Analysis of Attitude Factors in Adolescents' Cyberbullying Behavior. The attitude factors in adolescents' cyberbullying behavior are mainly influenced by cognitive evaluation, moral beliefs, and the social environment.

How adolescents perceive cyberbullying, and its potential consequences largely determine their behavioral choices. Their cognitive evaluations might come from various channels, such as personal experiences, peer sharing, or media reports. If adolescents believe that cyberbullying can lead to severe consequences, like punishment or social ostracism, they are likely to avoid such behavior, and vice versa. Therefore, clarifying and correcting adolescents' misconceptions about cyberbullying to make them aware of the natural consequences is crucial for changing their attitudes and behavior patterns.

Moral beliefs, the sum of their values, beliefs, and ethical standards, are deeply influenced by family, school, and social culture. When cyberbullying behavior conflicts with adolescents' moral beliefs, they are more inclined to resist such impulses.

The social environment also has a significant impact on their attitudes and behaviors. Peer pressure often drives adolescents into cyberbullying, especially in social groups that consider cyberbullying as "normal" or "fun." Additionally, adolescents might be exposed to other forms of bullying or invasive behavior in their family or school environments, which could also affect their attitudes toward cyberbullying.

Analysis of Subjective Norm Factors in Adolescents' Cyberbullying Behavior. The subjective norms of cyberbullying differ from bullying in real life. The internet provides adolescents with a relatively anonymous and indirect environment, leading to cognitive biases when evaluating the consequences of their actions. In the online environment, there is a sense of distance between bullies and victims, making it difficult for bullies to see or feel the direct consequences of their actions. This anonymity or indirectness might make some adolescents more likely to launch attacks because they do not directly confront the emotional responses of the victims, potentially underestimating the severity of their actions [12].

Negative emotions suppressed by morality are amplified in heterogeneous groups and are reinforced by the disappearance of a sense of responsibility [13]. On some social networking platforms, bullying behavior may receive support or encouragement from peers, such as through "likes" or supportive comments, leading adolescents to believe that cyberbullying is acceptable or even popular, further reinforcing misguided subjective norms.

To prevent and reduce cyberbullying, it is necessary to emphasize the natural consequences of online behavior, reminding adolescents of the negative impact their cyberbullying actions have on others and society.

Analysis of Perceived Behavioral Control Factors in Adolescents' Cyberbullying Behavior. In the context of the modern digital age, adolescents' interactions with technology are deeply embedded in their social and cognitive ecology. The level of technological familiarity and the anonymity of the internet are two aspects influencing the perceived behavioral control factors of adolescents' cyberbullying behavior.

On the one hand, adolescents' early and ongoing exposure to network information technology has led to a specific technological familiarity, enhancing their sense of control over the online environment. The fluency of technology might create an illusion of evading responsibility when engaging in cyberbullying, and the rapid evolution of technology also means that the forms and strategies of cyberbullying could become more complex and diverse over time.

On the other hand, the immature psychological traits of adolescents also make them more prone to cyberbullying. Due to their still-developing minds and weaker emotional control, they are prone to extremes and often express themselves irrationally [14]. Therefore, they are more likely to post aggressive comments through online media compared to other age groups.

3 Design of an Anti-cyberbullying Intervention Device for Adolescents Based on the Theory of Planned Behavior

3.1 Design Concept of the Device

The Theory of Planned Behavior suggests that attitude, subjective norms, and perceived behavioral control collectively determine a person's behavioral intentions, thereby influencing their actual behavior. In this context, this paper proposes the design of an educational and persuasive device, aiming to materialize adolescents' emotional expressions in cyberspace and educate them about the consequences of their actions.

The device uses a balloon to simulate the act of breathing, intended to reflect a person's emotional fluctuations during social interactions. The inflation and deflation of the balloon represent the cycle of positive and negative emotions, providing users with a tangible, physical outlet for their emotions. The device uses ChatGPT's deep learning model for emotional analysis, to identify and extract subjective information from text, such as emotional attitudes, polarities, and intensities. When a user posts excessively negative, aggressive comments on ChatGPT, the device responds by altering the inflation state of the balloon, allowing users to see the impact of their virtual behavior in the real world. This helps adjust users' attitudes and makes them aware of the significance of their online expressions. The design considers the social environment's influence on adolescents' behavior. The "breathing" state of the balloon can be observed by those around, thereby creating a form of social monitoring. When the balloon inflates to its limit and bursts, it sends a clear signal, indicating that the user's aggressive online behavior has reached a threshold. Thus, the device simulates the social feedback mechanisms found in online communities, encouraging users to value others' opinions of their behavior. Although the device cannot fully control the user's behavior, visualizing the user's emotional state, provides a real-time feedback mechanism. Users can see how each of their comments affects the state of the balloon, thus gaining immediate awareness of their emotions. This perceived behavioral control helps them adjust their behavior and understand their interactions with the social environment and the device.

3.2 Design of the Device Form

1. Safety: Safety is essential for ensuring users' physical well-being [15]. For parents, the health and safety of their children are of paramount concern. In the design of the anti-cyberbullying intervention device for adolescents, the safety of the device should be comprehensively considered, including the safety of materials (using safe, harmless, green materials is a basic requirement), the safety of form and structure (maintaining a smooth design to prevent injuries from sharp edges), and the safety of

structural functions (high overall structural stability with well-sealed connections of circuits, motors, and air tubes, inaccessible to adolescents).

2. Fun: Opposing cyberbullying is a lengthy process. Safety is just the premise for encouraging adolescents to experience the device, but it does not guarantee consistency throughout the process. More positive factors are needed to create user stickiness and provide continuous appeal. Considering adolescents' curiosity, the device should include some fun and engaging features that can add emotional content, making it appear lively and responsive to different interactions, thereby increasing their willingness and anticipation to use it.

3. Aesthetics: Adolescents are forming their aesthetic judgment and gradually developing independent thinking and judgment abilities. Products they frequently encounter play an important and subtle role in shaping these abilities. A device aimed at combating cyberbullying, it must be designed in a style that is aesthetically pleasing, elegant, and artistic, to aid in cultivation children's aesthetic sensibilities.

4. Usability: Considering adolescents' limited experience in preventing cyberbullying and their relatively weaker judgment and stress response capabilities, the design of the device must emphasize usability. The product should be easy for people to understand, with users requiring little or no special training to use it proficiently [16]. This will help reduce cognitive load and ensure that adolescents can use the device easily, even unconsciously, to ensure its effectiveness.

3.3 Hardware Design of the Device

The hardware of the device mainly includes an Arduino UNO board, Sensor Shield v5.0 expansion board, inflation pump, deflation pump, solenoid valve, etc. The schematic diagram of the hardware wiring of the experimental device is shown in Fig. 3.

The Arduino control board and expansion board are stacked through corresponding sockets, with the power supply connected to the Arduino board. Each component's power supply pins and ground pins are connected to the multi-channel power supply and ground pins of the expansion board. The inflation pump is connected to pin 9 of the expansion board for inflating the balloon; the deflation pump is connected to pin 10 for deflating the balloon; the solenoid valve is connected to pin 11 to control the inflation and deflation states.

The physical device consists of a plastic waterproof box with a diameter of 9 cm and a height of 19 cm and five soft tubes externally connected to pneumatic gloves weighing about 1 kg. The internal hardware connections are shown in Fig. 4, and the physical device is shown in Fig. 5.

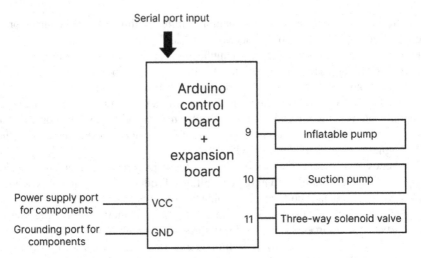

Fig. 3. Schematic Diagram of Hardware Wiring for Experimental Setup

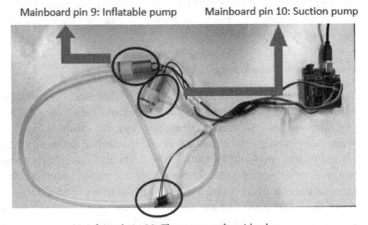

Fig. 4. Internal Hardware Connection Diagram of the Device

3.4   Software Design of the Device

Software Framework Design.   The software part of the device is a multi-layer architecture involving natural language processing, user interface design, and embedded hardware control. The overall design integrates ChatGPT, Python, and Arduino technology stacks to achieve fine control and feedback on user emotions.

The core of the ChatGPT module is the use of a pre-trained ChatGPT for user interaction and emotional analysis. Customized scenarios and response formats enable ChatGPT to perform quantitative emotional assessments of user feedback. Through this method, the system can not only parse user text inputs but also assign an emotional score to these inputs.

Inflation state   Deflation state

Fig. 5. Appearance and Status Illustration of the Device

A user interface is created using the Python programming language, integrating the API interface of ChatGPT. This allows users to interact with ChatGPT in real time. Regular expressions are used to extract emotional scores from ChatGPT's responses. If the emotional score exceeds a certain limit, the data are sent to the Arduino controller via serial protocol.

The Arduino side is programmed to operate the device and receive serial data from the Python user interface. Once Arduino receives an emotional score, it decides and controls the working state of the device based on predefined logic, reflecting the user's emotional changes (Fig. 6).

ChatGPT API   Serial Communication

Fig. 6. Software Framework Schematic

Software Process Design. Firstly, ChatGPT is provided with prompt words and preset story backgrounds to ensure interaction with users in defined scenarios. Additionally, the response format of ChatGPT is standardized for more consistent and predictable outputs. When users input their dialogues, ChatGPT not only generates corresponding story developments based on the preset background but also provides an emotional score for the user's input statements, ranging from 0 to 10. Here, 0 represents the most negative emotion, and 10 represents the most positive emotion.

Secondly, the interaction with ChatGPT is completed using Python. Users dialogue with ChatGPT in real time through a Python-written interface. The Python interface extracts emotional scores from ChatGPT's output. If the score is below 5, the Python interface sends commands to Arduino via serial communication.

Finally, the control process of the Arduino device is as follows: after powering up, Arduino defaults to the following cycle:

5. The inflation pump operates for 3 s.
6. The solenoid valve opens for 0.5 s, preparing for deflation.
7. The deflation pump and solenoid valve work together for 3 s.

When Arduino receives a command from the serial port indicating an emotional score below 5, it immediately activates the inflation pump for 3 s, then returns to the default operation cycle (Fig. 7).

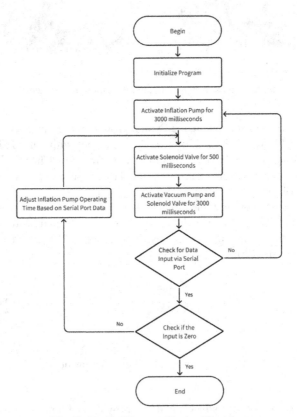

Fig. 7. Device Program Design Flowchart

4 Experiment on Adolescent Anti-cyberbullying Device Design Based on Theory of Planned Behavior

4.1 Purpose of the Experiment

In today's digital society, the complexity and uncertainty of online communication make every individual susceptible to either becoming a perpetrator or a victim of verbal violence. Adolescents, in a crucial stage of physical and mental development, are profoundly influenced by online interactions, shaping their values and behavioral patterns. To mitigate the negative impacts of cyberbullying on adolescents, this study aims to cultivate their awareness of cyberbullying through carefully designed intervention measures, encouraging active participation in building a more respectful and understanding online community.

4.2 Experimental Procedure

Experimental Design

1. Questionnaire Design and Selection.

Firstly, this experiment involved selecting questionnaires (see Appendix 1) adapted from the Adolescent Online Aggressive Behavior Scale (AOABS). The original scale contained 20 items, but this study modified and added some items according to the research group and focus, resulting in a new scale with dimensions like "online debates," "online harassment," "online exclusion," "online stalking," "online impersonation," "defamation," "fabricated slander," "exposing fraud," "happy handcuffing," and "malicious voting." The questionnaire's reliability and validity were ensured through tests. After validation, several adolescents were invited to fill out the questionnaire.

2. Participant Grouping

Based on the questionnaire results, participants were divided into two groups: frequent online commenters and infrequent users. This classification considered online activity level as a critical factor in differentiating user groups.

3. Experiment Design

Four experimental conditions were designed based on the two user types, each with specific variable combinations, to explore the effects of the anti-cyberbullying device more deeply. The conditions were as follows:

- Group 1: Frequent online commenters with the anti-cyberbullying device. This group would help understand if the device reduces cyberbullying among highly active online users.
- Group 2: Frequent online commenters without the anti-cyberbullying device. This control group would compare the impact of the device on cyberbullying behavior.
- Group 3: Infrequent online commenters with the anti-cyberbullying device. This group would help understand if the device is equally effective for less active users.

- Group 4: Infrequent online commenters without the anti-cyberbullying device. This control group would compare the device's impact on infrequent commenters.

To simplify the experiment, Groups 1 and 2 were mainly chosen for comparative experiments. This design allowed a comprehensive understanding of the device's effects across different user groups, providing robust data for further research and improvements. The experiment would offer important insights into addressing cyberbullying in the AIGC trend.

Experiment Preparation. Prior to the study on the Adolescent Anti-Cyberbullying Device Design under the AIGC trend, detailed preparations were made to ensure scientific and effective experimentation. The preparation steps included:

1. Ethical Review and Approval: To ensure ethical compliance, the experiment adhered to ethical review requirements, safeguarding participants' rights and privacy.
2. Participant Recruitment: A group of adolescent participants representing the target user group was carefully selected. Factors like age, gender, and online habits were considered to ensure diversity.
3. Experiment Environment Setup: An appropriate environment, including computer equipment, internet connection, and software installation, was arranged for the experiment.
4. Material Preparation: Various materials needed for the experiment, such as emotional scales, AIGC scenarios, and the anti-cyberbullying device, were prepared following specific standards for reproducibility.
5. Experiment Guidance and Training: Experiment hosts were trained to introduce the experiment theme and rules accurately to participants and address their questions, ensuring consistency and credibility.
6. Data Collection Plan: A detailed data collection plan was developed, including participants' emotional data, conversation records, and device status. This facilitated better management and analysis of experiment data.

These preparation steps laid a solid foundation for the study, ensuring its scientific, ethical, and controllable nature, enhancing understanding of the device's impact on adolescents, and providing support for improvements and educational interventions.

Pilot Experiment. A pilot experiment was conducted to understand the design needs of the Adolescent Anti-Cyberbullying Device under the AIGC trend, assessing the target group's initial reactions. The purpose was to gather preliminary feedback to guide subsequent design and research.

In the pilot experiment, a small group of adolescents, representing part of the target user group, interacted with a simulated device based on AIGC technology. Participants engaged in dialogues and interactions with the virtual device and provided feedback on its design and experience.

The pilot results revealed vital findings. Most participants were interested in the concept and believed it could enhance their awareness of online safety. They also showed keen interest in the device's emotional assessment and feedback mechanisms.

These findings provided valuable preliminary guidance for design research, highlighting users' positive attitudes and expectations towards the anti-cyberbullying device.

This feedback would be incorporated into the design process to ensure the final device meets the needs of adolescent users.

Main Experiment. To thoroughly understand the effects of the Adolescent Anti-Cyberbullying Device under the AIGC trend, the following experimental process was designed and divided into experimental and control groups.

- Experimental Group:

  1. Filling in the Scale: Before the experiment, participants filled in an emotional scale (see Appendix 2) to record their emotional state.
  2. Language Input: Participants connected to the anti-cyberbullying device and entered a virtual environment set up with AIGC. They engaged in verbal dialogues with the AI as in real online interactions.
  3. Language Preprocessing: AIGC intelligently analyzed user input, assigning emotional scores based on the Positive and Negative Affect Schedule (PANAS, see Appendix 3).
  4. AIGC Score Determination: Based on the emotional score, AIGC determined the device's status. If the score was below 5 (a passing grade), the device inflated; the lower the score, the more inflation. Frequent negative words triggered multiple inflations until the balloon exploded.
  5. Filling in the Scale Again: After the experiment, participants refilled the emotional scale to record their emotional changes.

- Control Group:

  1. Filling in the Scale: Similarly, control group participants first filled in the emotional scale.
  2. Language Input: Control group participants also freely inputted language in the AIGC virtual environment.
  3. Refilling the Scale: After the experiment, they refilled the emotional scale to record any emotional changes.

This experiment design allowed the comparison of emotional changes between the groups, assessing the device's effectiveness in reducing cyberbullying. Interactions with the virtual environment helped understand the device's impact on adolescents' emotions and behavior, guiding future improvements and dissemination to protect adolescents from cyberbullying.

Experimental Data Processing and Results. In this study, SPSS software was used to perform paired sample T-tests on each question before and after the experiment for both Group 1 and Group 2, totaling 60 subjects. The purpose of this step was to analyze the p-values of each question to assess whether the differences in emotional states before and after the experiment were significant. The results showed that all the questions in Group 1 had p-values less than 0.05, indicating a significant improvement in emotional states. Meanwhile, Group 2, serving as the control group, had only one question with a p-value less than 0.05, with the remaining nine questions having p-values greater than

0.05, indicating no significant improvement in the emotional states of subjects without the anti-cyberbullying device (Tables 1 and 2).

Table 1. Paired Sample T-Test Results for Group 1

Paired Variables	Mean ± Standard Deviation			t	df	P	Cohen's d
	Pair 1	Pair 2	Paired Difference				
Q1	3.5 ± 0.827	2.8 ± 0.834	0.7 ± −0.006	2.896	29	0.009***	0.648
Q2	3.8 ± 0.951	2.45 ± 1.05	1.35 ± −0.099	3.701	29	0.002***	0.828
Q3	3.7 ± 0.801	2.95 ± 0.686	0.75 ± 0.115	3.29	29	0.004**	0.736
Q4	3.85 ± 0.875	3.1 ± 0.788	0.75 ± 0.087	2.68	29	0.015**	0.599
Q5	3.5 ± 1	2.3 ± 0.801	1.2 ± 0.199	4.66	29	0.000***	1.042
Q6	4.1 ± 0.852	2.65 ± 0.875	1.45 ± −0.023	5.081	29	0.000***	1.136
Q7	3.8 ± 0.768	2.55 ± 0.826	1.25 ± −0.058	5.483	29	0.000**	1.226
Q8	4 ± 0.858	2.95 ± 0.999	1.05 ± −0.14	3.804	29	0.001***	0.851
Q9	3.85 ± 0.875	2.85 ± 0.745	1 ± 0.13	3.343	29	0.003***	0.748
Q10	3.95 ± 0.759	2.65 ± 0.933	1.3 ± −0.174	4.212	29	0.000***	0.942

Note: ***, **, and * denote significance levels at 1%, 5%, and 10% respectively

Table 2. Paired Sample T-Test Results for Group 2

Paired Variables	Mean ± Standard Deviation			t	df	P	Cohen's d
	Pair 1	Pair 2	Paired Difference				
Q1	3.767 ± 0.679	3.7 ± 0.596	0.067 ± 0.083	0.441	29	0.662	0.081
Q2	3.5 ± 0.731	3.6 ± 0.77	−0.1 ± −0.039	−1.361	29	0.184	0.248
Q3	3.867 ± 0.819	3.8 ± 0.887	0.067 ± −0.067	1.439	29	0.161	0.263
Q4	3.833 ± 0.986	3.533 ± 0.681	0.3 ± 0.304	2.34	29	0.026**	0.427
Q5	3.833 ± 0.834	3.7 ± 0.651	0.133 ± 0.183	0.941	29	0.354	0.172
Q6	3.7 ± 0.794	3.5 ± 0.572	0.2 ± 0.222	1.293	29	0.206	0.236
Q7	3.7 ± 0.988	3.667 ± 0.844	0.033 ± 0.144	0.239	29	0.813	0.044
Q8	3.633 ± 1.033	3.7 ± 0.837	−0.067 ± 0.197	−0.441	29	0.662	0.081
Q9	3.533 ± 1.106	3.5 ± 1.106	0.033 ± −0.001	0.273	29	0.787	0.05
Q10	3.667 ± 0.844	3.533 ± 0.73	0.133 ± 0.114	0.941	29	0.354	0.172

Note: ***, **, and * denote significance levels at 1%, 5%, and 10% respectively

5   Discussion and Analysis

The experimental results reflect the positive emotional impact of the anti-cyberbullying device under the AIGC trend among adolescents. We can see that the intervention of this device has significantly improved the emotional state and responses of adolescents. This indicates the potential of the device to help adolescents better cope with cyberbullying incidents, enhancing their emotional health and psychological resilience. Secondly, the results emphasize the potential application of AIGC technology in cyber safety education for adolescents. With the increasing incidents of cyberbullying, we need more innovative methods to help adolescents identify and deal with these issues. The anti-cyberbullying device under the AIGC trend offers a new approach, combining intelligent technology and emotional management, and is expected to play a key role in raising cyber safety awareness among adolescents.

However, we must also acknowledge the limitations of the study. Firstly, the experiment's duration was short, and we could only observe short-term emotional improvements. Future research could consider long-term follow-ups to assess the lasting effects of the device. Secondly, the sample size was relatively small, which might introduce some selection bias. Future research could expand the sample size to enhance the representativeness and generalizability of the study. At the same time, facing various forms of cyberbullying, targeted measures should be taken, and a multi-dimensional approach should be adopted. This study focuses on solving the psychological health issues caused by cyberbullying from the perspective of the perpetrator, and subsequent research should also consider the perspective of the victims to refine the design.

In summary, the study on the design of the adolescent anti-cyberbullying intervention device under the AIGC trend provides new ideas and methods for the field of cyber safety education for adolescents. The short-term effects of this device are significant, offering important support to help adolescents better cope with cyberbullying issues. We look forward to future research that can further explore the long-term effects of this device and investigate more innovative educational intervention methods to create a safer and more respectful online environment.

6   Conclusion

This study aimed to explore the design of an anti-cyberbullying intervention device for adolescents under the AIGC trend. With the rapid development of the internet, cyberbullying has become one of the serious issues facing adolescents, posing a significant threat to their psychological health and safety. Adolescents, being in a critical period of physical and mental development, need effective tools to face this challenge and cultivate awareness of cyberbullying. Through this study, we explored an intelligent device combining AIGC technology aimed at enhancing adolescents' awareness of cyber safety and their ability to counter cyberbullying. Our experimental results show that this device had a positive impact when interacting with adolescents, helping to raise their awareness and aversion to cyberbullying and providing an effective intervention tool.

However, while this study has reached certain conclusions, there are still many future challenges and opportunities. Future research could further optimize the design of the device to better adapt to the needs and cognitive characteristics of adolescents. At the same time, we need to continuously update AIGC technology to provide more accurate emotional assessment and feedback mechanisms. Additionally, we need to pay attention to the long-term effects of the device's use by adolescents to ensure its feasibility and sustainability in practical applications.

Meanwhile, we hope this research will inspire more studies on cyber safety education for adolescents and contribute to building a safer, friendlier, and more respectful online environment. In the future, we will continue to work hard, constantly improving the device's design to protect adolescents' cyber health and safety better!

Appendix 1

1. Online Debates.

1.1 When I encounter views different from mine on the internet, I try my best to persuade the other party.

(1 Completely Disagree 2 Disagree 3 Neutral 4 Agree 5 Completely Agree).

1.2 On the internet, I initiate debates actively and challenge others' opinions.

(1 Completely Disagree 2 Disagree 3 Neutral 4 Agree 5 Completely Agree).

2. Online Harassment.

2.1 I have persistently bothered or mocked someone on the internet.

(1 Completely Disagree 2 Disagree 3 Neutral 4 Agree 5 Completely Agree).

2.2 I persist in harassing someone over disagreements or differing opinions.

(1 Completely Disagree 2 Disagree 3 Neutral 4 Agree 5 Completely Agree).

3. Online Exclusion.

3.1 I have intentionally ignored or excluded someone on the internet.

(1 Completely Disagree 2 Disagree 3 Neutral 4 Agree 5 Completely Agree).

3.2 I intentionally do not reply to someone's messages to exclude them online.

(1 Completely Disagree 2 Disagree 3 Neutral 4 Agree 5 Completely Agree).

4. Online Stalking.

4.1 I follow someone's activities on the internet and keep an eye on their updates.

(1 Completely Disagree 2 Disagree 3 Neutral 4 Agree 5 Completely Agree).

4.2 I search for and collect someone's personal information on the internet.

(1 Completely Disagree 2 Disagree 3 Neutral 4 Agree 5 Completely Agree).

5. Defamation.

5.1 I have posted comments on the internet that damage someone's reputation.

(1 Completely Disagree 2 Disagree 3 Neutral 4 Agree 5 Completely Agree).

5.2 I have spread false information or rumors about others on the internet.

(1 Completely Disagree 2 Disagree 3 Neutral 4 Agree 5 Completely Agree).

6. Fabricated Slander.

6.1 I have fabricated stories to slander others on the internet.

(1 Completely Disagree 2 Disagree 3 Neutral 4 Agree 5 Completely Agree).

6.2 I use the internet to twist facts to slander others.

(1 Completely Disagree 2 Disagree 3 Neutral 4 Agree 5 Completely Agree).

7. Exposing Scams.

    7.1 I expose others' fraudulent behaviors on the internet.

    (1 Completely Disagree 2 Disagree 3 Neutral 4 Agree 5 Completely Agree).

    7.2 I have publicly exposed someone's dishonest behavior on the internet.

    (1 Completely Disagree 2 Disagree 3 Neutral 4 Agree 5 Completely Agree).

8. Schadenfreude (recording violent actions and uploading them online for others to watch).

    8.1 I have recorded violent actions and uploaded them online for others to watch.

    (1 Completely Disagree 2 Disagree 3 Neutral 4 Agree 5 Completely Agree).

    8.2 I have enjoyed watching videos of violent actions on the internet and found pleasure in them.

    (1 Completely Disagree 2 Disagree 3 Neutral 4 Agree 5 Completely Agree).

9. Malicious Voting (organizing or participating in malicious votes online, like voting for the ugliest or most annoying person in class).

    9.1 I have organized or participated in malicious voting online (such as voting for the ugliest or most annoying person in class).

    (1 Completely Disagree 2 Disagree 3 Neutral 4 Agree 5 Completely Agree).

    9.2 I support and participate in malicious voting activities online.

    (1 Completely Disagree 2 Disagree 3 Neutral 4 Agree 5 Completely Agree).

10. Online Impersonation (using someone else's account to leave prank messages or pretending to be a victim and publishing false statements.)

    10.1 I have used someone else's account online to leave prank messages.

    (1 Completely Disagree 2 Disagree 3 Neutral 4 Agree 5 Completely Agree).

    10.2 I have pretended to be a victim online and published statements.

    (1 Completely Disagree 2 Disagree 3 Neutral 4 Agree 5 Completely Agree).

Appendix 2

1. In online debates, I sometimes strongly refute the other party's opinions.

    (1 Completely Disagree 2 Disagree 3 Neutral 4 Agree 5 Completely Agree).

2. In online social activities, I may be indiffe.

    rent to people I don't like.

    (1 Completely Disagree 2 Disagree 3 Neutral 4 Agree 5 Completely Agree).

3. If I find someone's behavior disagreeable, I may publicly express my dissatisfaction.

    (1 Completely Disagree 2 Disagree 3 Neutral 4 Agree 5 Completely Agree).

4. When I see opinions I disagree with online, I may directly express my opposition.

    (1 Completely Disagree 2 Disagree 3 Neutral 4 Agree 5 Completely Agree).

5. In the online communities I participate in, I may engage in activities that make others uncomfortable.

    (1 Completely Disagree 2 Disagree 3 Neutral 4 Agree 5 Completely Agree).

6. If I know someone is being attacked online, I may choose to participate.

(1 Completely Disagree 2 Disagree 3 Neutral 4 Agree 5 Completely Agree).

7. I think some arguments and conflicts online are just harmless jokes.
   (1 Completely Disagree 2 Disagree 3 Neutral 4 Agree 5 Completely Agree).

8. When I see someone's reputation being attacked or slandered online, I may choose not to ignore it.
   (1 Completely Disagree 2 Disagree 3 Neutral 4 Agree 5 Completely Agree).

9. I think exposing online scams may not have much impact because there will always be people who are deceived.
   (1 Completely Disagree 2 Disagree 3 Neutral 4 Agree 5 Completely Agree).

10. I think some tracking behaviors online are just harmless expressions of interest.
    (1 Completely Disagree 2 Disagree 3 Neutral 4 Agree 5 Completely Agree).

References

1. Yu, H.: A multidimensional approach to governing online violence: emphasizing criminal law. Jianghan Tribune 128–135 (2023)
2. Hou, Y., Li, X.: Cyber violence in China: its influencing factors and underlying motivation. J. Pek. Univers **54**(01), 101–107 (2017)
3. Chen, Y.: Understanding and addressing the root causes of online violence. Legality Vis. 145–147 (2022)
4. Rong, C.: Analyzing the justification for criminalizing online verbal abuse. J. Swupl **20**(02), 63–72 (2018)
5. Legal Daily: The Challenges in Exposing the Hidden Perpetrators of Online Violence. http://www.news.cn/legal/2023-02/23/c_1129388620.htm. Accessed 23 Feb 2023
6. Tencent News: Woman Suffers Cyberbullying and Possible Suicide Attempt After Giving a 200 Yuan Tip; Delivery Worker Distressed and Sleepless. https://new.qq.com/rain/a/20220407A08IEQ00. Accessed 07 Apr 2022
7. Sohu News: The Sulli Case - A Fatal Consequence of Online Harassment. https://www.sohu.com/a/347491491_186350. Accessed 16 Oct 2019
8. Liu, C.-G., Luo, J.-F., Xu, J.: Analysis of the domestic and foreign standards on structural safety of children's furniture. Stand. Sci. 73–76 (2017)
9. Xu, X., Tian, K., Li, W.: Evolution, opportunities, and future of next-generation AI technology (AIGC). Rev. Ind. Econ. 5–22 (2023)
10. Wang, B., Niu, C.: Bridging ChatGPT and GovGPT: Building a Generative AI-Driven Government ServiceEcosystem, E-Government:1–14 http://kns.cnki.net/kcms/detail/11.5181.TP.20230425.0901.004.html, 2023/07/20
11. Fishbein, M., Ajzen, I.: Belief, attitude, intention, and behavior: an introduction to theory and research. Philos. Rhetoric, **10**(2) (1977)
12. Tang, B.: Cyber violence and its influence on youth deviance: an analysis from the perspective of risk society theory. China Youth Study, 44–47+53 (2015)
13. Liyuan, Y.: Decoding adolescents' ethical disarray in the virtual world. Yinshan Acad. J. **25**(01), 27–31 (2012)
14. Fan, L., Wu, J.: The Critical Role of Media Literacy Education for Youth: A Joint Responsibility of Home and School. Wenhui Daily, 2021–08–22 (001)
15. Zhou, C.: The importance of safety in product design. Sci. Technol. Innovation 84–85 (2015)
16. Dongdong, Y., Shiguo, L.: Understanding user needs and design strategies in interactive design. Packag. Eng. **34**(08), 75–78 (2013)

Author Index

P.-L. P. Rau (Ed.): HCII 2024, LNCS 14702, pp. 425–426, 2024.
https://doi.org/10.1007/978-3-031-60913-8

Printed in the United States
by Baker & Taylor Publisher Services